IN THIS PROFOUND memoir… a brutal tour of modern American racism at its worst, a case study of traumatized youth and drug addiction, and a stark reminder of the human capacity for redemption, Meeink and Roy's account is a shocking but ultimately reaffirming read.
  – *Publishers Weekly* Starred Review

FORMER NEO-NAZI'S STORY offers profound lesson in Trump era.
  – Lisa Falkenberg, *Houston Chronicle*

FRANK MEEINK IS the real deal! *Autobiography of a Recovering Skinhead* will captivate you and open your eyes to the struggles of racism. His story is a lesson for everyone.
  – Gustavo Alvarez, author of *Prison Ramen: Recipes and Stories from Behind Bars*

THE BOOK'S LASTING impression is of the brutality of Meeink's earlier incarnation, and one wonders if those drawn to white supremacy and hatred could take any lessons from it before their beliefs come to harm others.
  – Caleb Powell, *The Rumpus*

FRANK MEEINK'S STORY is inspiring, compelling and moving. It has the power to change lives. We should all be grateful to him for sharing it.
  – Morris Dees, Founder and Chief Trial Counsel, Southern Poverty Law Center

FRANK MEEINK'S BOOK is a candid and captivating story of upbeat transformation of a raw racist into a courageous citizen, which has much to teach all of us. Don't miss it!
  – Dr. Cornel West, author of *Democracy Matters: Winning the Fight Against Imperialism*

POWERFUL, ABSORBING, STUNNING and sobering, this book is an unvarnished, revealing, sad, and painful portrayal of a struggle that continues, and of a tortured but hopeful soul striving to do good.
  – Barry Morrison, Regional Director, Anti-Defamation League

AS A WHITE MAN, trying to stand in solidarity with folks of color in the struggle against racism, I am heartened by Frank Meeink's story. His narrative confirms that we as white folks have a choice when it comes to how we wish to live in this skin. We can remain silent, or even collaborate with the subordination of peoples of color, or we can become allies in the fight for justice. Meeink has made his choice. May we all have the courage and fortitude to do the same. Nothing less than the fate of our nation depends on it.

    – **Tim Wise, author of** *White Like Me: Reflections on Race from a Privileged Son*

FRANK MEEINK'S STORY is so brutal, so visceral, so unflinching, and in the end, so soul-wrenchingly, specifically American, that it should from this moment on be required reading for anyone who wants to understand the origin of race hatred in these United States of America. *Autobiography of a Recovering Skinhead* stands out as more than a great memoir. It is testament to a great heart, to a man willing to own up to his own violent past and, ultimately, shine a light of hope on this sick, pigment-fixated, demented nation we inhabit. The writing is phenomenal and Meeink's tale will keep you riveted. In the end, like all true testaments, what the author has to offer is hard-earned, down-to-the-bone hope. I loved this book.

    – **Jerry Stahl, author of** *Pain Killers* **and** *Permanent Midnight*

I WAS UNABLE to put this book down. Frank's story pulled me in to the point I felt I was living it with him, like I was skating alongside him as he overcame the odds and changed his life, and along the way, proved how hockey and other sports can change other kids' lives, too.

    – **Bobby Ryan, Anaheim Ducks, National Hockey League**

FRANK'S TRANSFORMATION PROVIDES us commanding proof that reconciliation is possible even for those most tightly bound by hatred.

    – **Jesse Dylan, Director of the Obama campaign's** *Yes We Can* **video**
    and the documentary *Reconciliation*

FRANK MEEINK'S LIFE story is a window into a world where hatred works like a drug. It is a compelling and cautionary tale.

    – **Kenneth Stern, Director on Anti-Semitism and Extremism, American Jewish Committee**

Copyright ©2017
Jody M. Roy, Ph.D.

All rights reserved. No part of this book may be reproduced in any form or by any electronic or mechanical means, including information storage-and-retrieval systems, without prior permission in writing from the Publisher, except for brief quotations embodied in critical articles and reviews.

Library of Congress Cataloging-in-Publication Data

Meeink, Frank.
Autobiography of a Recovering Skinhead :The Frank Meeink Story/ as told to Jody M. Roy.
2nd Hawthorne ed.
p. cm.
ISBN 978-0-9970683-7-5 (alk. paper)

1. Meeink, Frank.
2. Skinheads – United States – Biography.
3. Neo-Nazis – United States – Biography.
4. White Supremacy Movements – United States.

I.   Roy, Jody M. PH.D.
II.   Title

[HV6439.U5M44 2010]

320.5′6 – DC22 [B]

2009027527

Hawthorne Books
& Literary Arts

9   2201 Northeast 23rd Avenue
8   3rd Floor
7   Portland, Oregon 97212
6   hawthornebooks.com
5   *Form*:
4   Sibley House, Portland, OR
3   Printed in China
2   through Print Vision
1

Set in Paperback

In the interest of privacy, names and identifying characteristics of some individuals and groups have been altered throughout this book.

For   Riley, Jake, Matt, Smooth D.,
        Little Nick, and Fargosrena.
        May you always, only, know love.

In memory of Josh

Autobiography of a Recovering Skinhead

The Frank Meeink Story
as told to
Jody M. Roy, Ph.D.

 HAWTHORNE BOOKS & LITERARY ARTS
Portland, Oregon | MMLXXVIII

Preface
Jody M. Roy, Ph.D.

THE TERM "SKINHEAD" CAME INTO COMMON USE IN Britain in the late 1960s. "Skinheads" referred to those young men, also known as hard mods, who shaved their heads and donned classic workers' attire in protest of the androgynous style trends and flagrant drug use popularized by soft mods such as Mick Jagger. Although notoriously violent, Britain's original skinheads were not defined by racism; rather, working-class pride and antielite sentiment bonded skinhead crews, in some cases even across race lines.

In the late 1970s, Ian Stuart, the lead singer of the legendary hard-mod band Skrewdriver, publicly affiliated himself with the National Front, a neo-Nazi organization. The antielite anthems Stuart had bellowed for years were replaced by aggressively racist lyrics. Stuart's transformation split Britain's skinhead subculture: while many skinheads followed their musical leader into the white supremacy movement, others turned on Stuart and became adamantly antiracist.

The skinhead scene was sharply divided into two camps by the time it crossed the Atlantic Ocean in the 1980s. For years, neo-Nazi skinheads and Skinheads Against Racial Prejudice, (SHARPs), battled for turf in major US cities. Bolstered by support from the adult white supremacy movement, neo-Nazi skinhead crews grew rapidly. By the late 1980s, several thousand young men had shaved their heads and dressed in the classic look of the British hard mods. They laced their Doc Marten boots in red to symbolize both the purity of the Aryan bloodline for which they fought and the minority, or "mud," blood they had spilled.

Frank Meeink was only fourteen years old in 1989, when members of a neo-Nazi skinhead crew ritually shaved his head and presented him with a pair of red-laced Doc Marten boots. In the years that followed, Frank emerged as one of the most notoriously violent racist skinheads in America. Today, he is one of the most inspiring antiracism advocates in the country. *Autobiography of a Recovering Skinhead* is Frank's story, a story at once poignant and painful, utterly unique and tragically typical.

The white supremacy movement and American youth culture both have changed since Frank's years as a teenage skinhead. The American political landscape and the technology through which we communicate also have changed. Yet, the social and emotional forces that originally drove Frank to hate are identical to those that influence many people still today. Whether expressed by joining a gang or an extremist group, by opening fire inside a school or house of worship, by blowing up a building or flooding venom through social media, the hate itself remains the same.

Hate is a process. Hate occurs when we think in absolute terms of "us versus them," when we stereotype them, when we scapegoat our problems onto them and, ultimately, when we dehumanize them to be not someone, but something, other than us, less than us. It doesn't matter much who they are or even who we conceive ourselves to be. People of any race, any religion, any nationality, gender, sexual orientation, socio-economic class, or any other demographic category can be hated. They can also hate. Sadly, hate itself does not discriminate; it can seduce any human by offering a heady illusion of power that promises to displace our fears and insecurities.

The world has changed dramatically since Frank Meeink became a skinhead, but hate hasn't changed at all. As such, Frank's story offers valuable insights into why some people hate, how the dynamics of hatred can be interrupted, and, of course, great hope that others can transform their lives just as Frank has. From 2004 to 2007, I worked with Frank to confirm key events in his past. We retraced the first thirty years of his life by interviewing a variety of his family members, friends, and former associates and, whenever possible, by cross-checking those interviews against official documents and media accounts. Among those interviewed for *Autobiography of a Recovering Skinhead* were: Frank's mother, father, stepfather, and half-sisters; his paternal grandparents, aunt, three of his four surviving uncles, and two cousins; members of the corner-turf gangs known as 68th and Buist, Second and Porter, and Third and Jackson; a founding member of Strike Force and members of the Springfield crew; Frank's ex-girlfriends and the mothers of his three oldest children; his wife, her parents, and brother; teachers, coaches, and school support staff personnel who worked with Frank during his childhood; the program director and former production crewmembers for the public-access television channel operated by Sangamon State University, now the University of Illinois–Springfield; members of the Springfield, Illinois, police department, public defender's office and state's attorney's office; the staff of Terre Haute's Catherine Hamilton Center; Terre Haute police officers; representatives of the Philadelphia regional office of the Anti-Defamation League; a variety of Frank's former and current neighbors, employers, coworkers, and associates in Philadelphia, Illinois, and Indiana; and several of Frank's friends from addiction recovery programs. In addition, I consulted ex-convicts, employees of the Illinois Department of Corrections, and a southern Illinois–based criminal defense attorney to confirm the plausibility of Frank's account of gang activity, violence, and contraband issues within the prison system at the time of his incarceration.

The original edition of *Autobiography of a Recovering Skinhead* traced Frank's life from 1975 until the spring of 2005. The nine new chapters added to this second edition, beginning with

"Hurry Up and Wait," include Frank's reflections on the events of his life from May 2005 through February 2017, as well as a few new insights about his earlier years gleaned from additional conversations with family and friends.

Autobiography of a Recovering Skinhead is, ultimately, Frank Meeink's personal recollection of the life he has lived and his intimate reflection on the lessons he has learned along the way. Frank's story is a raw telling of one young man's journey through some of America's most devastating social problems. Significantly, Frank Meeink himself is living proof that those problems can be overcome.

Introduction
Elizabeth Wurtzel

THIS IS THE TRUTH: I READ *AUTOBIOGRAPHY OF A RECOVER-ing Skinhead* with my mouth either actually or metaphorically agape, because I just could not believe anyone could be this much of an idiot and live to tell the story so clearly and cleanly. I don't know what the worst of it is: the racism, the anti-Semitism, the sexism, the alcoholism, the addiction, the depression, the abuse, the violence, the homicide, the suicide – or just the way all these maladies coexist. Frank Meeink's story is upsetting and crazy, but it is above all a strangely absurdist drama that forces us to ask a troubling question about American life: Why, in a land with so much opportunity, is a critical mass of young people choosing hatred over possibility?

Frank Meeink speaks for those people, the ones you don't know and don't want to know, the ones who walk around with the creepy feeling they were born to lose. The only thing these people have to hang onto is their taste for blood, their desire to kill. When President Obama, at a campaign fundraising dinner in San Francisco, made the error of referring to those folks in Pennsylvania who cling to their guns and religion because it's all they've got, he wasn't wrong: meet Frank Meeink – he bashes in skulls for kicks. At the book's turning point, Frank finds himself doing time in the same Illinois state prison as John Wayne Gacy and suddenly realizes: this is no mistake – he is exactly where he belongs, with the worst of the worst.

But to begin with, Frank Meeink is just an Irish-Italian kid in a row house in South Philly with a big extended family full of people with names like Big Louie and Little Nick. He's anybody's neighbor. To read *Autobiography of a Recovering Skinhead* is to understand that evil is the end result of nothing more than the boredom and emptiness we're all too familiar with, at one time or another.

Frank Meeink and I are contemporaries, but I grew up in Manhattan's Upper West Side, I went to Jewish schools until college, and even though my father disappeared when I was young, my mother invested heavily in my education and upkeep. I could not have been more depressed or suicidal, but all this negative energy led me to academic overachievement and eventually Harvard, not Neo-Nazism. Frank's broken down family is quite a different story: all of his assorted parents are addict-alcoholics, his mother and stepfather are drug dealers, and the most memorable interior design quality he describes of his childhood home is a living room full of holes in the furniture from cigarette burns as a result of all the nodding-off junkies. "Wardens and gang chiefs had parented me more than my parents had," he reports. Frank Meeink, too, could not have been more suicidal or depressed, but all his negative energy leads him to white separatism and eventually the American Nazi movement. Harvard and Nazism don't have much in common really, but both are refuges for compulsive people seeking regimentation and authority and prestige. That the former is considered a good place to end up and the latter is believed to be the worst kind of dogma to get caught up in is merely a reflection of time and place: Frank's setting is, blessedly, the United States in the late twentieth century, not Germany in the late 1930s.

But that's what makes Frank's life so familiarly tragic: he is smart and brash, and he can't find anything better to do with his adolescent frustration than deposit it into a black hole of bully politics. As the book unfolds and Frank's life unravels, he starts to meet people of different races, religions, and ethnicities – in prison, in sports, and at work – and he discovers that his hate is ill founded, that it's just stupid and ignorant. His favorite people in jailbird football are black, and his favorite boss is Jewish. "Understanding is the first step toward prevention," explains Frank's first mentor in his lessons in tolerance. Slowly and then suddenly, Frank just kind of stops being a Nazi – he even gets the five-inch swastika tattoo lasered off of his neck. Frank goes from being the leader of Strike Force, a Nazi youth gang that he started with a buddy, to speaking at universities and conventions for the Anti-Defamation League; from preaching hate to praising love.

But the moment Frank Meeink is on the verge of some kind of secular enlightenment, he gets so caught up in drinking and drugging that it almost doesn't even matter. He has such a tenuous – if any – relationship to contraception that he gets three different women pregnant before his twenty-first birthday. What becomes clear is that this isn't really a story about Nazi ideology – it's about a life that is swinging way out of control. And that's the reason *Autobiography of a Recovering Skinhead* is not just a crazy story – it's also a good book and a great read. Because we all have our moments when the world just doesn't make much sense – for Frank Meeink that feeling was so palpable that he actually created a life that made no sense. But he turned it into a narrative that truly does. Over time and over pages, the pieces pull together, and the fractures and fragments turn into a person I would actually like to know.

Meet Frank Meeink – he knows the truth.

AUTOBIOGRAPHY OF
A RECOVERING SKINHEAD

The Confessional

ON THE MORNING OF APRIL 19, 1995, I SQUEEZED PAST THE meat counter of a corner deli, grabbed a pre-wrapped hoagie, and made my way to the cash register. The clerk was glued to a small television set behind the counter.

"What's going on?" I asked.

"Somebody blew up a building."

"No shit? Where?"

"Oklahoma City."

Within minutes of the blast, the world was huddled around television sets. Even me and my fellow drug dealers abandoned our corner at Second and Porter to follow the story. We piled into the front bedroom of a ratty South Philly rowhouse.

"What kind of an asshole does that?" somebody asked.

Little conversations erupted around the room.

"Youse think it's terrorists?"

"Like in Israel?"

"No fucking way. That shit don't happen here."

"It happened in New York."

"This ain't the same thing. It's fucking Oklahoma."

"I still say it's terrorists."

"I think it's some fucking nut job."

"I bet I know who did it," I said.

The room fell silent.

The Second and Porter boys had taken me in a few months earlier when not a lot of people wanted anything to do with me.

I hadn't seen most of them since grade school, but they accepted me back anyhow. I was one of them. Like every other dude on that corner, I was a South Philly Catholic cocktail. I was a little darker than the pure Irish guys, a little taller than the full Italians, and a lot skinnier than everybody except the kooksters who'd given up food for cocaine. But to the Second and Porter boys, I was still Frankie Meeink from the old neighborhood. They overlooked everything else. Or maybe they never really believed the stories until the day of the Oklahoma City Bombing, when they heard me say, "I bet I know who did it."

For the first time that day, everyone turned away from the television. Every dude in that room stared at me as if he was really seeing me for the first time since I'd reappeared in their lives. I felt their eyes lock on the five-inch swastika tattooed on my neck. I glanced nervously at my hands. The tattoos on my knuckles accused me: "S-K-I-N-H-E-A-D."

Finally, someone cautiously asked, "Who?"

"I ain't saying I can name the name, but youse just watch: it's going to end up being somebody tied to the movement."

I knew. Deep in my gut, from the second the story broke, I knew. I recognized the plot. It's from *The Turner Diaries*, the "novel" by Andrew MacDonald. The thing is, Andrew MacDonald isn't the author's real name; his real name is William Pierce. And, in 1995, William Pierce was still head of the National Alliance, and his book was still at the top of the white supremacy movement's "must read" list. When the cops finally apprehended Timothy McVeigh, they found copies of pages from *The Turner Diaries* in his car. My copy was tucked away in the back of a closet. I'd read it cover-to-cover during my skinhead years, and while I read it, I wanted to blow something up. And I knew how, thanks to that book and others like it. I'd just never had the right opportunity.

The other Second and Porter boys wandered back to the corner later that night, but I stayed in front of the television. I didn't leave the house for days. I barely even got high. I just sat there, flipping channels, catching all the angles on the story, unable to look away. One image seared itself into my mind: a firefighter carrying a bleeding baby girl out of the rubble. Every time I saw that picture, I thought of my little girl, the little girl I hadn't seen in more than a year, and I wept.

As the body count mounted, I felt so fucking evil. For the first time ever, my victims haunted me. The kid in Springfield desperately trying to catch his own blood so I wouldn't make good on my threat to shoot him if he stained my carpet. The unarmed gay men I beat with an Orangina bottle. The college student I held down so another skinhead could pry a hammer from his head. Timothy McVeigh and Terry Nichols killed 168 people. How many of my victims had wished for death while I brutalized them?

Once, when I had glanced down at the bloody face of a college student, I had been seized by a horrible realization: "He could be my Uncle Dave," my childhood hero, the guy I could've been, should've been, if everything in my whole fucking life had been different. But I'd shaken that thought off the second it flashed across my mind, and I kicked that poor college kid more, harder. I laughed at his suffering. I attacked others that same night, and so many others in the years that followed. And for years, for five fucking years, I believed I was fighting a holy war. I was raining down God's justice on an evil world. Timothy McVeigh and Terry Nichols believed that, too. That belief killed 168 people in Oklahoma City. Nineteen of them were innocent little kids, like my baby girl. I couldn't shake that. I couldn't bear that.

I knew if I didn't talk to someone I was going to lose my mind. But I had no one to talk to. No one in my life outside the white supremacy movement understood what the movement was about. No one in my life outside the movement had a clue how far in I'd been. My parents, grandparents, my buddies on Second and Porter, none of them knew the truth about me: for five years, I would have blown up a building.

It took almost a week to figure out who I could talk to

without needing to translate every term, who probably knew enough about me to believe me.

THE LOBBY WAS impressive, but the offices were plain. A framed photo of an Eagles fullback stood proudly on a table. I'd expected wanted posters.

"How can I help you?" asked the clean-cut kid at the front desk. He looked like he'd probably played football in high school. I watched his eyes survey my tattoos like he'd been taught at Quantico.

"I need to talk to somebody."

"What's this in reference to?"

"Oklahoma City."

Within about a minute, I was sitting on a metal chair in a windowless room. Unlike the kid working the front desk, the agent across from me in the interrogation room was no rookie. His dark, wavy hair framed the wrinkles cutting into his forehead. From the looks of the bags under his eyes, he hadn't slept since the truck exploded.

"Do you know Timothy McVeigh?" he asked.

"No."

He came at the same question from different angles until he was satisfied I really did not know McVeigh.

"I'm not here to rat nobody out," I said.

"Then why are you here?"

"I didn't know where else to go."

"For what?"

"I didn't know Timothy McVeigh." I paused for a really long time trying to find the right words. Then I said, "For a really long time, I wanted to be Timothy McVeigh."

I confessed to that agent like he was a priest.

Welcome to South Philly, Baby

I WAS CONCEIVED ON MY NANNY BERTONE'S KITCHEN floor a few hours after the Philadelphia cops killed one of my dad's best friends. My dad was nineteen. My mom was seventeen. I was the accident that drove them to the altar.

The oldest son of a big, loving Italian family from Southwest Philly, my dad, Frankie Bertone, had been a star basketball player, a promising boxer, and a chess champion until his younger brother, Steven, was electrocuted on the train tracks. They were playing together when it happened. Fourteen year-old Frankie blamed himself. He withdrew into his grief and guilt, then tried to drown them in a bottle. When that didn't work, he tried to poison them with drugs. Drunk, high, or more often both, Frankie took to the streets. Before long, the young boxer had earned a reputation as one of the meanest streetfighters ever to battle for the 68th and Buist boys.

My grandparents had already lost one son; they weren't willing to stand by while they lost another. For two years, Nanny and Pop tried to persuade my dad to change, but he refused. The night he came crashing through the back door on the run from the cops, Pop kicked him out. He was sixteen.

My dad says the cops picked him up thirty-five times before he turned eighteen and shipped out with the Navy. The Navy could have been his fresh start, a chance to reclaim who he might have become had everything been different. But he slammed that last window of opportunity shut one weekend when he came home on leave. A few hours after he learned the devastating news of his friend's death, Frankie quietly let himself in his parents' back door; he wasn't alone. In a drunken fit of rage and desire, he knocked up a seventeen year-old Irish girl who popped Quaaludes like Chiclets.

Margaret Meeink had been raised to keep up appearances. When my mom was a kid, her parents refused to patronize the boozy Mummer halls that are the community family rooms of South Philly. Instead, they secluded themselves in a tidy row-house and drank their beers in private. My mom spent most of her childhood on her knees scrubbing floors, doing her part to maintain the family illusion. Over the years, the cleaning regiment scoured most of the love out of her. From everything I've heard, my mom played along with the family lie for a long time, embraced it. She drank heavily throughout high school and used her parents' example to hide her drinking even from them. She hid the Quaaludes the same way she had been taught to hide her emotions, behind a bleached exterior. The night she met Frankie Bertone, petite, fair-skinned Margaret Meeink didn't look like the budding addict she actually was.

Although few realized it, my mom was past the point of rebellion when she met my dad; by then she was shopping for retribution. With his shaggy hair and shady eyes, Frankie Bertone was just what Margaret needed. Margaret's parents hated "dirty Italians." At nineteen, Frankie had become their worst stereotype: a drunk, drugging, promiscuous, violent "dago." Of course, my mom had become most of that by then, too. Drunk and stoned at a Phillies game during the heyday of their courtship, she attacked my dad so violently security kicked her out of the stadium. Yet she still thought she was the one slumming, and she rubbed it in my dad's face and in her parents' faces.

I WAS BORN Francis Steven Bertone on May 7, 1975. I don't think my teenage parents were thrilled about my arrival, but the Philadelphia Flyers sure were. A couple weeks after I was born, they celebrated by winning their second world championship. I like to think I had something to do with that, like I was their good luck charm. Or maybe it was fate that Philly's notorious "Broad Street Bullies" brought home the Stanley Cup the same month my parents brought home the baby who would become one of Philly's worst bullies.

Frankie and Margaret gave marriage and me the best shot they could. Parenthood tamed their desire for each other, but not their cravings for booze and drugs. They loved me between binges, did their best to remember to get a sitter before they got too far gone.

We lived in a second-floor apartment over a market in the heart of Southwest Philly. The entire Bertone clan was at the ready to look out for me. My twelve year-old uncle babysat me on Saturdays until the afternoon my parents promised to return within two hours, only to disappear until the wee hours of Sunday morning. After that, Nanny Bertone kept me at her house most weekends.

Neither my presence nor my absence ever really affected my parents' social life. If they could find a sitter, they went out; if not, they stayed in. Their friends still talk about the wild parties they threw in the apartment over the market.

I survived my parents' brief marriage with a lot of help from the Bertones and the neighbors. And my parents survived each other, although both were bitter and bruised by the time my mom walked out. She was nineteen and I was two when we moved in with her parents deep in South Philly's Irish quarter. At first, my dad tried to visit me, but my Grandfather Meeink always slammed the door in the face of the "dirty Italian" who had soiled his "pure" Irish daughter.

Not too long after my mom and I moved in with her parents, she got a good job as a runner for a stock brokerage and started saving up money so we could get our own place. She pooled resources with her best friend, another single Irish mother with a half-Italian son. Together, they managed to rent a tiny rowhouse on Tree Street.

Tree Street is narrow, even by South Philly standards. To be polite to their neighbors, native South Philly drivers park halfway up on the slivers of sidewalks and halfway out in the street, otherwise nobody can get through on streets like Tree. On wider streets, people still park half up over the curb, so there's room for other people to double-park next to them. If there's not enough street left after that, drivers edge two wheels onto the opposite sidewalk, being careful not to rip their front bumpers off on a stoop. Pedestrians are on their own. In South Philly, even if you're standing on your front doorstep, you either get out of the way or you get clipped.

Nearly two years after she'd taken me back to her old neighborhood, my mom finally agreed to let my dad have visitation. The condition on my occasional overnight visits was that I had to stay at Nanny and Pop Bertone's home, not at the apartment my dad shared with his best friend and fellow 68th and Buist bruiser, Crazy Cha-Cha Chacinzi. My grandparents welcomed both me and my dad, but usually only I stayed the whole night. I think I was more than my dad could handle for very long, especially by himself.

Like my dad, my four Bertone uncles were amazing athletes, but they were all still living at home, still going to school, still racking up the trophies Pop displayed like a shrine. Nanny and Pop's house always felt full, full of men, food, accomplishment, fun, mostly love. But I always felt a little bit empty there after dinner, after my dad took off to party with his friends. Nanny and Pop must have recognized the hole my dad left in me each time he disappeared, because they loved me like loving me would take them back in time to before the tragic day they lost one son to the traintracks and another to the streets.

It felt like six months passed between each visit with my dad. And sometimes six months did pass. The waiting made me crazy, especially the time I had something amazing to show him.

My mom had given me the coolest present ever: a San Diego Chargers jersey with my name printed on the back. My dad took one look at it and his eyes flashed with rage.

"I don't ever wanna see youse wearing that piece of shit again."

"I know it ain't the Eagles, but . . . "

"Take it off!"

Tears filled my eyes as I pleaded, "But, Daddy, Mommy gave it to me."

"Yeah, she gave it to youse all right. She gave youse a shirt with somebody else's name on it."

"No, Daddy, it's got my name on it." I spun around so my back was to him, so he could read the printing again. "See? It says 'Meeink.'"

"I can read, Frankie. I know what it says."

To my dad, that jersey said *fuck you*. It was my mom's special message to him, and I was the unknowing messenger.

Years later, my dad's sister told me what had happened. Apparently, the papers authorizing my mom to change my name from Bertone to Meeink had been buried in the middle of stacks of divorce, custody, and child support documents. My dad signed everything in the stack as fast as he could, without really reading any of it. By that point in their nasty breakup, he would've signed anything to get rid of my mom, and he did. Without realizing it, he signed away my name and his namesake.

My mom swore she only changed my name to protect me from the anti-Italian prejudice in her old-school Irish neighborhood; a name like Bertone was like a bull's eye in that part of South Philly back then. Hell, it wasn't the first time that name had been changed. When Pop was a kid, dumped in an orphanage, the nuns had changed the spelling from Bertoni to Bertone for the same reason my mom gave for changing it all the way to Meeink. I'm sure being a Meeink instead of a Bertone probably did spare me a few black eyes. But as I got older, I realized there was probably at least some truth to my dad's theory—my mom changed my name to punish him.

MY MOM ALMOST always had a Virginia Slim in one hand and a beer in the other while she watched TV in the evenings. After I'd go up to bed, I'd hear her switch off the set; moments later, the familiar sounds of her favorite Jethro Tull album would drift up the stairs, and I'd smell the funny-smelling smoke. I'm sure there was a time when I didn't know the distinctive odor of marijuana, but I can't remember that far back. Our row house on Tree Street always smelled faintly of pot. And pot smelled like Jethro Tull sounded. Unless my mom was really depressed about being alone; then pot smelled like Air Supply.

I tried not to let my mom see how much I missed my dad. I felt like a traitor whenever I fantasized about running away to live with the man my mom said didn't give a rat's ass about either of us. But one night she heard me crying in my bed. In a voice so gentle it startled me, she asked if I missed him. It was the only time my mom ever asked me how I felt about my dad and the only night I can remember her ever holding me. She cradled me in her arms until I finally cried myself to sleep. Something about seeing me that way inspired her to change the rules. After that, I got to spend one weekend a month at Nanny and Pop's, whether my dad showed or not.

The weekends my dad ditched me broke my heart, but they made the weekends he did show even more special to me. Sometimes, on Saturday afternoons, he took me to his favorite bar for a couple hours. Every time he threw open the door for me, the sudden flash of midday light temporarily blinded the regulars. The smoky darkness inside stole my vision. I had to half-feel my way to the bar before my eyes adjusted enough to make out the faces of the men saying, "There's our Little Frankie!" and "Where youse been hiding out, kid?"

When I wasn't playing the bar's bubble hockey game, I got the best seat in the house: the stool between Crazy Cha-Cha Chacinzi and Fat Mike DeRenzio. I always thought Cha-Cha was what a mad scientist would end up with if he mated a human with a cuckoo bird. With his crazy hair and crazier smile, Cha-Cha looked every bit as insane as his name promised he'd be, and he was, mostly in a good way. The giant known as Fat Mike looked gentle, but he wasn't, not to his enemies. I was his little buddy, though, and he couldn't have been sweeter whenever I squeezed in next to him.

I always drank Coke at my dad's bar. He and his friends sometimes ducked into a dirt lot they called The Boneyard to snort coke or smoke weed, but inside they just drank beer. The more the 68th and Buist boys drank, the more I learned. My dad taught me everything he knew on those afternoons. Mostly, he taught me how to fight. He taught me what kinds of hits to use because they do the most damage to the other guy, and what kinds not to use so I wouldn't bust my hands. He taught me the importance of scanning a room when I enter it, to know where my escape routes are, where someone might be hiding, what they might use as a weapon against me and what I could use as a weapon against them. He schooled me in the martial arts of beer bottles, pool cues, and lead pipes. In time, he introduced me to the finer points of knives and also guns.

I NEVER GOT into any serious fights when I was little, at least no more than any other kid in South Philly. Mostly, I hung out with my cousin Jimmy and I knew better than to start trouble with him. We were a good team: we both loved to skateboard and we both lived for Philadelphia sports.

Jimmy loved the Flyers as much as any kid who grew up thinking cheese-steak is a food group, but I was the die-hard hockey fan. The one thing I wanted more than anything was to get inside the Spectrum, the Flyers' home arena. I was born loving hockey. I would've given anything I had to go to a Flyers game, but I never had money for a ticket. The closest I ever got to the Spectrum was a fort Jimmy helped me build by Walt Whitman Bridge. I spent one whole summer laying on the roof of that fort, staring out at the Spectrum, dreaming about what it would be like to go there someday.

I played hockey every chance I got, even though the rink in our neighborhood sucked. The City didn't always maintain the ice on the indoor rink, so about half the time kids had to settle for roller hockey on the concrete rink outside. It took balls to play on that outdoor rink, and not just the wadded balls of electrical tape we used for pucks. Some sections of the boards didn't even exist, meaning a good check could send a dude flying out into the parking lot, and a great check could send him into traffic. The boards still hanging were so rotten that nails stabbed at us whenever we slammed into them. The Flyers were better hockey players than we were, but I doubt they were tougher. I've never heard of anybody in the National Hockey League taking a nail to the face during a game, but that shit happened all the time in our league.

The P.O.W.

THE BOYS ON CORNERS LIKE THIRD AND JACKSON SMACK-talked everybody who passed by, except the older women in the neighborhood. In South Philly, talking shit to somebody's grandma can get you killed. Mostly, the Third and Jackson boys aimed their mouths at hot girls, rival corners, and total strangers. They were the kind of crowd that scared lost tourists. They fascinated the hell out of me.

And no Third and Jackson boy fascinated me more than Nick, my oldest cousin on my mom's side. Nobody near Third and Jackson wanted to get on Nick's bad side. He was a good-looking guy with bad acne, but not once did I hear a single person tease him about it. Every teenager in our neighborhood knew Nick wasn't the kind of guy you wanted to pick a fight with. I don't ever remember Nick fighting, but Nick seemed like he'd be a hell of a fighter, so no one ever pushed him too far, not even Jerry, my asshole of a cousin-by-marriage. Battling for the honor of Third and Jackson was Jerry's job, but picking on little kids like me was his favorite hobby. He loved to pin me down under his hulking weight and drool all over my face. Nick would only let Jerry mess with me just so much, though, before he'd bark, "Enough!" But one time Nick issued his command too late: my wrist snapped under the pressure of Jerry's knee.

I never forgave Jerry for breaking my wrist, but I forgave Nick for not saving me fast enough. I would have forgiven Nick anything because he was everything to me. I felt like a celebrity just being related to the guy. But it went deeper than that. I felt safer out on the streets knowing Nick was around, the same way I felt with my dad, like I had my own private bodyguard.

Of course, I wasn't with my dad very often. I got to see him once a month, if he remembered to visit during my stays with Nanny and Pop. When he did, when he whisked me off for an afternoon at the bar, I felt invincible. I was second-generation 68th and Buist. I was Big Frankie Bertone's son. Even ten years removed from his days on the corner, my dad could still bust skulls if the need arose. I loved sitting at the bar between Cha-Cha and Fat Mike, watching the women flirt with my dad while he mixed their drinks and the men watch their backs around him. My dad was a badass dude. He was Rocky Balboa reality. But, he wasn't around much.

Nick was around, though. When I was still really young, not more than eight, Nick's parents decided to move out of the city. Uncle Nick and Aunt Catherine bought a little farm in Lancaster County. When they got it, the "farm" was a trailer parked on a hilly lot next to an Amish guy's actual farm. My aunt and uncle set to work on it, though. They used the trailer as their base and built a new house around it. From the front it looked like a one-story ranch. But that view lied. Around back, the house climbed down the hill until the rooms on the lowest level opened onto a patio through sliding glass doors.

Uncle Nick and Aunt Catherine's kids couldn't see their parents' vision of what that trailer could become. None of them wanted to move to the farm, but only Nick was old enough to put up a real fight. I wasn't there for the big showdown, but I think maybe his parents finally caught a glimpse of the "don't fuck with me" stare that had made him a legend on the corner. When he said, "Youse can't make me leave South Philly," they knew he was dead serious. So they struck a room-and-board deal with my mom to let Nick move in with us.

The only thing better than having Nick move in with me was getting to go along with him for weekend visits to the farm.

Seeing as I grew up thinking the concrete slab underneath I-95 was a park, going to that farm was like going on safari to Africa. Nick's little brother, Shawn, was my field guide. Shawn was a few years older than me, but still more kid than teenager. I was totally cool with following his lead because I was lost out in Amish country. Street smarts don't count for shit once you turn off the paved road.

Shawn and I spent most of our days outside exploring and playing. We had run of the farm. If there were other kids around, we'd play football or softball. If it was just the two of us, we'd make up our own games. Some involved chasing balls, others involved chasing the Amish neighbor's cows. By mid-afternoon, sweat would mat my scraggly hair, sticking it to the back of my neck like a scarf, but I kept running, always trying to keep up with Shawn as he led me toward our next adventure. We would play right up to the point of dying from exhaustion, then we'd lie quietly by the creek until the salamanders would decide we were rocks and come out of hiding. We captured some once and stuck them in peanut butter jars, hoping to start our own zoo. It ended up more a salamander cemetery.

Back in Philly, Nick's steady snore was my night music. Before Nick moved in, I'd felt really alone at home, even sitting across the kitchen table from my mom. She didn't have a lot to talk about with a little kid. Nick was old enough to hold her interest, though. When he moved in with us, he was fourteen going on fifteen and hardened beyond his years. And while my mom seemed ancient to me just for being my mother, she really wasn't. She was only twenty-five, and she regretted giving up her youth to have me. I knew she felt like that not because of what she said or did to me, but because of what she didn't. I'd see my friends showing their moms pictures they drew or homework with a star on it, and their moms would hug them and say stuff like, "You're such a good artist," or "You're so smart," or "I'm so proud of you." My mom never said shit like that. Her eyes never lit up when she saw me. She treated me like laundry, another chore she had to check off her list before she could get on with her life.

It was different with Nick. My mom talked with Nick in ways she couldn't, or wouldn't, talk with me. And he talked with her, too, like she was one of his friends, not just his aunt. Nick opened his heart to my mom the night one of his buddies got murdered. When I walked in on her holding him, stroking his back as he cried, I felt like a peeping Tom, like I was watching something I wasn't supposed to see and yet I couldn't look away. I'd never seen Nick cry and it scared me. And I'd only ever seen my mom so tender once, on the night I'd confessed how much I missed my dad. But her tenderness toward Nick was still there when we all woke up the next morning.

When Nick first moved in, I was too young to understand the whole truth about why my dad was shaving a few more hours off my visits to Nanny and Pop's with each passing month. No matter how badly I wanted him to stay there with me, he always had to leave, always had to hook up with the 68th and Buist boys. It wasn't just his friends my dad was so loyal to; it was the drugs he did with them out in The Boneyard. Like any child of an addict, I felt the effects of addiction long before I knew the word. From one visit to the next, I could feel my dad slipping even further away from me into something far darker and more dangerous than the shadows of 68th and Buist. I didn't know what was pulling my dad away, only that it was stronger than me.

The more my dad withdrew into addiction, the more I leaned on Nick as the main man in my life. Nick was the perfect fill-in father, even if he was still a kid himself. He thought like my dad, and his boys on Third and Jackson fought like my dad. Nick was even half-Italian. But when my dad started ditching all my visits, I begged off spending weekends with Nanny and Pop just to avoid being stood up. Not even Nick could fill the hole in my heart after that. Nobody could have. I wanted my dad. Not my cousin, not Pop, not my uncles, and definitely not one of the guys my mom dated off and on.

MY MOM HAD never sounded so happy or so alive as she did the first time I heard her talking about her new boyfriend, John. Not too long after that, I was playing alone in our cramped cellar when I heard footsteps on the rickety stairs.

"So this is where they keep you," a man's voice said.

I knew immediately he had to be John.

As he ducked his head to clear the stairwell, I couldn't help but compare him to my dad. Even though his street name was Big Frankie, my dad wasn't a big guy; he just seemed big, especially if he was ticked off about something. My dad had the kind of classic Italian looks that made a lot of women giggle whenever he so much as smiled at them. I couldn't see women going crazy like that around John. On the scale of tall, dark, and handsome, height was all John had going for him. He was an okay looking guy, an average looking guy. Mostly, though, he was an Irish looking guy. If Grandpa Meeink were still alive, he would've been thrilled.

John introduced himself and pulled a chair next to me by my electronic football game. He flipped the "on" switch, and we silently watched the little linemen vibrate into each other. John helped me set them all back up for another play, then he started talking. He explained that things were getting pretty serious between him and my mom and that he liked her a lot.

"I better never hear you disrespecting your mother," he said. I liked that; it told me he really cared about my mom. Then he said he was moving in with us.

"When?" I asked.

"About an hour ago. You got a problem with that?"

"No." I really didn't.

John stayed with me for a few minutes, playing the football game, checking out my Matchbox cars, and talking to me about the Eagles. Then he said he needed to go back upstairs and finish settling in. He told me he'd see me at dinner, then he added, "I'm the only man in your mom's life from now on."

That was okay by me. John seemed like a good man. And he

seemed like a good match for me. From our short conversation, I could tell John loved sports as much as I did. But at dinner that night, I learned something even better about John. He wasn't just a sports fan; he'd been an honest-to-God athlete, a serious boxer during his years in the Navy. I believed it. His nose looked like it'd been busted a few times and his gnarled knuckles looked like they'd smashed in more than a few noses. Even though he wasn't boxing anymore by the time he moved in with us, John was still the kind of guy I could brag about to my friends. And even though he wasn't my dad, John seemed like the kind of guy who'd make a pretty cool stepfather if he and my mom ended up making it legal. I had really high hopes for John the day he moved into our house.

Those hopes lasted maybe a week, at the outside. I was fixing myself a snack in the kitchen when John walked in to get a beer from the three-case stack he'd erected next to the refrigerator.

"We need to talk," he said.

"Okay," I replied, fiddling with a cereal box.

John slapped the box out of my hands.

"When I talk you listen! You don't screw around with shit, and you don't interrupt. You listen. That's all you do. You got that?"

Under the circumstances, I didn't know if I was supposed to answer or not. I kept my mouth shut.

"What are you, some kind of retard?"

I still didn't know what to do.

"Answer me!"

"Yes."

"Yes, you're a retard?"

"No. I mean, yes, I got it."

"Don't you forget it. And don't you forget this either, Frankie. You lost the battle the minute I moved in. This is *my* house now. You're my prisoner of war."

I was ten. I didn't have a clue in hell what John was talking about. He taught me soon enough.

God knows I was no saint as a kid, but John didn't punish

me for my sins. He punished me for the sheer hell of it. If I got an answer wrong on my homework, John would ask, "How'd you get to be such a retard?" Then he'd rip up my assignment and ground me for a day or two. Sometimes he locked me up for weeks and ordered me to copy words out of a big black dictionary. When I was on lockdown, everything was off limits except school and that dictionary. I couldn't watch TV. I couldn't talk on the phone. I couldn't eat dinner with everybody else. After they were finished, John would give me permission to come downstairs. There'd be a lukewarm plate of leftovers on the counter. I'd eat alone in the kitchen while John and my mom curled up on the living room couch with their beers and the *TV Guide*.

My mom looked so happy with that creep's arms wrapped around her. I didn't fucking get it. How couldn't she see him for what he was? He was a total asshole to everybody. He said rude shit to my aunts and uncles whenever they came over. He even said mean things to my mom and treated her like a slave. She worked crazy long hours. John occasionally picked up work at a steel mill, but mostly he made a career out of drawing unemployment and disability checks. Still, he never helped around the house. He laid on the couch all day drinking and watching TV, waiting for my mom to get home and cook his dinner. If he was drunk by then, he was all lovey-dovey with her. But if he was still sober, he wasn't so nice. No matter what she said, he'd say, "You don't know what you're talking about." Sometimes he called her "stupid."

Nothing John said seemed to bother her, except for the one time John called my mom "Bitch" like it was her name and she slammed the telephone into his head. He didn't hit back. He didn't say anything. They just went to their separate corners for a while to cool off, then they fell back into their routine on the couch with their beers and the *TV Guide* like it'd never happened.

Eating alone in the kitchen, sometimes I'd overhear John talking about me to my mom. I don't recall ever once hearing her stand up for me when he bitched about how stupid I was or how much trouble I caused him. Sometimes I wanted to run out into the living room and scream at her, "Why aren't you sticking up for me?" But I couldn't. I wasn't allowed to leave the kitchen until John told me I was done with dinner. Just like I couldn't eat dinner with everyone else because John told my mom, "The sight of your rotten kid makes me too sick to eat." The sight of John made me sick, too, so I didn't mind eating alone.

What sucked most was I couldn't play sports, not even the one John had signed me up for. Right after he moved in, John convinced my mom to let me do something I'd wanted to do for years – join the Philadelphia recreational football league. John told my mom it would be good for me. I didn't know about that; I just wanted to play. The league went by weight, not age, and neighborhood, not school. I played with the seventy-five pounders for EOM, the Eddie O'Malley team. Being on EOM was as Irish as playing college ball for Notre Dame. I was really good at football. It was the only good thing John ever gave me and the first thing he took away.

After a year, my room felt like a cell. I thought I finally understood why John called me his "prisoner of war." Little did I know, I had yet to see war. The first time John hit me, he thought I'd lied to him about my homework; he smacked my vocabulary copy book so hard across my face the metal spiral binding dug into my cheek, leaving a dark purple welt by the next morning. I told my friends at school I got hit by a hockey puck.

John started slapping me around pretty regular after that. If I got an answer wrong on my homework, he'd call me a "retard," like always, but then he'd slap the side of my head before he sent me to my room. If he caught me trying to sneak some pickles or a TastyKake out of the kitchen, he'd call me a "fucking mooch," like he always had, but then he'd shove me into the edge of the counter before storming away. His speed was contagious. After a few months, my ducks and bobs got faster, but never fast enough.

My mom and John had been together for about two years

when my half-sister Kirsten was born. When she was still a little worm of a baby, I barely noticed her. But once she started walking, everybody in our cramped rowhouse had to go on high alert, including me. I was lying on the couch watching TV one afternoon when Kirsten came toddling along the edge of the coffee table. She still hadn't mastered walking without hanging on to something and even then, she usually didn't make it more than three or four steps without landing on her butt. I just knew she was going to hit her head on the sharp edge of that table, so I put her up on the couch with me and pinned her behind my body so there was no way she could fall. Kirsten was having a great time pacing the back of the couch. She was giggling like a little monkey. Regardless of who her father was, she was so cute I couldn't resist loving her. I kept reaching back to tickle her so she'd giggle even more. I still can't believe Kirsten didn't smash into the coffee table when her dad's fist slammed into the back of my skull and sent me rolling onto the floor. Instead, she kind of slid down the cushions and landed on my stomach. She thought that was fucking hilarious.

"You stupid son of a bitch!" John screamed. "She could have fell off that couch the way you had her!"

I looked into Kirsten's little eyes. She was okay; she was still giggling. I cradled her in my arms and staggered to my feet. As I shook my head to clear away the sting of the blow, I realized I was okay, too.

But John wasn't okay. He stood rubbing his hand, staring at me with half disbelief and half rage. I thought of all the lessons my dad had taught me those afternoons we'd spent together at the bar, and I thought, "You stupid son of bitch, don't you know you never use your fist on the back of a guy's head? That's a good way to break your hand." And it was.

John never punched me in the back of the head again, but once he got his cast off, he punched me about everywhere else. The lingering ache in his hand made him hate me more and hit me harder. The era of slapping was over. From that point forward,

John beat me like a man beats another man in a bar, as if I were his age, his size, his competition. But I couldn't compete with a former boxer who had nearly a hundred pounds and twenty years on me. I didn't even try to fight back like my dad had taught me. I knew my best hope was to try to survive.

No one outside our house knew how bad things were. I was a tough kid who played tough sports in a tough neighborhood. Kids like me were always bruised and cut. I was too ashamed to tell anyone the truth about my injuries. Nick saw some of it go down, of course, but even he wasn't strong enough to make John stop. But he kept me sane. Late at night, alone in our room, he'd whisper to me across the darkness, "You're okay, Frankie. John's the asshole."

My mom refused to see the truth – probably because John never hit me in front of my mom. She never saw the beatings, only the bruises. And like me, she pretended I got them playing hockey. She couldn't do that anymore after John stormed up the stairs screaming, "Margaret, your idiot kid just made me break my hand!" There was no more denying what John was doing to me. So my mom started in on why he was doing it. John was smacking me around because I was a smart mouth. I was an idiot. I was a brat. John was a good man doing what any good man would do to try to save a rotten kid like me from ruining my life. If it weren't for John, I'd end up no better than my no-good father. And if I weren't such an ingrate, I would be thanking John instead of whining about him to my mother. The lecture got a little longer every time she bandaged up a new round of my battle scars, but she always finished with the same advice, "If you'd just stop upsetting him, he wouldn't have to hit you."

In the end, my mom was the one who got upset. About halfway through seventh grade, I finally figured out that John was going to smack me and ground me the same for not doing my homework at all as he would for doing it wrong. So I saved myself the trouble: I quit doing my schoolwork. John knew, because he punished me for it, but apparently he never told my mom, so when my school called her in for a conference, the news blind-sided her. That pissed her off even more than my failing grades.

Everything I know about what went down immediately after that meeting I got from Nick, but not until weeks later. My mom was enraged by the time she stormed through the door. When she told John I was flunking, he pretended he didn't already know, then he went off on one of his riffs about how I was a retard. My asshole cousin Jerry was there too and egged them both on, saying I needed a lesson I wouldn't forget.

Things didn't seem right as soon as I stepped through the front door. Cigarette smoke wasn't hanging over the first floor like smog. The house was quiet as a tomb. I paused for a second to wonder where everybody was, and that's when John got me. It was a perfect ambush. John had tucked himself against the wall behind the door. He waited until I was exactly where he needed me to be before he punched me square in the side of my head and knocked me across the living room. Before I even realized what had hit me, he was on top of me. He dragged me to my feet and pinned me to the wall with one hand; with the other, he proved he really could've been a contender. It was the most savage beating he ever unleashed on me, so brutal I knew I had to make a run for it.

I took the first chance I got. When he pulled both hands off me to set up for a combination, I broke free. I sprinted up the stairs, thinking if I could just make it out the bathroom window, I could jump onto the kitchen roof, drop into the alley and run away. But John was too fast. I couldn't make it into the bathroom, so I cut hard right, into my room. He grabbed me from behind. He yanked my shirt up part of the way over my head, pinning my arms. I was completely defenseless.

My stepfather opened round two with a quick series of hooks to my ribs and an uppercut to my jaw that made me see stars. I felt the room start to spin. I heard my dad's voice: "Always know what you can use for a weapon." I shook myself back to reality and peeked beneath my shirt, scanning the floor for anything I could use to fight John off me. I guess John was doing the same thing, because when I slipped out the bottom of my shirt and lunged toward my hockey stick, he hurled my most beloved possession, my E.T. lamp, down onto my back. Shards of E.T. skittered across the room. I screamed and slumped to the floor. Then I rolled myself into a ball and I prayed.

John's heaving breath was the only sound I could hear over the pounding of my heart. I could tell he was exhausted, but I knew he wasn't finished with me. I'd let him corner me, and he wasn't backing away. After a few seconds, I heard him moving into position above me. Something deep in my gut told me I was about to die. By then, I was ready; I just wanted it to be over. I drew in what I assumed would be my last ever breath and waited for his final blow. It wasn't what I expected.

"That's it!" John said. "You're outta here! I fucking hate you! Your mother fucking hates you! I don't want you in my fucking house no more! Pack your shit."

John paced the hallway outside my bedroom door like a pit-bull in a run. I grabbed what I could. He was on my heels as I marched down the stairs, a duffel bag of clothes in one hand, hockey stick in the other.

My mom's timing was too perfect to be accidental. She walked in the front door just as I stepped into the living room. She said not one word to me as I dialed the telephone. She wouldn't even look at me. But I couldn't take my eyes off her. Never in my thirteen years had I ever seen her eyes so hard or her scowl so callous. That's when I finally understood who had been calling the shots.

"Mommy's kicking me out," I said into the telephone. Mommy. What a fucking word for me to call her. What a joke. Kind of like Daddy. But it's what I'd always called them. "Can I live with you?"

A few seconds of silence feel like hours when you don't know the answer you're going to get.

"Of course," my dad replied. He sounded drunk. I didn't care.

As I walked out the door, John sneered at me. "So long, retard."

My mom didn't say a goddamn word. Neither did I.

The whole bus ride across town, I kept thinking to myself, "You ought to be really upset. You just got the shit kicked out of you. You just got kicked out of your own house. Your own fucking mom hates you."

But I wasn't upset. I was relieved. I was thrilled. I was free.

The Neo-Phyte

COLD SOBER, MY DAD COULD READ THE TRAIL OF ANOTHER fighter's hooks and jabs like a Boy Scout could read a map. Of course, it had been a lot of years since my dad had been sober. Still, I knew he wasn't going to buy, "It happened in hockey."

"John shoved me around a little," I said on my way in the door.

My dad eyed me suspiciously.

"It was nothing." I lied.

If I'd confessed the truth at that moment, my dad might have gone after John. I like to think he would have if I'd told him. But how in the hell could I tell my dad the truth? That every precious afternoon with him at the bar had been a waste of time? That I hadn't put even one of his lessons into practice to save my own ass? That I hadn't looked to see where somebody might be hiding? That I'd let John attack me with my own goddamn lamp? How could I tell a 68th and Buist boy his only son had let himself be a prisoner of war and a punching bag for nearly three years?

He took me to the bar. Cha-Cha, Fat Mike, and the other guys sensed something was up; they left us alone in a corner booth. I sipped a Coke in silence while my dad worked his way to the bottom of a pitcher.

"So, youse wanna talk about it?" he finally asked me.

"No."

He started to get up from the booth.

"I can't believe she fucking kicked me out instead of him."

I didn't expect much of a response from my dad, maybe

not any response. What could he say? He didn't know what John had been doing to me. He didn't know John. Hell, he barely knew my mom. I wasn't expecting him to give me some mind-blowing insight. But he did.

"She chose dick over you."

That's all he said, but it was enough. It knocked the wind out of me. It was so brutally, undeniably true. My dad knew my mom better than I did. And he knew I needed to see her for what she really was if I was going to make it through even my first night without her.

After my mom left him, my dad spent several years jumping from one bed to another. His binge of one-night stands resulted in the birth of one child, one we know about anyhow, a little girl he barely ever saw. Then he married a woman named Sally who he met at his bar and became the stepfather to her three sons. The whole crew shared a glorified one-bedroom apartment in Southwest Philly with Cha-Cha Chacinzi, who made his bed in a converted closet.

The night I moved in, I didn't have a clue about how many drugs my dad was on or how he had to use one to bring himself down from another. But after a few days, I saw enough to know without doubt he was an addict. I saw the white powdery residue on the table, the empty pill bottles by the sink, the little bags in the trash can, the cut straws on the nightstand where he always stashed his weapons. I wasn't an idiot. The adults tried to hide the hard stuff from the kids, but they were too fucked up to pull it off. They didn't even bother to hide their drinking or their pot-smoking. Beer was their water; joints were their Marlboros.

I still don't know what went wrong when my dad signed me up at Pepper Middle School, but I somehow managed to jump from seventh grade classes to what felt like eighth grade on my bus ride across town. I had no clue what was going on in any of them, but I didn't care. I had a bigger problem. Pepper was pretty far from my dad's house, too far to walk, and there were

only two trolley stops anywhere near it. One was in front of one of
the worst housing projects in Philly; between the second stop
and the school stood a dense tangle of trees and brush where the
local crack dealers did their business. I rode the trolley each
morning with some of the Italian kids from my dad's neighborhood. We got off at the first stop to avoid the crack forest, which
meant we had to run for our fucking lives through four blocks of
projects controlled by the gang called the Junior Black Mafia.
We'd run in a pack, hoping there was truth in that old saying about
safety in numbers. There wasn't. The Junior Black Mafia got
at least one of us every damn morning. I was usually pretty lucky.
I was fast. But not always fast enough.

I hate to admit it, even to myself, but I came to appreciate
John in a weird sort of way after I transferred to Pepper. After
years in the ring with a full-grown boxer, I knew how to take a
punch. Short of stabbing me or shooting me, there was nothing
the gangbangers could do that I hadn't already survived before.

THE ONLY PLACE I actually felt comfortable was on the softball
field. I was the only white kid who made Pepper's softball team
that year. I was the shortstop. Softball didn't thrill me like hockey
or even football, but it served its purpose. I was a pretty good
player, good enough I had a hunch my teammates would keep me
from getting killed in a pinch, at least until after the season
was over.

After practice one day when I hadn't been on the team more
than a week, I went back into the school. I was hoping the boys'
bathroom would be empty. There had been so many attacks over
the years the authorities had removed all the doors from the
stalls. At Pepper, you only got to drop a deuce in private if you were
the only one in the john. Since it was after four o'clock, I figured
I'd have the place to myself. I was wrong.

The hallway door no sooner thudded shut behind me when
a voice said, "There's another one." Several guys, I couldn't tell
how many, were crowded into one stall. One of them was glaring

at me. I recognized him; I'd seen him before, hanging with the
Junior Black Mafia. When he started moving toward me,
I caught a glimpse of the kid on the floor. From the looks of things,
the JB Mafiosos had wedged the kid against the toilet to keep
him from sliding away when they kicked him. Blood poured from
his nose and huge red welts scarred his cheeks. If I hadn't
ridden the trolley to school with that same Italian kid every morning, I don't think I would have recognized him through the
swelling. The JBM dude was almost on top of me when another
voice echoed from the back of the stall: "Frankie's cool." The guy
charging me stopped dead in his tracks.

DeShawn Cooper emerged from the stall with a big smile on
his face. We looked like twins in our matching softball uniforms.

"You're cool, aren't you, Frankie?" DeShawn asked.

I knew what he meant.

I glanced down at the kid on the cold tile floor. He was shaking violently. Through the blood and the bruises and the
swelling, his eyes begged me to do something, to get somebody,
to do anything I could to save him. I looked back up at DeShawn.

"I'm cool," I said.

I kept my eyes on DeShawn and his friends as I backed out
of the bathroom. My footsteps echoed in the long, abandoned
hallway, as I walked toward the exit, trying to look cool in case
they were watching. But when I threw open the front door,
I bolted. I ran all the way back to my dad's house. I snatched off
my filthy uniform and climbed into the shower. I reeked of
sweat and something worse. As the hot water rained down on my
body, I knew I'd never be able to scrub off the stink of how
rotten I felt for leaving that kid on the disgusting bathroom floor.
I knew I would never be able to wash away the memory of how
degraded he looked when he locked his eyes on mine. We both
knew I wasn't going to go get help, because we both knew
I couldn't. I had to be cool, or I'd have been lying in a pool of my
own blood, too.

I did not go back to Pepper the next day. I never went back again.

IN EARLY JUNE, a month after my fourteenth birthday, I called Uncle Nick and Aunt Catherine to see if I was still welcome at the farm.

"You don't ever have to ask," my mom's sister said.

A few days later, Uncle Nick drove into the city to get me. Aunt Catherine was the only one home when we pulled in the rocky driveway. She mauled me with hugs, then told me to take my stuff to Shawn's room where I'd be bunking. My cousin had redecorated since my last visit. The plain curtains that once covered the sliding glass doors had been replaced by two flags: a Confederate battle flag and a black swastika on a red background. The symbol of the Nazis. Newspaper clippings about skinheads wallpapered the room. I knew a little about skinheads, because there were skinheads on South Street, Philly's alternative district. Every time my cousin Jimmy and I went down there on our skateboards to check out the punks, he warned me to watch my back around the skinheads. They were hardcore street fighters, and they didn't like skaters, especially long-haired skaters like us. I'd seen the South Street skinheads around enough to know that you couldn't tell who they were just by their hair. Most of them did have their heads shaved, but some just had their hair cut short. To tell if a guy was a skinhead, you had to go by how he was dressed. Skinheads wore matching flight jackets with suspenders and combat boots, unless they were going to the clubs; then they usually wore suits. They stuck out on South Street because they always looked so pulled together, and because they were one of the few groups in Philly that seemed completely integrated. Some of the skinheads were Irish, some were Italian, some were black, but no matter what, they were all tight, kind of like a corner, only they had all of South Street.

I had no clue why Shawn was taping up articles about

skinheads at the same time he was flying a Confederate flag. From what I'd seen, the skinheads on South Street were about as "Yankee" as you could get. I scanned a couple articles more closely and kept seeing the phrase "neo-Nazi." I knew about the Nazis, and Hitler, and WWII from school and all but I wondered, "What's a 'neo'?" I figured I'd ask Shawn once he got home. The worst he could do was call me a "retard" for not knowing. If he did, I figured I could call him a "retard" right back for thinking the Civil War had anything to do with skinheads.

While I waited for Shawn to come home, I sat in the kitchen scarfing down a homecooked meal and talking with Aunt Catherine and Uncle Nick. They didn't ask me about my mom kicking me out so I returned the favor: I didn't bring up anything about the flags flying in Shawn's room. Aunt Catherine warned me he was going through "a phase," though. Then she said to me in that low voice ladies use when they talk about divorce or cancer, "The move was real hard for Shawn."

A few hours later, Shawn clomped through the kitchen door and completely blew my mind. He looked like the skinheads on South Street. His head was completely shaved. His combat boots glistened. It was too hot for a flight jacket, but his narrow suspenders looked like the ones the skinheads in the city always wore, except his were red and I thought theirs were usually blue. My mouth dropped straight to the floor when I saw him. I couldn't get over how different, how good, Shawn looked. It wasn't just the clothes, either, or that he'd been lifting weights. Something in Shawn's eyes looked different. He had this intensity I'd never before seen in him.

Shawn's friends had the same look when they showed up later that night. They snuck in through the sliding glass door in Shawn's room, careful not to snag either of the two flags on the cases of beer they were carrying. Bob Reynolds and Tim Kleinschmidt were both around seventeen, a little older than Shawn but a lot older than me. I figured they wouldn't want a kid like me hanging around with them, but Tim tossed me a beer.

"I've been looking forward to meeting you, Frank," he said, shaking my hand. "Shawn says you're a stand-up guy."

I blushed and glanced toward Shawn. My cousin was beaming at me.

"What's going on in Philly these days?" Bob Reynolds asked.

"Not much, I guess."

"It's okay," Shawn said. "You can talk to these guys."

"What do youse want me to talk about?" I asked. The only thing going on in Philly was bullshit with my parents. And if Shawn thought I was going to spill my guts about that to strangers, he was crazy.

"I want to hear about that school you go to," Tim said. "Shawn says it's almost all niggers. They ever jump you?"

I puffed up a little and said, "I hold my own."

Tim and Bob smiled at me. Shawn said, "Tell them about the time you saw that nigger shoot one of us by your mom's house."

So I did.

"Tell them about all the coon crackheads by your school."

Okay.

It went on like that for hours. Every time I told a story about life in Philly, Bob, Tim, and Shawn added their own commentary.

That conversation was the first time I thought about my life in Philly in terms of race. I'm not saying I'd been colorblind; that ain't even possible in Philly. I'd noticed race. Especially after I moved in with my dad and I saw black guys beating the shit out of white guys almost every day. Especially on the days I was the one they were wailing on. But I had never really thought about it as a *race* thing. Growing up in the inner city, I understood it as a *gang* thing. To my mind, the black kids at Pepper were vicious because they were gangsters. But the more I talked to Bob, Tim, and Shawn that night, the more they got me thinking maybe I had it all backwards: maybe the kids at Pepper were vicious gangsters because they were black.

Looking back, I'd be lying if I said those guys planted a seed in me that night; the truth is they just added water and beer to a seed already inside me waiting to grow. I had been raised to hate. I was a Catholic mulatto, a half-mick-half-dago who'd never felt more than half-accepted anywhere, especially not in my own home. I didn't realize it, but by summer of 1989, I had fourteen years of rage bottled up. And I had three years of rage built up from John beating and humiliating me. I had three months of rage building inside me from having to run through a freaking gang gauntlet every day to get to Pepper Middle School. Worst of all, I had this God-awful guilt eating away at me for leaving that kid bleeding under the toilet the day I saved my own ass and ran out of Pepper for good.

By the time I met them in the early summer of 1989, Bob Reynolds and Tim Kleinschmidt were obsessed with the white supremacy movement, and they'd already recruited Shawn and a couple of other guys in the area. And they knew what to do and say to snag the interest of a fourteen-year-old half-Irish, half-Italian kid from Philly whose real dad was an addict, whose stepdad was an asshole, whose mom was indifferent, whose school was a war zone, and whose only real desire was never to feel like a fucking victim again: they gave a shit about me.

These three guys who looked too cool even to talk to a kid like me actually cared about me. Shawn and Tim were both very good-looking guys, real ladies' men. Bob had muscles I didn't even know the names of all cutting his clothes. They could have hooked up with the hottest chicks in Lancaster County any night of the week, but they chose to spend most of their time with me instead. The Lancaster County white supremacists talked to me like they cared about what I thought and what I could become. Then they told me I had a destiny. They told me I could become a warrior. They told me all I had to do was look in the mirror and see the truth: I was white and that was all that mattered.

After a couple of hours with those guys, I understood why Shawn had a Confederate flag hanging in his room. And I got the connection with the Nazis, even if I still didn't know what "neo" was all about. But one thing still had me confused: the whole skinhead thing.

"So if youse guys hate blacks so much, why do youse have all this skinhead shit?" I asked.

Bob exploded. "We *are* skinheads! *Real* skinheads! Neo-Nazi skinheads!" He jumped to his feet and thrust his right hand toward the ceiling. "*Sieg Heil!*" Shawn and Tim followed suit.

I probably would have been freaked out by that if I'd been sober. In fact, if I'd been sober, I probably would have realized the thing I was about to say may have been an invitation to getting my ass kicked. But I was drunk off my ass by then, drunker than I'd ever been before, so the words just spewed out: "I'm pretty sure the skinheads in Philly ain't Nazis. Half the skinheads in Philly are black."

The veins in Bob's anaconda neck pulsed so hard I feared he was going to have a stroke. "Those nigger motherfuckers are not skinheads! They're nothing but mud. They're fucking SHARPs, and so are the fucking nigger-loving race-traitors who hang out with them." He was right up in my face when he growled, "Don't you *ever* let me hear you call them skinheads again!"

I felt like hell when I woke up the next afternoon. My head throbbed as I tried to piece together everything that had happened the night before. The drinking and the lecturing had gone on until dawn. I only remembered pieces of what Shawn and his friends had taught me, but I remembered enough to know better than to confuse a neo-Nazi skinhead with a Skinhead Against Racial Prejudice, a.k.a. SHARP, again. Of course, I didn't realize then that I'd just survived my first night of indoctrination into the white supremacy movement. I just knew I liked hanging out with those guys and hoped they'd show up again.

They showed up almost every night. Usually, we'd hang out in Shawn's room drinking and talking until three or four in the morning. Sometimes, we'd pile into Tim's truck and meet up with some of their other friends for a party. The Lancaster County skinheads showed me good times the summer of 1989. But it wasn't all about fun. They spent hours explaining complicated theories to me. They were patient. Even when I got stuff turned around, not once that summer did anybody call me a "retard."

Bob and Tim began by teaching me about something called Identity Theology. Having been raised Catholic, I was pretty suspicious of anything religious coming out of the mouth of any dude who wasn't a priest, but I had to admit that a lot of what the skinheads said made sense, especially after they pointed out verses in the Bible that proved their points. Everything they said was basically the opposite of what I'd been taught at Our Lady of Mount Carmel, but it was all right there in the Bible when the skinheads showed me where to look. The twelve tribes of Israel were the ancestors of today's Europeans, the "Aryans." They were the only true children of God, the humans created in His image through the lineage of Adam. The other races were the bloodlines produced by Eve's carnal sin with the serpent; they were the descendents of Cain, the literal son of Satan. The skinheads assured me the pure Aryan blood of the twelve tribes, *God's* blood, coursed through the veins of every white person in the world, including mine. They told me it was a sin against God for whites to desecrate His sacred bloodline by race-mixing with the sons and daughters of Satan.

"Why didn't I learn this at mass?" I asked, holding the Bible in my hands.

"God chose for you to know now," Tim replied. "The question you should be asking is, 'What am I going to do now that I know?'"

Whenever the skinheads talked about Identity, I felt like I was being called to join God's army. It was my duty as an Aryan, as a child of God, to fight against the forces of Satan. And those forces were enormous, according to my new friends. The skinheads told me that even though it looked like the black, Asian, and Hispanic "mud" were taking over the world, it was really the Jews who threatened Aryan survival.

"The Jews are Satan's generals. The fucking Jews call the

shots for all the mud. They fucking control everything, the cops, the government, the media. It's all Z O G; the Zionist Occupational Government. Z O G s everywhere. And most whites have totally fallen for it. Most whites are too fucking blind to realize they're helping set up their own genocide."

I grew up on the streets of South Philly; I was a hard sell even at fourteen. I asked those skinheads about a million questions, and they had an answer for every one. I tried to trip them up, to show them up, to prove them wrong, but I couldn't. After a while, I just gave myself over to them, and the minute I did, everything started making sense, even the hell of the first fourteen years of my life. Z O G had all but destroyed the white working class in America, stealing our jobs through Affirmative Action and our rightful place in society through Civil Rights laws. In the name of "liberalism," Z O G forced working-class whites to live amid "mud," who brought gangs and drugs into what had been moral neighborhoods. Z O G had humiliated men like my father so much that they turned to dope to escape their pain, and men like my stepfather so much that they unleashed their rage on innocent children. Worst of all, the Jews who controlled Hollywood were brainwashing whites to think "race-

mixing" was cool.

That summer was the first time I enjoyed learning about something other than sports. It wasn't like in school where everything the teachers said sounded like gibberish. I don't know what it was about those theories, but once I got the gist of them, white supremacy made perfect sense to me. It was like I'd been born already knowing about Z O G and Identity and all the skinheads did was remind me it had been inside me my whole life. Remember that movie, *Field of Dreams*: "If you build it, they will come"? Well, once you believe it, the evidence will come. By July, I believed it, and suddenly everywhere I looked I found proof of everything the skinheads were teaching me. The more proof I uncovered, the harder I believed. And the harder I believed, the more I wanted to follow the skinheads into battle.

The problem was there wasn't really anybody to battle in the middle of bumfuck nowhere Pennsylvania. Hell, by virtue of being full Italian, Uncle Nick was the closest thing to a minority within ten miles of the farm. The Lancaster County skinheads spent a lot of time talking about jumping some black kid in the city of Lancaster, but they never did. That whole summer, they never laid so much as one finger on a minority. Instead, they laid into what they called "long-hairs," better known to the rest of the world as skaters. I'm not sure the Lancaster County skinheads ever actually realized I was a skater, or maybe they did and they just overlooked it because I was Shawn's cousin. They gave me a lot of crap about how long my hair was, but that was the extent of it. "Long-hairs" not related to Shawn suffered a far worse fate. The rural skinheads were absolutely convinced that all long-hairs were ZOG dupes. I swear, if Jesse Helms had skipped a couple of barber appointments, those farm boys would have thought he was a Jewish communist.

Midway through the summer, the skinheads took me along with them to a concert in the city of Lancaster. They knew some other skinhead crews from up around Allentown were coming in for the night, so they warned me to stick really close to them.

"They'll think you're a long-hair," Shawn said, "So we're going to have to keep an eye on you."

I couldn't wait to get to the club, expecting something like the Trocadero on South Street. I'd been trying to sneak into the Troc since I was ten. But the Lancaster "club" was nothing like the Trocadero. It was a small bar hosting a punk rock night open to underagers. The place was packed. A lot of long-hairs were there, but I noticed right off that they all were crowded against the back wall. As we made our way into the crowd, I saw why: the mosh pit at the base of the stage teemed with skinheads, all thrashing in time to the music and slamming themselves into each other. I'd glimpsed mosh pits in action before through propped exit doors at the Troc, but never anything like that. There must've been thirty or forty skinheads in the pit that night. It was a blood orgy of the brotherhood.

"You'll be safe up here," Bob Reynolds said as he grabbed me under my armpits and hoisted me onto his shoulders. "Whatever you do, don't fall off me, 'cause they'll kill you with that damn hair of yours."

"Are you sure this is a good idea?" I screamed over the roar.

"You see anybody in there bigger than me?" he asked.

He had a point. In that pit, being the biggest guy with a shaved head meant acceptance, even if you did have a long-hair riding on your shoulders.

I have no idea how many mosh pits I've been in, hundreds at least, but none ever compared to being up on Bob's shoulders in that pit of skinheads. Every skinhead in the pit and every long-hair along the back wall was staring at me, wondering, "Who *is* that kid? Who's the long-hair with his own skinhead bodyguard?" I felt like a celebrity, totally safe up on my perch.

Maybe seeing me floating above the crowd is what inspired another long-hair to brave the pit. Maybe seeing me riding high on Bob's shoulders is what kept the other skinheads from attacking that long-hair the second he stepped inside the circle. Bob saw him before I did. He nudged my leg to get my attention, then pointed across the floor. The other skinheads had moved away from the kid like he was a toxic spill, all looking to Bob for some kind of signal.

I nearly lost my balance when Bob took off across the floor. He rammed into the kid from behind, caught him by the hair, then spun him around to face us. Bob wrapped both his enormous paws around the long-hair's neck and held him firmly in place. The kid looked like he was going to shit his pants.

"Kick him, Frankie," Bob ordered.

It was my moment of truth: was I a long-hair or was I a skinhead? Everyone in the club was watching me. It felt like everyone in the whole fucking world was watching.

I drove my foot directly into the kid's face. Blood sprayed from his nose. Bob released the kid's neck; the long-hair's body slumped to the floor. Every skinhead in the mosh pit smiled at me. Then, without saying a word, they fell back into formation, swirling around the pit like bald, brawny dervishes.

A few nights later, the Lancaster County crew gathered in Shawn's bedroom. They took turns with a pair of electric clippers until my head was shaved clean. Tim Kleinschmidt presented me with an old pair of his Doc Marten combat boots. He explained that they were laced in red to symbolize both the sacred Aryan blood in my veins and the ZOG blood I had spilled in the mosh pit.

I was fourteen, and I was a neo-Nazi skinhead. For the first time in my life, I felt like I mattered.

The Boys Who
Would Be Führer

IN THE LATE 1980S, SKINHEADS WERE THE HOTTEST TOPIC on the talk show circuit thanks to a few show-stopping guest spots by Tom Metzger, head of White Aryan Resistance, and his son, John, the white-power wunderkind. The appearance everybody remembers is the time Johnny Boy went on *Geraldo*. John Metzger faced off center stage with a Jew and a black dude. He wasn't alone; he had two other young neo-Nazi leaders on stage with him and dozens of skinheads in the audience.

Geraldo kicked things off by introducing a white guy with a black eye who claimed he'd been viciously attacked for no reason on the train by a pack of skinheads in front of his wife and baby, who were sitting next to him on the set. The guy's story sent the other panelists into overdrive. Before long, Metzger's comments got the black panelist so riled up he came out of his chair, wrapped his hands around Metzger's neck, and tried to choke him. That's when all hell broke loose in Geraldo's studio. This enormous brawl erupted on stage, in the audience, everywhere. Geraldo's security guards came flying onto the set, but not quite fast enough to save their boss. One of Metzger's boys hurled a chair across the stage; it slammed into Geraldo's face and broke his nose.

I guess none of the adults in my life watched *Geraldo*, because when I returned from Lancaster County, not one of them realized I'd become a skinhead even though my head was shaved clean and I was parading through South Philly in a flight jacket and combat boots. My dad didn't say anything about the change in my appearance. When my mom finally saw me, she told me she thought I looked a lot better without long scraggly hair. John was more blunt: "At least now you don't look like a retard." His reaction surprised me only because I hadn't counted on him saying anything. I figured he'd just beat the crap out of me. But he didn't.

Only other kids understood that my new look was a political statement, not a fashion statement. My first night back in the city, I showed up at Nanny and Pop Bertone's house for dinner. Uncle Dave, the superstar athlete of the Bertone family, was still home on summer break from college. When I stomped into Nanny's kitchen in my Doc Martens, Dave looked at me like I'd sprouted a second head. I wondered if that's how I'd looked when I first saw Shawn in Aunt Catherine's kitchen. All through dinner, Dave just stared at me. He didn't say anything in front of Nanny and Pop, but he cornered me once we were alone.

"You're going to get yourself killed," he said.

I assured him I would be proud to give my life to protect the survival of the Aryan race. I stared right into my childhood hero's eyes and saluted, "*Sieg Heil!*"

"Jesus, Frankie – do you even know what that means?"

"God chose me to know," I replied. "I know exactly what's going on. I know the fucking kikes and niggers are trying to take over. And I know we're not going to take it anymore."

"Who's telling you this shit?" Dave asked.

"My white brothers."

"Your white brothers are full of shit."

"You're full of shit!" I screamed at my uncle. "You and all the rest of the fucking dupes laying down in front of ZOG. You make me sick."

I stormed out of the house without even saying goodbye to Nanny and Pop. I headed over to Finnegan's Park, where I'd always spent my free time in my dad's neighborhood. I helped myself to a beer and settled in for the night. Since I'd been gone for nearly two months, the guys wanted to know what I'd been doing. They weren't too interested in what I had to say about National Socialism, but they liked the story about how the skinheads had carried me into the mosh pit and I'd kicked the "long-hair" in the face. They had me re-tell it every time somebody new joined the crowd. After a while, one of the guys pulled me aside and said, "You ought to meet Louie Lacinzi."

"Who's he?" I asked.

"Some kid from St. I's who's been around this summer. He's a skinhead."

"He's probably a fucking SHARP from South Street," I replied.

"A what?"

"A SHARP. A nigger-lover."

"Trust me, dude, Louie Lacinzi ain't no nigger-lover."

A few nights later I was hanging around by the baseball field drinking and bullshitting about nothing with the guys when I saw Louie Lacinzi for the first time. I tried not to look like I was watching him approach, but I was watching him, just in case he was a SHARP.

"Cool, another skinhead," he said. "I heard youse were hanging out down here. Thought I'd come see if the rumors were true."

"What rumors?"

His lips curled into a slight smile. "That there's finally somebody else around here who's sick of niggers taking over what's ours."

So I wasn't the only neo-Nazi skinhead in Finnegan's Park. Louie Lacinzi was a skinhead, too. And by the end of the night, he was my best friend.

Louie and I had only been palling around for a few days when someone told us a group of skinheads hung out most nights in the Wise Potato Chip Company's parking lot across the street from McCreesh Playground. Since the guy who told us wasn't a skinhead, I wasn't sure he knew what he was talking about. The Lancaster County skinheads said there'd been a really hardcore neo-Nazi crew in Philly a few years back, but they seemed to think it had broken up. So when Louie and I heard about the guys at Wise's, we were skeptical. We headed over to check them out for ourselves. After we spied on them from a distance to check out their colors and make sure they weren't actually Sharpies, we decided to introduce ourselves.

Most of the ten or twelve guys in that parking lot were in their early twenties. Most of them weren't skinheads, but four were. And they were the real deal, the kind of neo-Nazi skinheads I hadn't met out in Lancaster County. Louie and I didn't have a freaking clue who we were dealing with that first night. When we asked those older skinheads what they did in Philly, they all sort of shrugged and said it'd been more than a year since they'd done any serious battling. Louie and me were too naïve to realize those guys were stonewalling us because they didn't trust us yet. And we were too cocky to think we could learn much from our elders. We were polite – they were pretty big dudes – but we basically wrote them off as white power retirees who stood around drinking beer in a parking lot. Of course, we were more than happy to stand around drinking beer with them, especially for free.

When we came back for more free beer the next night, we got our first lesson in East Coast skinhead history. A few years earlier, back when Louie and me were still in grade school, the guys in the Wise's parking lot had been founding members of The Uprise, the first neo-Nazi skinhead crew in Philly. The Uprise had been really violent, so they were notorious with the Philly cops within a couple of months of organizing. But their leaders, the Windham brothers, hadn't been content just to be local legends. They formed a white power band and distributed their recordings all over the U.S. and even Europe. In neo-Nazi circles, the guys from The Uprise were celebrities. But having their own band wasn't the only claim to fame The Uprise veterans had to share with us. They asked us if we'd seen the big skinhead brawl on *Geraldo*.

"You remember that bastard who said he'd been attacked by skinheads on the train?"

Of course, we did. He was the white guy with the black eye. He claimed he'd been minding his own business when a group of skinheads jumped him.

"He wasn't lying," an Uprise vet said. "Well, he was lying when he said the skinheads started it, because they didn't. He did. He was ripped up drunk and started calling them 'jarheads' and talking shit. The idiot tried to rub one of their heads. That asshole was praying for an ass kicking; they just answered his prayer."

"Who did?" we asked all wide-eyed.

The older skinheads exchanged glances like they weren't sure if they could tell us.

"It doesn't matter now," one said to the others. Then he turned to Louie and me and said, "Those were our boys on that train."

They told us that Scott Windham and another member of The Uprise were still doing time in Rikers Island for that attack. The other Windham brother was in prison, too, as were at least half the members of the original crew. All of them had been sent up for crimes they had committed in the name of The Uprise. The remaining members explained to Louie and me that back when they formed the crew there hadn't been too many SHARPs in the city, so The Uprise hadn't had to fight the anti-racists for turf. Instead, they had directed almost all their violence at blacks who'd started moving into their neighborhood.

"The cops don't give a shit if you roll on some other white kids," they said. "They don't know the difference between us and Sharpies. They don't know who's who. But you start laying out niggers, and the fucking Jew lawyers'll come running down off their thrones to make sure you get locked up for good."

By the time we met, only four of the original twenty or so members of The Uprise crew were still hanging together in the Wise's parking lot. They were the ones who taught me that the Lancaster County skinheads really didn't know shit about the white supremacy movement, at least not about the role skinheads played in the movement. The Uprise had been an incredibly hardcore neo-Nazi crew. They knew the ideology and history of white supremacy inside out. They hadn't just read pamphlets from groups like Aryan Nations, some of them had gone out to Idaho to train at the Aryan Nations' compound. The Uprise veterans were like white power Ph.D.s, and after I'd been their student for a couple nights, I realized the Lancaster County skinheads couldn't have passed a neo-Nazi GED.

In those days, though, I still was thankful to have met the Lancaster County skinheads because they introduced me to the movement and the movement was everything to me. But I was even more thankful to The Uprise veterans for taking me to the next level of my education. In one way, I remain thankful to The Uprise – I figure I owe my life to them. The guys from The Uprise taught me something the Lancaster County skinheads never could have taught me out in Amish country: they taught me what it takes to survive as a skinhead in the gang-infested inner city of Philadelphia. It takes a crew.

Although some vocabulary expert will probably disagree with me on this, back in the late 1980s, most skinhead crews were basically just local gangs. They were a lot more formal than a group like the Third and Jackson boys, but they weren't networked in the way gangs like the Latin Kings were, gangs with branches all over the country. All that started changing, though, right around the time I joined the movement.

Romantic Violence was the first American neo-Nazi crew. They formed in Chicago in 1984, and other crews started organizing soon after. This was a decade before the internet, so it took a while for everybody to get connected. Still, within a few years, the crew leaders found each other, mostly at white-power concerts or at rallies held by groups like Aryan Nations or the KKK. In time, some of the crew leaders started taking some of their cues from their enemies. Nazi skinheads hated minority gangs like the Latin Kings and the Gangster Disciples but they couldn't deny that the structure of those gangs was what was help-ing them spread so quickly into new turf, including the once all-white neighborhoods the skinheads wanted back. So in the late 1980s, some skinhead crews followed suit. The crew leaders started building the alliances that became national gangs by the mid-1990s.

Even though The Uprise had never had branches in other cities, its remaining members helped Louie and me understand that the world of skinheads was a lot bigger than we'd imagined. According to those guys, there were several thousand actual neo-Nazi skinheads in the United States then, and by "actual" I mean guys who'd gone through formal training and initia-tion periods with real crews like the Eastern Nazi Alliance. As "freshcuts," or initiates, they had worn white laces in their Doc Martens to declare that they were willing to fight for the Aryan bloodline. Not until they had spilled the blood of some Sharpie "ZOG dupe" or some minority "mud," had they graduated to red laces and full rank within their crew.

Louie and I had both been blood red from the start, and we were hell bent on keeping it that way. Before the summer of 1989 rolled to a close, Louie and I came to an understanding about our future together as skinheads. We were going to form our own crew, and our crew was going to blow The Uprise the hell out of the record books. It was our silent pact, because kids who grow up in places like South Philly don't talk about their goals. They see too many dreamers get burned to set themselves up for public humiliation. In South Philly, dashed dreams are right up there with deformities for getting a guy pegged with an embarrassing nickname for the rest of his life. I could just see myself thirty years into the future if I'd shot my mouth off about my Nazi aspirations then failed to deliver. I'd wind up hanging on some corner bitching about my arthritis to Tommy "Earbow" Petanzi and Mikey "Muffin Ass" McCarthy.

"Shut up about it already, Eva Braun," they'd say.

That's when some young corner punk would pipe up and ask, "Why do youse guys call him 'Eva Braun'?"

"Frankie got fucked by Hitler, too."

Thankfully, Louie and I didn't have to talk about our vision for the future to know we totally agreed on what it ought to look like.

Most nights, we scammed beer and history lessons off The Uprise vets for a few hours. When they got bored with us, we'd head over to South Street and scam beer and club passes off the older punks who still remembered me as one of the little skater kids from back when Jimmy and me used to show off our Ollies for the dudes waiting in line to get in the clubs. There were about a dozen SHARPs on South Street then. They thought they owned the place because the skaters and the young punks feared them. Then Louie and I showed up. We didn't care that the SHARPs had us outnumbered; we got in their faces. That's when we realized most of those South Street SHARPs commuted in each night from their pretty houses out in the suburbs. Louie and me reeked of South Philly. We weren't commuters.

For about a month, we glared and dropped threats, nothing more. It was enough. South Street buzzed about how Louie and I had put the SHARPs in their place. Kids the SHARPs had always bullied started sticking real close to us. We sure as hell weren't geniuses, but we were smart enough to recognize a brilliant idea. Maybe we didn't have to find other skinheads to form our own crew – we could just create our own skinheads. The more the skaters and punks gravitated to us for protection, the more I flashed back to that mosh pit in Lancaster. I had been a "long-hair" on my way into the pit that night, a "long-hair" with my own skinhead bodyguard, but when I came out of that pit, I was a Nazi. Security breeds loyalty, and loyalty is everything. By the end of summer 1989, my loyalties were clear: Louie Lacinzi was my brother, and the white supremacy movement was my family.

MY MOM AND John must've been in shock after they heard I got promoted to ninth grade, because they invited me to move back home. Now, moving back in with my asshole of a stepfather was the second to last thing in the world I wanted to do. I knew I could survive John because I'd done it before. But I wasn't so sure anymore about the Junior Black Mafia. In fact I was pretty sure I'd be dead the second they saw my shaved head. So the weekend before school started, I took my mom and John up on their offer since it meant I could go to Furness High School, deep in the heart of the Irish district. I noticed right away that things had changed on Tree Street while I'd been gone. I'd been living with my dad; I knew what a house looked like once drugs moved in. I didn't know then exactly what John and my mom were taking, only that whatever it was glazed over their eyes and slurred their speech. Even the house had changed. The house had never been fancy, but my mom had always kept it clean. It was a disaster. It looked like my dad's house, like a crack house. But it wasn't a crack house; it was just a Percocet house then.

John no longer had the strength or desire to beat on me. He just gave me a speech about how I was going to have to live by the rules, especially since my mom was pregnant again and she couldn't handle pregnancy, baby Kirsten, and me running wild all at once. Even while they lectured me, I could tell the rules weren't going to matter anymore, so long as they kept using. But I remembered what it had been like in the past. I'd watched enough *Wild Kingdom* as a kid to know you still watch your back around a lion even after you shoot him with a tranquilizer. I made a good show of buckling down, good enough, at least, to convince two drunks on downers they could trust me.

At first, I confided the truth about them using to only a couple people. Louie was the only skinhead I really trusted with that information. Drugs were a big issue in the movement, one I couldn't afford to be associated with so soon after joining even by association with my parents. Neo-Nazi skinheads hate drugs because they think drugs are a "nigger" thing. Part of the

ZOG conspiracy theory says that some whites, especially poor whites like my parents, get caught up in drugs because there's this big plot to use drugs to weaken white resistance. That part of the theory gives white addicts a little bit of an out; they're not just druggies, they're actually victims of ZOG. But you only hear that part of the theory getting bounced around among skinheads when they're having a really serious bull session. The other 99.9% of the time, they see a stoned white person, and they call them a "wigger."

My cousin Jimmy was the only other guy I talked to about my mom and John. I trusted him with my secret. I trusted him with my life. And I trusted that if I played my cards right, I could get Jimmy to become a skinhead, too. Even though the skaters and the young punks on South Street were loving Louie and me for backing off the SHARPs, and even though my cousin Jimmy was a punk who loved to skate, I knew that tack wasn't going to work on him. Jimmy didn't fear SHARPs. Jimmy was a rare breed, a near perfect blend of seething rage and brass-knuckle balls. Louie and me needed guys like that if we were going to form a real skinhead crew. Of course, we also needed those guys to sign on to the whole movement philosophy, and that's where we ran into trouble with Jimmy. When it came to hatred, Jimmy didn't need any of our theories, and he didn't want any of our lectures. He didn't give a rat's ass about race politics. Jimmy hated *everybody*, because at some point in his life, everybody – black, white, liberal, conservative, jocks, brains, everybody – had picked on him. I knew getting Jimmy to hate SHARPs and minorities would be a total no-brainer; getting him not to kill other Nazis was going to be the challenge. And, for a while, it looked like that might include Louie and me. Every time we tried to preach Identity to Jimmy, he got that Tasmanian devil look on his face. Then he'd spit. For Jimmy, spitting was more than just a habit; it was punctuation. When he hocked an exclamation point onto the sidewalk, I knew I should back away slowly without making sudden movements.

Jimmy and I reported to Furness High School together when school started back up. He cruised through the front doors in his Mohawk; I marched in wearing my Doc Martens. I'd been sulking through mandatory counseling sessions at school in between fights for about two months when Jimmy tipped me off that some black kids planned to jump me. He'd overheard a couple of them talking about what they were going to do to "that skinhead." He didn't know when it was going to go down, only that it was.

I saw them coming before they even moved toward me. They weren't standing where they usually stood in the lunch line. They were watching me too closely. There were three of them. I'd survived worse odds and better fighters in my dad's neighborhood. I glanced down at the polished stone floor, smiled at my shadowy reflection, and thought, "Bring it on." They circled me, talking crap about my shaved head. The cafeteria fell silent. I just stood there, watching, keeping all three of them in sight at all times, waiting for someone to throw the first punch so I could claim self-defense, feeling my brass-knuckle knife inside the pocket of my flight jacket, knowing it would be more than enough if my fists weren't.

Then from out of nowhere this hard plastic cafeteria tray came flying up against the side of one of the black guy's heads. I was as surprised as he was. Jimmy was holding the tray like a club. He looked like a freaking rabid dog, crazier than I'd ever seen him look. If Jimmy had actually foamed at the mouth it wouldn't have surprised one person in that lunchroom. He drew the tray all the way back, then smacked it across the face of one of the other kids.

"Get your motherfucking nigger asses away from Frankie!"

That was classic Jimmy: drop two guys to the ground with a tray before thinking to tell them to back off. The one black kid still standing inched away from us. The two still rubbing their heads didn't look like they had any interest in getting up off the floor.

The guidance counselor called me into his office first thing the next morning. The principal was standing next to his desk when I arrived.

"I didn't lay one finger on nobody."

"That's not why we called you in," the principal said. "We pulled your records in hopes of getting some insight into the problems you seem to be having here at Furness. You did not complete all four quarters of the eighth grade."

I wanted to say, "Dude, I didn't even pass all four quarters of the seventh grade." But I thought that might be shooting myself in the foot. So all I said was, "My mom got a letter saying I was in the ninth grade."

"Well, you're not," the principal replied. "Some type of error was made and I've arranged for it to be resolved. Report to the front office of Sharswood School before first bell tomorrow."

So much for ninth grade.

THAT EVENING AT home, I was playing in my room with Kirsten when Jimmy called.

"Yo, I shaved it," he said.

Once Jimmy shaved his head, he started spending most of his nights and weekends down on South Street with Louie and me. We claimed a nasty back alley as our turf and hung out drinking beer that we either scammed from my mom and John or sweet-talked punk girls into buying for us. One weekend, Shawn and a couple of other guys from the Lancaster County crew drove in to party with us in "Skinhead Alley." They must've told everybody they knew about the good time they had, because within a few months, there were at least a half-dozen Nazis, sometimes as many as fifteen or twenty, coming into the city from one suburb or another nearly every weekend. Between the parties in Skinhead Alley and the parties we got invited to in other towns, Louie, Jimmy, and I became regular social butterflies.

But for some reason, Jimmy wasn't with us the night Louie and I first met John Cook, one of the most legendary skinheads on the East Coast then. Cook was this huge dude in his mid-twenties, tattooed from head to toe in movement symbols. He was a big deal inside older skinhead circles; he was an enormous deal to a couple of kids like us. So Louie and I were totally flattered when Cook invited us to spend a weekend at his house outside Reading. And we nearly wet ourselves when he introduced us to the Invisible Empire of the Ku Klux Klan.

When we pulled into the driveway of the old farmhouse, I thought the place was abandoned, maybe condemned. We parked among at least a dozen other cars and trucks, some missing doors or engines, others new and polished to a high gloss. Cook led us behind the ramshackle house where a large, sided Army tent was already set up. Inside, neat rows of folding chairs faced off with a Confederate battle flag and men were beginning to take their seats. The elderly leader of the klavern told Louie and me we were welcome to join the Klan so long as we promised not to stir up any trouble and got our parents to sign off on our application forms. If you're under eighteen, you can't join the Invisible Empire without a parent's or guardian's signature. Klansman are surprisingly fussy about stuff like that for guys who made their name off lynchings.

Louie and I promised we'd ask our mothers for permission to join the Klan. Back in Skinhead Alley, Louie forged my mom's name on my form, and I forged his mom's name on his. We hitchhiked back to the country a week later and took our vows with Cook looking on like a proud godfather, but Louie and me were streetwise enough to take those country Klansmen with a big grain of salt. We knew when we signed up that they weren't what we wanted to be. But they had stuff we wanted. That particular Invisible Empire klavern only had a handful of members, but they were on the mailing lists of every white supremacy group in the United States. That old house was a library and as members, we were free to borrow anything we wanted. That house was also an arsenal. And as members, we were free to shoot anything we wanted. The old dudes in the klavern had grown up in the country; they'd been shooting deer and beer cans since they could walk. They taught us how to handle shotguns and even semiautomatics. My favorite was a Simonov SKS carbine. The Klansmen let us spend entire afternoons shooting at the pictures of Martin Luther King, Jr. they'd nailed to trees as targets. They never asked us to pay for our ammunition or even our food. For a couple of city boys, the place was like summer camp. But just as it had been with the Lancaster County skinheads, it wasn't all about fun and games. Everybody in the Invisible Empire was seriously into Identity Theology. I knew the basics about it from the time I'd spent with the Lancaster County skinheads, but those Klansmen put Louie and me through seminary. Sitting through sermons was the price we had to pay to get to play with really big guns.

Louie and I went up to the Invisible Empire camp together at least every few months. If he wasn't around or up for the trip, sometimes I'd go alone and meet up with skinheads from other parts of the state who'd started visiting the Klansmen. Usually I'd hitch a ride out in the morning then hitch another back late afternoon so I wouldn't have to miss a night on South Street. Jimmy went with me a few times; Louie had signed for his mom, too. But none of the other South Street skinheads ever went out to Klan country. Most of the other skinheads who regularly hung on South Street then were from middle-class suburban families, and every goddamn one of them chickened out on the Klan when he found out he'd have to get a parent's signature.

"My mom won't sign this!" they'd say, offended we'd even think they would.

"So don't show it to her, you moron. Sign it yourself."

Then they'd really freak out. "My mom would kill me if I forged her signature!"

These guys spent Saturday nights bragging about how they couldn't wait to beat the hell out of the SHARPs, and they were pissing themselves about getting grounded. It made Louie and Jimmy and me wonder who would actually have our backs if all hell broke loose.

Everybody came to think of Louie and Jimmy and me as the leaders of the skinhead scene on South Street, partly because we were the only ones with big enough balls to forge our mommies' signatures so we could join the Klan, but mostly because we were from South Philly. The suburban skinheads thought we were dangerous, and compared to them, I guess we were. But compared to the kinds of guys we'd grown up around, guys like my dad, for instance, we weren't even on the same block as dangerous. We were just city kids, as dirty and mean in a fight as the streets we'd been raised on, and that alone secured our rank.

We had a hell of a good time being neo-Nazi skinheads in those early days. We battled the SHARPs enough to have fun with it, but not so much we had to fear for our lives. We talked about ZOG enough to remember why we hated everybody else, but not so much that it interfered with our partying. We let a lot of the punks hang with us then, and the skaters. So long as they weren't friends with the SHARPs, we figured we might be able to turn them into Nazis. Most just wanted our beer, but we converted a few of the harder-core punks. A kid named Dan Bellen was one of the first punks to shave off his blond hair. He was from one of the townships on the outskirts of the city, but he fought like he'd been raised in South Philly. So did Matt Hanson and Brian "Stug" Stugen, two suburban skinheads who came to practically live on South Street. They were the only three guys we trusted to have our backs in battle. The other guys who partied in Skinhead Alley were our friends, our fellow Nazis, our followers, but only Dan, Matt, and Stug were our brothers-in-arms.

Then there were our sisters. Girls started wandering back into Skinhead Alley once word spread that we always had beer. There weren't any actual skinchicks on South Street then, just a bunch of punk-rock chicks and skater girls. Even without the beer, we were like magnets for some of those girls. Guys who couldn't have bought a date off a prostitute before they shaved their heads found themselves juggling three or four girls at a time. Of course, they also got their asses beat down by some of those girls before they learned the cardinal rule of dating on South Street: never cheat on a punk girl who's spent more time in mosh pits than you have.

I didn't consider myself much of a ladies' man when I was fourteen. Like any boy that age, I was self-conscious about my looks even though a few girls had told me I was cute. Mostly, I was self-conscious about my age, though. I was younger than just about everybody on South Street, but only Louie and Jimmy knew it. Everybody else assumed I was at least sixteen because I was one of the skinhead leaders. The girls who came into Skinhead Alley assumed I was older, too. At first, I didn't correct people's assumptions, then I started telling people I was actually two years older than I really was. Eventually, I realized I'd made a royal mess for myself by lying about my age. It was bad enough that I was a fourteen year-old virgin; now I'd turned myself into a sixteen year-old virgin. I lived in fear of one of the girls on South Street tasting my innocence while she was kissing me. I could just imagine her telling all the other girls, them telling all the guys, and me ending up the laughing stock of Philly: the big, bad Nazi dude who couldn't get himself laid even once in sixteen years. What could I say? "Hey guys, leave me alone. It hasn't been sixteen years; I'm only fourteen." I would've choked myself on Kirsten's pacifier before I would've admitted I was the baby of my own gang.

I don't know if it was the skinhead-mystique thing I had going for me, or the Italian-stallion genes I got from my dad, or both, but something fooled the South Street girls into thinking I was a lot more experienced than I actually was. None of them ever acted like they suspected I was only fourteen, and none of them acted like they thought I was a virgin. Almost every weekend, I'd meet up with some punk girl or another in a dark corner of Skinhead Alley. She'd start kissing on me, and I'd start kissing her back. Usually right about the time I'd start trying to get her clothes off, she'd realize we were leaning up against a nasty ass brick wall in a hell hole of an alley with a dozen or so sweaty skinheads drooling along at the show. Not exactly the kind of romance a girl reads about in *Seventeen* magazine.

There wasn't any privacy within forty blocks of Skinhead Alley, so I spent a lot of nights pacing South Street, trying to give myself a mental cold shower. I'd imagine the most unsexy things I could think of, like Kirsten's poopy diapers or John passed out drunk on the couch. Once I finally got myself back under control, I'd go back into Skinhead Alley in hopes of finding some other cute little punk girl who might not be so shy about having an audience.

Makin' Nazi Love

I GOT KICKED OUT OF THE EIGHTH GRADE AT SHARSWOOD
School after I beat the holy hell out of a black student named
Sheldon Jones who'd been terrorizing some of the Irish kids I'd
grown up with. The next day, bored, I stopped by Furness High
School looking for Jimmy. The cop who guarded Furness's front
door knew I wasn't a student there anymore and wouldn't let me
in. When I snarked off about that, he patted me down and found
my knife. A couple hours later, two Philadelphia police officers
escorted me home. Right in front of me, my mom asked the cops
if there was something she could sign so they'd take me away
somewhere. They said there wasn't.

Those cops hadn't wedged their cruiser more than a block
down Tree Street before my mom and John kicked me out
again. I didn't bother calling my dad this time. I just threw some
clothes in a duffel bag and started walking. Hanging around
South Street, I'd gotten to know this older punk dude named George.
He and his wife Rachel had an apartment that was the first
floor of a rowhouse not far from Tree Street. I'd partied there a
couple times. While George and Rachel's place was party
central, it was also a real home. They already had one kid and
Rachel was pregnant. So there'd be all these punks crowded
in, listening to music and drinking and playing with the kid.
Except for her belly, Rachel looked like she hadn't eaten in
a year, but she'd make amazing food for everybody, and George
would do dishes like a maniac, suds splashing up onto the skull

tattoos on his arms, trying to keep up with Rachel, who was basically an anorexic Julia Child with a mohawk. I showed up on George and Rachel's stoop hoping only for some food and sympathy before taking up residence on South Street with other homeless kids. But George and Rachel weren't having any of that. They insisted I stay.

Since I didn't have to get up for school or anything else anymore, I partied seven nights a week. If I wasn't officially an alcoholic before I moved in with George and Rachel, I became one there. There was almost always somebody hanging around the apartment to drink with. If there wasn't, I drank alone. I'd get myself half in the bag every afternoon before heading down to South Street to get really wasted. One night at a club, I was standing with George when this black punk friend of his leaned over to me and whispered, "Check her out, man!" I followed his finger to where he was pointing on the other side of the room. This girl was completely focused on the band, bopping to the music, totally oblivious to everything. She looked cute as hell in her pleated plaid miniskirt and Doc Martens.

"Dude," the black punk said to me with complete sincerity. "You two should get together and make Nazi love."

So that's how it came to pass that a black dude set me up on my first date with a neo-Nazi skinchick. Lauren was fifteen. She didn't know I was only fourteen, and she didn't know I was a virgin. She only knew I was a skinhead, and that was enough for her. Lauren was the first girl I met who was seriously into National Socialism. She was a skinchick because she was a Nazi, not just because she was hot for skinheads. That girl knew as much about the theory behind National Socialism as any skinhead in town. Whenever any of the guys got in her sweet pudgy face even a little bit about her being "just" a skinchick, she'd word-whip them something fierce. Lauren wielded quotations like Jimmy wielded cafeteria trays.

Another girl around the scene was Rachel's best friend, Amy. She was eighteen, same as Rachel. She was a true anarchist punk, opposed to anything that looked like conformity, and you can't get much more conformist than Nazism. I had a hell of a crush on Amy long before I actually met her. She was one of the most beautiful women I'd ever seen, even when she was snarling her lips and hurling slams about skinheads. I drooled every time she prowled past the mouth of Skinhead Alley. But Amy had never so much as spoken to me on South Street. She had to speak to me at George and Rachel's, though. My first morning there, when she stopped over for coffee, I was leaning against the cabinet where Rachel kept the cups.

"Move, Nazi fuck," Amy said. At least she was talking to me.

After a few days, she stopped calling me "Nazi fuck." By the end of the week, she and Rachel were including me in their girl talk out in the kitchen. Once Amy started talking to me like I was actually a human being, I fell at least a little bit in love with her. Relaxed in her best friend's kitchen, her lips loosened into a soft smile I found even sexier than her South Street sneer. But I wasn't a fool; I knew Amy was about a million miles out of my league. And besides, I had Lauren.

Amy devoted a lot of time to me while I lived with George and Rachel. We would spend hours talking about everything from music to why I was into the white supremacy movement. Amy really listened to what I had to say, even when she didn't agree with me. Nobody else had done that since I'd become a skinhead. Nobody else had paid me the respect to explain why they didn't agree with my racism; everybody else who disagreed just wrote me off as stupid or evil. Amy wasn't like that. She treated me like her equal, even though I knew I wasn't. Amy and I got close enough after a few weeks that I confided in her that Lauren and me were having problems. It wasn't anything earth shattering, just teenaged couple crap. But it was bugging me one night, so I told Amy about it.

"How did you and your last girlfriend get along?" Amy asked.

"I haven't really had a 'girlfriend' before Lauren."

I could tell she was surprised. "That's part of the problem.

You haven't had any practice being somebody's boyfriend. You're not used to thinking about how somebody else is going to react because you've never had to think about your actions as half the actions of a whole. I'm not saying you're selfish, at least not intentionally. Guys can be really selfish sometimes and not even realize."

"Like by doing what?" I asked.

"Like when a guy's really sweet to his girlfriend at a party or somewhere, and they go off and fuck, then they come back to the party and he ignores her the rest of the night. Most guys are too dickheaded to understand how that makes a girl feel like a whore."

I must have blushed or something. All of a sudden, Amy looked at me like a scientist who'd just discovered a new species of mold.

"You know what I mean?" she asked, dipping her toe in the water.

"Sure," I said, trying my damnedest to sound cool. Amy wasn't buying it.

"Are you a virgin?"

If it had been anybody else in the world asking, I'd have lied. But I trusted Amy.

I looked away. Panic washed over me, and I turned back and pleaded, "You're not going to tell anybody, are you?"

Amy gave me a big hug. Her bobbed hair tickled my shoulder when she said, "Of course not. It's nothing to be embarrassed about anyhow, but I promise I won't tell anybody." Now, this absolutely gorgeous eighteen year-old was still hugging me at this point, and she whispered in my ear, "Maybe, if you play your cards right, I'll take that virginity from you one day." Amy gave me a really innocent little kiss on the cheek, and went back into the kitchen to see what Rachel was doing.

I must have paced up and down the alley behind that apartment for three freaking hours. Kirsten's diapers after she eats peas. The hair growing out of Pop's ears. Puke crusted on the side of a toilet. The time Kirsten spit up on my shirt and it looked like cottage cheese. I didn't think my erection would ever go soft.

After that, every time Amy came over to the apartment, she'd pull me aside and whisper in this creepy boogeyman voice, "You better watch out, Frankie. I'm going to get your virginity." We'd crack up. It was our inside joke. And what a joke it was: the hottest punk chick in Philadelphia hooking up with the homeless skinhead virgin!

I took the advice Amy had given me about Lauren. I was sure I wasn't doing anything to make Lauren feel like a prostitute, seeing as I wasn't doing anything much other than kissing her, but I tried to think more about her feelings. It must have worked, because we stopped fighting.

Lauren came over to the apartment early one Saturday afternoon for a pre-party George was throwing. A couple carloads of South Street punks were heading to Allentown for a concert that night, and they'd offered to let Lauren and me ride along. We'd been drinking for a couple of hours when Lauren said, "I need to talk to you for a minute."

I grabbed a fresh beer and followed Lauren to the basement, which was the only place you could get away from the party at George and Rachel's.

"What's up?" I asked once we were alone.

She answered me with a kiss. We kissed for a long time, long enough that I started unbuttoning her shirt. I was prying open her bra when I felt her go for the top button of my Levi's. We weren't leaned up against some nasty-ass brick wall in Skinhead Alley with a crew of Nazis watching us; we were leaned up against the nasty-ass brick wall of a rowhouse basement, but we were alone. Lauren and I were sickeningly sweet the rest of that afternoon at the apartment. When it came time to leave, we slid into the backseat of George's car. Amy climbed in the back with us. I got stuck with the hump; I was in the middle, with Lauren on one side and Amy on the other. Allentown is about an hour and a half drive from South Philly. George was blaring the stereo the whole way. I couldn't hear anything anybody in the front seat was saying. To make matters worse, for the first half-hour or so, Lauren and Amy were screaming across me in the backseat, trying to hear each other over the thump of the speakers in the window behind our heads. My head felt like it was going to explode before they finally gave up trying to talk. Lauren dozed off. Amy stared silently out the window.

We'd been driving for almost an hour when Amy leaned in close to my ear and asked, "Did you fuck her?" Her voice was a strained whisper fighting the loud music. She didn't want Lauren to hear. Amy wasn't the type to embarrass a younger woman like that.

"I'll tell you later."

"I said, did you fuck her?" Amy's lips contorted into the snarl I hadn't seen in weeks. This time, Amy's voice didn't sound strained; it sounded pissed. This wasn't the opinionated, theory-spouting anarchist who'd taken me under her wing. This wasn't the mature older woman who'd gently counseled me on how to be a better boyfriend. This was a fucking hellcat who sounded jealous. I was confused, scared, and turned on.

"Later." I pleaded with my eyes for Amy to back off in case Lauren might wake up and realize we were talking about what had happened in the basement. Amy glanced over at Lauren, and so did I. She was propped against the door, still dozing. She'd had a lot of beer that afternoon, and the crowded car was hot. She wasn't really sleeping, though; her eyes opened a little when we hit a bump. Amy didn't care. She started tracing her fingers down my chest.

"Did your little friend even have a fucking clue what she was doing?" Her hand dropped down onto my crotch.

"Jesus, she's fucking sitting right there," I said, but I didn't try to move her hand.

Lauren half-opened her eyes and looked at me. I smiled at her. She smiled back, then dozed off again. Amy never took her hand off my cock. If I hadn't been completely drunk, I would have come right there in the car.

When we poured ourselves out of the car in the club parking lot, Lauren took my hand. Amy shot me a look that made me a little worried about Lauren's safety. I squeezed Lauren's hand. She squeezed mine back. We got in line to pay the cover charge. It was chaotic until the last few feet, where it dropped to single file so the bouncers could stamp people's hands. Being the polite and respectful boyfriend Amy had taught me to be, I motioned for Lauren to go in front of me, ladies first and all. When I dropped Lauren's hand so she could pass through the gate, I felt Amy press up against my back. Her breath was a blowtorch on the nape of my neck.

The second Lauren stepped inside the club, Amy yanked me out of line. We barely made it into the alley behind the club. There was none of the sweetness there had been with Lauren that afternoon. For a few seconds, Lauren and I had almost made love. Amy and I just fucked. It was the best fifteen minutes of the first fourteen years of my life.

When I finally made it inside the club, Lauren nailed me. "What did you do with her?"

"You know you're my only girl." Then I hugged her, which was stupid because I reeked of Amy. Lauren and I never made love a second time.

Amy and I fucked almost every day for the next two months. Then Amy broke off our nasty affair without warning, which left me with nothing to do during the day. None of the suburban skinheads came into the city during the week. Jimmy and Louie both still went to school. And with the birth of their second child just weeks away, George and Rachel were too busy to hang out. Whether I was lonely or just bored out of my skull, some days I'd cruise over to my dad's neighborhood to see if anybody was lolling around in Finnegan's Park. Usually, since I was in the neighborhood already, I'd show up at Nanny and Pop's just about the time Nanny was putting dinner on the table. By then my grandparents knew I'd become a skinhead, and they knew what that meant. Nanny and Pop in no way approved of what I was doing with my life, but they weren't willing to cut me out of theirs. They'd tried that tack once before with my dad, and it had been a disaster. Nearly twenty years later, the ghost of who my dad could have been still haunted my grandparents. No matter how bad I got, no matter how much trouble I got into, every time I showed up at their back door, they welcomed me into their lives. And every time I stopped by they tried to convince me to step away from the white supremacy movement.

"If you hate everybody you'll end up hating yourself," Pop warned me. His barreled chest heaved when he said, "This thing is taking control of you. You aren't yourself anymore."

"I'm afraid you're going to get hurt," Nanny said. "You're too good of a boy to let your life be ruined by this. Please don't do this to yourself. Please don't do this to us. We love you."

I respected my grandparents too much to call them "ZOG dupes." I knew they were worried about me. I just didn't care. Nothing mattered to me as much as being a skinhead, and I wasn't going to let anybody take that away from me, not even Nanny and Pop. I'd been stopping in for dinner and a lecture a few nights a week for several weeks when Nanny finally got suspicious about why I was there so often. When she dropped the question I had been hoping to avoid, she dropped it like a bomb, right on target and without warning.

"When did your mom kick you out?"

"A few months ago."

"Why didn't your father tell us you were back?"

"He doesn't know."

"He doesn't know you moved in with him?" Nanny knew her own kid; she knew it was possible my dad was on a bender and too messed up to notice something like me moving back into his house.

"He doesn't know I got kicked out," I said. "I'm not living with him."

Nanny looked like she was going to throw a pot across the kitchen. "Are you telling me your mother put you on the street and your father doesn't even know?"

"I'm not on the streets. I've been staying with friends."

Nanny shook her head.

There was no sense in lying at that point, so I spilled the whole story, which didn't seem to surprise Nanny; she'd lived through almost the same story with my dad two decades earlier.

"Do you want to live with us?" Nanny asked. "We love you. You're always welcome here."

"I love you, too," I said. "But I'm okay. I'm doing fine."

I HAD MY thumb up by the side of the road for a ride home from Louie's one evening when a middle-aged guy pulled over to pick me up. It was always middle-aged guys who stopped. Women don't pick up hitchhikers. Young dudes are too cool to stop and really old dudes are too scared. This guy looked like every other guy who'd ever given me a ride – still young enough to feel safe with a stranger in his car, but old enough to feel sorry for a scrawny kid standing on the side of a highway. Like the rest of them, he seemed nice enough, a regular Joe, salt-of-the-earth and all that. We were speeding east on Highway 3, shooting the shit about sports, when he reached across me, opened the glove box, pulled out a revolver, and shoved the barrel into my temple. He held the steering wheel with his knee and used his free hand to unzip his pants.

"Suck me," he said.

"No fucking way."

"Your choice, kid." He pulled back the hammer.

He kept that fucking gun cocked, jammed into my skull, the whole goddamn time. When it was over, he dumped me on the side of the road. I memorized his license plate as he sped away.

A few hours later, I stumbled into my dad's bar more desperate for him than I'd ever been. He offered me a beer. I asked for whiskey. I must've downed a half dozen shots before I could bring myself to confess that I'd sucked another man's cock just because he'd held a gun to my head. I needed my dad to tell me I wasn't a pathetic little pussy. I needed him to have one of his boys track down that plate. I needed him to show that motherfucking asshole what the 68th and Buist boys did to perverts who rape kids.

"Bad shit happens," my dad said.

That's all he said. I was fourteen years old, slamming back Jack Daniels to try to wash the taste of some asshole's cum out of my mouth, and the only thing my father could think to say was, "Bad shit happens."

Later that night, I jumped a random queen in Center City. I bragged to the other skinheads about how I'd brutalized him, but I never breathed a word to them about what the man in the car had done to me. The skinheads closest to me could tell something was up, though – my drinking got even heavier, my moods even darker. I paced South Street like a wounded lion; Philly felt like a cage.

Matt Hanson misread my mood when he came into the city that Friday night after his school let out for the summer.

"We should go on vacation," he said.

"Dude, where am I supposed to fucking go? Beverly Hills? Youse know I ain't got no money."

"We don't need money. You up for a little trip to the shore?"

"Jersey?"

Matt grinned. "There's always somebody down there from South Street. We can get by."

OTHER THAN CASINOS, Atlantic City's got nothing on Wildwood. The Wildwood boardwalk is classic East Coast, Jersey's very own Coney Island, only it's not an island. It's block after block after block of wide wooden decking crammed so tight with souvenir shops, carnival rides, and junk food joints that in some stretches it's easy to miss seeing the Atlantic Ocean. Still, you can't escape the ocean in Wildwood. Every gust of wind whips off the waves, crosses the beach, then side-checks the boardwalk. Along the way, the salt air mixes with the sand, the fast-food fumes and the sweaty, suntan-lotion stench of tourists so that it's thick and sticky by the time you suck it in. One good breeze in Wildwood and I knew I was on vacation.

No other Nazi skinheads lived at the Shore full-time that summer. In fact, it had been a few years since any Nazi skins had really laid claim, which is how the SHARPs had managed to get a foothold. With no Nazis around to counter them, the SHARPs had done to the boardwalk in Wildwood what they'd once done to South Street in Philly: they'd terrorized every alternative white kid in town. Matt and me decided it was time to take back the beach. We had about the best support troops imaginable for this mission. The Axis Skinheads out of central Jersey were the most brutal Nazi crew on the East Coast back then. I was brutal enough myself by this point, but I was fucking terrified of the Axis Skins.

Early in the summer, a couple of them came down to visit. They hadn't been there more than a few hours when they grabbed this homeless guy and dragged him under the boardwalk. It was like a scene out of a movie. It happened so fast, and they didn't say a word, not to him or to each other. They shot each other this look and leapt into action like they were following a script. I'd seen a lot in my fifteen years, but I hadn't ever seen anything like that. A few minutes after the Axis guys disappeared with the homeless dude, they reappeared on the boardwalk. One of them had a puckered face that made him look like an old man who forgot his dentures. That Axis skin wasn't missing any teeth, though. He flashed Matt and me a smile that would've made a dentist proud. Then he claimed he and his crewmate had stabbed the homeless dude. I don't know if they did or if they were screwing with us, but either way, it left an impression.

The only reason the Axis Skins had ever let the SHARPs so much as touch the Wildwood boardwalk was because it was inconvenient for them to police it. They had their own boardwalks to patrol in other parts of Jersey, and they patrolled them like the Nazi stormtroopers they were. But some weekends, when they were sure everything was under control on their home turf, they'd ride in to Wildwood and clean house. Word of those raids traveled fast and far.

In the late 1980s and early 1990s, Nazi skinheads and SHARPs were waging serious turf warfare all up and down the Eastern Seaboard. Pennsylvania, Maryland, Virginia, and New Jersey were home to enormous crews on both sides of the race issue. The Eastern Nazi Alliance owned Jersey from Camden to Newark. After the collapse of The Uprise, our South Street crew started unifying all the Nazis in Southeastern Pennsylvania. The Axis Skins ruled central Jersey like a gulag. And Nazi crews in Baltimore, DC, and Virginia Beach were pushing the new era of white supremacy closer toward the Old South.

Of course, damn near every town that had even one Nazi also had a SHARP, and the tension between those two lone wolves is how the rival crews were born. Kind of like how it happened with Jimmy and me at Furness. Jimmy wasn't a Nazi at all when he slammed that cafeteria tray into those black kids' heads; he was just my cousin and loyal friend. So when he saw me outnumbered and in danger, he jumped in on my side. That made him a Nazi to everybody in that cafeteria, and, when I look back on it, that made him a Nazi to me and to him, too. SHARPs had the same thing happen the first time they got into a fight with Nazis. If they had buddies loyal enough to jump in and help them, those buddies became SHARPs the second that fight was over. Once you bleed for a cause, you may as well sign up.

By summer of 1990, guys were bleeding on both sides, from New York to Richmond. The more Nazi crews that sprung up on the East Coast, the more SHARP crews sprung up, or tightened up, to counter them. In a lot of parts of the country, SHARPs weren't very organized. Then again, neither were Nazis. Most American Sharpie crews were loose knit groups of guys who were proud of their working-class roots, into Ska, and wished like hell they'd been born in England. In some places, the SHARPs were only a "crew" because they liked the word; it was British.

But in some areas, the SHARPs were more organized. The tightest Sharpie crews I ran into hailed from Delaware, Manhattan, Baltimore, and DC. There were SHARPs in pockets around Jersey and SHARPs on South Street in Philly, and a few dudes in those crews were hardcore fighters. But it was the Delaware, Manhattan, Baltimore, and DC SHARPs we really had to watch out for. They would've denied they were a "gang," but they fought like gangsters.

With the Axis Skins' blessing and our own boys from Pennsylvania on call if we needed them, Matt and I laid claim to the Wildwood boardwalk for the white supremacy movement and became its round-the-clock security guards. We were only there a couple weeks when the inevitable happened: some kid on vacation from Baltimore went home and talked about his trip, and the Baltimore SHARPs caught wind there were Nazis in Wildwood.

Fifteen of them showed up on a Friday night. Fifteen of them versus Matt and me, who combined couldn't top 300 pounds, and two Richie Rich suburban Nazis who happened to be on the Shore with their parents. The four of us were sprawled on the benches of the Douglas Fudge Pavilion when the Baltimore Sharpies materialized out of the never-ending parade of tourists. Fifteen versus four, assuming the two dudes from the suburbs knew how to fight, which we didn't know because we'd just met them.

"This is our boardwalk," I said, without bothering to stand up.

The leader of the SHARPs moved nearer the entrance to the pavilion, but he didn't step inside. He jutted his chin out, trying to look tough, knowing he had us outnumbered. But

numbers alone don't always add up; there was no way that dude
was going to risk stepping too close until he knew for sure who
we were.

"Are you Axis?" he asked. That still cracks me up. Fifteen
SHARPs from Baltimore, probably the toughest SHARPs in the
nation, against four of us. But those Sharpies wanted to know
before they even thought about starting anything if we were Axis.
That's how notoriously ruthless the Axis crew was.

We used some girl's long-distance phone card to call the
Axis Skins. If they'd sent even two of their best guys that
probably would've been enough for us to handle those SHARPs.
But they didn't send two. Axis turned out in force, nearly half
their crew, about two dozen of the meanest Nazi skinheads in
America. The next night, the Baltimore SHARPs were not given
the option of backing down; Axis didn't give options.

That brawl on the beach was the nastiest fight I'd been in
to that point. It was a real, honest-to-God rumble. No guns or
knives, just fists, combat boots, and anything within grabbing
range. I got clocked in the head with a beer bottle; I returned
fire with a chunk of loose railing one of the Axis monsters had
ripped off the boardwalk stairs with his bare hands. When it
was all over, every last one of those fifteen SHARPs was rolling
around in agony on the sand.

The Axis crew spent the rest of the night celebrating with us
in the pavilion. Everybody got totally shitfaced. As usual, I was
one of the drunkest guys at the party. But I wasn't so drunk that
I forgot one of the Axis leaders had told me I was a hell of a
fighter. I don't think I could have been more proud if Bobby Clark,
the Flyers' legendary captain, had turned up at the South Philly
ice rink to tell me I was a good wingman. I passed out that night
feeling like I'd just won the Stanley Cup.

Goddamn Gerbils

TOWARD THE END OF SUMMER, MATT AND I CAUGHT A RIDE out of Wildwood. He moved back home and I moved in with Dan Bellen, who lived in one of the townships on the outskirts of Philly. I'd crashed at Dan's a few times since he made the switch from punk to skinhead. When I showed up in August carrying my duffel bag, his mom realized I didn't have anywhere else to go. She offered to let me live with their family on the condition that I had to go to school, not just register. It seemed like a fair trade: a little bit of homework in exchange for sharing a roof with Dan, his mom, and his grandma.

A few days after I moved in, I got a job cleaning cages at a pet shop. It wasn't glamorous, but it let me give Dan's mom some money. She didn't ask me to pay her, but it seemed like I ought to. Besides, I liked working at the pet shop. I gave half of my first paycheck to Dan's mom and spent the rest on my own gerbil family.

I dug an old leather trunk out of a back corner of Dan's pigsty of a room and turned it into a gerbil mansion. By the next morning, I understood why the pet shop kept gerbils in metal cages. We had gerbils running all the hell over the place. Dan's grandma pitched a fit when one ran between her feet. I did everything I could to convince her it wasn't a rat, but she wasn't buying it. She screamed at Dan and his mom to get the rats and the rat-boy out of the house. Dan's mom ordered us to round up the rodents before his grandma blew an artery.

I put about a week's worth of food out in what was left of

the gerbil mansion, hoping to lure my little buddies back to me. The next morning, most of the food was gone, but the mansion was still empty. The next afternoon when I got home from work, I found little chalk outlines of gerbils on the kitchen floor.

"You're a riot, Dan," I yelled out into the living room. I knew he was trying to be funny drawing those outlines, but it ticked me off anyhow. I liked those gerbils, and I was worried they were going to get hurt running loose in the house.

"I hate to be the one to break it to you," Dan said, as he clomped into the kitchen. "But we brought in an exterminator."

"Yo, Frankie!" Louie Lacinzi leaned his head through the doorway. "Youse should've seen those things explode when Danny and me whacked 'em with a tack hammer."

The room started spinning. I felt like I was falling, like Alice in Wonderland, only I ended up on Tree Street. I saw this vision of my asshole stepfather beating my little gerbils to death with my E.T. lamp. I'd never had pets on Tree Street because I knew John would kill them. I shook my head, came back to reality. I wasn't on Tree Street with John. I wasn't a prisoner of war anymore. I was with my friends; I was free. And my friends had just murdered my gerbils.

"You fucking assholes didn't have to kill them!"

"My grandma was losing her mind about it," Dan said.

I knew she was. She'd been terrified. I don't know if she was in the early stages of Alzheimer's or if it was something else, but little things upset her, scared her. Gerbils loose in the house scared her. Nazi skinheads loose in the house scared her.

"It was the gerbils or you," Dan said. "Somebody had to go."

"You should have had me do it," I said. They were my gerbils; if they had to die, I would've at least shown them some respect and not drawn outlines around them.

"There ain't no way you could've killed 'em," Louie said.

He was right. It would've broken my heart to kill those gerbils. It broke my heart to know Dan and Louie had killed them, even though they did it for me. After Dan and Louie went back into the living room, I lingered in the kitchen, pretending to fix myself a sandwich. I tried to keep my eyes focused on the bread, cheese, and pickles I'd set out on the table, but I kept sneaking glances down at the little outlines on the floor and slipping back in time. Early evening on Tree Street, and I was eleven years old, fighting back tears from the sting of John slapping my copy book against my face. Mid-afternoon on Tree Street, and I was twelve years old, reeling from the blow of John's fist crashing into my skull. Late afternoon on Tree Street, and I was thirteen years old, curling myself into a ball on my bedroom floor, staring at the shards of my own fucking lamp, waiting for John to strike his final blow. I hated John. Even more, I hated the fucking pussy victim John had turned me into. I hated victims. I wiped my eyes on a dish towel. Goddamn gerbils probably hadn't even tried to fight back.

I STARTED CLASSES at a school so Spic-n-Span spotless it could've passed for a hospital. That township school was unlike any school I'd seen in Philly. It had shit I'd only seen on TV, like lockers that had locks on them. Even the stalls in the boys' bathroom had doors and locks.

I don't know how, but I ended up in the ninth grade again. I didn't stand a chance of passing, but I gave school more effort than I had before, because that was my deal with Dan's mom, and I didn't want to break my promise. I went out for football, thinking that'd be a real stand-up thing to do, and earned a spot on the JV squad. I hardly ever ditched classes, at least at first. I did my best to learn, but I didn't know how to learn. I didn't know how to study and remember. I didn't know how to move numbers around and show my work. I didn't know how to write essays.

"I don't know what youse want me to do," I said to my English teacher.

"I want you to realize that "use" is a verb, not a pronoun," she instructed.

Soon after, the principal called me into his office. I was

either suspended for a while for fighting with a couple SHARPs or expelled for good. It didn't matter what he said. I was done with school. Dan's mom didn't throw me out; I didn't make her. I knew the terms when I moved in, so I packed my bag that night, thanked her for everything she'd already done for me, and grabbed a bus back to the city.

It was late September, maybe early October, still warm enough outside that it didn't bother me to curl up in Skinhead Alley for the night, especially after a cute runaway curled up next to me. Louie, Jimmy, and Matt heard the news by the next morning and came looking for me.

"We gotta get youse off the street," Louie said.

"I'm all right."

"No, you ain't," Jimmy said with a spit for emphasis. "You can stay with us."

But I couldn't. Jimmy's mom was my mom's sister. And I didn't want to stick my aunt in the middle of our feud.

"I'm cool. Really."

"Geez, Frankie, will youse drop the act already? You're living in a fucking alley. Now will youse grab your shit, or are we gonna have to drag your ass outta here?"

I bounced back and forth between Louie's mom's basement and Matt's mom's couch. Although I never stayed at my mom's house, I visited sometimes. Kirsten was almost three already, and my new half-sister, Hayley, was learning to walk. I loved my baby sisters, even though I hated their father. I loved my mother, too, even though I hated who she'd become. She'd become a full-blown addict by then, as had John. They washed their Percocets down with Busch pounders. My mom still dragged herself out of the house every morning to work some secretarial gig she'd scored in the neighborhood, but there was no way that one paycheck was covering everything, even with a little help from the government. They were dealing the same stuff they were using, hustling enough to keep themselves supplied and the girls fed.

If my mom was that bad off, I couldn't even imagine the

shape my dad must be in. I hadn't seen him in about six months when I decided to pay him a surprise visit. It was a shock to both of us. His hands shook violently as he struggled to take a drag off his smoke. I could barely make out his words. He mumbled for me to meet him at the bar later that night.

When I showed up, he was better; he was high. He'd gotten to the point where he seemed more normal fucked up than sober. But even totally whacked out, he wasn't who he had been, even when I was a kid and he'd been high. Things didn't register with him anymore. I didn't register with him anymore. He talked to me like I was one of his boys from 68th and Buist, not like I was his fifteen year-old kid. It didn't cross what was left of his mind to ask me, "Are you okay? Do you have a place to live? Are you hungry? Are you lonely?" No. No. Yes. Yes. I didn't get the chance to tell him the truth; he was past the point of remembering a dad should ask his kid those things.

I wasn't okay, but at fifteen, I was too cocky to admit it, maybe too stupid to know. I judged my welfare in comparison to others, and by comparison I came off great. I drank like a fish almost every day and, thanks to a punk chick, I'd tried acid, but I wasn't an addict like the rest of the family. I didn't have an address, but I had friends with couches, so I wasn't homeless. I had not a clue in hell where my next meal was coming from, but I hadn't starved to death. I'd been kicked out of three schools, but I wasn't in jail. I was fifteen and making it on my own, with a little help from my Nazi brethren. I was okay. I believed that when I was fifteen.

I thought my biggest problem was transportation. I didn't have a car, of course. Hell, most days I didn't even have bus fare, so I started making out with this enormous skinchick nick-named Muffy because she had a car and a crush on me. She drove me anywhere I wanted so long as I gave her some action. Usually by the time she rolled me into the backseat I was too wasted to care that she looked like a bulldog in a kilt.

One night I got so drunk I actually fucked her. The worst

part was she told people about it. I took unbelievable amounts
of shit from the guys in Skinhead Alley once word spread that I
had spread the Muff. But that didn't stop me from crawling into
her backseat at least a few nights a week so she'd keep hauling
my ass around Philly. The Muff was a pimp, her Dodge Dart was
her Cadillac, and I was her bitch.

Muffy had just dropped me off at Dan Bellen's for a party
one night when I heard one of the guys use the term "terror
squad" for the first time. I loved how that sounded. That was what
we'd been waiting for, what we wanted to be, what we could be.
We only had to yank our heads out of our asses and do more than
sit around drinking and shooting the shit. Of course, we had to
sit around drinking and shooting the shit about the whole idea
of the terror squad for a couple of weeks before we actually did
anything. When we did, it got really bad, really fast.

Although we occasionally included a few other guys in our
raids, the core of the terror squad was Dan, Matt, Stug, Jimmy,
Louie, and me, in other words, the real streetfighters of the South
Street crew. The purpose of the terror squad was just what
the name suggested: to strike fear into the hearts of everyone we
hated. We announced our presence by spray-painting a swastika
and "*Sieg Heil*" on the side of a Polish-American club. Looking
back on it, it was kind of a stupid target. Hitler took over Poland,
but he didn't hate the Poles. We weren't thinking about that when
we picked the Polish-American club – we targeted the building
because it had a big open exterior wall just begging for some graffiti,
it was dimly lit at night so we wouldn't get caught tagging, but
visible by day, so everybody would see our message. It had the
desired effect: the very next morning, everybody was freaking
out about having Nazis in their neighborhood. The outrage stoked
our fire. By the second night, we were Nazi commandos. We
were Aryan warriors. We were cruising the suburbs in Dan's car,
loaded again and still half-cocked, when we saw a poster
advertising a reggae concert going on at that very moment at a
nearby college.

We read that poster like a burning bush. The God of Identity had sent us a sign: he was pointing us toward the enemy. Filthy-rich white private school kids spending their daddies' money to listen to a bunch of ganja-smoking Rasta niggers wailing about oppression! Fucking Jew bastards who ran the universities trying to mind-fuck another generation of Aryan youth! Fucking frat boys looking down their country-club noses at us like we had no right to even walk in front of their Ivory Towers! Fucking idiot fucking ZOG dupes paying to listen to nigger-motherfucking mud! Terror, you Jew rats! Terror, you nigger-lovers! Terror! Terror! Terror!

I felt like I was going to freaking explode. I knew every single Nazi walking with me was screaming the same thing in his mind. Terror! But the only sound in the whole quad was the echo of our combat boots marching in goose-step formation down a dark stretch of sidewalk. Terror! Right. Left. Terror! Right. Left. Terror!

We were ripped up drunk and armed old-school style. Louie had a bat. Matt had a hockey stick. Dan had his tack hammer. Stug had a pipe. I was wearing my weapon: my vintage Doc Martens, twenty holes and steel toes. Right. Left. Right. Left. Terror!

I felt the rage boiling inside me until I thought I was going to puke or scream or die. Right. Left. Right. Left. Terror!

We are footsoldiers in God's army. Right. Left.

We are the enforcers of God's law. Right. Left.

Our race is our fucking religion you fucking mud scum! Right. Left. Right. Left. Terror! Terror! Terror!

Two white students leaving the concert, walking away from the rest of the crowd, walking away from anybody else who could be a witness, walked toward us. We could see them coming, their shapes backlit by the distant streetlights. They seemed startled to realize they were not alone in the darkness.

Stug's dinner-plate face looked so innocent when he asked, "Got a dollar?"

"No, man, sorry."

"Wrong answer."

Terror!

Stug cracked his pipe over the guy's head. Louie followed with his bat. The other student started screaming, running for help, running for his life. He didn't get twenty feet before I landed a flying kick into his back. The force of my entire body channeled through my boots and sent him reeling. His face bounced off a fire hydrant; his body slammed to the sidewalk. He used the last bit of strength he had left to try to cover his head with his arms. I punished him with my combat boots. He rolled onto his back. His hands fell away from his head. His head was wide open when Dan brought the hammer down. Terror! Hammer. Kick. Hammer. Kick. Terror! The screams were inhuman, the sound of hell splitting open. Dan's final blow was so savage the small, pointed end of the hammer got stuck. Blood gushed from the kid's head.

"Give me back my hammer, you motherfucker!" Dan screamed. I pinned the kid's neck to the ground with my boot to give Dan the leverage he needed. With one vicious jerk, Dan freed his weapon.

I still had my boot on the kid's throat when I finally saw him, I mean really saw him. Underneath the blood and the gore, beneath the ZOG theory and the Identity theology, he was just a college kid. For all I knew, he may have been the best student on campus. He may have been the star athlete. He may have been the kind of all-around great guy kids looked up to.

He could have been my Uncle Dave.

I almost puked.

"Cops!" one of the skinheads screamed, shaking me back to reality. It was our turn to run for our lives. We were faster than our victims.

Looking back, I realize Dan's final blow could not have been fatal, but when we fled the scene, we didn't know. If it had been, the cops would have hunted us down. Even though it had been dark and there hadn't been any witnesses, they would have tracked down the monsters who brutalized that poor kid if he hadn't survived. But I remember speeding away in the car, cracking open beers. We were all laughing ourselves sick at the memory of Dan yelling, "Give me back my hammer!" to the bloody mess on the sidewalk. We beat the crap out of at least three or four other people that night. I can't say who, where, or why because by then I was so drunk they ran together, a blur of faces at the end of my steel-toed boots, a collage of victims who all made me want to vomit when they begged me for mercy, who made me hit them even harder because they showed me how pathetic and weak they really were.

That's how sick I was then. I couldn't see it, of course. Then, I thought the rest of the world was sick, sick from the parasitic infestations of ZOG, sick from the plague of race-mixing, sick from denying the truth of white supremacy. The whole world was sick, everybody but us Nazis, everybody but me.

I truly believed I had a permission slip from God to kick anybody's ass if they disagreed with me, looked at me funny, didn't look at me at all. I thought I was doing God's will by raining down "justice" on those who violated his commandments. The thing is, I only enforced the "commandments" Identity preaches; I never thought twice about the other ten, the ten God handed down to Moses. I blew at least half of those on a daily basis.

This Ain't South Philly, Kid

THE TERROR SQUAD HAD BEEN RIDING PROUD FOR SEVERAL months already when Louie and I wound up completely shitfaced at a post-rally Klan party in West Chester. Our ride had ditched us, so we were looking to make some new friends.

A few skinheads from Baltimore were the only other teenagers in the sea of middle-aged Klansmen. They seemed really cool by comparison, at least while we were tanked. We invited them to spend a few days with us in Philly just so they'd drive us home. In the sober light of the next afternoon, the Baltimore skinheads didn't seem quite so cool. They were real stand-up guys; they were just boring. We took them down to South Street hoping maybe the action in Skinhead Alley would wake them up. It did.

By their second night in Philly, they wouldn't shut up about how they needed something like Skinhead Alley in Baltimore. Louie and me gave them some pointers on how they could liven up the Nazi nightlife over in Maryland, but they didn't think they could pull it off on their own. They were right, so I decided to give them an on-site demonstration. It's not like I had anywhere else in particular to be, seeing as I was homeless, jobless, and expelled from the ninth grade.

As it turned out, those guys weren't shitting us when they said it was boring as all hell to be a Nazi skinhead in Baltimore. The month I spent in Maryland was the most mind-numbing month of the first fifteen years of my life. I talked to the Baltimore skinheads about how they could sign on more guys if they threw some parties, real parties, with beer and girls. I talked about how they could form their own version of the terror squad. I talked about getting down and dirty, about living the skinhead life hardcore. A couple of local girls I barely knew and didn't particularly like kept me fed and drunk. In return, I bounced back and forth between their two beds. I promised them I'd pay them back for real for my food and phone calls as soon as I could get some cash. One night, I tried to jack a car stereo. That plan didn't work out too good. The guy who owned the car caught me – it's a miracle the cops didn't bust me.

The disaster with the car stereo made me hate Baltimore more than I already did. I wanted to go home. I felt oddly homesick, considering I'd been homeless for more than a year. One evening when my roommates went out, I called Nanny Bertone. It had been nearly a year since I'd last heard her voice. When she answered the phone, I got so choked up I could barely say, "It's me, Frankie."

"We've been so worried. I was afraid you were dead. Where are you?"

I considered lying to her, but changed my mind.

"I'm in Baltimore. I'm getting sick of it, though. I'm not doing so good."

"Come home. Now. You are moving in with us."

It was an order, not an offer. My own room. A clean bed. Three hot, home-cooked meals a day. Access to all the sports equipment in Nanny and Pop's front hall closet. I felt like I was being sentenced to prison at the Ritz Carlton. Nanny wired me bus fare, and I was settled into my grandparents' house before dinner that next night.

Nanny and Pop did everything they could to make me feel at home, including laying down the law about how I was going to have to behave while I lived there. No throwing my clothes on the floor. No sleeping all day. No showing up late for dinner and expecting Nanny to cook for me. No cursing, drinking, or girls in the house. No "*Sieg Heil*-ing" in the house. I could live with all that because I didn't plan to be in the house very much.

Nanny and Pop made me promise I would return to school in the fall, but they couldn't do anything about the rest of the spring semester. I hadn't dropped out; I had been expelled from at least two, maybe actually three schools in less than twelve months. I wasn't welcome in any public school for at least another year, and I think my grandparents knew it would have been flushing money down the toilet to pay for parochial school. Besides, one look at my permanent record would have sent the local nuns screaming into the nearest bar.

I spent my days puttering around the house with Pop and eating myself sick in Nanny's kitchen. In the evenings, I'd tell my grandparents I was going to go visit my dad or my cousins. They'd tell me to be careful and not to stay out past midnight. Then I'd meet up with Louie in Finnegan's Park. Nanny and Pop proved to be a little more observant than I thought they were going to be. They busted me sneaking in after curfew several times. Every time I broke the rules, I got a lecture, but they never threatened to kick me out. They'd tried that with my dad. Nanny and Pop blamed themselves for what he'd become, even though not even my dad thought it was their fault. But the guilt had been building up inside them for nearly twenty years, and it influenced how they handled me. I was their second chance, their do-over, their mulligan. They weren't sure what to do with me; they only knew kicking me out wasn't an option, and I took horrible advantage of that.

ONE NIGHT, I hooked up with Louie, Matt, and Stug in Skinhead Alley. We headed toward Center City. We marched shoulder to shoulder in our matching flight jackets, our heads shaved, our Doc Martens laced in red. The closer we got to the downtown district, the farther away from us people moved. Center City yuppies weren't used to sharing their streets with Nazis. Sidewalks cleared in front of us. We'd drained a twelve pack in Skinhead Alley before we set out, tucked loose forties inside our flight jackets. We made only one stop along the way. Louie was a complete freak for Oranginas, those orange sodas that come in the little round bottles. He insisted on stopping at a market for Oranginas so he'd have chasers for his beer.

I felt like I was living *A Clockwork Orange*. I loved that movie; all the skinheads did. We watched it every chance we got. Our favorite part was the scene where the guys croon "Singing in the Rain." I haven't seen that movie in years, but I remember that scene: they made the guy they were beating on sing the "bomp bomp bomp" part of the song while they attacked him and raped his girlfriend. The first time I saw that scene, I thought it was fucking hilarious in a sick kind of way. Do people really do that kind of psycho shit? I wondered.

They do. And I felt it that night, deep in my bones. That night, the boys and me didn't have to say anything or do anything to back people away from us; we gave off this vibe that sent those powerful Center City suits and their trophy wives scurrying out of our path. But we weren't stalking them in Center City that night. We were hunting for the people most of those yuppies had probably never noticed living among them. All across America, the homeless haunt the wealthiest neighborhoods because rich people don't rob the homeless; they just pretend not to see them. In places like Center City, the homeless are like gutters; people step over them instinctively without noticing they're there, so nobody notices when one disappears.

Louie, Matt, Stug, and I were hunting the homeless that night. We were looking for some black wino or some Puerto Rican junkie nobody would miss. It was a terror squad night: we weren't looking for a fight – we were looking for a victim. We stormed through Love Park, jumping up and down off the concrete walls and benches wailing "Singing in the Rain" at the top of our lungs. But we didn't find what we wanted. We marched in formation around City Hall, yukking it up, goofing on everybody we passed. But still, we couldn't sniff out our perfect prey. The longer we searched, the quieter and more focused we got. By the time we settled into the front edge of an alley, we were like a pack of lions, bloodthirsty, ready to pounce on the first victim to stumble past our den. We'd been so focused on hunting we hadn't realized we'd become the hunted.

"You SHARPS?"

This is not a good question for Nazis to hear echoing from the street when they're standing in a dark alley that deadends into a brick wall. All four of us spun around to face the voice. All we could see was the shadowy outline of one really big guy standing about fifteen feet away from us out in the street, and the shadowy outlines of two even bigger guys standing right behind him.

In the darkness, I could see their combat boots and flight jackets, but I couldn't see what color laces were in their Docs, and I couldn't read the pins and patches on their jackets. Cornered inside that dead-end alley, I couldn't tell if the three guys blocking our exit were Nazi skinheads like us or the three biggest SHARPS I'd ever seen.

"We ain't no fucking Sharpies. Are you?" I replied, stepping into the street and into their range. I made out the swastika patch on the lead dude's collar, but I didn't recognize him.

He looked me up and down, checking the color of my laces and the patches on my jacket to make sure I wasn't lying. I looked him up and down to size up what I'd gotten myself into. The guy must have been about twenty-five and must have weighed around 250 pounds, solid muscle. He locked his eyes on me.

"So if I don't know you and you ain't a SHARP, who are you?"

"I'm Frankie Meeink." I waved behind me and added, "And this is Louie, Matt, and Stug."

"Where you from, Frankie Meeink?" he asked without so much as glancing at my three friends.

"South Philly."

I sheepishly took another step forward. That's when he

closed in on me. He was just inches away from me, so close I could taste his breath, when he said, "This ain't South Philly, kid."

The tone of his voice made it sound like he was trying to decide if it was worth his trouble to kill me. I could tell from the look in the guy's eyes that he wasn't just smack-talking; this was one serious, badass Nazi, and he clearly thought we were invading his turf. If he'd been another teenager, I wouldn't have put up with the attitude he was giving me. But I'd learned my lesson about respecting my elders from my run-in with The Uprise veterans in the Wise's parking lot. Those guys had been a lot further into the movement than we'd given them credit for that first night, but this dude was a whole different ballgame. The guy staring me down on the edge of that alley was about ten times more hardcore than anybody we'd met in the Wise's parking lot. This dude was a good three times more hardcore than the Axis Skins and, until that very moment, I'd thought those guys were the most ruthless dudes on the planet.

"So what are four boys from South Philly doing in Center City?" he asked.

I sure as hell wasn't going to correct him and let him know two of the guys behind me grew up in the suburbs. He seemed like the kind of guy who might have a pretty serious problem with guys from the suburbs, or with guys who corrected him for that matter.

"Just looking for something to do," I said as politely as I could.

"Like what?"

"Maybe a bum bash?"

The two guys behind him snickered. He almost grinned at me.

"They don't have bums where they're from," he said. "They're country boys. They came all the way up from Texas to welcome me home."

"Are you from Philly?" I asked.

"Yeah, but I've been away for a few years."

"Texas?"

"No, Rikers Island." He let it sink in for a second, then he said, "I'm Scott Windham."

I seriously just about shit my pants. Scott Windham was a fricking god among skinheads. Scott Windham was the co-founder of The Uprise. Scott Windham was the ringleader in the infamous train attack, the dude whose crime they'd been talking about on *Geraldo* when the chairs started flying. And at that moment, Scott Windham was actually shaking my hand.

"I thought you were in prison."

"I was," he said. "Now I'm not."

Even though I'd switched over to one of Louie's Oranginas right after we'd tucked ourselves into the alley, I'd downed more than a few forties already that night. I was half tanked. Meeting Scott Windham sobered me up faster than a full pot of coffee could have. I couldn't believe I was actually talking to the guy. Usually, when a bunch of followers tell you about their long-lost leader, they exaggerate. But everything the guys in the Wise's parking lot had told me about Scott Windham was true. If anything, they hadn't done him justice. Scott Windham was the kind of guy no man wants to fuck with and every woman wants to fuck. There was something magnetic about him, something almost magical, that drew me in completely. I would have respected him just as much that night if I hadn't had a clue about his legendary past. Hell, I might have respected him if he'd been a SHARP.

Scott Windham was the most hardcore white supremacist I'd met since I'd joined the movement. He didn't just know the theories and talk the theories, he enacted the theories; I think he may have invented some of the theories back in the early days of The Uprise. Scott Windham was fresh out of Rikers Island. The red laces in his Doc Martens dripped blood. Scott Windham was the Aryan warrior the Lancaster County skinheads had promised me I could become. He was the Aryan warrior they would never be. He was the ideal, the hero, the fantasy, and he was shaking my hand and talking to me, telling me he was proud to know that guys like me had been keeping his dream alive while he'd been gone. I was totally star-struck; I would have done anything he asked.

Scott was just making the rounds of introducing us to his friends, two Nazi Alliance members from Dallas, when we heard this big commotion: a rush of footsteps, then a shrill voice let out a shriek. We thought somebody was messing with a woman.

Two doors down from the mouth of the alley sat a small hole-in-the-wall bar. We'd walked past it earlier that night, but the neon beer signs hanging in the window got lost in the glare of the next door restaurant's bright lights; when we walked by, the place just hadn't registered with any of us as anything more than just another mom-and-pop shop. We hadn't noticed it was a pop-and-pop shop. We figured that out once we realized the "woman" screaming was actually a man. He and two other guys, all white and all dressed up very fancy, were pitching one royal hissy fit out on that sidewalk. There was no way we were going to pass on front row seats at a gay love-triangle spat, so we sprinted down the street to check it out.

We were just a couple of yards away from them when we saw what really had them so bent out of shape. This old black man, who looked like he'd been living on the streets since before they were paved, was trying to panhandle the three gay guys. We could smell the dude from ten feet back; he reeked of booze and piss. He was everything Louie, Matt, Stug, and I had been hoping to find in Center City. I could just hear him slurring "bomp bomp bomp" in time to my boots cracking his ribs.

"C'mon, ladies, spare a quarter."

"Get away from me you nasty thing," one gay guy said.

Those three gay guys were talking to that black panhandler like they were a bunch of Southern debutantes and he was frickin' Kunta Kinte trying to ask them to the prom. For some reason, that really pissed us Nazis off. None of us skinheads said it, but I think we were all thinking the same thing once we got a look at him. He wouldn't have been much fun to bash, not compared to three gay guys. We were dogs looking to play: the black bum was a busted stick lying on the ground; the three gay guys were tennis balls bouncing all the hell over the sidewalk, begging to be chased.

"You don't have to take that shit off faggots," Louie said to the old black man.

Scott Windham muscled his way in between the homeless guy and the three gay guys. "Leave him the hell alone."

One of the gay guys started to say something like, "You can't tell us what to ... " but Scott decked him before he finished his sentence. The guy reeled backwards and slid down the exterior wall of the bar. Scott jumped on top of him. He didn't get more than three or four punches in before both Nazi Alliance dudes piled on the same guy. The next thing I knew, Matt, Stug, and Louie all threw themselves on the second gay guy. There were two separate piles, each with three Nazis on top and one gay guy underneath; it looked like a scene out of an s&m porn movie.

I was just standing there holding my Orangina bottle, watching all hell break loose on the ground right in front of me, when the third guy started screaming, "Stop it, you bastards!" I looked up at him. He looked over at me. I looked down at the rock-hard, perfectly round Orangina bottle in my hand. I looked back up at him. He let out the kind of shriek I thought only six year-old girls could make, then hightailed it back into the bar. I took off after him.

When he threw open the door, everybody inside heard the screaming out on the sidewalk and turned to look. I caught a glimpse of a couple horror-stricken faces before the door slammed shut on its automatic hinges. When I jerked it open again about two seconds later, I saw a sea of panic. Everybody in the bar was crowding toward the door to get a better look outside. But because they were all pushing forward, the guy I was chasing couldn't get more than about three feet inside. I took one step past the threshold and whacked my Orangina bottle down on top of his head. He fell straight to the floor, leaving the first guy who'd rushed over for a look wide open. He lunged at me but got tangled up in the guy heaped on the floor. Just as he tripped and fell forward, I clocked him on the back of the head with the Orangina bottle.

There were two guys dazed, one on top of the other at my feet, and I looked at that crazy Orangina bottle and thought, "What the hell do they make these out of, iron?" I guess I must've actually held the thing up in the air a little ways to marvel at it because that's when the next guy headed my way with his fists up caught sight of the bottle and stopped dead in his tracks.

"Oh, shit," he said, but the words sounded funny, too slow for how fast his mouth was moving, kind of like an old 45 record set on the wrong speed. That dude and I were both staring at the Orangina bottle, him wondering if I was about to whack him with it and me wondering if it'd break if I tried throwing it up against a concrete wall, when somebody yelled, "The cops are on their way!"

I sprinted back outside. Windham and the Nazi Alliance guys were still wailing on the one guy. Louie and Matt were bent over on the sidewalk, catching their breath, while Stug was holding the other guy down on the ground. I jogged over to Stug, shoved him out of the way enough to open up an angle, and smacked the Orangina bottle over that guy's head.

"This fucking bottle won't break for nothing," I said to Stug, holding it up so he, too, could admire it. "This is the third guy I've clocked with it, and it ain't even cracked."

The guy underneath us started struggling to get away, but he wasn't going anywhere. Nobody could get out from under Stug without help from a crane.

It's not very often that Nazi skinheads beat up gay guys like they're defending the honor of a black homeless dude they don't even know. I think Louie was kind of offended the wino wasn't cheering us on. He said to him, "Get out of here or you're next."

"You get out of here," the old black man replied.

Every single shaved head spun around at that moment. Even Scott Windham and the Nazi Alliance stopped pummeling their victim long enough to see why the black wino was bossing Louie around.

"You guys got to get out of here," the old man said. That's when I heard the sirens.

I don't know who said it, but one of the skinheads actually yelled, "Thanks, brother," to that black dude when we took off running down the street. Three police cruisers slammed around the corner just as we hit the intersection. One ran right into Matt; he rolled up onto the hood, laughing like a lunatic. The rest of us were still trying to get away, but we were laughing, too, and stumbling all over the place. Meeting the legendary Scott Windham had sobered us up enough to beat the fuck out of some drunk gay guys, but we were all way too shit faced to get past a three-car police barricade.

Not more than fifteen minutes after Scott Windham introduced himself to me, he was handcuffed and sitting in the back of a police car. He and the two guys from the Nazi Alliance were all over eighteen and they all had records. For Scott, that fight wasn't just a felony; it was also a parole violation. I couldn't imagine how much time he was facing.

As the first squad car pulled away from the curb, Scott Windham smiled at Matt, Stug, Louie, and me through the back window. The cops had the four of us lined up in our matching flight jackets and combat boots. Shoulder to shoulder with my comrades, back up against the wall, awaiting my first trip to juvie in the glow of Scott Windham's approving smile, I felt proud, truly proud, for the first time.

The Most Valuable Player

IF HE HADN'T BEEN A RACIST, MATT HANSON COULD HAVE scored a stand-up comedy gig opening for Eddie Murphy. His poor mom was his favorite straight man. Vivien Hanson was this super sweet, totally normal mom who was hoping she could pray her son out of his skinhead phase. Matt called her "Nazi Viv."

"I'm home, Nazi Viv!" he'd say on his way through the door.

"Matthew, I told you not to stay out so late. You have school tomorrow. And stop calling me Nazi Viv!"

"You know you love it, woman. You know you're down with Hitler. Come on, Nazi Viv. Say it for me. Say 'I'm down with Hitler.'"

Good old Nazi Viv. Saint Viv was more like it.

I'd been laughing my ass off at the Matt and Nazi Viv show for more than a year when the cops handed Louie, Stug, Matt, and me over to the jailhouse guards. Matt kept running his mouth nonstop about how he was going to sue the cops for running him over and their mamas for giving birth to them. After a couple hours, the guards at the jail didn't think he was too funny anymore. By then even the rest of us skinheads were praying they'd gag him. Finally, they moved him to his own cell, hoping maybe he'd pass out if he didn't have an audience.

It didn't work. Matt amped up the volume. I struggled to hear my own thoughts. I couldn't shake the memory of what Scott Windham had whispered to me a couple hours earlier. I'd been standing where I'd been told to stand on the juvie side of the precinct's booking room when the cops brought Scott through on his way to the main holding cells. The officer escorting him had stopped to drop off some forms at the desk, and in the few seconds that took, he parked Scott, still handcuffed, next to me. Scott didn't look at me when he whispered, "Tell them I did it all. I'm done. No sense in you guys going down, too." But I never would have rolled on Scott Windham.

"You fuckers don't know who you're messing with," Matt was yelling at the guards. "I'm Charlie Manson, and I've got the swastika to prove it. It's just not on my forehead anymore. I had it relocated to my dick. Come on, copper, suck my swastika! You know you want me." We all started cracking up again. Matt Hanson had lost his mind. He was still rolling on his Manson impersonation when I finally dozed off.

The next morning, when the guards walked us into the juvie hearing room, I saw Louie's mom sitting in the front row. Stug's mom was two rows back. The bailiff lined us up in front of the bench. After giving us a lengthy speech about the evils of drinking and the consequences of violence, the judge said, "Mr. Lacinzi and Mr. Stugen, your mothers are present. I am releasing you into their custody until your case comes before the court. Mr. Hanson, your mother is on her way into the city as I speak. You will be detained downstairs until she arrives.

"That brings me to you, Mr. Meeink," the judge said. I knew what he was going to say before he said it.

"Your mother was made aware of the scheduled time for your appearance before this court. At this time, she has not indicated when she will be able to sign for your release. You will remain in the custody of the juvenile detention system until such time as your mother appears on your behalf."

I don't know what was worse: knowing she wasn't going to show or knowing the other guys knew it, too. The guards barely had time to transfer Matt back down to the cells before his mom came to take him home.

When he passed by my cell, I said, "Be nice to Nazi Viv."

"I will, dude." He sounded like he meant it. The guards hustled him on toward the exit, but he turned back and said, "Your mom'll show up soon."

I wasn't so sure.

I had a lot of time to think that afternoon. My thoughts traveled back to the campus of a chi-chi private college out in the suburbs. I'd been thinking about it ever since the night we fled the scene, leaving that poor kid laying there bleeding from the head. Sitting in that holding cell, I knew for sure: the cops didn't know it was us. It had been dark and there hadn't been any other witnesses, but I finally knew without doubt that when our victims recovered, they hadn't been able to give the cops any information that might identify us. If they had, the cops would have recognized us outside the gay bar. They didn't know.

The second-shift guards came on duty late in the afternoon. I was relieved when one of them unlocked my cell and told me he was taking me to processing. I was also shocked; I'd figured my mom would make me spend at least another night in detention before she sprung me. When we got to the main desk, I scanned the waiting room.

"Where's my mom?" I asked the guard. She had to be the one to sign for me because she was my only legal guardian. My dad had signed that power away in the same stack of papers where he'd given up my last name.

"She's not here, son," the guard said. "We're moving you up to Sleighton Farms."

Sleighton Farms was the guarded compound of dormitory-style housing where Philly stockpiled kids whose parents refused to sign for their release during the two-month wait for their hearing. I never figured out for sure who all was actually in Sleighton Farms and why. From the way some of the other guys talked, it sounded like they'd been convicted already, but maybe not. Maybe they'd already done time for something else and now were back waiting for a new hearing. All I know is that's why I was there.

The other inmates had already been locked down in their
single-man rooms for the night when I arrived. The intake
guard watched me unlace all twenty holes of my knee-high combat
boots. It takes a while to get out of those things, even if you hurry.

"Same routine every night," the guard said. "Put 'em in there."
He pointed to a box big enough to hold a refrigerator. "You'll get
'em back in the morning."

When I dropped my boots into the box, I noticed there wasn't
another pair of Doc Martens floating around anywhere in that
sea of $100-a-pop basketball shoes. The next morning, I took my
place at the end of the line of boys waiting to dig for their shoes.
A black kid at the head of the line held my Docs up over his head.

"Who's the fucking skinhead?"

I held my shaved head high as I marched barefooted to the
front of the line of blacks and Puerto Ricans. If there was
another white kid in my unit, he wasn't waiting on the shoe line
that morning. I held out my hand. The kid who'd called me out
sneered at me, but he gave me my boots. It didn't take a genius
to notice that there were some serious racial tensions brewing
at Sleighton Farms long before the Nazi arrived. Blacks sat on one
side of the mess hall, Puerto Ricans on the other. Blacks
congregated in one end of the rec room, Puerto Ricans in the other.
It was like the Korean Peninsula with me and a handful of other
white inmates sitting in the DMZ called the middle of the room.
The only place the two sides ever met up was in the yard. Every
afternoon an all-black team took on an all-Puerto Rican team in
football. When I finally got yard privileges, I didn't know this,
so I stood in the middle of the unmarked lawn minding my own
business. I noticed the Puerto Ricans were huddled up having
a big debate about something. After a few minutes, one of them
ran over to the blacks. Then a couple of the blacks ran with him
back over to the Puerto Ricans. After a few more minutes, one of
the black kids sprinted up to me.

"You're playing for the Puerto Ricans."

"Playing what?" I asked.

"Football."

I didn't care. And I didn't mind playing for the Puerto Ricans. It'd pass the time. Besides, there weren't enough white inmates to field a third team. I joined the Puerto Ricans in their huddle. I didn't know going into the game, but there wasn't one single guy on the Puerto Rican team who'd been at Sleighton Farms long enough to remember when their losing streak had started. The problem wasn't that they were bad players so much as it was that a couple guys on the black team were really good players. We couldn't have been more than three plays in when I broke through the line and ran for a touchdown.

It was like I was Jesus walking on water. The second I crossed into the end zone, my teammates forgot about my politics. They started screaming and cheering and jumping up and down. I wouldn't have been surprised if one of them would have asked me to start dating his sister.

When it was all over, the black players slunk back toward the barracks with their heads hanging low. The Puerto Ricans gathered by the fence, rehashing every play of the game. I went back to my spot in the middle. I was trying to scrape some of the mud off my Docs when a black kid who'd sat off by himself during the game called out to me.

"Yo, skinhead!"

I looked his way.

"You didn't drop one ball, did you?" he asked.

"Dropping balls is against my religion."

"Then I'm thinking the brothers need to get themselves converted."

I couldn't help but laugh. I said, "I don't think 'the brothers' would like my church."

"I don't know, man. If you kick their asses like that again tomorrow, they're either going to convert or kill you."

"Then I guess they're going to have to convert," I said.

Locked up in my room that night, I kept replaying the game and the days leading up to it. I'd always been a pretty good

football player, but I'd never played like that before. I let all my
rage come steaming out of my feet. I just ran and ran and ran,
and there wasn't a single guy on the field who could catch me.
I was too fucking pissed about being locked up in Sleighton
Farms to be caught.

I kept playing for the Puerto Ricans. I liked some of them
better than most of the white guys I met at Sleighton Farms.
At least the Puerto Ricans and me could talk football. The other
white dudes in there were lumps. I sat with them if I didn't feel
like sitting alone in the mess hall, but that was about it. Yard time
playing for the Puerto Ricans was all the social life I needed.

I never again played football like I did that first day, but I
played well enough to even the field a little. The Puerto Ricans
and me won at least a couple games a week. And after they got over
being pissy about it, I think some of the guys on the black team
kind of enjoyed having me around to compete against. A kid I'd
stiff-armed in my first game stayed pissed off, though. His name
was Maurice, and he was a leader of the black kids at Sleighton
Farms on and off the football field. Maurice never missed a
chance to bump into me in the halls. I'd been at Sleighton Farms
a couple weeks when two new white kids arrived from
Kensington, the section of North Philly that's home to the heroin-
infested slum known as the Badlands. They spotted me right
off and tried to snuggle up next to me. I guess they thought the
lone Nazi would be their savior if all hell broke loose. They
thought wrong. I would've taken a punch for any Puerto Rican in
that joint before I would've broken a toenail for doped-out
wiggers from the Badlands.

They showed their true colors the next day when they cozied
up with Maurice and his buddies in the mess hall. I kept my
distance, stayed in the middle by myself, but I went on full alert
whenever those Badlands jerks came near me. I knew in my gut
they were trying to start trouble. One of my Puerto Rican teammates confirmed my suspicions.

"They're working with Maurice. That dude's got it out for you."

"I figured. Youse know when they're gonna move on me?"

"Sorry, man," he said. "But if I hear more, I'll let you know."

THERE WERE A shitload of restrictions on phone calls in juvie lock up. As best as I could tell, I could only make calls on my own dime, and I could only take calls from my lawyer or my mom since she was my official guardian. Well, I didn't have a dime in my pocket the night I got arrested, and it's not like I could call anybody to send me money without one. I also didn't have a lawyer, at least not one I knew about. And my mom took her sweet time checking up on me. I must have been at Sleighton Farms close to two months before she finally got in touch.

I wanted to scream, "Where the fuck have you been, bitch?" But I had an even more important question to ask.

"Did you let Nanny and Pop know I'm okay?"

"I called them right after the cops called me," my mom said. "I told them your dad was going to have to cough up the money to get your sorry ass out of this mess. I haven't heard from him."

I was so relieved that Nanny and Pop knew I was okay. I'd been thinking about them every damn day while I was at Sleighton Farms. It had killed me to think they'd spent two months worrying that I was dead in some alley. My mom, of course, hadn't been worried I was dead. She'd known exactly where I was the last two months, and she was pissed – time had done nothing to calm her down. She fucking unloaded on me over the phone. I was a spoiled brat. I was a no account piece of shit like my father. I was ruining her life just like I always had. But once she got it out of her system, she promised she'd sign the papers to get me out so I could be home in time for Easter. Easter was only a week or two away.

I made the idiot mistake of telling people I was getting out. Thank God for my friend from the football team. He gave me the heads-up that Maurice was going to get me while he still had the chance. Then he told me to sneak upstairs and put my bar of soap out on my window ledge, so it'd be cold and hard as a rock by the time everybody came back up to the unit after dinner.

"Stick it inside a sock," he said. "Wind the sock around your knuckles, and, man, whatever you do, don't take your eyes off that door."

After dinner, I left my door slightly open, shoved my pillow under the covers, and turned off the light. To anyone peeking in from the hallway, it would look like I'd dozed off early. I stood next to the door, my back plastered against the wall, the rock-hard soap tucked into the toe of a tube sock, the sock twisted around my hand.

Maurice was the first to cross the threshold. When he lunged for the bed, I slammed the door behind him so I wouldn't have his friends jumping me from behind. I jumped Maurice from behind, though, while he was trying to jump me in my sleep. I pounded the hell out of him with that soap-sock. Shut out in the hall, his friends, the same guys who'd been planning to jump me, too, started screaming for the guards. "That Nazi bastard's got Maurice!"

The guards were kind of rough with me when they first busted into my room. I was on top and definitely getting the better of Maurice. Then Maurice put the nail in his own coffin.

"I was just minding my own business, and that fucking skinhead jumped me."

"You were minding your own business in his room?" a guard asked. Busted. Maurice and his cronies got sent to Sleighton Farm's version of solitary confinement. I never saw them again; I got released before they did.

I didn't get home in time for Easter, though. My mom never did show up to sign the papers for me. The only reason I got out of Sleighton Farms was because my case came up. I was transferred straight from Sleighton Farms to my hearing. Nobody gave me anything different to wear other than what I'd had on the night I was arrested. I did what I could to make my skinhead get up look less like a skinhead get up. I rolled my flight jacket into a ball and tucked it under my arm. I'd been wearing one of my good Fred Perry shirts and luckily it didn't have any patches on it. I uncuffed my Levis so they'd cover most of my Docs.

When I arrived at the courtroom, I saw Louie, Matt, and Stug all dressed up like little princes, sitting in a row at the defense table with four guys in suits. I figured the suits had to be the lawyers, even though one of them looked like he could've still been in high school. "Maybe he's a helper," I thought. I turned to scan the crowd. My mom was sitting in the back row looking like she wanted to kill somebody. The guard sat me down hard on the empty chair at the end of the table. Louie reached over and tapped my leg.

"Youse all right?" he asked. At that moment, that meant the world to me. Louie cared what the hell had happened to me the last two months even if my own fucking mom didn't.

"Hello, Mr. Meeink," the high-school looking suit said to me. "I'm with the Public Defender's Office. I'll be representing you today."

"Great," I thought, "Doogie Howser, PD, is the only thing standing between me and three years in juvie."

"There's no need to be worried," he said. "I've reviewed the files very carefully. We should be able to clear this up this afternoon."

I wasn't so sure about that, but what did I know? I don't remember nobody telling me anything about my case until that moment. And most of what was said at the hearing went over my head. The parts I did understand, like "assault," didn't sound too good for me. Even worse was the way all the other defense lawyers seemed to be trying to make the thing out like it was all my fault, like I was the ringleader since I was the one from South Philly and the other three guys were from the suburbs. That was such total bullshit. Louie's mom had bought a house in the suburbs all of maybe eighteen months earlier and he didn't even sleep there half the time. And Matt and Stug would've battled like South Philly thugs even if they'd grown up in Paducah.

But from the way the judge kept looking at me, I don't think he cared.

As it turned out, neither did Doogie. When he finally got his turn for his big speech, he talked about inconsistent witness testimony, the absence of any prior criminal records in reference to his juvenile client, and Scott Windham. He talked a lot about Scott Windham and the Nazi Alliance dudes who'd been with him that night. He talked about how they were much older than I was, how they were hardened criminals, and how they were responsible not just for the attack, but for dragging all the minors, including Mr. City-Boy me, into the middle of it. The other defense lawyers must have liked the theory, because in the end they joined up with Doogie and all four of them did exactly what Scott Windham had told me to do–they rolled like a ball.

It worked. The judge threw out the assault charges. Nobody was going to juvie. But nobody was getting off free, either. The judge rattled off the string of minor charges he wasn't going to drop. Most of them had to do with us being underage and blind drunk. The judge released us one at a time, taking a few minutes to give each of us and our parents a lecture. I was last in line. He was letting me go, but he clearly hadn't let go of the hired-gun lawyers' idea that I was more at fault than the other guys simply because I was the only official city kid.

"You will keep your Nazi friends out of Philadelphia!" he said.

Then the judge turned his attention to my mom. He asked her if she was willing to allow me to be released into her custody during my probation. I held my breath.

"If he changes his ways," she replied.

"If he doesn't, ma'am, just let me know," the judge said. He gave her a telephone number. "If he fails to comply with any of the conditions of his probation, call that number and we'll come get him." Then he turned back to me and asked, "Do I make myself clear?"

"Yes, sir."

"Good. I don't ever want to see you back in my courtroom again."

"Me either, sir." I meant it.

Stricken

I HAD NO CHOICE BUT TO MOVE BACK IN WITH MY MOM AND JOHN; IT WAS THE PRIMARY CONDITION OF MY PROBATION. JOHN HAD A FREAKING FIELD DAY WITH ME. WHEN I WALKED THROUGH THE DOOR, HE ASKED, "SO, JAILBIRD, HOW'D THEY TREAT YOU UP AT SING-SING?" I KNEW HE DIDN'T GIVE A DAMN; HE WAS JUST FUCKING WITH ME. BUT HE WOULDN'T DROP IT. ALL DAY EVERY DAY, ALL I HEARD FROM JOHN WAS "SING-SING" THIS AND "SING-SING" THAT UNTIL I ACTUALLY THOUGHT IT MIGHT BE WORTH THREE YEARS IN JUVIE TO GET A GUN AND BLOW JOHN'S FUCKING MOUTH RIGHT OFF HIS FACE.

I'd only been back home about a week when the great skinhead high holy day arrived: April 20, Adolf Hitler's birthday. We threw an enormous bash in an abandoned soap company warehouse on the outskirts of the city. Every skinhead within fifty miles was at that party, drinking to the memory of Adolf. We even had a birthday cake.

Of course, I was drunk long before the skinchicks cut the cake. By midnight, I was too far gone to remember I had a court-ordered curfew, not that remembering would've mattered. I was back with my crew. The judge, my mom, and that phone number he gave her could all go fuck themselves. So when Louie pulled me aside and asked, "Wanna go on a mission?" I didn't hesitate.

It was my first terror squad ride in four months. From what I can remember, we didn't actually hurt anybody that night. We just leaned on a few people we didn't like the look of, including one white guy whose only mistake was walking down the street carrying a fresh twelve-pack. We gave him some crap about being part of the conspiracy, but it didn't make sense. We were so tanked Hitler himself wouldn't have understood what we were talking about. But the guy handed his booze over anyhow. It was like he threw a raw steak to a pack of Dobermans; we didn't give a crap about the dude once we were sucking on beers. We piled back into the car and returned to the party.

I woke up late the next morning and realized I was lying on Louie's mom's basement floor. Skinheads and skinchicks were passed out all around me. I crawled over them to get to the phone.

"Mommy, it's Frankie," I said. It wasn't the first time in my life "Mommy" caught in my throat. I knew the woman on the other end of that telephone line wasn't going to give me the kind of break I thought a "mommy" would.

"I am so sorry, Mommy. I fell asleep. I swear I just lost track of the time and fell asleep. Please don't call the cops on me."

I settled myself into a comfortable position to listen to how I was a brat, an ingrate, a no good piece of shit just like my father.

"I don't need to call the cops. They've already been here. Did you strong-arm rob somebody last night?"

Did I strong-arm rob somebody last night? I was only half hungover because I was still half-drunk. I couldn't remember more than bits and pieces. Old warehouse. Beer. Super hot little skinchick out in the back alley. Beer. Cake. Beer. Beer. Car ride. Beer. Somebody yelling, "Frankie, get your stupid ass back in the goddamn car!" Beer out of a twelve-pack. Shit.

I returned my focus to the phone, where my mom had started in on how I was a brat, an ingrate, a no good piece of shit like my father.

"What did you tell the cops?"

"Told 'em you weren't here all night even though you were supposed to be back before midnight."

Shit. Even if the cops didn't get me for the robbery, my mom had given me up for a probation violation. I took a deep breath.

"Did you tell them to take me back to Sleighton Farms?" I asked.

"No," she said. I exhaled. "But I'll tell them the second you step foot in this house."

For the first time, I actually felt homeless. Both times before when my mom and John had kicked me out, they'd at least given me a couple of minutes to throw some clothes into a bag. This time, all I had were the clothes on my back. I was worried about the cops, too. I didn't want to go back to Sleighton Farms. So instead I went back to the Jersey Shore for another summer with Matt Hanson. A lot more Nazis came to visit us that second year. The Axis Skins and our boys from South Street came down almost every weekend. Quite a few guys from the Eastern Nazi Alliance showed up, too.

Now, in 1991, Scott Windham and John Cook were still probably the most legendary skinheads on the East Coast, but Joe Morgan was the most popular, bar none. Joe Morgan's dad owned a beer distributorship. There's just nothing like free and unlimited access to beer to give a guy social clout among skinheads. But Joe Morgan would have been beloved by skinheads even without the booze connection. I'd met up with him a few times in Philly, and every meeting left me liking him more. In addition to being an all-around good shit, Joe Morgan was one of the highest-ranked members of the Eastern Nazi Alliance and he was starting to become a legend himself within the white supremacy movement. He was the lead singer of a white power band that was starting to get a lot of notice. Thanks to word of mouth and bootlegged tapes, by the summer of 1991, skinheads all over North America were gushing about Joe Morgan. He was the most popular skinhead on the East Coast, if not in the whole country. Other Nazi Alliance skinheads literally would have killed for him. Even skinheads from other crews were intensely loyal to him. I was intensely loyal to him, which suggests I must have been out of my mind when I decided to start fucking one of Joe's women behind his back.

Adrienne wasn't Joe's girlfriend. If I'd fucked Joe Morgan's actual girlfriend, I wouldn't have lived through the night. Adrienne was just one of the girls who hung around Joe. I guess, looking back on it, I'd call her a groupie. I didn't know what their relationship was beyond that, only that I never saw any of the other guys approach Adrienne even though she was really hot. I couldn't help myself.

I never once thought of Adrienne as my girlfriend. She and I just hooked up sometimes when nobody was looking. I never did figure out what if anything she and Joe had going, but I always respected whatever it was whenever anybody else was anywhere near us. I basically ignored her if anybody else was around. Not one person ever let on that they were onto what we were doing. But about a month or so after our first hookup, I noticed Joe staring at me funny, methodically stroking his trademark goatee as if he were trying to come to a decision about something. After that, whenever I was around him, I felt his eyes on me.

When I wasn't sneaking around with Adrienne, I was scamming tourist chicks. One cute little blond showed up on the boardwalk with a weird dude in John Lennon glasses who looked like he'd been partying since Woodstock. They invited me to go for a ride in the guy's Bronco. I invited Louie, Matt, and another skinhead named Kevin to come along, too.

Matt and Louie had enough sense to get out of the truck in Allentown, but not Kevin and me. By this time there were two cute little blonds in the Bronco and we followed our dicks into a shitload of a mess. Turned out the crazy dude had stolen the Bronco from his boss. By the time he told us this, we'd already crossed two state lines in the hot car roadtripping along with him and the chicks to Virginia Beach. We weren't there more than two days when they ditched us. Kevin and I would've hitchhiked back to Philly, but the weather was too sweet to leave.

For a while, Kevin and I slept under a pavilion near the water. But one night, we crashed a party at one of the beachfront hotels and met the foreman of a traveling construction crew. The guy offered us jobs and even a room in their hotel block. Kevin and I busted our asses siding a new government building. At the end of ten, sometimes twelve hour days in the Southern sun, we were exhausted. Most weeknights, we just laid around our air-conditioned hotel room drinking beer. Kevin was still pretty new to the movement, so I schooled him in Identity. He was an eager student.

I HEADED BACK to Philly at summer's end. It had been almost exactly two years since I'd first returned from Lancaster as a skinhead. In those two years, I'd been at the center of the rebirth of the neo-Nazi movement in Philadelphia. But, except for our in-house code phrase, "terror squad," our crew had never had a name. We were just the skinheads from Philly. Our only official designation, actually, was with the Invisible Empire of the Ku Klux Klan. Over the previous year, Louie, Jimmy, and I had finally convinced most of the other skinheads on South Street to grow some balls and join the Klan, too.

Klansmen young and old turned out for a party John Cook threw in Reading. A few weeks later, Klansmen, young only, showed up for an animal rights fundraiser concert in Pottsgrove where we got into a knock-down, drag-out with some SHARPS in the parking lot. We were on a roll by the time we finally made it inside. The mosh pit was out of control, then it spread up on stage. We destroyed the band's equipment, then started in on the band. When the local media reported how neo-Nazi skinheads had ruined an animal rights event, they made it sound like we'd stormed the place screaming, "Puppies to the gas chamber!"

A few days later, the elderly Klansmen who'd sworn us into the Invisible Empire called Louie and me up to the camp to tell us they were kicking us out. They said skinheads were giving the Klan a bad name. Getting the boot from the Klan drove our egos over the edge. We were unstoppable after that. Within just a few days, Louie and me and some of the other guys decided that from that point forward, our crew would be called Strike Force.

No more kid stuff. No more dicking around. The time had finally come for us to go big time.

We spread the word about Strike Force to the other major East Coast crews and announced that we were preparing to expand. Guys like John Cook were all over the idea and started encouraging kids in their areas to use the new name, too. Before long, we struck a deal with the Eastern Nazi Alliance. Rather than divide turf geographically, we were going to divide it by age. Joe Morgan and the Nazi Alliance would focus on organizing all the veteran skinheads on the East Coast, the guys in their twenties, and Strike Force would work on the next generation. The plan was for Louie to head up all of Strike Force, spreading it nationwide from our bases in Pennsylvania, Delaware, Maryland, and New Jersey. He would travel around to get other young skinhead groups to affiliate as Strike Force Chapters. My job was to stay home, take the reins of our flagship crew, the Pennsylvania Chapter, and show the whole freaking world just what Strike Force could do.

I did my job well. Too many nights were terror squad nights once I became a Strike Force crew commander. I had as many as forty guys in Southeastern Pennsylvania actually in or at least running with the chapter. Forty skinheads can do an unbelievable amount of damage, and we did. I can't say with certainty how many people we attacked; it's not like we kept records. I rarely went more than a week without beating on somebody, whether SHARPs or minorities. The other guys in Strike Force were beating on people, too, some even more so to try to prove themselves and earn rank. I had rank. I didn't need to prove shit. I was beating the shit out of people because I wanted to. It made me feel good. It made me high. Some kids cut themselves because they only feel alive when they're bleeding. I cut other people. I felt alive when they bled. I craved the power I felt surging through my veins every time I slammed my boot into some dude's face.

THE HOST OF an apartment party out in the suburbs was this punk named Donny who had wicked asthma and a bunch of other medical problems. His bathroom was a pharmacy. I went in there to piss and ended up swallowing every pill he had. About an hour and a six-pack later, I almost fell down the stairs. Louie caught me.

"You ain't that drunk, are you?" he asked.

"Not drunk," I slurred. "Just medicine."

"What're you talking about? You ain't sick."

"Just a little some of Donny's pills," I struggled to say. My legs collapsed.

"What the fuck did you do?" Louie screamed at me. Then he screamed for Donny to go check the bathroom and for somebody else to help him carry me to the car. The last thing I remember clearly is Louie asking, "Jesus, why?"

"I really don't wanna be here."

I have a vague memory of being in the backseat of a car, thinking that if the pills didn't take me out, Louie was going to; he damn near slapped me to death before we got to the hospital. He knew what to do. He wouldn't let me fall asleep, and he brought all the empty bottles along to the emergency room. While the doctors stuck a tube down my throat, Louie filled out my paperwork. Under "Parent," he wrote, "You can't get in touch with them. They're crackheads." But he called my cousins, and they had sense enough to call Nanny and Pop.

My grandparents were at my bedside when I finally came to.

"Where's Mommy?" I asked, through the haze.

"She'll be here soon," Nanny said, but she didn't look too sure.

Several times, when I had my eyes shut, I overheard the nurses grilling Nanny and Pop about why my mother hadn't come in or returned the hospital's calls.

"I don't know," Nanny replied. It sounded like she was crying.

"Can't we take him home with us?" Pop asked.

But a nurse explained that they couldn't release me without my mother's signature because she was my legal guardian.

She finally showed up late the second day, maybe the third. Her first words to me were, "Do you know your idiot friend told them I'm a crackhead?" She sounded like a crackhead the way she went off on me about that. The nurses had a hard time calming her down. Once they finally did, they explained the options: she could either sign me out and take me home with her, or she could sign a form to have me committed to a psychiatric hospital for more intensive observation. My mom picked door number two.

I not only had my head shaved, but also my eyebrows shaved off. I looked like Pink in the movie *The Wall*. I did that sometimes because it looked so totally hardcore, at least when I was wearing a flight jacket. Wearing a hospital gown, locked up in a mental ward, it made me look like a complete lunatic. Even the shrink did a double-take when he first came in to interview me. He asked why I'd taken the pills.

"I just really didn't want to be there," I said. "Not for Christmas. I wanted to go home for Christmas. I just want to go home."

"Where is home?"

"My mom's," I said automatically. I heard the words roll off my tongue, and added, "I guess."

I'm sure he already knew the answer from the visitor records, but the doctor asked, "Has your mom come to see you?"

He might as well have stabbed me. My dad's words echoed through my memory: "She chose dick over you."

"She'll come," I said.

"What about your father? Has he come to visit you yet?"

"I called him earlier. He said he's coming tonight."

"What did your mom say when you called her?"

I didn't answer. The doctor didn't push the knife in any deeper.

When my dad showed up a few hours later, the doctor asked to speak with him in private. They walked down the hall together. Any number of things may have happened in that meeting. Knowing what the doctor knew by then about my mom, he may have decided to bend the rules about legal guardian signatures. Or maybe my mom had signed me away for good a few days earlier and nobody'd had the heart to tell me, seeing as I was already suicidal. But it's also possible my dad leaned in close and whispered a little medical advice of his own, something like, "Youse wanna stay healthy, Doc, you're gonna let me have my kid." Whatever happened down the hall, when my dad came back to my room, he helped me get dressed, and then he took me home with him. It was December 23rd.

I guess I was still suicidal on Christmas Eve because after my dad left for the bar, I headed across town to see my mom. She barely even spoke to me. John took one look at me, burst out laughing, then made me stand in front of the Christmas tree so he could take a picture of "hairless Santa." Then he shocked me and pissed off my mom by inviting me to spend the night.

I awoke on the couch Christmas morning to squeals and giggles. Kirsten and Hayley were up early and looting under the tree. I made them wait until my mom and John could get down the stairs. I watched my baby sisters open their gifts. I watched John and my mom open their gifts.

"I got this special for you," John said. He handed me a beer.

Marked Man

I WAS SPORTING A NEW TATTOO, "STRIKE FORCE," ON THE
back of my neck in time for my cousin Jimmy's wedding. He'd
fallen hard for a girl from the old neighborhood, and they'd spent
months planning their big day. Two huge Catholic families and
every friend the bride and groom had made since birth crowded
into a South Philly Mummer hall for the reception. There were
more shaved heads than flowers at that shindig.

One of the bride's uncles was a notorious doped-out drunk,
and he was beyond sloshed by the time they wheeled out the
cake. He stuck his hand in the icing and smeared it on my cousin
Shawn's head. The bride's guests thought it was funny, but dozens
of skinheads took offense. Tension rolled across the room like tear
gas. Then both sides just fucking exploded.

The older guests and little kids ran for cover. I dove into the
middle of the brawl with everything I had. Someone grabbed
me from behind so forcefully he nearly jerked me off my feet. He
wrestled my arms behind my back. I didn't need to see his face:
I recognized the handprint of the bruises already forming around
my wrists and the stench of his beer-soaked breath.

"What's it going to be?" John asked. "Your family or these
fucking skinheads?"

My mom appeared before me, wagging her finger in my face.
Over her shoulder, I saw the bride's uncle take a swing a Louie.

"Get the fuck out of my way!" I twisted free from John's grip
and pushed past my mom. I ran to Louie.

OUT OF RESPECT for Jimmy, Shawn, and me, no skinhead would have ever knowingly hit one of our family members. But once the brawl spilled out into the middle of Second Street, the skinheads couldn't tell who was who, only who wasn't one of them. One jumped my cousin Nick from behind.

"No!" I screamed, but I was too far away to stop it.

Jimmy's wedding reception riot had spread almost a block down Second Street before the cops crashed the party. Louie and I yelled for the other skinheads to follow us. We herded as many guys as we could back to Jimmy's apartment. We were trying to decide how we could get the skinheads out of South Philly without anybody getting killed when Jimmy showed up in his shredded tuxedo. He was crying.

Jimmy spent his wedding night with me. The South Philly side streets seemed darker than usual while he and I crept around our old neighborhood, finding the other guys' cars, driving them back to the apartment, and then guarding the out-of-town skinheads while they loaded up. On one of my runs, I swung by Third and Jackson to make sure Nick was okay. Jerry saw me before Nick did.

"Get your fucking pussy ass out of the car! I'm going to rip your fucking head off, you fucking retard!"

Nick still ruled Third and Jackson. He waived his hand at Jerry to signal, "Enough!" Jerry slunk away.

Then Nick walked over to me and said, "Your boys are fucked up."

I started in about how the bride's uncle had started it all, but Nick cut me off.

"Shut up! What's wrong with youse is what I want to know? Jumping guys three or four to one like some little punk? That's just not right. And fucking with family? Fucking with *us*?" Nick glanced over his shoulder at the other Third and Jackson boys. They were all keeping their distance, but they wanted to kill me.

"You didn't see what started it," I said. "We were just sticking up for Shawn."

Nick looked away from me, away from the corner, into the shadows of the side street. He stayed silent for a long time, before he turned back to me and asked, "Why?"

"What do you mean, why? Because it's Shawn."

"Because he's our family or because he's one of your fucking Nazis?"

There was no way in hell I was going to answer that question. The truth would have killed Nick. The truth might have gotten me killed. Nick stared me down, waited me out, but I refused to answer. He walked away from me in disgust and stepped back inside the tightly-knit circle of Third and Jackson boys. I thought he was done with me, but then he came back over to the car, leaned through the open window, and hissed in my ear, "You used your only pass tonight, Frankie. Do you understand what I'm saying to you?"

I understood.

"Now you get your ass back to wherever your pussy friends are hiding and you tell them we'll be waiting for them."

As I drove back to Jimmy's apartment, I wrestled with what I should do. Third and Jackson had called out the skinheads. My cousin had just warned me I'd already broken the code, the code you only get to break once with guys like Nick. I had to deliver the skinheads to Third and Jackson to prove my loyalty to the cousin who'd all but raised me. But the guys still tucked away in Jimmy's apartment weren't Axis or Nazi Alliance. Most of them were just young kids from the suburbs; they wouldn't have stood a chance against the Third and Jackson boys. Hell, if it weren't for Nick, I wouldn't have stood a chance against the Third and Jackson boys that night. Only Jimmy was safe. Not even our asshole cousin Jerry would've busted Jimmy's chops after the shitty day that poor kid had just had. So, with Jimmy by my side for added protection, one carload at a time, I escorted all the other skinheads out of South Philly.

I CRASHED OUT in the suburbs for a month or so, and eventually wormed my way into floorspace at a skinhead flophouse in Allentown. I have no clue whose name was on the lease or who paid the rent, only that my arrival pushed the roommate count to fourteen. I don't think one dude crashing there had a job. Since we were all broke, nobody got all prissy about stealing being "beneath" Nazis. We stole shit all the time. Food. Beer. Weapons.

Of course, being skinheads, theft wasn't our crime of choice. Every dude living in that house was violent. One night, two of my roommates came home bragging they'd just killed a homeless guy. Not to be outdone, the next night, three other guys walked in the door covered in blood and announced that they'd stabbed a cabbie for the hell of it.

I didn't kill anybody while I lived in Allentown, but I changed up my look around that time. I went on a tattoo binge. The best ink man in the movement was a skinhead named David Conover who worked out of a shop in Reading. Conover wasn't just a tattoo artist for the movement, though; he was a John Cook type, a high-ranked older skinhead with deep ties to adult white supremacy groups. John Cook had turned me into a Klansman, but it was David Conover who turned me into a walking Nazi art exhibit.

He started by inking "Made In Philly" across the front of my head, right above the hairline, if I'd had any hair. Then he drew a portrait of Joseph Goebbels on my chest. Of course, I got *the* Nazi symbol, too. But I didn't get just a regular swastika. David Conover laid a five-inch circle swastika into the left side of my neck. David was one of the few skinheads on the East Coast who could authorize giving somebody that particular patch. It was the original White Combat symbol, and it required a certain amount of rank inside the movement to wear.

I'd earned my rank by then. And I feared that rank had earned me a certain amount of notoriety with the authorities, especially in Philly. After I got my cool new tats, I became even more paranoid about getting busted, just not paranoid enough to change my ways. After every terror squad mission, I practically gave myself an ulcer worrying my victim would report, "One of the guys had a bigass swastika on his neck," or "He's got 'Made In Philly' on top of his head."

But being the genius I was, I didn't think twice about the cops nabbing me if they saw my picture in the newspaper. A writer for one of the Philly papers came out to Reading to interview John Cook and David Conover for a story about the growing number of teenaged skinheads in Pennsylvania. The paper ran the article with a picture of John and David posing next to two of their favorite teenaged skinheads: Louie and me. The article inspired one of the morning television talk shows in Philly to do a segment on skinheads. John Cook did most of the talking, but Louie and me made for real good visual aids, with my tattoos and Louie missing one of his front teeth from a fight.

I was convinced I had more warrants out on me than I could count. But warrants or not, I was determined to celebrate my seventeenth birthday on South Street. I was riding shotgun in the Muffster's Dart, not ten minutes away from Skinhead Alley, when Muff got nabbed for DUI. For once, I was actually sober and totally innocent. But seeing those cherries spinning in the rear-view mirror was more pressure than I could take. If I'd given the cops my real name, and if they'd run it, I would've been screwed. I had to get out of Philly.

I hitched a ride to Jersey that night. The first and only skinhead I saw on the Wildwood Boardwalk was Joe Morgan. He said I looked nervous. Of course I looked nervous; I was nervous.

"Let's take a ride," Joe said.

"That's it," I thought. "I'm dead. Joe knows about Adrienne and me, and he's going to whack me now while no witnesses are around." So what did I do? I said, "Okay Joe" like he'd invited me out for an ice cream cone. I climbed into the car with him, proving I must have still been at least a little suicidal.

To this day, all I know is that Joe Morgan was a good shit, at least to me, when I was desperate. After I told him about how much the Philly cops probably had on me, he spent the rest of that night on the phone making arrangements to get me off the East Coast. The next morning, Joe drove me to the Greyhound terminal in Philadelphia. All I had were the clothes on my back and a wad of cash in my pocket.

"They'll meet you in Indy," Joe said. "Just do what they tell you, and don't do anything stupid."

Caught on Tape

FROM THE SECOND I STEPPED OFF THE BUS, INDIANAPOLIS made me queasy. The sky was too far away. In the bright blue glare of mid-afternoon, the sparkling high-rise buildings reflected each other like funhouse mirrors. I took a deep breath hoping to steady myself, but that only made it worse.

Five members of the Nazi Alliance met me at the bus station as promised. Joe Morgan had called them not more than twenty-four hours earlier and said he needed them to take me in. Joe out-ranked them, so they obeyed, but they weren't exactly happy about hosting a seventeen-year-old. The Indy Nazi Alliance guys were all in their mid to late twenties. They weren't just skin-heads anymore; they were hardcore Aryan nationalists. I wasn't the first rogue race warrior they'd protected inside their safehouse, but I think I was the youngest. They seemed to hold that against me.

When I arrived, they were fine tuning their plan to rob banks to fund the race war in Yugoslavia. That impressed the shit out of me. I'd met some skinhead legends on the East Coast, but I'd never actually come face-to-face with Bob Matthews' descen-dents. Back in the early 1980s, Matthews and his followers in The Order had pulled off a string of bank robberies for the move-ment; they'd scored more than a million bucks and even murdered a famous Jewish talk radio host before the feds caught up with them. Bob Matthews went down shooting. The rest of The Order was locked up in a federal supermax penitentiary by the time I became a skinhead. If guys like Joe Morgan, John Cook, and Scott Windham were legends among skinheads, Bob Matthews was a god.

The members of the Indianapolis Nazi Alliance spent damn near every waking minute working out the details of their plan to follow in Matthews' footsteps. They had books about guns scattered across the stained shag carpet in the living room and piled high on the kitchen table. They had guns all over, too. Of course, I could barely see the guns because their townhouse was always dark. The Indy Nazi Alliance guys were so paranoid they were pushing towards schizophrenia by the time I met them. And me showing up made it worse. They'd boarded up their windows from the inside in case of a raid and hung thick drapes over the boards in case of spies. I thought it might be nice to see what was in my cereal bowl, so I opened one of the drapes about an inch to let a beam of sunshine in between the cracks in the armor, and you'd have thought I'd outed myself as undercover FBI.

They really went freaking berserk a few days later when I left the house. They rarely ventured out during the day. They just couldn't believe I was stupid enough to walk down to the Walgreens in broad daylight for no good reason. I thought I had a great reason: I was bored out of my fucking mind from listening to them yammer nonstop about their big plot.

My hosts would take me out for air sometimes after dark, though. One night, we vandalized a black church. Another, we jumped a junkie shooting up near the old train station downtown. I'd been living in the safehouse for about a month when my guardians took me with them to Aryan Fest, held that year at the Alabama farm of Bill Riccio. I can't tell you who all Riccio was in bed with, but I can tell you he seemed like one very big dog, or at least one very loud dog, in the white supremacy movement back in the early 1990s, big and loud enough that a film crew came down to Aryan Fest to make a documentary about him. I didn't see the cameras or Riccio my first day at the festival; apparently he was taping interviews inside his house while skinheads partied down outside to a battle of white power bands. The second day, I was too polluted to notice the cameras. They noticed me, though. If you ever get a chance to check out the documentary *Skinheads USA*, the tattoo of "Strike Force" in the opening scene is a close up of the back of my neck. A little while later, I'm the one with the big swastika, *Sieg-Heiling* in one scene and waving a Confederate battle flag in another. Toward the end of the movie, I'm the one tilting sideways, clinging for dear life to a beer bottle, right on the cusp of passing out.

Like I said, I don't know what all Riccio was into, but the cops busted him for some of it while Aryan Fest was in full swing. To the skinheads in attendance, Riccio's arrest was further proof of the ZOG theory: it was the Zionist Occupational Government trying to silence one of our heroes. The crowd went insane, but since we were out in the middle of nowhere, there really wasn't much we could do other than get even more drunk than we had been the night before and bash the shit out of each other in the mosh pit.

Spending a long weekend with skinheads who knew how to let loose only made Monday morning back in Indianapolis all the more awful. I couldn't take sitting around in that cell of a safehouse anymore. I busted out again and signed up for work on a concrete crew. The Nazi Alliance had a cow, but they got over it once I offered to fork up some rent money. I used the little cash I had left over to bribe the Indy skinheads into giving me rides. One Saturday, we all went to Chicago for a concert. I have almost no memory of that night: I don't remember the band that played, where it was, nothing. I don't even remember the trip back to Indy. All I remember is that standing in line waiting to get into the concert I got drunk with a couple of young skinheads from Springfield, Illinois, and when I woke up back in Indy the next night, I had their phone numbers stuffed in my pocket.

After that, I spent most of my weekends in Springfield, which is about a three-hour drive from Indianapolis. If I couldn't get a ride from one of the Indy guys, the Springfield skinheads would make the six-hour roundtrip to get me on Saturdays, then make it again early Monday morning to get me back in time for work. They were so pumped about having a big-city skinhead from the East Coast hanging with them that I think they would've driven me to Alaska if I'd asked. Hanging around those small town skinheads made me miss Philly less. They weren't exactly the terror squad, but they were young, fun, and fearless.

There were only a handful of guys in Springfield who considered themselves skinheads when I first went over for a visit, and only one had any actual ties to the movement. He was a redneck in his early twenties and had connections to Aryan Nations, which was the Vatican of Identity Theology then. The Springfield Aryan Nationalist wasn't just devoted to Identity, he was obsessed with it, which was both a blessing and a curse for the rest of the skinheads. He was a goldmine of information for people who wanted to listen, but he was a total turnoff for those who didn't. And that made him a real problem when it came to recruiting, because he tended to go fishing with a club.

I knew better. I knew how to bait a hook, and I knew how to bait and switch. It only took me one walk around Springfield's White Oaks Mall to find my angle. Springfield had skaters. Springfield had punks. Springfield had goths. And wherever you find skaters, punks, and goths, you can bet you'll find preps and jocks who like to bully the crap out of them. I'd long since learned there are two ways to form a skinhead crew: find skinheads or make skinheads. I found about half a dozen on my first visit to Springfield, then I convinced them we needed to make some more.

TOWARD THE END of one especially boring week in Indy, I couldn't wait to get back across the state line. So when I overheard my boss talking about going to Illinois, I asked if I could hitch a ride. He said he'd be happy to give me a lift so long as I didn't mind making a pit stop along the way.

My boss was in the process of relocating to Terre Haute,

which is right on the Indiana-Illinois border. He'd leased a new apartment on the second floor of an old dump of a house. He warned me before he dropped me off that the place was empty. He wasn't kidding. There was a ratty couch and a clock radio. That was it, other than the twelve pack of beer he bought me. He told me to cool my heels in the apartment while he hooked up with his girlfriend and promised he'd have me in Springfield in no time.

I tried to tune the clock radio to something, anything other than country music. After an hour or so of fighting it, I gave up. I turned the radio off and listened to the analog numbers flop over, flop over, flop over, every sixty seconds, for hours. I watched the sun set on Terre Haute.

After ten o'clock at night, Terre Haute, Indiana, is as quiet as a tomb. In the dead silence, that fucking clock dripped like a faucet. Then it ticked like a bomb.

I ran out of beer around eleven. I hadn't eaten since the night before, so a dozen beers fucked me up more than usual. I rooted through the closets, hoping to find a gun so I could shoot that fucking clock. The closets were empty. I was empty. I felt dead. I looked out the window to see if the world had ended and nobody told me. A car meandered down the street.

What street? I wondered. What street am I on? I'm in Terre Haute, but where? What's my boss's last name? I didn't know.

A freaky thought popped into my head: no one will know who I am if I die at this moment. I had no ID on me. I'd given my boss a fake name and social security number when he'd hired me. I hadn't told the Indianapolis Nazi Alliance I was leaving; I hadn't told the Springfield skinheads how I was getting there. The only people in the world who could rightly identify my body were in Philadelphia. Would they ever even find out if I died in that empty apartment? Would they care?

I staggered into the kitchen and ransacked the cupboards. They were grimy but empty. I tried the drawers. When I shoved my hand to the back of one next to the sink, I felt a wooden handle.

I followed it with my fingers: the blade was wedged so tightly into the seam of the drawer I nearly busted the countertop getting enough leverage to pry it loose. When it broke free, I took that as a sign: I knew what I was supposed to do.

I was wearing my best Ben Sherman shirt and the only Levi's I owned that weren't in shreds, so I stripped first. I stood in the middle of the kitchen, naked except for my boxers, staring at the blade. It was dull and rusty. I had to stab at my wrist to get an opening, but once I sawed a few passes back and forth, the blood flowed real nice.

I had blood smeared all over my face and chest by the time I walked out to the balcony. If I hadn't been so wasted, I probably would have fainted. Instead, I leaned over the railing and watched blood drip from my fingertips down onto the sidewalk. I watched the droplets merge into a small puddle.

My boss's neighbor screamed when he saw me. Then he apparently called 911 to report I'd murdered somebody. Minutes later, squad cars swarmed the street, and the cops kicked in the apartment door. Two cornered me on the balcony and ordered me to get down on my stomach while the others ran frantically in and out of rooms. It wasn't until they tried to handcuff me that they saw the gashes and realized the blood was mine.

The emergency room doctors stitched me up and pumped me full of antibiotics. They gave me a tetanus shot that hurt worse than the damn rusty knife had. In the meantime, the cops calmed down the neighbor and assured him the bald, bloody, tattooed stranger he'd seen on the balcony had not actually killed anybody. Then the cops tried to figure out who the bald, bloody, tattooed stranger actually was. I was in no shape to give them a name, real or otherwise. All they knew was I sure as hell wasn't local.

I woke up the next morning in a starched white bed in a sterile white room. My wrist felt like it was on fire. I pulled it out from under the covers and saw the blood-stained gauze. Then I remembered what I'd done. A nurse came in, escorted by a burly orderly. She took my temperature, changed my bandages, made me swallow some pills, then asked me if I felt like eating. I said sure. She asked me for my name, and, without thinking, I gave her my real one. She asked for my address; I gave her the only one I could remember: Tree Street.

"Can I leave? Really, I'm feeling okay. Just a little sore," I said. "I've got people waiting for me."

"I'm sorry," she said. "It's a seventy-two hour hold."

"For this little cut? Seriously, it doesn't even hurt."

"I'm glad," she said, smiling gently at me. "But it's not the cut so much as why you cut yourself that we're worried about."

That's when it hit me: Toto, we ain't in Kansas anymore.

"Where am I?" I asked, knowing I did not want to hear the answer.

"You're at the Catherine Hamilton Center, sweetie," the nurse said.

Later that day, another patient confirmed that I really was where I feared I was. "Most folks around here call it Crazy Cate's," he said.

They didn't pump me for much information that first day. The second day, they must have pumped me full of drugs, because I played along. Taking all those quizzes, I felt like I was back in school. I guess I must've flunked, because nobody was talking about letting me go early.

At my big meeting with the head shrink, he shared the results of my tests – I was alcoholic and depressed. No shit, Freud – they brought me in drunk off my ass with slashed wrists. It's what he said next that made me lose my mind.

"We've asked the police to help locate your mother."

"You called the cops on me?"

"There's no reason for you to become agitated, Frank," he said in his annoying shrink voice. "The police only want to help you. They brought you to the emergency room, remember?"

"I don't have fucking amnesia. They brought me in. I didn't hurt nobody. Why are you calling the fucking cops?"

"Because you hurt yourself. The police aren't pursuing this as a criminal matter. They're simply trying to help us locate your mother. They're working with the Philadelphia police."

"The Philly cops?" I panicked. When I shot up out of the chair, the doc looked like maybe he was panicking a little bit, too, even though he still didn't have a fucking clue about who he was talking to. If that doc had known all the shit I'd done, he wouldn't have come into that room alone with me. Nobody knew except me, some skinheads, and, I feared, the Philadelphia police.

"Please try to relax. Everyone is trying to help you. You told us you were from Philadelphia. Isn't that accurate?" He flipped frantically through my file. I hadn't been there forty-eight hours, but the thing was already close to two inches thick from all those stupid tests. "Here it is. Tree Street for your mother, right?"

"Yes." I sunk back into the chair.

"We haven't been able to get an answer by telephone. The police will dispatch an officer to your mother's home. It's okay, Frank," he said. "It will speed the process along. This way, you'll be reunited with your family sooner."

Great, just fucking great. If I had as many warrants out on me as I should've had, I was totally screwed. The Philly cops weren't going to call my mom. They were going to have the Terre Haute cops arrest me.

"Am I allowed to make phone calls?" I asked.

"Of course. This is a hospital, not a jail."

"Not yet," I thought.

"I want to see if maybe I can reach my grandparents," I lied.

I PEERED OUT the small safety-glass window of my room into the shadowy parking lot two stories below. "Hurry the fuck up, guys," I thought. I distracted myself with a freshly sharpened pencil. What a stupid thing to give to a guy who'd stabbed himself in the wrist. But who was I to set psych ward policy? I doodled a few swastikas on some notebook paper left over from one of my evaluations. Then I pulled out a clean sheet and scrawled,

"Sorry. You were going to put me in jail instead of help. Thanks, Doc. P.S. Just another problem for me."

Moments later, I heard the muffled but familiar cadence of combat boots marching up the driveway. I wrapped myself in a bedsheet just as a hail of bricks spider-webbed the glass. I screwed my eyes shut and crashed through the remnants of the window, dropping nearly twenty feet to the ground below. The two overweight orderlies who came thundering outside looked like they were going to shit themselves when they finally realized what was going on. I guess they didn't know whether to chase me or call the cops, so they just stood there wide-eyed while I sprinted past them. Those poor guys had spent their careers babysitting neurotic housewives and high school bulimics – lucky for me, nobody'd ever trained them on the finer points of locking down a neo-Nazi skinhead.

In Springfield, a girl with ember eyes and olive-oil skin tended my wounds. Jessica didn't treat me like a boy who'd tried to check himself out for good; she treated me like a man who'd broken free. At first, I loved her just for that. Then I fell in love with her.

I moved in with a guy named Jake who wasn't interested in the white supremacy movement so much as the music that came with it. If Jake had been in Philly, he probably would've been a straight-up punk on South Street. But seeing as he was stuck in Springfield, the local skinhead crew was the closest he could get to a hardcore scene. Once I got settled in Jake's apartment, I got down to business. If I was going to stay in Springfield, the Springfield skinheads were going to have to get a little more organized. The guy from Aryan Nations was thrilled by this, of course. He sent off to the Aryan Nations compound in Idaho for more flyers. He was ready to tape their recruiting posters on every telephone pole in central Illinois.

I had a slightly different plan, though. I asked one of the skinheads if his high school had lockers. He looked at me like I was an escaped mental patient. I reminded myself I wasn't in

South Philly and rephrased my question, "The lockers, do they have slats, air vents?" He said they did. A few days later, he slipped about a hundred of my homemade recruiting flyers through those slats. He just went down a hallway, sliding them into every locker he could without knowing whose locker was whose. In the parking lot after school that afternoon, black and white players alike from the varsity basketball team threatened to kick the shit out of him.

The next afternoon, when the basketball players walked outside, they found a half-dozen skinheads leaning up against their cars. Not surprisingly, they didn't give us any shit. When we came to the parking lot again the next day, I noticed that all the alternative kids were huddled up under a tree. It was a fine hangout spot as hangout spots go, but it wasn't big enough for all of them. They were crammed next to each other like sardines, so I asked what was up.

"The tree breaks the fall when they throw shit at us."

Right about then, I heard something whistle through the air, catch in the branches, then bounce downward: plunk, plunk, plunk, one branch at a time. The kid was right: the tree broke the fall, sort of. Even slowed by the branches, the D battery was still a dangerous missile when it smacked a girl in the shoulder. She shrugged it off like it didn't really hurt, but I could tell it did. I picked up the battery and walked over to the crowd of jocks leaned up against the most expensive cars in the whole parking lot, laughing like a pack of idiots.

"Who the fuck threw this?" I asked.

The laughing stopped.

"I said who the fuck threw this? Youse ain't got big enough balls to even answer a question? There's twenty of you and one of me."

Silence.

"There's six of us," one of the skinheads said behind me.

"There'll be more tomorrow," I said. "And if I ever see so

much as bird shit drop out of that tree again, I'm going to fucking rape one of youse. You hear what I'm saying?"

Silence.

That was October. By November, there were more than a dozen skinheads in Springfield. I didn't need to bother recruiting racists. All I did was befriend kids who were pissed off about being picked on day in and day out. I trusted them to pay me back with loyalty. I trusted that I could turn their humiliation into hate. All I had to do was redirect their rage until it came thundering back out as racism.

I know it's scary to think it's really that easy to turn a nerd into a Nazi, but it is. Even easier was getting that kid's friends to follow him into the movement. I always devoted the most time to recruiting guys who owned their own cars. In the Midwest, guys with cars literally drive their buddies' social lives. Guys without wheels either follow along or sit home alone. Once I started, all I had to do was sit back and wait for my first-round draft choices to drive up with my next wave of followers.

White Oaks Mall became our South Street, and the parking lot outside of the Sears became our Skinhead Alley. After I beat down two SHARPs in the mall parking lot, I got "SHARP KILLER" printed inside my bottom lip. I think watching me get that tattoo inside my mouth scared the rural skinheads even more than what they'd just seen me do to the SHARPs. I'd been on a tattoo binge ever since I'd climbed off the bus in Indy because they were so much cheaper to get in the Midwest than out East. I'd already had the letters S-K-I-N put on the knuckles of my right hand, and H-E-A-D on my left, so that people could read who I was when my fists came flying their way. Soon after, I got "4-Skins," the name of one of my favorite bands, on one forearm, and a South African Swastika on the other.

By the time I got "SHARP KILLER" hidden inside my lip, I was plenty easy to spot, and I wasn't in Philly anymore. I was in Springfield, Illinois, a city of only about 100,000 people; the cops didn't have much of anything better to do than to close in on me. And before long, they knew all about me thanks, in equal part, to the local media and my ego. After about a dozen kids shaved their heads, the newspaper decided to do a story about the Nazi threat. They even asked if they could interview me. The paranoia about getting busted that had led me to jump out the window of Crazy Cate's disappeared in the glow of the media spotlight. Being the cocky young idiot I was, I not only agreed to the interview, I gave the reporter my real name. When the article came out, it talked not just about me and the sudden increase in local skinheads, but also about the national white supremacy movement. It didn't actually say I'd been planted by the movement to start trouble in Springfield, but it kind of sounded that way if that's what you wanted to think. And that's what the panicked people of Springfield seemed to want to think once the story hit the newsstands.

Ironically, it was right after the story came out that the national movement contacted me; it was *because* of the story that they even found out I was in Springfield ready to stir things up. A leader of one of the big adult Aryan nationalist groups sent me a letter at the PO box I'd set up to receive mailings from groups like his and to list on the bottoms of the flyers we were distributing. He said he was proud of the work I was doing and wanted to help me out however he could. He also advised me that a lot of skinhead crews on the West Coast were putting the media to work for them in recruiting. He told me just what to do to attract more journalists to publicize our crew. He also told me how I could go about getting my own show on cable access television. Within a week, I stopped by Sangamon State University's Telecommunications Department and filled out the paperwork to request production assistance and airtime. The program director damn near passed out when I told her I wanted to call my show *The Reich*. But there was nothing she could do to stop me. Thanks to my pen pal mentor, when she tried to stonewall me, I had my legal arguments ready.

The first episode of *The Reich* wasn't much more than a bad

imitation of *The Tonight Show*, Nazi-style. First, I did a little mono-
logue about the evils of ZOG. Then a bunch of skinheads lip-
synched to some white power songs and proved beyond a shadow
of a doubt the truth of one racial stereotype: white men cannot
dance. We concluded with a spoof on the Klan that would have
gotten us into deep shit had John Cook been in the vicinity:
the Klan probably came out looking worse than any minority we
mentioned.

Of course, the central Illinois viewing public didn't see it
that way. People went ballistic. They swamped the television
studio with phone calls demanding that our show be banned; the
program director had to explain over and over that she could
not "ban" a public access show so long as it met the guidelines,
which ours did. The local Jewish league launched a counterof-
fensive and scheduled airtime for a show of their own. Then a
radical black Muslim launched a counter-counteroffensive
and invited me onto his public-access radio show so we could
go after the Jews together. Meanwhile, all the mainstream
media flipped into a feeding frenzy; Nazi TV was the scoop du jour.

The more the community publicized the evils of hatred,
the more kids wanted to sign on as skinheads. Even some of the
jocks I'd threatened to rape for throwing that battery started
showing up to drink with us outside White Oaks Mall. By December,
there were at least twenty freshcuts wandering the streets of
Springfield, and dozens of other kids, both alternative kids and
popular kids, acted like we were rock stars and they were our
groupies.

But the bigger our group got, the more the core crumbled,
the more I crumbled. Bullshit bickering I would've ignored
back in Philly felt like an earthquake in Illinois. Jessica and the
Springfield skinheads were all I had. Even with them, I felt so
damn alone. I couldn't and wouldn't let myself trust anybody, and,
God knows, by then nobody should've trusted me. Somewhere
between Terre Haute and Springfield, any shred of conscience I

still had left withered up and died, and everybody around me paid the price.

I loved Jessica more than I'd ever loved anyone, but every time I got tanked when she wasn't around, I screwed whoever was. When the cops hauled me in for questioning about a home invasion me and the boys pulled, I gave them names: Rudolph Hess and Adolf Hitler did it. Worst of all probably, when I look back on it, I used my connections with the Aryan Nations dude to import a shipment of illegal guns into a city so small fistfights still made the newspaper.

I was so broke then I probably should have sold some of those guns for cash. But I hadn't wanted them for the money. I'd wanted them for the same reason I'd always carried a knife in Philly. Just because. Just in case. Just like my dad taught me. Some of those guns were stashed in the apartment I shared with Jake and another skinhead. On Christmas Eve night, 1992, Jake came home all excited about some electronics he'd bought off a kid we both knew, a kid I hated. I'd heard the kid had been talking shit about me behind my back. He didn't dress the part, but something in my gut told me he was a closet SHARP. If there was one thing I hated worse than a SHARP, it was a SHARP too fucking chickenshit to show his true blue colors in public.

Jake wasn't far enough into the movement's ideology to share my Sharpie paranoia. So I gave him a different reason to hate the kid. I convinced Jake the kid had sold him stolen goods. Just in case that wasn't motivation enough, I snuck our rent money out of its hiding place then told Jake the kid had stolen it. That did it. Jake and I asked the kid to come over, said we were having a little party. When he arrived, I said I needed to speak with him in private. I led him back to my bedroom and fed him a line about how Jake and I were pissed off at the other skinhead sitting out in our living room. That's all me and that kid discussed behind closed doors. But when I led the kid back to the living room, I gave Jake the signal, the one I told him I'd give if the kid confessed to being our thief. The kid must've thought Jake was insane when Jake started screaming at him about being a thief and a traitor and owing us big time. The kid was hunkered down on the floor, leaning away from Jake's torrent, the first time I kicked him in the face.

We kept him in our apartment for what felt like all night, and what must have felt like eternity to the kid. But it was only a couple of hours. Still, it was long enough. We caught the highlights on tape, thanks to the third skinhead and a handheld camcorder. While the videotape rolled, Jake and I took turns beating the kid. One of us would offer commentary while the other one pummeled him and kicked him. Then we'd swap.

"We should kill this fucker," I said to Jake, loud enough that the kid heard every word. "Tie him up with some duct tape, haul his sorry ass out in the woods, and just take him the hell out."

I left Jake to do the beating while I went into my room. I returned with a shotgun. I put the barrel of the gun dead center of the kid's forehead and said, "We could kill you and no one would care." When he flinched, I added, "This gun is loaded. Youse wanna see?"

We didn't kill him; we just tortured him. At one point, our cameraman complained he wasn't getting enough blood in the shots, so Jake cracked the butt of the shotgun across the kid's back, and I kicked him in the face so many times I couldn't believe he still had teeth. The gore thrilled our cameraman, but not me: the kid was bleeding all over the place, so much I was afraid he was going to stain our wall-to-wall carpet and get us in deep shit with the landlord. I picked the kid up off the floor by his shoulders and propped him against the wall.

"If you bleed on this rug, I will kill you. You understand me?"

He moaned and nodded "yes" as best he could. He cupped his hands underneath his chin, desperately trying to catch his own blood while I twirled the gun and weighed, aloud, the relative advantages of taking him into the woods to kill him or just blasting his knee off right where he sat.

"You can't shoot him here," the cameraman said. "I'm gonna get hit with the spray if you unload that thing inside."

So I didn't shoot the shotgun. Instead, I nudged the kid to make sure he was still conscious, and I picked up the telephone. He heard the whole message I left on a national movement hotline calling out for anybody willing to do a hit on the kid and also his girlfriend. Then the kid listened to me asking a buddy of mine if I could borrow his 9mm for an hour or two.

In the end, we decided to let him go, it being Christmas and all. As the kid struggled to limp out of our apartment, Jake warned him he had forty-eight hours to pay us back or he would be dead for real. I warned him not to call the cops if he planned to keep breathing. He didn't get ten feet down the sidewalk before I had a second thought and called him back inside.

"Youse gotta scrub that blood off, dude." I shoved him toward the bathroom. "I wouldn't want anybody thinking you been in an accident or something."

There was one death threat already waiting on his answering machine by the time the kid staggered home. More Christmas "greetings" came in throughout the night. Santa never made it down that kid's chimney, but me and a few of my elves stopped by late Christmas morning while he was out, probably at the hospital. We erased the messages from his answering machine and ransacked his apartment. While my little helpers broke everything they could get their hands on, I pulled my knife and slashed his waterbed.

The kid didn't get a chance to call the cops; his downstairs neighbors beat him to it. When water started pouring through their ceiling and they couldn't get an answer at his door, they dialed 911. Of course, we were long gone by then. We gathered the whole crew together for a party on Christmas night and promised we'd have some surprise entertainment. Once everybody settled in with a beer, I walked over to the television. The camcorder was connected to the set.

"This," I said dramatically, "is what happens to people who

stab me in the back." Then I pushed play. A few of those dudes nearly puked just watching it.

I didn't think too much about the closet SHARP or the video-tape after that. I just went about my business, trolling the mall for more recruits, preparing future episodes of *The Reich*, and try-ing to keep the peace with Jessica. The tattoo itch hit me again in early January, but I didn't have enough cash for what I wanted, even at Illinois' cheap rates. So I asked my tattoo guy if he took trades, and he asked me what I had to offer.

"I've got a camcorder I'm done with," I said.

He scrolled "*Sieg Heil*" on the back of my head in exchange for the camcorder. It never once dawned on me to pop that thing open and make sure there was no tape in it. When I showed up at the television studio about a week later to record another episode of *The Reich*, the program director met me in the waiting room. She looked more nervous than before, which seemed weird to me. She'd actually been pretty cool once she'd decided I wasn't going to murder her. I figured she was probably just having a bad day, and I thought I knew why. There were quite a few people crowded onto the couches in the cramped waiting room. I had a hunch they were there to give her hell about letting me tape *The Reich*. I shot her a look to let her know if any of those other guys gave her any crap while I was there, they'd live to regret it.

That's when I saw her eyes dart over my shoulder. It was already too late.

"Francis Meeink, you are under arrest for … "

The detective who'd snuck up behind me slapped cuffs on me and rattled off a string of charges that started with assault with a deadly weapon. I didn't bother to resist, not much anyhow, once the people on the couches jumped to their feet. They weren't there to give the program director trouble. They were all there for me; they were all undercover cops.

Big Time

THE JUDGE SET MY BAIL AT $750,000. ONLY ABOUT $749,999 more than I had to my name. Getting sprung early wasn't an option. Getting sprung ever wasn't looking like much of an option, either. The State's Attorney's Office had the videotape I'd left in the camcorder. They also had the statement the closet SHARP had finally given to the police more than two weeks after the attack. They even had statements from Jake and the skinhead cameraman, who'd both run their mouths like hoses. When I found that out, I started talking, too. All's fair in love, war, and a holding cell.

Of course, the authorities had way more on me than they did on anybody else. Thanks to my own bigass mouth, they had all the statements I'd given to local media and all the sermons I'd preached on *The Reich*. Because I was in that limbo-land called "age seventeen," they had access to my juvie records from Philly. And they had the eyewitness accounts of my recent escape from Crazy Cate's. I didn't find out until later, but they even had surveillance logs: the cops had been watching me since the first week I'd moved to town, including on the night I took delivery on that shipment of illegal guns.

Me? I had another public defender.

A lot of dudes get religion in lock up. Most of them have PDs. I was no exception. That I'm not still in prison to this day is proof that miracles happen. By my count, I could've been facing close to a dozen felony charges. I might've even been looking at federal charges on that gun deal, since the guns weren't just hot, they were imported across state lines. But the prosecutor decided to focus all his time and energy on what I'd done on tape to the secret Sharpie. I was facing actual charges on only two counts: aggravated unlawful restraint, which is kidnapping, and assault with a deadly weapon. And on those two counts, I was toast. Under the circumstances, my PD advised me to take any deal the prosecution offered. "If a jury sees that video ... " he said, shaking his head in despair. Not even Johnny Cochran could've gotten me off with that footage replaying in a jury's mind.

I was still in booking when I promised my lawyer I'd keep an open mind. I was also still in denial about how much shit I was really in. In my mind, it was going to be Sleighton Farms revisited. But I wasn't a "juvie" anymore. I was seventeen, and I'd used a firearm in the commission of a violent felony. By Illinois law, that meant I was an adult; I would be tried as an adult, and I would serve time as an adult, even while awaiting trial.

Reality started hitting me when the guards escorted me to my cell in Springfield's Sangamon County Jail. Compared to Philly, Springfield is a village. But it's the county seat, the state capitol, and also home to part of the federal court system, so its local jail is surprisingly large and un-fucking-believably hardcore. It was the back wing, three or four stories high, of the same massive red-block building that housed several courts. I guess that made it easy to transport people to hearings: us inmates didn't even need to go outside to get in front of a judge. And we never got to go outside for anything else, either. The day the cops handed me over to the guards at the Sangamon County Jail was the last day I breathed in fresh air for nearly three months.

As the guards ushered me along the cellblock corridors, I caught glimpses of my fellow inmates peeking out at me. They were men, not boys. Some were big time gangbangers from East St. Louis and Chicago awaiting trial on federal drug charges. Some were parole violators waiting to be shipped back to the prisons where they'd spent the last decade or two of their lives. Some were rapists. Some were murderers. But only one dude in the whole joint was a seventeen year-old Nazi kidnapper with his own TV show who'd recently escaped from a mental institution after a suicide attempt.

I'm pretty sure my adventures in Terre Haute are what landed me in the maximum security segregation cell block of the Sangamon County Jail. My private quarters featured only a blue rubber mattress atop a concrete slab and a stainless steel toilet-sink combo. Through the slot in the metal door that the guards used to deliver my meals, I could glimpse the rows of cells housing other high-risk inmates. Through a small, lonely window, I could look down several stories onto the back entrance to the building. I wouldn't have been able to fit through that window, and I wouldn't have been able to survive that jump.

The guards watched me 24-7 via closed circuit camera, for my own safety. They could've quit watching. Unless I'd figured out how to drown myself in the pint-sized toilet, suicide wasn't an option. And unless the guards had tried to off me, I was as safe as could be because I was on constant lockdown. For more than a month, the authorities secluded me completely from the other inmates.

Except for court appearances and meetings with my lawyer, I was allowed to leave my cell for only two reasons: showers and visitors. I got shower privileges two or three times a week, visitation rights only once a week; neither lasted more than a few minutes, and both required that I be accompanied by guards. Jessica and a couple of the skinheads came to see me every week. One week, between visits, she sent me a letter. It said she was pregnant.

Thinking about what kind of father I'd make occupied my mind during the 166 or so hours of each week I spent alone in my high-security cell. I wanted to be the kind of father my grandfather was. I wanted my kid to feel the kind of love Pop radiated. I hoped my kid would respect me like my uncles respected Pop. They didn't stay out of trouble and make smart choices because they feared Pop, but because they feared disappointing him.

Pop was Ward Cleaver, the perfect dad. But I'd only had one weekend a month in the best years to observe how Pop pulled that off. Most of what I knew about being a father I caught from my dad and my stepfather, two alcoholic-addicts, one who seemed to forget I was alive and one who seemed to want to kill me. With those two for my role models, what chance did I stand of turning out like Pop? What chance would my kid stand of surviving me?

My cell didn't look like my tiny bedroom on Tree Street, but it felt like it. Late at night, I'd startle awake from nightmares of my years as John's prisoner of war. In my daze, I'd look across the room, expecting my cousin Nick to be there. Of course, he wasn't. This time, Nick wasn't lying across from me, whispering assurances so I wouldn't lose my mind. This time, no one was there.

My only company was a worn copy of the Bible. At least it wasn't John's damn dictionary. I opened that Bible the first time simply to dull the boredom. I filled the endless hours searching for verses that said what I wanted to hear. I was a footsoldier in God's army; that's why I had to beat down that sneaking closet-Sharpie ZOG dupe. I was a martyr for the white race; that's why I was rotting in a ZOG jail.

I'd been locked up a few weeks before my public defender delivered the prosecution's opening offer: fifteen years.

"I'm only seventeen!"

"They have the videotape," he replied. "They watched you torture that kid."

Against my lawyer's advice, I opted for a jury trial. He told me that was suicidal and promised he'd keep trying to work a better deal with the State's Attorney. Prison overcrowding was a serious problem in Illinois then. That and my age were the only arguments my PD had to work with.

I hadn't spoken to my mom since before I'd left Philadelphia, but she knew I was in jail. Jessica had called her for me, which made me love that girl even more. What a fucking call to have to make: "Hello, ma'am, my name is Jessica. I'm dating your son.

I thought I'd call to introduce myself and fill you in on what Frankie's been doing in the six months or so since you saw him. Basically, he fled his outstanding warrants by moving to Indiana where he stayed in a safehouse operated by a hate group, then he tried to kill himself, escaped from a mental institution, formed a new gang, starred in a television show called *The Reich*, beat the shit out of God-knows how many people, then kidnapped and almost killed one. Now he's in jail and it's not looking so good for him. I've got the telephone number and mailing address of the jail for you, in case you might want to get in touch with him. By the way, I'm pregnant. You're going to be a grandma before you turn thirty-five, isn't that great? So, anyhow, enough about all that. How are you today?" Even my mom didn't deserve to get a call like that from a stranger.

Under the circumstances, I wasn't surprised when she didn't mail me a care package. But as the weeks wore on, I was surprised she didn't even write me a letter. Just a few hours after my lawyer delivered the prosecution's plea offer, I asked the guards for permission to use the telephone.

My mom responded better than I thought she would. When the operator said, "You have a collect call from Frankie. Will you accept the charges?" my mom didn't slam down the phone, which I'd kind of expected. Instead, she said something like, "I was wondering when you were going to have the balls to call me yourself."

I tried to sound as normal as possible: I asked how everybody back home was doing. My mom said, "Fine," then asked what exactly I'd done to land my ass in jail this time. I told her. She asked me if I was bullshitting her. I assured her I wasn't.

"Mommy, the lawyer says I'm going to prison. Pretty much for sure." My voice broke a little. "Maybe for fifteen years."

"Oh my God, Frankie. What have you done?"

Neither of us said anything for a long time, then I asked, "Does Daddy know?"

"I told your grandparents. I'm sure they told him."

"Does he know how to reach me?"

"You know he does." The soft, sad tone of her voice frightened me, as it had ten years earlier, the night she'd held me and asked if I missed him.

I'd felt alone most of my life. But in my cell that night, I felt a kind of loneliness I'd only ever felt once before. And this time, there was no rusty knife stuck in a filthy cabinet to keep me company. There was only a blue rubber mattress, a metal toilet, and a Bible. I couldn't tie the mattress around my neck, and I couldn't fit my head into the toilet, so I got down on my knees, folded my hands, and bowed my head.

"God, please fucking help me!" I began. I'm sure it wasn't the most eloquent prayer the Almighty ever heard, but it was sincere. Prayer was nothing new for me. I'd been praying ever since the nuns at Our Lady of Mount Carmel had taught me how. As a kid, I'd prayed for new hockey skates that actually fit. I'd prayed to win free season passes to Flyers games. I'd prayed for my dad to visit me. I'd prayed for John not to kill me. I'd prayed for someone to kill John. I'd prayed a lot as a kid. And I'd kept praying as I got older; I just prayed differently. The Lancaster County skinheads, and later, the Klan, had taught me how to pray like an Aryan. I'd prayed for God to reveal the "truth" of white supremacy to the world. I'd prayed for God to reveal his will to me and all the other white warriors battling ZOG out in the streets.

Alone in my cell, hundreds of miles away from Our Lady of Mount Carmel and the Invisible Empire, I prayed like never before. I didn't remind God I had just been trying to do his will. I didn't make any promises I knew I wouldn't keep if he'd just cut me a break. I didn't even ask for forgiveness. All I did was open my heart.

I MADE MY debut in the general population common room accompanied by two guards. My hair had grown out a little during my stint in solitary, so "Made in Philly" and *Sieg Heil* were hard to read, but the big swastika on my neck was clear to the dozen or so black and Latino inmates gathered around the television.

"It's him," someone said.

Whispers followed as I made my way toward my new cell.

"He's the Nazi with the TV show."

The voices sounded more curious than threatening. One actually sounded a little concerned: "He's just a kid."

The first few days, everyone talked about me, but no one talked to me. Even though I was free to come and go, I mostly stayed in my single-man cell, studying my Bible, looking for answers to questions I couldn't put into words. I felt like God was trying to tell me something, but what? Sometimes a shadow would darken the page I was reading. I'd look up to see a giant of an inmate standing in front of my doorway, blocking the bright overhead light from the hallway, silently watching me. Whenever I met his gaze, he'd saunter away. Eventually, I ventured back out into the common room. I poured myself a Dixie cup of Kool-Aid, the Dom Perignon of lockup. I found an empty spot as far away as possible from the crowd around the television and leaned my back against the wall so no one could take me by surprise. I tried to ignore a group of black and Latino inmates playing Spades at a nearby table, but after a few minutes of me just standing there, one asked, "Know how to play, Aryan Boy? Want dealt in?"

"Okay." There's nothing quite like boredom to shatter a dude's political convictions.

I got damn good at Spades thanks to the Sangamon County Jail. And I got the scoop on the Illinois prison system. If I got lucky, I'd get sent to Big Muddy, which was air-conditioned. If I got fucked, I'd get sent to Menard, which was hotter than hell and home to Satan himself: John Wayne Gacy, the notorious serial killer.

The card players were divided on whether or not I should've taken the fifteen-year offer. The guys who'd already done hard time thought I was insane to turn it down, especially after I told them about the videotape. But the younger guys, the ones who still had hope, agreed with me. Except when the table talk turned to gory predictions of what my life was going to be like in a hellhole like Menard State Penitentiary, playing Spades with those guys helped distract me from the mess I was in. When I was alone in my cell, my mind wandered to places darker than Menard. Alone in my cell, I kept drifting back to Tree Street. After all the years and all the hell, my mom was still too busy fucking the warden to check on the prisoner. She didn't write. She didn't call. She sure as hell didn't climb on a bus to come visit me. "She chose dick over you," I reminded myself. And she was still choosing. I assumed my dad was still choosing drugs over me. I didn't know for sure because I hadn't seen him for about a year. All I knew was that my mom had told Nanny and Pop how to reach me and they would've told him. Nanny and Pop wrote me faithfully. My dad never wrote me a single word.

I WAS HUNCHED over my Bible, praying that I'd get out of prison before my baby was an adult, when the shadow once again descended on my cell.

"Yo, skinhead!" His voice was as deep and dark as the Mississippi River. The Spades players had told me all about him. His name was Abel. He stood nearly 6′6″ tall. He'd been a drug kingpin in East St. Louis before he'd been born again behind bars. The feds didn't care about his conversion; they'd transferred him from his prison home up to Springfield to try him on new charges that would add even more years to his sentence.

"I see you reading the Bible in here by yourself all the time." Abel paused, like I was supposed to answer him, even though it hadn't been a question. I waited.

"You know, skinhead, we have Bible study in my cell every night at eight. You ought to come down."

Facing fatherhood and fifteen years in prison had re-opened my heart to God, but it hadn't opened my mind. I would play Spades with minorities, I would take prison survival tips from minorities, but I wasn't going to study the sacred word of the God of Identity with "mud."

"I hope you join us," Abel said, then he walked away. The light returned to my cell.

Later that day, I wound up next to Abel during a body count. Once the guards cleared us, he leaned down to me and said, "See you tonight."

"No way in hell," I thought. I guess Abel knew something I didn't. I don't know what changed my mind, but a few minutes after eight I found myself at Abel's door. He and five other black inmates were standing in a circle, holding hands, reciting the Lord's Prayer. The two men closest to the door silently opened the circle to me. They took my hands gently in theirs. I finished the Lord's Prayer with them.

"What's your name, skinhead?" Abel asked.

"Frankie."

"Lord, thank you for bringing Frankie to us on this night," he prayed.

I attended Abel's Bible study almost every night after that. Abel would lead us in prayer, asking God to bless our meeting and guide us toward understanding and love. He'd offer specific prayers on behalf of fellow inmates facing jury selections or verdicts the next morning. After the prayers, we'd discuss a passage from the Bible and how to apply it in our lives. To close the meeting, the brothers would sing gospel songs. I'd croak along as best I could, thankful that Abel's booming voice drowned me out.

Before I started going to Abel's Bible study, only the Spades players treated me like a human, and even they never called me by my name. But everybody in the jail seemed to relax around "Aryan Boy" once they saw me going to Abel's cell each night. That's not why I went. I went because the hour I spent there every night was the only hour of every day when I didn't feel like I was dying.

Everybody was basically cool with me by the time a voice

came over the intercom and announced, "Frank Meeink, please report to the guard station. You have a phone call." I'd been in general population close to a month, and not one other inmate had ever been paged to take a phone call. I felt like the king of lockup. Everybody in the common room gave me the same weird look. "Jealous," I thought. The other inmates watched me bound toward the guards' station like I was expecting a bouquet of roses to be waiting. The guard at the desk didn't make eye contact. He just said a call had come in for me a few minutes earlier, and I needed to return it right away. He escorted me to a telephone and handed me a note with a number scrawled on it. My mom's number! My mom was finally checking up on me. Then my mom picked up the phone, and I finally understood: the weird look I got from all the other inmates hadn't been jealousy; it had been pity.

She was sobbing so hard she couldn't even say, "Hello."

"What's wrong?"

"Nick's dead!"

"Not Uncle Nick!" I cried in disbelief.

"No!" she said. "Not Uncle Nick! *Nick!* Nick is dead!"

She rambled on about how some junkie named TJ had shot my cousin Nick so full of China White that he'd never had a chance, about how there was no way Nick would've overdosed on purpose or even by accident, about how she didn't know how she was going to survive this, about how she couldn't fucking believe I was rotting in jail in bum-fuck-nowhere when my family needed me back in Philly, about how she was going to call the Red Cross to see if they could spring me for the funeral like they did with soldiers. But I couldn't follow her. Nothing she'd said after "Not Uncle Nick!" really registered with me. Nothing in the whole fucking world made sense.

I clung to the receiver even after my mom hung up. Tears streamed down my cheeks. My shoulders shook. I sank to the floor. I have no idea how long I stayed like that before my Spades partner, an older Latino, threw his arms around me and dragged me to my feet. He buried my head in his chest and held it there so that no one could see my face. Then he started walking me toward my cell.

"Don't cry," he said in a gruff whisper. "Don't let anybody see you cry." He kept moving me toward my cell, shielding me from the view of the other inmates, knowing my moment of weakness could make me a target. He didn't even know what I'd just heard on that phone call, only that it was tragic. Jailhouse veterans know that all incoming calls to jail are bad news. Only I hadn't known.

"You can't lose it in here. You gotta put it out of your mind." That's what Nick would've said if he'd been there. But, of course, he wasn't. He never would be again.

I didn't get to go to the funeral. I had no clue if my mom had actually tried to get the Red Cross to fly me home, because she didn't call me back. It didn't matter. I wouldn't have gone even if I could have. I wouldn't have done that to Aunt Catherine and Uncle Nick. They didn't need to see their nephew in shackles next to their son's grave.

If I hadn't known Jessica was pregnant, I would've been praying for the death sentence. Only the thought of her and our baby made me want to keep breathing.

After close to three months in jail, my day in court finally was in sight. In preparation, my lawyer had me speak to a psychiatrist. The doctor asked me if I'd ever experienced any trauma. I said, "Not really, just life, you know?" So we talked about my life: South Philly, my mom, my dad, John, skinheads, being on my own, being suicidal, being on the run, going to prison, becoming a father. Every couple of sentences, he'd interrupt me with, "You didn't find that traumatic?"

Finally, the doc asked, "What *would* you consider traumatic?"

I thought about it for a few minutes, then I asked him, "Does being raped count?"

My case never made it to trial. Right before we were scheduled to begin jury selection, my public defender had another meeting with the prosecutor. That PD had one hell of a shit-eating grin on his face when he asked me, "Would you be willing to take three-to-five?"

B25509

NOT MANY WHITE SUPREMACISTS ACTUALLY LAND IN prison. Groups like the Southern Poverty Law Center figured out years ago that the best way to break up a hate group is to break their bank, so the real powerbrokers are more likely to get sued into oblivion than incarcerated. Of course, some of the big dogs get chased by the FBI or the ATF. If they don't go down shooting like Bob Matthews or Randy Weaver, those guys disappear forever inside the federal system. Regular old rank-and-file white supremacists rarely do time, because they rarely get arrested – most adults in the movement are all talk. And since a lot of skinheads are under eighteen, the worst they usually get is a stint in juvie. Unless of course they pull a shotgun while they're beating the dude they've kidnapped, then forget to take the freaking videotape out of the camcorder.

Less than a week after the ink dried on my plea agreement, I rode a Department of Corrections bus to the intake facility at the Graham Correctional Institution. I was photographed, finger-printed, body-searched, and renamed: B25509. Then I changed into my prison-issue blues and followed a guard to my temporary home in the intake-observation cell block.

My cellmate was a Gaylord. The name ain't what it seems: the Gaylords are one of the meanest gangs in the Midwest. They formed in Chicago in the 1950s. The gang's real name is Great American Youth Love Our Race Destroy Spics, which is a shitload to tag on the side of a train car. So they go by the acronym Gaylords, which sounded cooler back in the '50s, but still sounds like trouble to anybody in the know.

I couldn't have asked for a better first cellie. I'd grown up around East Coast corner boys and skinhead crews, not Midwestern gangs and sure as shit not prison gangs. I needed to learn my way around fast, before I made a mistake that might cost me my life. My cellie had grown up in Chicago. He was only in his twenties, but he'd done stints before, as had most of the other Gaylords waiting for him in general population. He looked how my cousin Nick would've looked if he'd been pure Irish. His street smarts reminded me of Nick, too, so I trusted him, as much as I was willing to trust anybody under the circumstances. Our first night together, he gave me a crash course on how things work behind bars.

Gangs control the prisons; any dude who tells you otherwise has never been on the inside or he's a warden. The truth is the system caters to the gangs, uses the gangs, because the gangs are the only thing standing between the guards and the bowels of hell. The gangs bring order to the chaos; they make the violence predictable.

My cellie gave me the rundown on all the big gangs within the Illinois prison system and where they all fit within the superpower alliances called People and Folk. To understand People and Folk, just think Cold War, 1960s-style, but with JFK and Castro wearing doo-rags. By the time I got sent up, the People versus Folk line divided most prisons right down the middle, and it was the only thing that consistently cut through the race lines that divided the gangs. The People included the white Gaylords, the black Vice Lords, and the Latin Kings, among dozens of others. Black Disciples, Latin Folk, and white Simon City Royals were among the Folk. So were the Crips. But the Bloods were People, which explains why it's a miracle Los Angeles didn't burn to the ground back in the 1980s.

Each side of the alliance lived by the same basic code: the integrity of the alliance itself trumped any frictions between particular gangs inside it. So Vice Lords and Gaylords may have battled it out sometimes, but if the Black Disciples started any shit in the meantime, the battle stopped until the war was over. Beyond just defense, there were certain courtesies extended between gangs within an alliance. Like, if a Gaylord were to shank a Vice Lord for no good reason, since they were both People, the head Vice Lord would tell the top dog Gaylord, "If you wanna keep the peace, you better take care of your boy." The next few days, there'd be one less Gaylord in the yard. Now, had that been a Black Disciple who'd stabbed a Vice Lord, the Vice Lords would've taken that dude out themselves, no questions asked, no warnings issued, black unity be damned.

People and Folk weren't just about war and peace; they were also about the bottom line. The prison black market in Illinois was enormous in the early 1990s. Food, cigarettes, homebrewed hooch, and narcotics were the top commodities, and the gangs traded them like Wall Street brokers. The most powerful gangs had connections on the outside and guards in their pockets. For the right price, they could get you anything short of freedom. I actually saw one dude take delivery on a bag of McDonald's. But I never saw People gangs doing business with Folk.

The peace treaties and trade agreements inside the two alliances made prison a lot safer and more predictable than I'd imagined it would be. If you abided by the warden's rules, you stayed out of the hole. If you abided by the alliances' rules, you stayed out of the grave. That's good shit to learn before the guards waltz your ass out into general population. So my first night in intake, I took full advantage of my cellie's knowledge.

"So is everybody People or Folk?"

"No. The super-hardcore Muslims, the Malcolm X types, they pretty much steer clear of all the gang shit." His eyes dropped to the swastika tattoo on my neck. "So do your boys."

The Aryan Brotherhood is the most notorious gang in the American prisons. By gang standards, they're unbelievably small. They're also unbelievably violent. The Aryan Brotherhood formed in the California prison system back in the 1960s. It spread across the country almost as fast as its reputation. It was the gang no other gang wanted to fuck with. It's still that gang. The Aryan Brotherhood answers to no one; everybody answers to them. All white inmates defer to the Brotherhood. No matter how badass they think their little gang may be, no white prison gang still in existence has ever refused a request from the Brotherhood. That's why the Brotherhood can run a prison even if they only have one or two guys there. But it's not just other white inmates who bow down to them. Most minority gangs get real quiet when the Brotherhood passes by. So do most guards.

The Brotherhood is so powerful it transcends the People and Folk alliances. But at least in Illinois in the early 1990s, the Brotherhood leaned toward the People. They did a lot of business with the Latin Kings, and they were tight with the Vice Lords. That shocked the shit out of me at first, seeing as the Aryan Brotherhood believes in white supremacy and the Vice Lords are all black. Then I learned that most Vice Lords are Muslims, meaning most of them hate Jews. The enemy of my enemy is my friend.

Other than some of the big white gangs like the Gaylords and the Northsiders, the two groups closest to the Brotherhood in most prisons aren't actually gangs, just groups. The first is the great white horde of outlaw bikers doing time for dealing meth and battering dudes who ride Kawasakis. The second group runs under the tag Aryan Nation. In prison, any guy who belonged to the white supremacy movement before hitting intake is considered part of Aryan Nation, even though most weren't actually in the real group by that name before getting busted. Some were Klansmen. Some were part of the National Alliance. Some had ties to White Aryan Resistance. A few actually had been members of the real Aryan Nations in their former life. But, at Graham, only one was a South Philly skinhead.

I was thrilled to learn from my cellie that there would be at least a few other Aryan Nationalists waiting for me once I got

out of intake. They'd be my family, my home base. I was counting
on those guys to keep me from losing my edge, my faith, my
mind. Those were the guys I could talk with about Identity and
ZOG and destiny. They were my brothers. The Aryan Brotherhood,
on the other hand, was totally out of my league. The Brotherhood doesn't recruit short-timers or babies, and by their standards,
I was both. But I was a skinhead, and a kind of famous one at
that because of the controversy about *The Reich*. So I had a hunch
the Aryan Brotherhood would step in if any minority inmate got
a bug up his ass to try to kill me, and I was hoping to God all the
minority inmates were thinking the same thing.

My second night in intake, I was shooting the shit with my
Gaylord friend when a monster of a guard appeared at our cell
door. If it hadn't been for the uniform, I couldn't have picked him
out of a lineup. He reeked biker badass every bit as much as the
badass bikers on my side of the bars.

"This is from a friend." He handed me a shoebox.

As soon as the guard walked away, my cellie asked, "Who
knows to send you a kite?"

"A what?"

"A kite. It's not real mail," he said. "You only get real mail at
call. That's from inside. Prison UPS."

I carefully unfolded the small paper football attached to
the top of my kite. "Welcome, Frank," the note began. It then
provided a list of inmates' names and their cell assignments and
instructed me to tell the guards to take me to any one of those
cells whenever I was ready to talk. The note was signed "Scooter."

When I read the name aloud my cellie said, "Dude, Scooter
runs the bikers." Then he leaned in close and whispered, "Word
is he speaks for the Brotherhood."

If there were any actual members of the Brotherhood at
Graham they were either on their way out of the system or on
their way back in. Except for its maximum-security intake and pre-
release units, Graham was a medium-security joint. It wasn't
the kind of place where the Aryan Brotherhood floated around

for long in general population. According to my cellie, that's exactly why the Brotherhood struck deals with guys like Scooter. He spoke where they couldn't, on the very front end of the system. Gaylord legend had it that guys like Scooter were kind of like the Brotherhood's welcome wagon. I didn't know enough about the Brotherhood or the prison system to know if that was myth or fact. All I knew was somebody'd finally sent me a care package. The shoebox contained a little bottle of shampoo, some toothpaste, a toothbrush, a comb, deodorant, matches, a huge stack of candy bars, and two small, easy-to-conceal marijuana joints called pinners.

"I never got nothing like this on intake anywhere," the Gaylord said. "Who the hell are you?"

He'd been so busy answering all my questions he hadn't paused to ask me who I was. He just assumed, since I was a kid, that I was, well, just a kid. So I told him about Strike Force and *The Reich*.

"I'm sharing a fucking cell with Adolf Hitler!"

"Dude, it's really not that big of a ... "

"Adolf fucking Hitler is my cellmate! My boys back home ain't gonna fucking believe this."

His eyes darted from me to the two pinners.

"So, Adolf, you gonna share?"

"Yeah, sure," I said. "What do I do?"

He assumed I meant how do I smoke pot in prison without the guards busting me. Of course, I didn't correct him; I just watched. I'd been around pot almost every day of the first fourteen years of my life, but I'd never paid any attention to how to light a joint, because I'd never wanted a joint. I'd only once ever even taken a hit off a joint, and I'd been really young, maybe fourth grade, and I only did that one hit so my older cousins wouldn't call me a baby. I hated that hit. I hated pot for the same reason I hated Jethro Tull: it reeked of Tree Street.

For a convict, I was a goody-two-shoes when it came to drugs. All I'd ever done was that one toke off a joint and a few hits of acid that had sent me on a guilt trip. As a skinhead, I didn't approve of drugs. Hell, I didn't even smoke cigarettes. I just drank. But Scooter hadn't sent me a case of Budweiser; he'd sent me two pinners. My cellie had no clue I was basically opposed to drugs when he started working his magic on my kite. He unrolled about four feet of the toilet paper and smeared deodorant all over it. He shoved it into the shoebox and lit the toilet paper on fire.

"That's prison incense," he explained. Then he fired up one of the pinners and took slow, steady drags.

Minutes later, half-stoned from my cellie's secondhand smoke, my whole anti-drug stance started to crumble. I was like one of those cartoon characters with a little devil whispering in one ear and a little angel chatting up the other.

The devil tempted me: "It's okay, B25509. You're stuck in fucking prison. It'll dull the pain."

"Don't forget who you are! You're only here because you're an Aryan warrior. Good Aryans don't do drugs," the angel reminded me.

"But they're from Scooter," said the devil. "He's got ties to the Brotherhood, and who the fuck are you to question the Aryan Brotherhood?"

I snatched the joint from my cellie and took such a long drag I nearly choked to death. I sputtered something about having a cold to try to save face, but it didn't matter. So long as I shared, my cellie didn't care that I was a weed virgin. Once I got myself back under control, he picked up the conversation we'd dropped when the guard delivered the kite.

"So like I was saying, man," he drawled through the haze. "The gangs run the store. It's all about who your friends are. What's that saying, 'no man is an island'? You can't be an island, man. In here," he rambled on, "you either sign on or bend over."

That sobered my ass up quick. The great dirty-little-not-so-secret of the American prison system: rape.

"You don't have friends to watch out for you," my cellie said, "you're fucked. All the gangs fuck with you. The psychos start eyeing you up. Even the guards fuck with you more if you're on your own."

A couple days later, I thanked my Gaylord cellie for all the lessons, and he thanked me for sharing Scooter's pot. We were sent to different cellblock houses in general population. My new cellmate was an older man whose accent I recognized on the first word.

"So what are youse in for, kid?" he asked.

"I beat a dude up and kinda kidnapped him. How 'bout youse?"

"I killed my brother."

After dropping the ending on me like a bomb, he started at the beginning of his story. Every twist and turn of his life growing up in Philly revolved around his brother. They had been more than brothers; they'd been best friends. They did everything together, always. As adults, they moved to Illinois together, found work together, made friends together, and hung out together every night at the same bar. It would've been a blessing if they'd died together. But when the cops showed up at the scene of the accident, my cellie's brother was already dead in the passenger seat, and my cellie was alive and uninjured behind the wheel. He blew nearly twice the legal limit on the breathalyzer while he watched the EMTs put his best friend into a bodybag.

When he finished his story, he asked me, "Youse drink much?"

I didn't have the heart to answer him; I just shrugged my shoulders. He snatched a big book off his bunk and said, "Youse ever wanna read this, help yourself."

I glanced at the cover. *The Big Book*. "What a fucking original title," I thought. Then I noticed the words printed near the bottom: Alcoholics Anonymous.

That afternoon, I took my first trip out to the main yard. It looked like a South Philly playground, an ocean of cracked concrete surrounded by weeds passed off as grass. I hadn't been outside more than a minute or two when a guy approached me.

I didn't recognize him from my block. His long black hair was slicked into a ponytail. Two huge goons lurked behind him.

"You get what I sent you?" he asked.

"Scooter?"

"Take a walk with me."

Scooter's bodyguards lagged behind enough to give us privacy when we were far away from other inmates, but they closed rank whenever we neared members of minority gangs. No one made a move toward us, though. Not even other bikers.

"I've heard about you," Scooter said, dragging hard on his smoke. He ran down a list of what all I'd done in the name of white supremacy since arriving in Illinois; he had more on me than the cops.

He waived his hand in the direction of a pack of young bikers. "Half those fuckers didn't know they were white until the blood drained out of their faces in intake. You're not one of them, not with that swastika on your neck." He offered me his cigarette.

"I don't smoke."

"You didn't smoke those two pinners I sent you?" He sounded pissed.

"I smoked those." I did not need Scooter mad at me my first day in general population. "I don't smoke cigarettes."

Scooter nearly busted an artery laughing at me. "Kid, this ain't a Marlboro." He flashed his hand open to reveal the pinner. He showed me how to hold it so it wouldn't be too obvious to the guards. I took a hit, then, being polite, turned to pass it to one of Scooter's boys walking behind us.

"No!" the bodyguard sharply corrected me. That dude shot Scooter a look that said, "Sir, I apologize for this idiot offering to let me smoke your weed."

That look taught me as much in one second as my Gaylord cellie had taught me in a week: no man is an island, but every island is ruled by only one man. I would've liked to have spent more time with Scooter simply to watch him work his Don-Corleone-on-a-chopper angle. He didn't have a drop of Italian blood in him, but that dude would have made a hell of a 68th and Buist boy. Unfortunately, my conversations with Scooter were short lived, because I was only passing through Graham.

Scooter must've seen the worry on my face. "No matter where you end up, they'll be there. They ain't gonna sign you on since you're just a kid, but they ain't gonna let anybody fuck with you, either."

"So how do I find them?"

Scooter shook his head and choked back a laugh. He tapped his index finger on the swastika tattoo on my neck. "Trust me. They'll find you."

A FEW DAYS later, I was transferred to Big Muddy State Penitentiary, the prison the Spades players in Springfield had made such a big deal about because of it being air-conditioned. When the bus stopped and the doors opened, I understood why: southern Illinois is a lot farther south than it looks on a map. It was July and I swear I thought my brain was going to melt walking from the bus into the building.

From what I've heard, Big Muddy is where Illinois warehouses sex offenders these days, but in the early 1990s, it was a regular maximum-security prison. At Graham, it had seemed like half the dudes I met were either on their way into the system or on their way out. Big Muddy inmates were just there: most had already been locked up for years; some would be locked up for life. Guys who count down by decades instead of days don't tend to worry about getting into more trouble.

In a twisted way, that made life pretty bearable inside Big Muddy. If the black market at Graham had impressed me, what I encountered at Big Muddy blew my fucking mind. Full-size joints replaced pinners. Instant soup took a backseat to hooch. If I'd wanted it, cocaine and heroin were there for the buying. So was porn. So were pretty-boy whores.

My first trip out to the yard at Big Muddy, I had my eyes peeled for Aryans of any stripe. There were little packs of white inmates lolling around in different areas, but I knew not all of them could be trusted. Some would be Simon City Royals. The last thing I needed was to have the Aryan Brotherhood's first impression being me talking to a Folk gang. I scanned ink to get my bearings, looking for the blood-drop cross of the Klan, the shamrock brand of the Brotherhood, or at the very least, Harley Davidson logos.

The Aryan Nationalists and the bikers were so tight inside Big Muddy that I don't think they even knew who was who for certain. They were like an old married couple that's been together so long they start looking alike. The head of the bikers was a rabid but unaffiliated racist who went by the nickname Peaches, and the boss of the Aryan Nationalists was a biker named Digger.

When it came to black market business, Peaches called the shots because he had unbelievable connections on the outside and the highest tolerance for pain of any human I've ever met. Peaches was one of those dudes like my dad whose attitude made his body seem a lot bigger than it was. But his attitude hadn't helped much when he took a bad tackle playing football in the yard. His shoulder snapped. From what I heard, he didn't even flinch. Then he turned the injury into the asset that let him corner the market at Big Muddy. Every week, when his old lady came to visit, she tucked drug orders into his cast. And every week, after his old lady left, his boys yanked that cast off his fractured shoulder to free the drugs, then they crammed him back into it. Needless to say, the shoulder never healed, so the cast never came off, not on doctor's orders; it only came off on Peaches' orders every week so his shipments could be delivered.

Digger didn't share Peaches' tough-guy reputation, but he had a lot of power because he had rank: supposedly, he'd actually been a sergeant-at-arms with the real Aryan Nations before getting sent up.

Ninety-nine percent of the time, Peaches and Digger called the shots on the day-in-day-out life of ninety-nine percent of

the white inmates at Big Muddy. But they didn't call the shots for
the other one percent. And whenever all hell broke loose,
they let that one percent call all the shots. Anytime there was big
trouble brewing, Big Muddy's small Aryan Brotherhood
contingent took over. I was never officially introduced to most
of them, so I can't say for sure, but Digger said there were seven
or eight actual members of the Aryan Brotherhood at Big Muddy.
Seven or eight's more than enough, especially when they've got
a couple dozen Aryan Nationalists standing to their right and a
couple hundred bikers lined up on their left.

As I made my way toward the white end of the yard, a voice
called out, "There's our boy!"

It was Digger, head of the Aryan Nationalists. As Scooter had
promised, he'd heard about me already. Digger made the rounds
of introducing me to the twenty or so white supremacists under
his command. He always opened with, "This is the kid with the
TV show." After I'd been introduced to all the Aryans, Digger parted
the nearby sea of bikers with his enormous girth and formally
presented me to Peaches.

"Anything you need, anything you want, all you do is ask me,"
Peaches said. He stroked his ZZ Top beard, nodded toward the
Aryan Brotherhood pack standing a short distance away, and
added, "You ain't ever alone in here."

For several weeks, I split my time at Big Muddy between
playing football with some of the younger bikers and explaining
to my Aryan brothers exactly what in the hell it was that Aryans
actually believed. Turned out, a lot of those guys hadn't really
been "in" the movement before getting sent up. They had never
been to rallies or meetings or had open access to a Klan library.
They were racists, but they didn't know much about the history
and theories of the white supremacy movement. So I gave daily
mini-sermons on Identity and earned a lot of respect from my
congregation on the bleachers in Big Muddy's yard.

I didn't spend all my time with the Aryans, or even with
other whites. I'd gotten totally hooked on Spades in the Sangamon

County Jail, so I'd throw cards with anybody up for a game. Before long, I was the regular partner of an old Vice Lord who said I cheated better than any white boy he'd ever met. None of the white guys, not even the Aryan Nationalists, minded that I played cards with the Vice Lords. Sometimes the enemy of my enemy is my card partner.

And no brand of Aryan got bent out of shape when I aimed a three-way phone scam at the Latin King market. In those days, the hot new commodity in telecommunications was three-way calling, and it was hotter than a red poker for inmates. If a prisoner called someone on the outside collect, and they had three-way, then that person could use their other line to link to somebody else. I used a Springfield skinhead's three-way to call people who wouldn't accept collect calls from me, like my mother. Another reason inmates wanted three-way access: the third number didn't register on the prison log.

I guess none of the Latin Kings at Big Muddy knew anybody with three-way calling, because once word got around that I was pulling it off, instead of copying my system, they became my clients. One afternoon, I set up a safe line for a King called Slick Rick.

"What do I owe you?" he asked when he was done.

"First one's on me."

"You're good shit." Rick shook my hand. Then he added, "I won't forget this. I'll hook you up."

Slick Rick showed up in my cell that same evening with a joint the size of a Cuban cigar. Even on the outside, I couldn't have bought incense strong enough to mask the fumes of that mongo doobie. I got so high I went completely stupid. I wandered out onto the tier, where I ran into the lieutenant of the guards, who was sniffing around like a bloodhound. Nothing happened that night. But the next morning I got a form in the mail telling me to report to the Internal Affairs Office the following day. There was a check in the box next to "urine test." I ran to find

Peaches, figuring the biggest dealer in the yard was my best source for advice.

"How hot are you?" he asked.

"I think I'm still fucking stoned."

"Tell them you won't piss. If they give you any shit about it, tell them you got religious reasons. Worst they'll do is throw you in the hole for a while for bullshitting them, but they can't make you pee."

I was still so stoned I figured that since I was going to get busted anyhow for refusing the test, I may as well get completely freaking polluted. I smoked a pinner I had stashed in my cell. Then I visited one of the bikers who brewed hooch.

I was blind drunk when I staggered home.

The damn Internal Affairs Office wouldn't stop spinning the next morning. I was holding onto my chair for dear life, reeking of booze and pot, when the IA officer asked me politely to pee into a cup.

"My religion forbids me."

A couple guards marched me to my cell to pack up my stuff, then they moved me into segregation, "seg," the hole, solitary confinement. It didn't matter what they called it, I'd been there before. I'd spent my first two months in Sangamon County Jail in solitary. Hell, I'd spent the better part of three years in solitary on Tree Street.

It was the first time I'd really felt incarcerated since entering prison, because prison was recess compared to county jail. Unlike jails, prisons had yards, big yards, with basketball courts, even football fields. In Graham and Big Muddy, I got at least three trips to the yard every day. When I wasn't outside, I had the run of all the cell blocks in my building. I had junk food from the commissary and all the pot and hooch I could want, thanks to the bikers and my phone scam clientele.

In the hole, all I had at first was a bastard of a hangover and a bad case of *déjà vu*. Then a guard came by with a library cart and told me to pick out a book. I chose Stephen King's *Pet Sematary* because I'd seen the movie. I read the first couple of pages, then tossed it aside and fell asleep. A few hours later, another cart rattling down the aisle awakened me. The small wire cage in my solid steel door opened, and a food tray appeared.

"You need anything?"

That wasn't a question a guard would ask. I bent over so I could peek out through the cage. From my odd angle, I couldn't see the face of the inmate-trustee delivering my rations, only the small blackish-green shamrock tattooed on his hand.

"I'm okay," I replied.

He asked the same question every day. After two weeks in segregation, I finally replied, "I'll take whatever youse got. I just gotta lose reality."

The next morning my breakfast arrived with a side order of yellow pills. I didn't know what they were, and I didn't really care, so long as they knocked me out. I swallowed them all.

I bugged out for two straight days. I hadn't made it past page ten of *Pet Sematary* in two weeks, but on those pills, I sped through to the end within hours. That's not a book you want to read when you're already seeing things. I spent the next twenty hours or so completely convinced that Gage, the creepy kid from the book, was hiding under my mattress.

Once I got past the worst of the crazies, I had sense enough to try to work whatever I'd taken out of my system. I had nowhere to run to, so I did push-ups. Thousands of push-ups. So fucking many push-ups I think I permanently altered my metabolism.

I still hadn't slept, but I was back in my right mind by the second night when my delivery man stopped by again.

"What was that?" I asked.

"Yellowjackets." That explained a lot.

"I'm in the hole, and you gave me speed?"

The day before my thirty-day stint in solitary came to an end, I was informed that I was being transferred. They never tell you where you're going or why, only that you are. The Gaylord next door told me not to sweat it.

"It don't matter where they send you," he promised. "If you're getting deliveries in here, you're gold anywhere there's barbed wire."

Satan Himself

EVERYBODY HAD WARNED ME ABOUT MENARD. THE SPADES players in the Sangamon County Jail. My first Gaylord cellie at Graham. The Aryan Nationalists and bikers at Big Muddy. Everybody talked about Menard in lowered voices, like they were at a funeral. But nothing anybody had said prepared me for how I felt as the bus pulled through those gates. There were thousands of guys warehoused inside, but only one mattered, and we all knew it. I tried not to think about him as the bus wound around the yard. I tried to focus on the buildings, the seemingly endless rows of modular cell blocks that descend the cliffs of the Mississippi River like stepping stones into hell, the towering limestone fortress of a main block that has haunted the nightmares of killers for more than a century. Nothing could have prepared me for how I felt when the guards marched me into the madman's castle in shackles. I was in his house now. Somewhere inside that tomb they call a prison, John Wayne Gacy was sitting on death row, waiting for his final trip to the execution chamber. But at that very moment, he was walking freely inside his cell, and I was the one in chains.

"How fucking rotten do people think I am?" I thought.

I never worried that Gacy was going to get me. It wasn't like that at all. I never even saw the dude. Nobody ever saw him except the guards. Even if the guards had lost their minds one day and turned him loose in the yard, it wouldn't have mattered. Gacy wouldn't have stood a chance man-to-man with any other inmate in the place. By then, he was nothing but a ball of blubber. Gacy never had been a fighter; he was just a fucking freak who had gotten more than thirty dudes so drunk and drugged they couldn't fight him off when he fucked them or when he dismembered them. It wasn't Gacy himself that messed with my head: it was the idea of being in Gacy's prison. "People think I belong here with him," I realized as I clanked along in my chains between the guards. "Normal people, nice people, regular people, look at me and think, 'Society is a better place if that no-good Frankie Meeink is locked up with John Wayne Gacy.'"

I could have handled that, but then this other thought flashed across my mind: they think I belong here because I almost killed that kid. It took a few seconds for the full effect to slam into me. When it did, it felt like a bomb exploded inside my chest. I thought I was having a heart attack.

"Oh my God," I thought. "I almost fucking killed that kid."

Menard broke the spell I'd been under since the day of my arrest, maybe since the day I became a skinhead. Menard kicked my ass back to reality.

Reality? I had almost killed that closet Sharpie in Springfield. Reality? I had almost killed a lot of people. As the guards led me toward my cell, I realized, "I belong here."

Nothing in the fucking world could have prepared me for that.

I DIDN'T DO the kind of God-awful time a lot of poor bastards do in Menard. I wasn't in the main block, where they kept Gacy and the other psychos; I was "on the hill," with the run-of-the-mill drug dealers, kidnappers, arsonists, rapists, and murderers. I got a nod from a member of the Brotherhood my first day. A couple weeks later, I got told to get back on the bus. As it turned out, Menard had only been a pit stop for me, but nobody bothered to tell me that. Inside the Illinois Department of Corrections, I never knew how long I was going to be anywhere or why I sometimes got told to get on the bus. I spent every waking minute

I was in Menard believing I was going to be in that hellhole for the remainder of my sentence. It was my shortest stay anywhere during my whole stint behind bars, but it was the one that got my attention.

I didn't let on to anybody that I'd snapped a little at Menard, or that my mini-breakdown had changed me a little. For the first time since I'd brutalized that Sharpie, I stopped being pissed at him for turning on me. A couple of times, I let myself get close to wondering if he was okay. That's the kind of squishy emotion that can make you a target in prison. Prison is a cage full of predators, and predators prey on the weak. I hardened my shell to compensate.

By the time the DOC bus pulled into Shawnee State Penitentiary, I had reclaimed my South Philly swagger. I wasn't some no-name, no-rank punk who felt just awful about his awful, awful crimes. I was B25509, the skinhead celebrity. No matter where the Illinois Department of Corrections put me, I'd have an audience of Aryan Nationalists, all the free dope I could want from the bikers, and if I ever needed it, the backing of the Brotherhood. Those were the credentials that would keep me alive in prison. Those were the credentials I planned to pull out in the yard at Shawnee.

Unfortunately, those were also the credentials the Department of Corrections flagged in the file they sent ahead of me to Shawnee's intake unit. The whole point of intake units isn't to let the new inmates settle in; it ain't like freshman orientation at college. The point is to give the system a chance to figure out who's who. The tattoos are the first giveaway, since most dudes have gang insignias scattered among their other ink. So the intake guards take photographic tattoo inventories before they even hand out temporary cell assignments. Then the guards watch how everybody interacts for a couple days or weeks. Who's got a really short fuse? Who's everybody else bowing down to? Who are the alpha dogs? The puppies? The bitches?

If anybody sees anything they don't like on an inmate's skin, in his eyes, in his actions, or in his file, the intake supervisor does a more extensive interview with him in hopes of figuring out where to place him in the maze of cell blocks so he'll do the least damage possible. I got called in for a special interview.

The intake supervisor lectured me about how I wasn't going to be a problem in Shawnee like I'd been in Big Muddy. I thought he was talking about the piss test. Then he drawled deeply, "We don't tolerate gangs here."

"Yeah right," I thought. But all I said was, "I'm not in a gang."

"Mr. Meeink, don't try to play games with me." He sounded like Boss Hogg from *The Dukes of Hazzard*. "Your gang activity at Big Muddy is well-documented." He dropped my case file on his desk for effect.

"I'm in a political organization."

He rolled his eyes. Then he trained them on me like a rifle sight. "You can call it the fucking Junior League for all I care, but it's a gang, and we both know it." He leaned across his desk, jabbed his fat finger at my face, and said, "We've got enough problems with your kind already."

Actually, my "kind" was almost nonexistent at Shawnee. Among the hundreds, maybe even thousands, of inmates housed in the sprawling prison, I met fewer than half a dozen guys who'd been members of the white supremacy movement before entering the system. And none of them were what I would consider serious. One was a no-rank Klansman from some backwoods klavern. One was a self-proclaimed "skinhead." He had a huge tattoo of Hitler running from his collar bone to his waist, but he'd never actually met a real skinhead crew member face-to-face until he met me in the yard. The rest of Shawnee's Aryan Nationalists were just guys who'd been on mailing lists.

Of course, there were plenty of racist bikers at Shawnee, and supposedly even a few members of the Aryan Brotherhood. But none of them turned out to greet me on my first trip to the yard. Instead, the chief of the Northsiders spotted me and filled me in. While I'd been cracking up over at Menard, a war between the bikers and the Latin Folk had gotten so out of control at Shawnee that the warden had placed most of the bikers and all of the Aryan Brotherhood in protective custody, not to protect them so much as to protect everybody else. They were all still in there, leaving the Northsiders as the only major white gang in general population. Fortunately for me, the Northsiders were freaking huge at Shawnee. The warden couldn't have put them into protective custody; they wouldn't have fit. The Northsiders were tight with both the bikers and the Brotherhood because they were all white and all badasses. And at least at Shawnee, the Northsiders also leaned toward the People. All that combined meant there was no question where they stood on the whole Biker versus Folk war. It also meant they had backing in the yard even after the bikers and the Brotherhood got sent to protective custody. The Latin Kings, the Vice Lords, the Bloods, and all the other minority People gangs at Shawnee were willing to risk their lives to protect the white Northsiders from the archenemy Folk. And once the leader of the Northsiders took me under his wing in the yard, the Latin Kings, Vice Lords, Bloods, and all the other minority People gangs knew it was their responsibility to at least keep an eye on me, swastika tattoo and all.

"You come to us if you need anything," the Northsiders' leader told me.

That was a relief. No man is an island. But when you're the only real Aryan Nationalist in the yard, and the Brotherhood and the bikers are in lockdown, it sure as hell feels that way.

"I appreciate it," I said to the Northsider.

"You just ride under our flag for now, until your boys make it back out." He motioned his hand toward the assemblies of Vice Lords, Bloods, and Latin Kings scattered about the yard. "They may not like you much, you being a skinhead and all," he said. "But they'll murder any Folk who so much as breathes on you."

As it turned out, some of the Latin Kings, Vice Lords, and Bloods did come to like me, in spite of the fact that I was a Nazi.

And I came to like some of them, too, in spite of the fact they were "mud" by Identity's standards. We all found this out only because of the tensions being so high at Shawnee.

When I first arrived, Shawnee felt like the main block at Menard looked. Almost every cell block was on restricted privileges and the guards were on edge. So when the war cooled a little and we finally got some freedom, we were all maniacs. We didn't want to walk the yard, we wanted to run laps around it. We didn't want to breathe the fresh air, we wanted to suck it in with heaving gasps. And there's nothing like a good game among convicted felons to get your heart pumping.

Sports were bigger at Shawnee State Penitentiary than they were at Penn State University. If Joe Paterno could've recruited out of our yard, he'd have gone undefeated his whole damn career. There's something magical about a barbed wire end zone and armed guards in the press box that gives a guy a real boost on the gridiron.

Everywhere else I'd been, the bikers fielded a team in every sport. But since most of the bikers were in lockdown and the Northsiders didn't seem interested in getting a team together, I asked if they minded if I joined somebody else's team. I had to do that because I was riding under their flag. They looked around the yard at all the black and Latin gang teams facing off, then they looked at me like they thought I was nuts. But they gave me their blessing and I spread the word I was a free agent. One of the Vice Lords I threw Spades with delivered an invitation for me to join their football team. I wasn't the only guy on the team who wasn't a Vice Lord: two of our linemen were Bloods. But I was the only white guy, and definitely the only Nazi.

The first game I played for the Vice Lords, I had to beg to even get out on the field. They finally let me in the game after the Gangster Disciples' team scored a touchdown on them; the Vice Lords said I could do the kickoff return. I was a Nazi skinhead playing tackle football in a prison yard with a bunch of black gangsters. This wasn't Pop Warner League. I hadn't expected the kid glove treatment. They were going to make me prove myself. I *had* to run that ball back. And I did, even though not one dude on my team blocked for me that first play. The Gangster Disciples took special aim when they tackled me. I looked like a fucking rag doll by the end of the second quarter. But I kept hauling my ass up off the dirt and going back in for more. There was no way in hell I was going to let those black players chase me off, not with the whole yard watching. So the harder they hit me, the harder I played. When I ran in for a touchdown during the third quarter, my teammates high-fived me. And when an opposing player hit me so hard in the fourth quarter that I actually went airborne, one of the Vice Lords helped me to my feet. After that, I wasn't the Vice Lords' token skinhead; I was their teammate.

At the end of our games, most of my Vice Lord teammates would be panting for air and rubbing their knees, and most of the Northsiders in the audience would be creaking their way down off the bleachers that ran along one side of the field. I on the other hand would be bouncing around like a puppy on crack. And two of my teammates, Little G and Jello, would bounce right along with me. The three of us would race across the yard to the basketball court to get in a little three-on-three time before the guards sent us back inside. Our team was all heart and no height. At 5′9″ I was the tallest of the three of us, if we didn't factor in Jello's fade. If the courts were full, we'd pace the sidelines, waiting until one of the games ended, then we'd challenge the winners. If nobody'd let us play, we'd just run. Some days we ran sprints; others we ran laps. But no matter what we did, we always did it at top speed and together.

None of our elders on either side of the race line gave us any shit about hanging out together so long as it kept us out of their hair. Like me, Jello and Little G were first-timers; they were also teenagers. Our energy exhausted the older inmates, and their words of wisdom depressed the hell out of us. No matter what color a guy's skin is, he doesn't want some old fart telling him that his girl is screwing another guy. I don't know what it is about old inmates, but they get their rocks off bursting the young bucks' bubbles. When you're eighteen and think you're in love and the only hope you're holding onto is that your girl will be waiting when you get out, it hurts like fucking hell to have some lifer declare, "I'll bet she's blowing your best friend right this very minute."

Little G and Jello never said shit like that to me because they too were eighteen and in love and hoping like hell their girlfriends weren't sucking some other dude's dick right that minute. They were the only guys I could talk to about Jessica. I read all her letters to them, and they read their girlfriends' letters to me. We analyzed every word.

"Look, here, where she wrote, 'I love you, baby.' 'You' is kind of smushed up. What do you think that means?"

"I don't know. Where's last week's letter?"

We'd dig through the stack, do some analysis. We were like twelve-year-old girls at a slumber party. If we'd done that in front of guys doing serious time, they would've busted our balls so bad we would've hit high notes like twelve-year old girls.

I would've lost my mind at Shawnee without Jello and Little G, because the closer Jessica's due date got, the more insanely jealous I became. No matter what she wrote about in her letters, I read between the lines until I found a reason to suspect her. I grilled her every time we talked on the phone.

"Frank, I'm eight months pregnant. Who'd want to fuck me?" she'd ask, laughing.

But I missed the sarcasm. I just plowed forward like a prosecutor, quizzing her about how she was spending her every waking moment. God forbid she did something with one of the skinheads, even though I'd personally asked a couple of them to take care of her for me while I was gone.

"He took you out to eat?"

"It was nice to get out of the house for a change."

"Did he try to kiss you?"

"Jesus, no! I look like a fucking whale. Who'd want to kiss me?

My voice would break a little. "I do."

"But you can't, can you?"

The electric chair would've hurt less than hearing Jessica say that. I couldn't kiss her. Prison rules forbid kissing during visits. Not that she visited often; she only made the trip twice, and both times, she got so pissed at me for acting jealous that she left early. Sometimes on the phone, if I asked her too many questions, she'd hang up on me.

Of course, every time she hung up on me, I became even more convinced she was cheating. But Little G and Jello always talked me off the ledge. And I returned the favor whenever their girlfriends hung up on them. We were three pretty typical teenage boys, obsessed with girls and sports. But we were inmates, so we had a few other things on our minds, like keeping safe and doing business. Our friendship bent the rules, but didn't break the rules: we were all on the right side of the People versus Folk line.

THE CIVIL RIGHTS Movement bypassed Shawnee's kitchen altogether: the white inmates got the perk jobs, and the black inmates got the shit jobs. Once they got out of protective custody, the bikers resumed their long-held positions as the executive chefs of the mess hall. I lugged industrial-sized ingredients around on their orders while they were cooking; once they were done, I manned a ladle on the service line. Being black, Little G manned a mop. Little G and I teamed up on a food scam simply because we got assigned to the same kitchen crew shift. But Jello was the real entrepreneur in our group. With the right investors, Jello could've turned Shawnee's kitchen into a national franchise, but all Little G and me could figure out was a straight up food heist.

Little G wasn't much taller or much wider than his mop handle. He fucking hated mop duty, but his mop bucket was the secret to our success. When the guards weren't looking, we stole as much food as we could grab and wrapped it tightly in plastic bags. Then we dropped the packages into the filthy water of the mop bucket. As the inmates filed through the line, they placed their orders with me, and I told them what to do to take delivery: take a seat, eat for a while, then spill their drink on the floor.

Whenever an inmate spilled something, the guards would signal the mop boy to go clean it up. Little G would push the bucket over next to our customer and start mopping, then he'd raise some bigass stink to distract the guards. Sometimes he'd go off about how mop duty was another name for slavery. Sometimes he'd start in about how he was going to get the NAACP to investigate Shawnee's kitchen. But no matter what spin he put on it, he always did it big and loud and moving toward the guards. And while the guards had all eyes on Little G to make sure he didn't attack them with his mop, our customer would reach down into the dirty water of the mop bucket Little G had parked right next to him, grab his order, and stuff it down his pants. We filled somewhere between three and ten orders at every meal, but the guards never caught on to what we were doing. At an average of fifteen bucks, cash or trade, per order, we made a good chunk of change. Of course, we had to cut in the gangs backing us, but the leftovers were enough to get us by.

ON A NOVEMBER day in 1993, I called one of my boys in Springfield and learned that I had a daughter. A few hours later, the prison counselor fixed it so I could call Jessica at the hospital.

"She has your eyes," Jessica said. "I wanted her to have your eyes."

I wanted to know what every part of my baby looked like. "What's her hair like? Tell me about her nose?"

"I've got to go," Jessica replied. "I'm so tired."

"I'm sorry. But I just gotta know what she looks like."

"She looks like Riley."

Riley. My baby girl was named Riley. But not Riley Meeink. Jessica had told me all along she was giving the baby her last name, but I'd spent nine months praying she'd change her mind. She didn't. My baby wasn't a Meeink. Then again, neither was I.

Jessica refused to bring Riley to see me. She didn't want Riley to meet her father for the first time in prison. I understood; I didn't want my kid to meet me for the first time in prison either. But my heart was breaking, and it came out as rage. I screamed into the telephone; I called my baby's mother a "bitch" and a "whore." It was the final straw. Jessica had put up with my temper and my jealousy since the day we'd met. She'd had her name dragged through the mud for dating Springfield's "Nazi threat." Her notorious boyfriend and her unplanned pregnancy had strained her relationships with family and friends. Now she was a seventeen year-old single mother trying to support a baby on her own because I was in prison. I was in prison nagging her, hounding her, distrusting her, demeaning her. I wasn't worth it for her anymore. She told me to go fuck myself and slammed down the phone.

I was a basket case. Jessica refused to take my calls, and she was wise to my three-way trick. The Springfield skinheads were my only source of information about the woman I loved and the baby I hadn't seen yet. They assured me Jessica and Riley were both okay, but they couldn't or wouldn't answer the questions that were driving me insane. How does it feel to hold Riley? Is Jessica screwing somebody else?

Riley was nearly a month old when I received her birth announcement in the mail. The tiny picture of my tiny girl was the most precious possession I'd ever had. I slept clutching that picture to my chest every night. Jello and Little G asked to see it almost every day. They made a huge deal over me becoming a dad. All the Vice Lords on the football team congratulated me. All those guys asked me how the baby was doing every time they saw me. If they hadn't made such a fuss over Riley, I'm not sure I would've noticed how little my fellow Aryans seemed to care. But I couldn't ignore the contrast. Almost none of the white inmates even acknowledged the news that I'd become a father.

THE ILLINOIS PRISONS were ridiculously overcrowded in the 1990s. As a result, a lot of dudes were getting paroled early just to make room for the newly prosecuted. I knew going in that if I kept my ass out of serious trouble, I stood a good chance of getting out even before my three years were up; that knowledge was motivating. I broke a lot of rules in prison, but I never got busted for anything serious, except refusing the piss test.

One Thursday, I received a letter informing me that I was scheduled for release the following Monday. The guards came to my cell on Friday and exchanged my regular uniform for a set of reds, the special jumpsuit prisoners wear in the days before their release. If you've got a lot of enemies, reds say, "Last chance to take me out." If you've got a lot of friends, reds say, "Last chance to say your goodbyes." I was lucky; I had a lot of friends.

Early in the morning of Monday, March 6, 1994, the guards locked down our tier. Then they popped the lock on my cell. They handed me a box to gather my personal items. I didn't have much, just Riley's picture and a few letters, mostly from Jessica and Nanny and Pop. As the guards escorted me through the rows of cells for the last time, my friends called out their goodbyes.

"Go hug that baby." My Vice Lord spade partner.

"Take care of yourself." Little G.

"We love you, man." Jello.

I was almost off the tier when a voice bellowed, "White is Right!"

Voices echoed down the row. "White is Right!"

"White is Right!"

The guards led me to an office and presented me with the clothes I'd been wearing on intake at Graham, the same clothes I'd been wearing when I got arrested in Springfield. I stripped off my reds and slid into my Levi's. I carefully attached my red braces over a t-shirt emblazoned with the words "Brutal Attack." Then, for the first time in more than a year, I wound my red laces through my twenty-hole Doc Martens. My legs quivered to the cadence of skinheads marching in formation through the streets of Center City, down the boardwalk on the Jersey Shore, across the quad of a fancy private college. The echo of the cell block rang in my ears: "White is Right! White is Right! White is Right!"

As I put one combat boot in front of the other, I said goodbye to the parallel universe that is prison. Prison isn't like the real world. Everything's different in prison. In prison, regardless of race, People are just people, and Folk are just folks. The door to that world slammed shut behind me.

I stood only two feet away from a second door, *the* door, the door back to the real world.

"Goodbye, Little G. Goodbye, Jello," I whispered.

The buzzer sounded again.

"Goodbye, B25509."

The door popped open.

"Frankie!" a skinhead screamed, running toward me with his arms wide open. He hugged me close and said, "I can't believe you're finally back."

"I'm back," I replied. "Trust me, I'm fucking back."

Daddy's Home

THE DEPARTMENT OF CORRECTIONS GAVE ME FIFTY BUCKS for bus fare, but since I had a ride, I blew half my wad on junk food at a convenience store not two miles from the prison. I think the dude working the counter thought I rode in on the short bus, because when he handed me my change, I just stood there staring at it. The prison economy runs on barter and bills; it'd been more than a year since I'd seen a coin. So I stood staring into my palm, marveling at the sight of loose change. On the ride home, my skinhead buddy filled me in on how the Springfield crew had fallen apart while I was gone. My driver was pretty much the only one of my guys who had stayed true to the cause in my absence. Some defected the day I got busted because they were scared they'd be next. Some held out until the jock and prep bullies at their high school realized I wasn't going to be waiting out in the parking lot anymore; those chickenshits buried their Docs in the back of a closet and went back to hiding for cover under a tree. The rest, the majority, just lost interest.

"So what're they doing instead?" I asked.

"Nigger shit," my driver said with disgust. "They're all into rap now and smoking weed."

"Jello and Little G would fit right in," I thought. So would I. But I didn't say that to my lone loyal follower.

A few days earlier, I'd left Jessica a message saying I was getting out Tuesday, so I could show up Monday and surprise her. Instead, she surprised me. She wasn't home. Neither was Riley.

Jessica's stepdad told me I could come in and wait for her, but that he wasn't sure when she'd be back. I wandered into her room and found a letter laying on her dresser. It was addressed to Clark, the guy she'd been dating before I first blew into Illinois. Toward the end, she wrote, "I hope we can stay as close as we've been even after Frankie gets back." That was all the proof I needed. I went ballistic. I was ransacking through her drawers looking for more evidence that she'd cheated on me when her stepdad called me to the phone.

Jessica welcomed me home with the words, "What are you doing at my house?"

"Is Riley with you? When can I see her?"

"She's spending the night with my sister. Don't go over there. It's too late. You can see her tomorrow."

"Can I at least see you tonight?"

She hesitated a long time before saying, "I guess." She told me where she was partying with the former skinheads.

"I'll see you in a while, then," I said. "By the way, I found your letter."

"What are you talking about?"

"Your letter to Clark? Remember, the one where you hope youse two can stay so fucking close now that I'm back?"

She didn't say anything.

"I knew you were screwing around on me!"

"You want to talk about screwing around? How fucking many girls did you screw behind my back? Can you even count that high?"

Barely. She'd heard the rumors from the beginning. She'd always known, but I'd always lied my way back into her heart. There was no sense lying this time.

Jessica'd already told me where the party was, and when I got there, she didn't greet me with open arms. She barely spoke to me the whole night. Not that she had much of a chance. The guys were swarming around me, welcoming me home and asking me about prison. Pot smoke hung over the room like fog. A couple guys who'd been pretty serious about the movement were now decked out like they were part of NWA. They apologized for the weed while they toked. I told them not to sweat it; I even admitted I'd smoked in prison. But I didn't smoke pot that night. I just drank. Hooch had scarred my tastebuds; it took half a case before beer tasted normal to me again.

Everybody was polluted when the party broke up. I climbed into the same car as Jessica. So did six or seven other guys. We all piled out at her house. She went straight up to her room, and the rest of us crashed in her basement. About half an hour later I snuck upstairs.

"What do you want?" Jessica asked.

"Just to talk. But not yet."

I sat silently in a corner of her room, watching her until her steady breathing steeled my nerves. When I was convinced she was asleep, I confessed all the shit I'd pulled behind her back. I told her how sorry I was for being such a jealous asshole. I admitted I was a shitty boyfriend and that she had every right to dump me and find somebody decent.

"But don't cut me all the way out, Jessica," I begged as she slept. "Let me be Riley's dad." I stroked her hair and gently kissed her forehead. As I rose to leave her room I prayed, "Please, God, let me be Riley's dad."

I met my daughter the next day. She was sleeping in a basinet. I picked her up softly without waking her. I never wanted to put her back down. She was still in my arms when her little eyes fluttered open. I gazed into my five-month old daughter's eyes and saw my own staring back at me.

I asked Jessica, "Does she smile?"

"She smiles at Clark."

God, that girl could hit below the belt. If it weren't for Riley, she would've met me at the door with a shotgun. But whether Jessica liked it or not, I was Riley's father, and I wanted to be her dad. I came to visit Riley every day. I held her. I played with her. I fed her. I even changed her diapers. Everything about Riley was sacred to me, even her poop. I spent hours every day with Riley, but I almost never got to spend time alone with her, partly because Jessica didn't trust me with her and partly because all the former skinheads spent almost all their time at Jessica's. During the day, they hung around watching TV and taking turns holding the baby. Once Riley was settled in her crib for the night, they partied in Jessica's basement.

I still loved the Springfield guys, even if they'd given up on being skinheads. I was grateful they'd been there for Jessica and Riley when I couldn't be. I loved them *because* of that. But it just about killed me to watch Jessica and Riley with those other dudes. Every time Jessica laughed at one of their jokes, my heart broke a little. And every time one of them made Riley giggle, part of me died. The one thing every inmate fears most had happened to me: life had gone on without me. Jessica and Riley had found a family amid the rubble of my Nazi crew. As time had worn on, the skinheads hadn't just drifted away from white supremacy, most had actually turned against it. Once I finally got back, those guys let me hang with them in spite of the fact I was still a skinhead, not because of it.

I left prison assuming I'd show up in Springfield and resume control of my crew, whip the boys back into shape, and take that gang as big-time as Strike Force in Philly. By my second night back in town, I gave up hope of trying to put the crew back together. I could turn nerds into Nazis, but I couldn't turn serious druggies back into skinheads. So I split the difference. Every night, I wore my Docs and my flight jacket to the party, then I toked weed while I drank myself straight to hell.

Somewhere in the middle of each of my nightly binges, I'd hit this point where everything felt okay, the point where I couldn't feel anything. The problem was the before and the after. Before I hit that point, I felt like total shit because I was still sober enough to realize Jessica didn't love me anymore and none of my crew really gave a shit about me anymore. Then I'd hit the sweet spot; for an hour or so, everything would be okay. If I could've just stayed in that spot, everything might've been different. But nobody can stay there.

By midnight or so, I was belligerent, and I aimed my mouth at Jessica. By two or three in the morning, I was dangerous, and I aimed my fists at any dude within striking distance. By dawn, I was a basket case, and I aimed my sob story at Jeremy, the former skinhead whose mom generously agreed to let me live at their house. By the next afternoon, I never remembered what all I'd said to Jessica or Jeremy or who all I'd bounced around. I didn't even remember the night I attacked Jeremy. Everything after the sweet spot always faded to black. There was never even a blur in my memory. Back in Philly, there'd always at least been a little trace the next day, if somebody reminded me. But by 1994, all traces were gone. Every morning was a morning after, and every morning after, I had no recollection of the night before. I'd jump into the shower and try to scrub off the stink of the booze and the haze of my hangover. Then I'd show up at Jessica's to see my baby girl, acting like nothing had happened the night before, because I never remembered. Jessica did, though. And after two or three weeks of it, she'd had enough. First, she put time limits on my visits. Soon after, she made it clear that I wasn't welcome at her basement parties anymore.

Most nights, I stayed home alone in my room. I'd down a twelve pack or more of beer alone while I licked my wounds. Some nights, though, I went out with whoever'd still have me around. I was cruising Springfield with one of Jessica's high school friends when a cop car flashed its lights behind us. Jessica's friend was a minor, behind the wheel, sipping a wine cooler. I grabbed the bottle from her, but didn't have time to ditch it out my window before the cop's face appeared in hers. He scanned the inside of the car and saw the wine cooler in my hand. Then he smiled the kind of smart-ass smile only a cop can pull off.

"Hey, Meeink. Long time no see."

I remembered the dude; he'd been part of the posse that

busted me at the television studio. He glanced at the bottle in my hand. "Glad to see you're staying on the straight and narrow."

I spent most of the rest of the night in the holding tank at the Sangamon County Jail. I think half the freaking guards on duty stopped by to ask me what in the hell I was thinking to violate parole less than a month after getting sprung. I wanted to ask them if they'd been talking to my buddies down at Shawnee State Penitentiary, because every one of those guards ended their visit with the same advice other inmates had given me: you better watch your ass, 'cause nobody's going to go easy on you the second time.

Sitting there in holding, I figured I was headed straight back to prison, but that's not how it works, at least not for something as minor as underage drinking and open intoxicants in a car, which is all they technically had on me. The cops released me early the next morning. At the same time, they forwarded my case to my parole officer. I was his problem now.

"Don't leave town," a cop said to me on my way out the door. "And stay by your phone, because your PO is going to be pissed if he has to track your ass down."

My PO found me later that day. He chewed me out for a while on principle, then admitted it was a minor violation in the grand scheme of parole violations. The Illinois prisons were still overcrowded. I went to bed that night pretty certain I wasn't going back to Shawnee.

I may as well have. After that, everywhere I looked I saw cops. It seemed like every time I left the apartment there was a cop on my ass. I saw cops on damn near every corner on my way to and from visits with Riley. When I picked up work on a construction crew, I would've sworn on a Bible cops were patrolling that job site. God forbid I went out after dark; everywhere I looked I saw red lights reflecting off windows. Partly, I was being paranoid. That comes with the territory for parolees. Partly, though, I really was being watched at least some of the time, especially when I went out at night anywhere near other kids. Springfield's

Nazi problem had all but disappeared in my absence. The Springfield cops weren't going to give me a chance to stir shit up again.
They didn't realize I'd already given up on that plan. The only plan
I had left was to try to keep far enough inside Jessica's good
graces that she wouldn't take Riley away from me. Seeing as Jessica
basically loathed me, that posed quite a challenge.

JESSICA PROMISED I could have Riley for part of the day on
Easter. It was my first holiday with my daughter, and I wanted
to make it special. I bought her a little basket and filled it with toys.
I hid plastic eggs full of candy all around the house. I had everything ready hours before Jessica was supposed to bring Riley
over. When she was more than an hour late, I called.

First, she said she forgot.

"How could you forget Easter?"

Then she said it was getting too late to drive the baby over.

"Come on, Jessica, it's the middle of the afternoon."

She hemmed and hawed for a while, then asked, "Why
should I let you see her?"

"Because it's Easter," I said, missing her point. "I've got
everything set up with eggs and all. Riley's going to love it."

"She can't even crawl yet."

"I'll help her."

"You can't help her. You don't help anybody. You just hurt
people."

She fucking unloaded on me. No little girl should have to
grow up having the police follow her every time she has to visit
her father. No little girl should have to grow up knowing her father
is the drunken, violent son-of-a-bitch who beat up her "Uncle"
Jeremy and threatened her "Uncle" Clark and keeps scaring off
all the good, reliable men she's come to love. No little girl should
have to grow up being "the Nazi's daughter." I thought I saw where
she was heading. The same ultimatum I'd heard before, from
my mom and John, Nanny and Pop, even my cousin Nick: your
family or the white supremacy movement. The choice had always

been crystal clear; it was crystal clear this time, too. This time, the choice would be Riley. But Jessica didn't let me choose. She wasn't giving me an ultimatum. I hadn't seen where she was going at all. She fucking blindsided me. "Everything you say about the white supremacy movement is nothing but fucking bullshit. You're not a 'race warrior.' You're a thug. Riley may be stuck with your DNA, but I'll be damned if that means she's got to be stuck with you."

I could've promised to try to do better by Riley. But wounded animals always bite, and Jessica's words had damn near killed me. I called Jessica names I'd never called a woman. If another man ever says to Riley the things I screamed at her mother that night, I'll end up on death row. I was screaming long after Jessica slammed down the phone. I was still crying long after I gave up screaming. When I finally calmed myself, the empty house was as silent as a tomb. Just like that goddamn apartment in Terre Haute. The silence closed in like hands around my throat.

It was early evening when I picked up the phone. Late enough, though, that I knew to call the bar, not the house. My dad sounded exactly the same as he had in our last conversation nearly three years earlier: groggy as shit, but happy to hear from me, like I was a long-lost 68th and Buist boy back for a reunion. He apologized, in his own way, for not keeping in touch.

"Youse know I don't like to talk to nobody when they're caged up."

I did know that. I'd heard it my whole life, whenever his friends got busted.

"It's too hard on me," my dad said.

It had been too hard on almost all my friends and family. Only Jessica and Nanny and Pop had written to me faithfully. Even Louie had stopped checking in on me after the first couple months.

"I understand." I said. Then I switched subjects and told him about his granddaughter, which seemed to thrill him.

"Jessica and me can't make it work. I fucked up too many times. She ain't gonna let me be Riley's dad."

I struggled to find the right words to explain to my dad that I wasn't thinking about leaving my kid, because I'd never leave my kid, because it would kill me to leave my kid, but what was the point of staying if I couldn't be her dad. The words didn't come out too good, but they didn't need to.

"You're preaching to the choir," he said. "What you gotta understand is this: it ain't leaving if nothing's left."

I ran the final fight with Jessica through my mind one more time, just to be sure. I choked back my grief and said, "There's nothing left here for me."

"What's your PO gonna say?" my dad asked.

"I wasn't going to tell him." I was afraid if I asked my PO for permission to leave the state he'd say no. I decided to go first then call him. I wasn't a murderer; I didn't think Illinois would waste the money to send somebody to Pennsylvania to haul me back.

"If you're gonna skip, you gotta do it clean," my dad said. "You got enough money?"

"I want to leave what I've got for Riley." I waited for him to volunteer, but he didn't, so I asked. "Youse think maybe you can help me out with train fare?"

"I'll call your mom. We'll get it together for you."

I called my mom the next morning expecting to hear that a ticket paid for by both my parents was already waiting for me at the train depot. Instead, I got another earful about my dad being the biggest asshole ever born onto Planet Earth. He'd quibbled about the fare she quoted him. She'd brought up the decade or so of child support he still owed her.

"I ain't talking to him again," she said. "So don't bother asking."

"Fine. Will you help me anyhow?"

"It's real tight around here. Let me and John talk about it."

Translation: no.

A couple days later, I asked the girl whose wine cooler had landed me in hot water to give me a ride to the train station. As we pulled into the parking lot at the depot, Jessica's friend caught me scanning the rows of cars.

"She's not coming."

"I know." But I still hoped she would. Deep in my heart, I couldn't bring myself to believe Jessica hated me so much she would deny me one last chance to see Riley.

"Make sure Riley knows I'll be back," I said. "I will. I swear I'll be back."

But the thing was, I only had enough money for a one-way ticket to Philly.

Fallen Heroes

MY MOM SHOCKED THE LIVING CRAP OUT OF ME. SHE actually met me at the train station in Center City. She ran toward me and gave me a big hug and a kiss like I'd just gotten home from college or war. She ruffled my hair, which hadn't been cut, let alone shaved, in six months. Then she asked, "What do you want me to cook tonight?"

I hadn't had a homecooked meal in close to three years, but just because my mom was acting like June Cleaver didn't mean I was counting on John to be Ward. The Warden was waiting for me on his favorite spot on the couch when I walked in.

"Welcome back," he said, raising his beer slightly in my direction.

Here it comes, I predicted. Any second now, he's going to add, "Speaking of back, I bet you had to watch that back end of yours real close up at Sing-Sing."

John rose to his feet. He reached out his hand to me. "Now I see where he's going," I thought. I'm going to shake his hand, and he's going to say something like, "Hey, what're you pawing me for? I ain't one of your boyfriends from Sing-Sing." What the hell, I coached myself, get it over with. I extended my hand.

"Glad you made it through okay," he said without a hint of sarcasm.

My little half-sisters mauled me in the kitchen. They weren't babies anymore. Kirsten was six and Hayley was five. I flashed to Riley. Will I get to see her again before she's that old? I flushed with panic. What if I never get to see her again? Tears welled in my eyes. I buried my face in the girls' long, soft hair and breathed in their scent until they finally wiggled away from me.

While my mom cooked dinner, I sat at the kitchen table, drinking beer with John and pumping them for everything they knew about what had happened to my cousin Nick. They stuck by the story my mom had given me over the phone when I was in Sangamon County Jail: some dude named TJ had shot Nick up with a huge dose of China White, one of the most powerful forms of heroin available. The dude was a total junkie, half dead already with AIDS, and he'd overdosed Nick. My mom and John both swore there was no way Nick would've ever shot that much heroin of his own free will.

After dinner, which I got to add was freaking fantastic, I headed down to Third and Jackson. The last words Nick ever said to me echoed in my mind: "You used your only pass tonight." I didn't care. I had to find Jerry. I busted into a circle of about a dozen Third and Jackson boys who hadn't seen me since the night of Jimmy's wedding reception riot.

"I gotta know what happened to him."

Jerry grabbed me by the elbow and steered me away from the crowd. "I already took care of it," he said.

"My mom swears he wasn't using, not serious anyhow."

"Your mom's flying," Jerry reminded me. Jerry knew all about my mom's pill habit. "Nick could've shot up at the kitchen table, and your mom and John wouldn't have noticed."

"So what are you telling me?" I asked.

Jerry shook his head with grief. "I'm telling you he did it himself."

"But you said youse took care of it."

"I did." Jerry's hard eyes dropped to the sidewalk. He shuffled his feet like a guilty child. When he spoke again, his voice was barely a whisper. "I feel real bad about that now. You gotta believe I do. I fucked that dude up hard. But I didn't have the whole story then. TJ didn't do it, I swear to you. So don't youse go after him, too."

There was no point in telling my mom her story about TJ was bullshit. She would've sworn on a Bible that Nick hadn't shot the fatal dose himself. Of course, this is the same woman who would've sworn to the Pope I got all those bruises as a kid playing hockey. When I got home, I begged off joining her and John for another beer. I couldn't bear the thought of listening to my mom rehash the lie. But before I made it upstairs, the Tasmanian Devil crashed through the front door screaming, "Yo, Frankie!"

My cousin Jimmy hadn't changed one bit since I'd left Philly. He plowed across the living room in full Strike Force regalia, lifted me off my feet, spun me around like I weighed about as much as a cafeteria tray, then hugged me so hard I'm surprised he didn't crush my ribs.

"It ain't been the same without you here. But I want youse to know one thing. It's the same now, you know what I mean?"

I did know. I just wasn't sure how I felt about it.

"I been running it without you, but I ain't got no ego about it. Strike Force ain't mine; it's ours."

"What about Louie?" I asked.

He glanced nervously over his shoulder at the skinchick standing just inside the front door. In all the excitement, I hadn't even noticed her until that moment. "Louie's a conversation for another time," Jimmy whispered to me.

The next night, Jimmy hosted a welcome home party for me in a woods north of the city. About thirty skinheads were already gathered around a bonfire when I arrived. Matt Hanson spotted me first and tackled me with a hug.

"What's with the hair?" he asked.

"No good barbers in prison."

By then the other skinheads had closed rank around us. I didn't recognize some of them at first. Guys who'd been scrawny freshcuts when I'd fled town were now fully sleeved in movement

tattoos and looked like they'd put on thirty or forty pounds of
muscle and beer gut. More than half the guys I didn't recognize
at all; they'd joined up while I was behind bars. I finally knew how
Scott Windham must've felt the night he cornered four of us
little newbies in a Center City alley. He felt like a fucking king.
That's how I felt when a kid whipped out a camera and asked if
he could get his picture taken with me. All night, dudes I barely
knew, even dudes I'd never met before, kept huddling around
me, telling me stories about my own freaking past. It was like they
were trying to prove they'd done their homework. It was weird.
It was also a total ego trip.

"When's Louie getting here?" I asked Jimmy.

He quickly herded me away from the others and said,
"I don't know how to tell you this, but, um, he's, um ... "

My heart stopped beating. Jimmy saw the color drain out
of my face and hurried to correct his mistake.

"He's ain't dead or nothing. He's just, well, he ain't one of us."

Like me, Louie'd gotten mixed up with drugs, but he
hadn't had the excuse of trying to lose reality while in prison.
To the more moderate skinheads, Louie Lacinzi had become
nothing more than a white trash wigger, just another South Philly
druggie. The radicals of the group viewed him as a full on race
traitor. Jimmy advised me not to mention his name to anyone else.

"Did anybody jump him out?" I asked, hoping they hadn't.

"He wasn't worth it." From Jimmy's perspective, that was
the end of the story: he spat on the ground.

For about two seconds, I was in shock; then I was outraged.
This wasn't some disposable freshcut Jimmy was talking about;
it was Louie. "Jesus, Jimmy! Did you at least try to talk him out
of it?"

"He made his choice. He ain't come back around since."

"You're telling me youse ain't even heard from Louie in a
year?" I imagined Louie ending up like my cousin Nick,
Jimmy's cousin Nick, and tasted puke in the back of my throat.

"Louie was our boy! It was Louie and me and you before there even was Strike Force!"

"There was just you and me before there was Louie," Jimmy replied. "And now it's just you and me again."

Jimmy dug up a lifetime of shared history with that one comment.

"I'm sorry, man. I ain't questioning that you tried."

"We're cool," Jimmy said. "You just gotta understand. A whole lot of shit went down while you were gone. Now it's over. Louie's history. Just don't go picking at the scabs, okay?"

Jimmy turned to head back to the party.

"Wait." I said. "I won't bring it up over there, but I gotta know if you heard anything at all? I mean, is he okay?"

"Depends on how you look at it," Jimmy said. "I sure as shit wouldn't want to be him, but I wouldn't mind having his car."

My confusion must have registered on my face. Jimmy burst out laughing.

"He ain't nodding off on skid row. He ditched us for the money, man. Louie's a fucking kingpin."

As the night wore on, I learned that Louie wasn't the only Philly skinhead who'd disappeared during my absence. Rumor had it Stug was totally strung out on heroin, but no one knew for sure because nobody'd heard from him in more than a year, either. Dan Bellen was gone, too. One day a skinhead called his house looking for him, and his mom said he'd up and joined the Air Force.

Things didn't feel the same without those guys around. Still, I felt less lonely at that skinhead party in the woods than I'd felt since leaving Philly in the first place. I don't think I'd realized how profoundly lonely I'd been until I finally stopped feeling it. I'd met some good people in the Midwest, but none except for Riley was my family. I had lots of family in Philly. Every skinhead at that party was my family.

A few days later, I visited my dad at his bar and learned I had killed a man. Or maybe two men. It depended on which aging

68th and Buist boy I talked to and how much they'd already had to drink. Not one of my dad's buddies, or my dad for that matter, knew what I'd really done to get sent to prison. And none seemed to care. They just kept sliding me drinks on their tabs and patting me on the back and saying shit like, "Our little Frankie's all grown up." As I had my whole life, I followed my dad and his boys out into The Boneyard; this time they offered me a hit off their joint. It was another moment of truth: was I a skinhead or just another South Philly druggie? I passed.

I spent a long time in the bathroom the next morning. When I was done, I called Jimmy.

"Yo guess what? I shaved it."

"Fucking A! Now you're really back."

"Like youse said the other night. Strike Force ain't yours or mine. It's ours."

I dove back into the Nazi scene with the idea that I'd be like the elder statesmen who'd brought me along when I first joined up with the movement. I'd be like The Uprise veterans in the Wise's parking lot or maybe even John Cook. I'd pass along my hard-earned wisdom. I'd help raise up the next generation of Hitler's youth. I'd rally the troops for battle. But I wouldn't be battling anymore. Battles are for the young. I wasn't young anymore. I had just turned nineteen.

ONE NIGHT, WALKING home from Skinhead Alley, I approached the intersection of Second and Porter and wondered if I'd actually wandered into a Sharswood School reunion. There must've been close to thirty guys on that corner, and I'd shared a hallway with at least half of them at some point during grade school. A lot of time had passed, but I recognized everybody immediately. No amount of hair could ever disguise Tommy "Earbow" Petanzi. And there's never been a pair of jeans made that could camouflage Mikey "Muffin Ass" McCarthy. Of course, I didn't need to see the face of the skinny, dark-haired dude sniffing lines of coke off the trunk of a parked car to know his identity: that little maneuver had John "Vicey" Sullivan written all over it.

They asked me what I wanted before they asked me where the hell I'd been for the past five or so years.

"I'll take a beer if you've got it."

"You sure that's all you want?" Hands flashed open to reveal a smorgasbord of drugs. Rainbows of pills. Tabs of LSD. Big bags of weed. Small bags of cocaine.

"Just a beer."

"Whatever youse want, Frankie." Someone put a forty in my hand.

"You were in prison for what, a year?" Earbow said.

"About."

"You were gone a hell of a lot longer than just a year. Where the hell were you?"

"No shit," Muffin Ass said. "We ain't seen youse since, geez ... " He turned to the other guys. It takes a while for thirty guys who're stoned off their asses to kick their memories into gear.

Finally, someone said, "Sheldon Jones! Remember? Frankie kicked his fucking ass!" That was the fight that got me bounced out of Sharswood for good.

"I can't believe we ain't really talked to you since then." Earbow said. "What the hell happened to you?"

I hit the highlights of the trip I'd been on since the day I beat up Sheldon Jones. It was a hell of a trip, even by South Philly standards. The guys could hardly believe even the sanitized version I gave them.

"So your mom just fucking kicked youse out after that?"

"Yeah."

"Youse really got totally into that Nazi shit?"

"Yeah."

"Youse ended up in fucking Illinois? On fucking TV? In fucking prison?"

"Yeah. Yeah. Yeah."

Vicey threw a boney arm over my shoulder and leaned in close to my ear. "You do anything to pass the time in prison?" he asked.

"I did what I had to do."

"Then why the hell ain't you doing it now?" He flashed me another view of his personal pharmacy.

"Same rules don't apply on the inside. Out here, it ain't who I am."

"If you change your mind," Vicey said, "youse know where to find me."

The next night, I laced up my Docs and headed toward South Street to meet up with the other skinheads. But before I got very far from home, I switched directions.

"You sticking with beer or you want something else?" Vicey asked me as soon as I rounded the corner.

"Sticking with beer."

After that, I spent most nights hanging with the Second and Porter boys, sticking with beer while they did and sold pretty much everything but heroin. I didn't bail on Strike Force, though. I still showed my face in Skinhead Alley a couple times a week, and I hit all the big Nazi parties. I got a tattoo of a crucified skinhead. I even wrote lyrics for a song called "Die Liberal Scum," and cut some vocals with a white power band.

I'd been back in Philly for several months when Jimmy told me he needed me to show for a big pow-wow. Some skinheads from New York City were coming down to talk about forming an alliance with Strike Force. That kind of meeting required both co-commanders of Strike Force be present. The plan was for the leaders on both sides to get there early and get the business out of the way before the rest of the Philly skinheads showed up to party. So around seven o'clock, I gave my head a fresh shaving, suited up in full-dress skinhead gear, and caught a cross-town trolley.

Another passenger on the trolley reminded me of Little G. My mind wandered back to Shawnee. I wondered how Little G and Jello were doing. I hadn't thought about them much since I'd stepped through the door leading back to the real world. The more I thought about them on that trolley ride, the more I realized all my good memories from prison were about the friends I'd made: Jello and Little G, the guys we played against in basketball, the other guys on our football team. Not one of those friends had been white. It was a strange thought to have crossing my mind on my way to a major skinhead bash.

The party that was supposed to start after the big meeting was already in full-swing by the time I arrived. I checked the clock. I wasn't late; the freshcuts were early. And they were acting like complete fucking idiots, trying to impress the visitors from New York. My arrival only made things worse, because now they were trying to impress me with how impressive they were being in front of our guests.

Those baby Nazis felt like they had cast-iron balls every time they spat out "nigger" or "spic." They felt like geniuses when they spouted off about how the ZOG-Jew landlords were handing North Philly over to the Puerto Ricans. They felt like gods when they bragged about what they'd done, as a pack, to a lone Puerto Rican kid in a dark alley the night before. I know for a fact that's how they felt, because it's exactly how I'd once felt.

But I didn't feel that way that night. That night, for the first time since I'd joined the white supremacy movement five years earlier, I listened to someone tell a racist joke, and I thought, "That ain't funny." For the first time in five years, I heard people flinging around theories about "mud" and I thought, "That ain't true."

I've been thinking about that night for more than a decade now, trying to figure out exactly what happened to me. If I could bottle it, we'd have world peace, and I'd be the richest man in history. But it wasn't that simple. There was no magic potion, just a freak set of circumstances that put me in the right mood, at the right place, at the right time to finally see the lies behind the "truth" I'd believed with all my heart since I was fourteen years old. Sitting in the middle of that party, surrounded by dozens of drunk skinheads spewing the same old stereotypes, I wanted to scream, "That's such fucking bullshit!" But I didn't have the balls. Instead, I got real quiet, so quiet one of the older skinheads came over and asked me if I was okay.

"I miss Riley," I said, which was true, but not the whole truth.

I found an empty spot on the end of a couch and started in on a twelve pack, hoping maybe it'd be enough to drown out the "nigger" jokes the freshcuts were screaming at the top of their lungs. It wasn't. It didn't drown out the "spic" jokes, either. Or the "chink" jokes. Or the one about the "fucking heeb rabbi."

And it sure as hell didn't drown out the New Yorker on the other end of my couch who started bragging about how he was *pure* Irish, a *real* Aryan, not some "fucking wop."

"Most Italians ain't really white," he said to an adoring audience of freshcuts.

"What the fuck are you talking about?"

It was the first time I'd spoken in nearly an hour. That alone caught everybody's attention. But so did the tone of my voice. The older Philly guys knew this was definitely a bad situation about to get worse unless that New York dude backed down immediately. But the dude didn't get it; he didn't know me. He met my eyes and got to his feet. I stood too. He had at least three inches on me. "I mean Italians ain't real whites like us Irish. What's your deal? Your name's Meeink, ain't it?"

"My name's Meeink," I said. "Thing is, it's also Bertone." You could've heard a pin drop in the middle of that party.

The dude glanced around to make sure the other New Yorkers were still in the room. They were, but he backpedaled anyhow: "You're half Irish, so you're white."

The big-mouthed New Yorker seemed to think our debate was over; he mumbled something about needing another beer. He was just about to walk away when I said, "My kid's seventy-five percent Italian. You gonna to tell me she ain't white?"

There's the kind of silence where you can hear a pin drop,

then there's the kind where you can hear a heartbeat. That New Yorker's heart was trying to pound its way out of his chest. The dude only had two options: save face or save ass.

He puffed up his chest and got out, "Then your kid ain't wh –" before my fist shut his mouth. The sucker punch stunned him, but it didn't stop him. He lunged toward me like a linebacker. I dropped him with an uppercut. He fell slowly, so slowly I would've had plenty of time to land two, maybe even three, shots to the back of his head. But there was no way I was going to waste my knuckles on that piece of shit. I waited for him to land. Then I let my boots do my talking.

A skinchick begged me to stop. "You're going to crush his fucking skull." I paused long enough to realize she was probably right. I sat back on the couch and opened a fresh beer.

"So much for our fucking New York connection," Jimmy said, slamming the door behind them as they huffed out, half-carrying my "pure" Irish victim.

"So much for any of youse having any balls," I said.

"What're you talking about?" someone asked.

"Half of youse are more Italian than me." I scanned their guilty faces. No one met my eye. "But I was the only one who said a fucking thing."

I walked out. No one followed me.

EVERYBODY CONNECTED TO Strike Force steered clear of me for a while after that. I think they were trying to give me space to cool off. What they gave me, though, was space to think. And they would've hated what I was thinking. It was like it'd been back in Lancaster County in summer of 1989, "If you believe it, the evidence will come." Only this time it happened in reverse. As soon as I started to question my racism, all this evidence appeared to prove I was on the right track. Thanks to the O.J. Simpson trial, every time I flipped on the television, there was a story on the news about DNA. I'd dropped out of school way before we got to that level in science class. So even though I'd heard the term before, mostly from other inmates bucking for an appeal, I didn't really know much about it. I became totally obsessed with what it was and how it worked. I remember staying up really late one night watching a documentary where a scientist scrolled down this long chain of genetic codes on his computer. He said only a couple of little links on that massive chain actually differed among human races, a couple little links on mile after mile of chain was all that separated whites from blacks. Not long after that, I caught a story about a white guy who'd nearly died when his body rejected an organ transplant. The donor had been a family member, but the guy was alive and well thanks to a successful transplant from a black stranger. Everything I'd ever been taught about Identity Theology, about how "mud" are a separate, inferior, subhuman species, told me that shouldn't happen. But it had.

The Second and Porter boys were the first people to notice I was changing. One night, somebody made a racist comment and looked to me for backup. I just shook my head and said, "I don't know. Maybe we're not that different." I'd dropped a couple of bombshells like that on the corner when one of the guys finally asked, "What's up, Frankie? First you hate everybody, now you love everybody?"

I thought about it for a minute, then answered truthfully, "Pretty much, I guess, except for the Jews."

Not even DNA evidence could dislodge my hatred of the Jews. I hadn't been taught that Jews were an inferior, subhuman species; I'd been taught that Jews were pure evil. Jews were ZOG. Jews were devious. Jews were greedy.

I, on the other hand, was flat broke and clueless about how I was going to find a job. Everywhere I went looking for work, people just stared at my tattoos. Some places wouldn't even let me fill out an application. But one day, a buddy of mine stopped by Tree Street with a lead. He'd been moving furniture for an antiques dealer across the river in New Jersey. They had a huge sale coming up and needed extra help.

"It's going to be fourteen-hour days," he said. "But it's yours if you want it. I already put in a good word for you with the boss. He said he'll go a hundred bucks a day if you work the whole weekend. You interested?"

I hadn't had two hundred dollars to my name in forever.

"Sign me up."

"There's just one thing," my friend said. "The guy's a Jew."

I rolled that tidbit over in my mind for a minute, then said, "I don't fucking care, so long as I don't have to talk to him."

My friend laughed and said, "That's exactly what he said about you."

A few days later, I showed up at this Jewish guy's fancy store with a swastika on my neck, and he didn't even bat an eyelash. Education? Ninth-grade dropout. Employment history? A job on a concrete crew before I got committed to a mental institution. Criminal record? On parole for aggravated kidnapping and assault with a deadly weapon. Even if I sugarcoated the truth, these ain't good people skills I was giving off in an interview. But after everybody else turned me away, Keith Goldstein hired me. An upper-crust Jewish antiques dealer hired an ex-convict with a swastika tattoo on his neck to deliver armoires to his suburban clients. I wasn't the first fucked up kid Keith tried to save with a delivery job. I wasn't even the first fucked up racist kid. I may have been the most fucked up, but that didn't matter to Keith. He liked the challenge.

I worked my ass off the weekend of his big sale. By Sunday night I was dragging and ready to head home. But I hadn't been paid yet, and Keith was nowhere in sight. I found my buddy.

"You sure this dude ain't gonna Jew me?"

The guy rolled his eyes at me. "He'll pay you. Relax, already."

But I couldn't relax. Every second I didn't see Keith Goldstein walking my way with two hundred-dollar bills in his hand reinforced everything the white supremacy movement had ever taught me about Jews. That bastard Keith was so devious, sneaking out like that when I was sweating my balls off for his business. That bastard Keith was so greedy, stealing my pay like that after I'd busted my ass carrying his goddamn furniture. That bastard Keith was so … so … so fucking ZOG.

Then that bastard Keith showed up and did something even worse than Jewing me out of my pay: he blew the living freaking crap out of the one and only stereotype I still had to hold on to. He thanked me for my hard work, paid me a hundred bucks more than the wage he'd promised me, and asked if I wanted to come to work for him full-time.

Part of me wanted to scream, "Stop being fucking nice to me!" Fortunately, the part of me desperate for money got control of my mouth. All I said was, "Yes. Thanks."

The next morning, Keith stomped on another one of my long-held beliefs about Jewish people: I didn't think there was a Jew alive who followed hockey. But Keith Goldstein lived for the Philadelphia Flyers. And if there's anything in this world that can cross a gap as wide as the gap between a Jew and a Nazi, it's loyalty to the legacy of the Broad Street Bullies. By the end of my first week at the store, Keith had filled me in on practically every play in every game I'd missed while I was in prison. And in between the play-by-play, I managed to carry what felt like a million pieces of furniture. When I clocked out Friday afternoon, Keith once again paid me in full plus a bonus.

Riding home on the bus, I realized something about the Jews: until Keith, I'd never met one. I'd spent most of my life in either South Philly or prison; there ain't a lot of Jews in either place. But I had a whole lot of theories about the Jews, and until I met Keith Goldstein, I would've sworn I had facts to back every one of those theories. Then I met Keith, and the fact was he disproved every theory I had. He was about the nicest, coolest dude I'd ever met.

That night after I climbed out of the shower, I stared at myself in the mirror for a long time. My tattoos screamed against my pale white skin. "*Sieg Heil*" on my head. The swastika on my neck. The portrait of Joseph Goebbels on my chest. A crucified

skinhead, nearly ten inches long, running the length of one forearm. The Celtic cross and other symbols of white supremacy
scattered elsewhere on my arms. I raised my fists to my own face:
"SKINHEAD" my knuckles declared, as if begging me to
remember my identity. I dropped my fists. I took in the full view
of my naked body. I still looked like a skinhead. But when I
looked deep into my own eyes, the hate was gone. I never officially
resigned my position as head of Strike Force; I just disappeared. None of the skinheads came looking for me. If they had,
they would've found me working for a Jew I considered a friend
by day, and partying with my Second and Porter druggie friends
by night.

One night, Vicey asked, "You *still* sticking with beer?"

For the first time since I'd been hanging on the corner,
I hesitated on answering that question. It was another moment
of truth: South Philly versus White Supremacy? Second and
Porter versus Skinhead Alley? Margaret and Big Frankie's baby
boy versus Hitler's Youth?

I made the choice with my nose. Within a few weeks, I was
snorting coke, smoking weed, or dropping acid damn near
every night. Some weekend nights, I did all three. But I tried to
control myself on weeknights so I'd be okay for work the next
morning. I didn't want to disappoint Keith, and I couldn't afford
to miss work. By then, I needed all the money I could get to
cover my growing tabs with the dealers.

ONE NIGHT IN early October, I was laying around watching TV,
thinking it was about time for me to wander down to Second and
Porter, when the phone rang.

"It's David Conover."

My blood froze. David Conover from Reading, the guy who'd
given me my most hardcore Nazi tattoos, by then the highest-
ranked skinhead in all of Pennsylvania. When I heard David's voice
on the other end of the telephone, I figured word had finally
filtered up the chain of command that I wasn't exactly fighting

the good fight in Philly anymore. I knew when I stepped away from Strike Force there was a good chance somebody'd jump me out. I was surprised it hadn't happened to Louie. Of course, that they'd let him go peacefully made it even more likely they'd come after me: one crew leader defecting is an embarrassment; two is a public relations nightmare.

"I need you to gather your troops," David said.

So word clearly had not spread up the chain of command.

"What's up?" I asked, playing it cool, like I still had troops. I leaned against the wall and prepared myself to listen to yet another skinhead diatribe about "Sharpie ZOG dupes" or some other bullshit I really didn't give a crap about anymore.

"We're going on a road trip. Some motherfucking nigger just killed Joe Morgan."

If it'd been anybody other than Joe, I might not have made the calls I made that night. But it was Joe Morgan, the same Joe Morgan who'd saved my ass by making the calls that got me off the East Coast when I was sure the cops were circling in on me.

Joe and his band had been playing at a white power music festival south of Milwaukee. When the concert ended, Joe and some of the other performers stopped by a convenience store to buy beer for a post-gig party. That's where they ran smack into a bunch of black guys. Sneers became words. Words became shoves. Shoves became punches. Then one of the black guys pulled a gun and opened fire.

The second David hung up, I called down the Strike Force roster. When they heard the tone in my voice, not one guy dared ask me where I'd been for more than a month. It didn't matter where I'd been or what I'd been doing; Joe Morgan was dead, and I was back in command of Strike Force, no questions asked. A few hours later I had close to twenty skinheads ready to move out on David's signal. While we waited, Matt Hanson tattooed "In Memory of Joe Morgan" on the back of my neck, just above "Strike Force." Then David called again.

"I just got off the phone with my guys. It's still too fucking hot. Cops are everywhere. We can't do anything right now."

My hand shook violently as I hung up the telephone. I leaned against the wall for support. I felt like my brain was imploding. For hours, all I'd wanted to do was kill the "motherfucking nigger" who'd killed Joe Morgan. For hours, there was no Jello, no Little G, no Keith in this world, only "mud" and "ZOG" and my steel-toed combat boots. For hours, all I heard inside my brain was "Kill! Kill! Kill!" All it had taken was one fucking phone call. One lousy, fucking phone call and I'd flipped right back into warrior-skinhead mode. I staggered across the kitchen and collapsed under the realization of how close to the edge I'd been. I'd only been one phone call away from going back to war, back to hate, straight to hell. I sat at the kitchen table, staring at the telephone. Then I broke down crying.

Joe's body was shipped back to the East Coast a few days later. Nearly every skinhead in a three-hundred mile radius turned out for the memorial service. Even my cousin Shawn and the Lancaster County crew came to pay their respects; it was the first time I'd seen Shawn in nearly three years. He nodded to me across the packed room as I waited in line to view the body.

Waves of skinheads marched up to the casket, saluting their fallen hero, "*Sieg Heil!*" I didn't salute Joe. I stood alone by his body for a few moments and remembered what he had done for me; he'd helped me when no one else could, or would. I hadn't come to the funeral home to pay respect to a skinhead; I'd come to pay respect to a friend. I leaned into the casket and kissed Joe's forehead. "Thank you," I whispered.

The skinheads threw a party in his honor. I hadn't planned to go; I had no desire to go, but Matt Hanson talked me into it, saying he missed me, assuring me everybody missed me since I'd stopped spending my nights in Skinhead Alley.

I walked up a long flight of steps to the second-floor apartment carrying the case of beer Matt had been told to bring. The host, a member of the Nazi Alliance, patted me on the back and said, "Glad you came." He asked me to put the beer in the refrigerator and waved me down a hallway toward the kitchen.

Three gigantic Axis Skinheads were leaning against the counter. Not one of them spoke to me. That's when I knew. I just fucking knew. I'd walked into a trap and there wasn't a thing I could do to escape. As I reached for the refrigerator door, the biggest one sucker punched me in the side of the head. Twenty-four bottles of beer shattered across the floor, leaving the linoleum as slick as ice. I knew it would be my only advantage. I lodged my shoulder into the Axis skin who'd hit me like I was checking an opposing hockey player. He teetered on the slippery floor. I clung to his shirt and used my weight to drag him down.

I only got in one shot before he screamed, "Axis Stomp!" That notorious battle cry has preceded many a bloodbath. It's their special code; it means all Axis Skinheads within earshot must jump in the fight. They all came running. So did all the other crews, who were jostling for ringside seats. As the first torrent of blows rained down on my head and chest, I heard the echo of a familiar tune in the back of my mind.

Bomp. Bomp. Bomp. "Singing in the rain … "

"So this is what it feels like," I thought, as Axis Skinheads punished me with their combat boots. Doc Martens looked like sledgehammers as they closed in on my thighs, my sides, my face. I curled into a ball and begged my back to endure the brunt of the blows. I tried to cover my head with my arms, but they kicked my only defense away. My arms fell helplessly, uselessly to my sides. Someone kicked me over onto my back.

"Just singing in the rain … "

I found Shawn against the far wall. I stared, as best I could through the blows and the blood, into my cousin's eyes. Five years had passed since he'd recruited me. He watched silently, shoulder-to-shoulder with the Strike Force skinheads I had recruited, as the Axis brutalized me. One lifted me off the floor. Maybe he was the same one who knocked me back down.

Maybe it was someone else. They were no longer individuals, just a blur of boots and fists.

Two Axis skins grabbed my feet and dragged me down the hall. I couldn't see the parade behind me, but I heard it. My eyes were trained on the stairwell dropping off only a few feet ahead of me. It moved in and out of focus, distorting and reforming before me like a reflection in a funhouse mirror. I felt Axis hands pawing at my torso, my legs. I smelled the stench of their sweat as they heaved me high above their heads. Then I felt their hands leave my body.

"What a glorious feeling ... "

I was floating. Just for a second, long enough to realize what would be next. Then I fell, rolled, careened out of control. My arms and legs caught on the railings, on the walls, on the steps, but I was moving too fast to stop the momentum the Axis unleashed when they threw me off the top step of that endless flight of stairs. I felt my body splatter, part by part, onto the concrete. My back slammed down first and my lungs emptied. There was no air left to carry my screams into the night as my legs, right, left, then my arms, right, left, struck the concrete. My head hit last. I was past the point of feeling, but I heard the impact. It was the "crack!" of the butt of a shotgun breaking across a back.

I have no idea how long I laid there. When I came to my senses, I saw dozens of skinheads looking down on me. Axis Skinheads. Eastern Nazi Alliance Skinheads. Lancaster County Skinheads. Strike Force Skinheads. Pure hatred shot from their eyes as they mocked me. Matt Hanson was the only guy who wasn't laughing.

"You're fucking dead to us, you fucking traitor!" someone screamed at me. Then they filed back into the apartment and slammed the door.

As I lay there, bloody and broken, it hit me. It's over. It's finally fucking over.

"I'm hap-, hap-, happy again."

Free At Last

"NO MAN IS AN ISLAND," MY GAYLORD CELLIE ONCE TOLD me. But I sure as shit felt like one, laying in a bloody heap on that sidewalk. The "family" I'd known since I was fourteen years old had just kicked me to the curb. Even my own cousins turned on me. The only skinhead who stayed friends with me was Matt Hanson. And he proved he was a true friend to me the night Axis jumped me out. He snuck out of Joe Morgan's funeral party to help me. Under the circumstances, that took balls the size of Jupiter.

"You okay?"

I answered with a moan.

Matt scraped me off the sidewalk and drove me back to his place. He swore he hadn't known he was walking me into a trap. I believed him. Matt was such a screwball, and he had such a big mouth. Hell, if I'd been setting somebody up, I wouldn't have let Matt in on it. The only thing the other skinheads had said to Matt was, "Invite Frankie and bring beer." That's all it took. He loved me too much to realize everyone else hated me. I should've seen it coming. To this day, I can't believe I walked into that party thinking it'd be okay because we'd all loved Joe. Even if guys like David Conover hadn't known I'd stepped down the night Joe got killed, everybody knew the minute I walked up to Joe's casket and kept my hands at my sides. I was the only "skinhead" at the funeral who didn't salute Joe with a *Sieg Heil*. That's when they realized they'd lost two comrades: one lying in a casket and one standing next to it refusing to salute. They took their grief and rage out on me. I should have seen it coming, because for a couple hours a few nights earlier, I'd been ready to do the same fucking thing. Axis beat any fleeting thoughts I still had about returning to the skinhead fold out of me. I was a traitor. There was no turning back.

Once I recovered from the jump out, I headed straight for Second and Porter to numb my pain. I didn't slip into addiction; I catapulted. I wanted to be fucked up all the time because it felt amazing, and because it was thumbing my nose at the skinheads. One night about thirty of us from Second and Porter went to the Trocadero Club on South Street. We hadn't been there five minutes when Matt Hanson came flying in the door.

"They heard you was down here. You gotta get outta here."

"Dude, *you* gotta get outta here," I said. "It's okay. I ain't alone."

"You ain't alone," Vicey Sullivan confirmed.

A few minutes later, about a dozen Strike Force skinheads marched into the Trocadero. I guess when they saw how many South Philly corner boys I had with me they had a nasty flashback to Jimmy's wedding reception riot, because they walked back out the door.

"You worried about this?" Vicey asked.

"I don't know, man. There's a couple of dudes out there who ..."

Vicey held up his hand to stop me. "Frankie, youse ain't alone."

IN THOSE DAYS, the biggest coke dealer in South Philly was a dude called Cork. Second and Porter was his home office. All night every night, cars pulled up to the curb, and Cork jumped in and rode off down the street. A minute or two later, we'd see him hop out at the next corner. Each time he strolled back to Second and Porter, the wads of cash in his pockets bulged out a little farther. One night Cork called me over to him.

"I'm totally backed up," he said, waving toward the idling cars lined halfway down the block. He handed me a pack of cigarettes. It felt empty, but I knew it wasn't; Cork concealed his stash inside empty packs. He flipped open the lid to show me the small bags of cocaine tucked inside. "You can sell these one bag for $20 or three for $50. Your cut is five bucks a bag. Got it?"

Thus began my career in pharmaceutical sales. Second and Porter was like a drive-through for every drug you could want: Xanax, Valium, cocaine, Percocet, weed, acid. Anything and everything, except heroin. Nobody on Second and Porter dealt heroin, and everybody swore they'd never use it. Heroin was what addicts used. We weren't addicts; we were just having a little fun and making a little money. At first, I only helped Cork, and only when he got really busy. Then Johnny Hawkins, the pot dealer, asked me to help him out, too. By day I was still moving furniture for Keith, which paid about three, maybe four hundred dollars a week. By night, moving drugs, I cleared about one hundred dollars an hour. Even a ninth-grade dropout can do that math.

Before long, I started my own business. Even though I was hated in Skinhead Alley, I still had a lot of connections on South Street. I used those to get a line set up with one of the older punks who wholesaled the best acid in the city. He charged me $90 for a 100-hit sheet; I sold hits for $5 each and cleared $410 per sheet. Some weekend nights, I sold as many as three sheets. If I hadn't been taking acid while I was selling it, I could've retired by age twenty-five. As it was, I ate a lot of the profits and sometimes couldn't remember the next morning where I'd stashed the rest.

If I got word there was a big rave going down in the city, I'd skip Second and Porter for the night, knowing I could double my business if I went to my clients instead of waiting for them to come to me. I raked it in for hours at one rave on South Street. I was on the verge of closing down shop when a large group of Italian guys, all dressed super-sharp, started filing through the door. "Cool, more business," I thought. Then I damn near fainted. The third guy in their line looked like he'd just jumped down off the cover of *GQ*, but I recognized him anyhow.

"What's up, dude?" I screamed across the room.

Louie Lacinzi's thin lips curled into a smile. He pointed at me and declared to his entourage, "This dude's closer to me than a brother."

We threw our arms around each other. Louie's boys kept their distance, but they never took their eyes off me while I talked to him. After a half an hour or so, one of Louie's guys walked over and whispered something in his ear.

"Hey, man, I gotta go," Louie said to me. "We gotta keep in touch, though."

"Where are you living?" I asked.

"I've got a house out in Chester County. How about you?"

"Tree Street."

"That fucking sucks." Louie hugged me again. "I'll be in touch."

A few nights later, I heard a knock at the front door. A well-dressed young Italian guy was standing on the stoop. He didn't say anything; he just pointed me toward the tricked out Mercury Cougar double-parked down the street.

"Is this really yours?" I asked through the car's open window.

Louie grinned at me. "Business is good."

We cruised around together for a couple hours, catching up and sharing a blunt, a cigar filled with weed instead of tobacco.

"I hear you're working Second and Porter," he said.

"Off and on."

"There ain't no future in that," he replied. Louie would know. Turned out Jimmy didn't have his facts straight about what all Louie'd been doing after he left the skinheads. He was a kingpin all right, just not the kind that works a corner, at least not for long. Louie was too big a dreamer to settle for small time hustling. The night he took me for a ride in his Cougar, he filled me in on his plan. The dude was talking about buying buildings and opening businesses. He knew every step he had to take, and he was sitting on enough cash to pull it off. He didn't say where the money came from and I didn't ask.

Nobody in my family had any plans to go legit. Every week,

my cousin Jerry dropped off at least ten times the number of Percocets and Xanax my mom and John actually used, and they used a lot. My mom alone was taking at least ten Percs a day. She sold the leftovers for Jerry out of our living room, covering not only the cost of her and John's habits, but also pretty much everything else the family needed to get by, which was good, since by then dealing was their only form of income besides state aid.

My mom gave me my first Percocet free of charge, family courtesy and all. When I came back for another the next night, she charged full price.

"Are you shitting me?" I asked.

"I ain't the fucking Goodwill," she said. "If you can't pay, work it off."

So I added xanies and percs as a sideline to my main gig dealing acid. The good thing about downers was I didn't eat up so much of the profits. Xanax especially fucked with my drinking. A dude's got to have his priorities.

Even though I was making a lot of money between my job with Keith and dealing, I kept living on Tree Street. It was close to Second and Porter, and I liked being around my little sisters. I set up a makeshift room in the dank basement. If somebody'd told me when I was thirteen that I'd end up voluntarily living in that rowhouse with John, I'd have laughed in their face. But John had changed a lot over the years. Booze and drugs, it appeared, had finally taken all the fight out of him.

I'd been living back on Tree Street for close to six months when a relative stopped by for a visit.

"So, how have you been?" she asked.

"I'm doing great."

"You're nothing but a fucking cellar dweller," John said from his nest on the couch.

It'd been so long since John had aimed one of his barbs at me, I actually thought maybe I'd misunderstood. "What did you say?" I asked.

"You're over there bragging about how you're doing so

fucking great. You're living in a cellar. You're a fucking cellar dweller. You couldn't even afford your own box in an alley."

"What's it been, ten years since you got off your lazy ass?"

"At least I ain't a fucking jailbird," he said.

"Here we go again," I thought. He's got an audience, so he's going to dust off all his stupid freaking Sing-Sing jokes. My little half-sisters sat next to each other on the far end of the couch playing with their dolls; I guess John figured they were finally old enough for his big comedy routine.

He was actually calling me out. "I said, you ain't nothing but a jailbird."

I glanced at my little sisters. They weren't looking at us, but they weren't dancing their Barbies around anymore either. "Drop it, John."

"You don't fucking tell me what to do in my own goddamn house, jailbird."

"Stop being a prick."

But he wouldn't. "I may be a prick, but I'm better than that fucking father of yours."

It was more than I could take. Everything I'd ever wanted to scream at John came pouring out of my mouth: "Don't you dare talk shit on my dad! You were a prick to me my whole fucking life. At least he didn't fucking beat me! You beat the living fucking shit out of me!"

"Margaret!" John yelled out into the kitchen. "You better get your ass out here and shut your kid's fucking mouth."

My mom stormed into the room and chose dick over me yet again. "I don't want to hear it anymore, Frankie! Stop lying! John barely touched you."

"You know that's a lie!" I replied.

"Shut the fuck up, jailbird," John said, staggering to his feet.

"Fuck you!"

John raised his dukes like he had in his boxing days and rushed me like he had in my victim days. I laid him out with one punch. I'd never hit someone that hard before in my life. John fell backwards over the same battered coffee table he'd knocked me over God knows how many times. He landed on top of my little sisters.

"You hurt my daddy!" Kirsten wailed, breaking my heart.

My mom grabbed me around the neck and wrestled me toward the front door. "Get the fuck out!"

The last thing I saw before my mom slammed the door in my face was John sprawled half passed out across the couch, as he'd been most of my life. But this time, blood poured from the gash under his eye. I'll go to my grave regretting that my little sisters saw it happen, but I'll never once regret throwing that punch.

Although I never moved back into the rowhouse on Tree Street, after a few weeks, once we'd all cooled down, I popped in to visit my mom and the girls. My mom acted like nothing had happened; she probably convinced herself John got hurt playing hockey. My little sisters knew the truth, though, and it showed in how they reacted to me. When I tried to hug them, they pulled away scared. That damn near killed me. John's reaction blew my mind. He came wandering in drunk about an hour after I got there and mumbled, "You got me good with that one, Frankie." He said it like a compliment from one fighter to another, but I wasn't ready to let my guard down.

"I ain't that little kid you used to knock around."

"I know you ain't." The scar still glowed bright red under his left eye.

"You ever pull that shit with me again," I said, "Or with those two girls, so help me God, it'll be worse next time."

He laughed the same drunken laugh I remembered from my childhood. He leaned in so close I could taste his putrid breath.

"I guess I kinda had it coming."

It was as close to an apology as I'd ever get from my stepfather.

I SPENT THE rest of that winter and the following spring living with Johnny Hawkins, the pot dealer, in a rowhouse about six down from my mom's on Tree Street. Every night, when I'd stagger home around three or four in the morning, he'd ask, "What'd youse do tonight?"

I'd rattle off whatever insane combination of drugs I'd managed to survive. Some nights it was just a lot of weed. Sometimes, mostly on weekends, it was weed plus mushrooms or acid. But no matter what it was, if it was a weeknight and I wasn't already half passed out, I'd wash down an extra perc with some beer so I'd have a chance of catching some sleep before the alarm clock rang. When it did, I'd snort a few lines of cocaine so I'd be awake enough to haul furniture.

One morning on my way to work, I walked into a deli to grab a hoagie. The clerk was glued to a small television set behind the counter.

"What's going on?" I asked

"Somebody blew up a building."

Born Again

THE CREASES IN THE FBI AGENT'S FOREHEAD SEEMED to deepen over the hours it took me to make my first confession. When I finally finished telling my story, he set his pen down and flexed his hand several times to get the blood flowing back into his fingers. He flipped through page after page of the notes he'd taken, then carefully laid them inside a folder. "I want to check a few things out," he said. He asked for my contact information and walked me out the door.

The whole experience was so weird. Not so much that I'd been talking to an agent, just that I'd talked about it at all. It was the first time I'd ever told my whole story to anybody. It was the first time I'd ever tried to make sense in my own mind out of the insane experience called my life. Thinking back on it, I probably should have been worried they were going to bust me for dealing. But none of that even entered my mind at the time. The only thing that mattered was finding somebody I could talk to. My past in the movement felt like poison inside me – I had to get it out of my system. I was grateful those agents had even let me in the door. I wasn't sure they would. Of course, so soon after the Oklahoma City bombing, they were probably willing to talk to anybody they thought might have any insight. I think my tattoos had been my calling card that first day.

About a week later, the agent called and asked if I'd be willing to come back in. This time, he walked me past the sterile interrogation room and led me to his private office. He offered me something to drink, sat me in a comfortable chair next to his desk, and tapped his finger on a file. I could see my name on the tab.

"Your story checked out," he said. "You were in pretty deep. How'd you get out?"

I didn't have much of an answer then. "I guess I just grew up."

"Are you willing to work with us?"

"I told youse the first time – I ain't gonna rat on nobody. I didn't come in here to name names. I just want it to stop."

He thought it over for a minute, then said, "I don't think we're who you need to talk to. Would you be willing to speak with the ADL?"

I burst out laughing. "There's no way the ADL's going to meet with me."

According to the white supremacy movement, the Anti-Defamation League is right up there with the Israeli government at the top of the ZOG conspiracy. The ADL isn't just an enemy; it's *the* enemy. And it's an aggressive enemy. For decades, the ADL has tracked the every movement of white supremacists. They monitor every publication, document every crime, and profile every leader.

For five years, I'd believed with all my heart that the ADL was a manifestation of the antichrist. So it took me a few days to get around to making the phone call.

"Hi, my name is Frank Meeink, and I need to speak… "

"Did you say your name is Frank Meeink? Please hold."

A minute or two later, the guy came back on the line.

"I'd like to come in… "

"No."

I was thinking, "I told you so, Mr. FBI man." But then the guy on the phone surprised me and said, "We'd prefer to meet you off site. You understand."

I cleaned up as best I could for my big meeting, but I still felt like a total dirtball walking into the fancy hotel lobby. I took a seat in a cushy chair. Center City loomed above me, but I couldn't enjoy the view through the glass ceiling of the atrium. I had to watch the door. Everyone who entered smelled like money and French cologne. I saw them dart their eyes in my direction, panic a little, then pretend they hadn't seen me. I waited nearly ten minutes. I was on the verge of leaving when I was approached by a middle-aged guy wearing a nice suit. He was followed by a very large bodyguard.

"My name is Barry Morrison," he said. "I'm with the ADL."

"I'm Frank Meeink."

"I know." The hint of a smile crept across his stern face. "We profiled you a few years ago, before you left for the Midwest."

Had I still been in the movement, that would've sent my ego into outer space. As it was, it freaked me out, in a Big Brother kind of way.

"You're no longer part of Strike Force?" he asked.

"No."

"Why is it you want to speak with us?"

"This whole Oklahoma City thing has me shaken up."

"It has us all shaken up," he said. Barry Morrison walked me to a deserted corner of the hotel lobby where we could talk without being overheard, then he quizzed me on every move I'd ever made as a skinhead. He put the freaking FBI to shame. But he wasn't hunting for information; he was testing if I really was the Frank Meeink he'd profiled. When he was satisfied I was who I claimed to be, he started working a new angle, a battery of questions about how, when, and why I'd left the movement. By the time he finally finished, I was exhausted.

"I want to verify a few things before we go any further," he said." But I'll be in touch soon."

Barry Morrison called me less than a week after that first conversation and invited me to come to the ADL office for a meeting with his staff. From the outset, I told them the same thing I'd told the FBI: I wasn't going to name names. But they weren't after names. They wanted something far more difficult to produce: they wanted to know why. Why did I hate? Why was I so violent?

Why did I target particular victims? Why hadn't I defected earlier? Why had I changed now? Why? Why? Why?

My answers weren't eloquent, just honest. I answered the only way I knew how: I stepped back into who I'd been when I was a skinhead and gave voice to "why" as only a skinhead can. I explained to a room full of Jews why I'd believed for so many years that God wanted me to eradicate them. I confessed in detail far more graphic than the normal content of an ADL profile what I'd done. When it was over, the ADL staff looked shell-shocked; I felt like hell.

"Thank you, Frank," Barry said.

"Thank you," I said. The elevator door opened, but I lingered. "I didn't think youse were going to talk to me."

The same hint of a smile I'd seen at our first meeting peeked through Barry's professional poker face. "You had good references," he said. "A federal agent called a few days before you did. He assured us you were sincere."

I left the ADL office feeling like I hadn't done much good, even though Barry said I'd helped just by sharing my story. "Understanding is the first step toward prevention," he explained. But I wasn't so sure. While I'd been sitting in that executive conference room yapping about my past, some skinhead some-where was preparing his next attack. What were my words doing to stop his actions? Hell, nothing anybody'd said had ever stopped me. So I wasn't convinced by what Barry said to me: after all, even though he'd said I'd been helpful, he hadn't said any-thing about me coming in again.

I returned to life as usual, moving furniture and drugs. Both my businesses were booming, so much so I no longer had time to commute to Keith's store in Jersey. It was Keith's fault he lost me. He gave me all the information and advice I needed to open my own booth in a consignment mall off South Street. I specialized in reproduction antique doll chairs, and I made a killing every Saturday and Sunday when the tourists strolled through. The tiny chairs reminded me of the tiny girl in Illinois I missed so desperately. I painted a wooden sign to hang over my booth: Riley's Antiques.

I planned to save the money I made at Riley's Antiques for my Riley, but by month's end, I rarely had cash left over to send to Illinois. I convinced myself the high cost of life in the big city was the problem. The truth was I snorted my little girl's support payments up my nose. I rarely let myself get close to that truth – it was easier to stay doped up enough that I believed my own lies.

One person saw through my sham, though. To help solve my commuting problem, Keith hooked me up with a buddy of his, Kyle Hirsch, a Filipino Jew who looked Puerto Rican and dealt used furniture out of a crammed storefront in an almost all-black section of West Philly. Kyle's shop didn't cater to the elite clientele Keith served in Jersey; he ran the kind of store where you could buy an eight-piece dining room set for two hundred bucks. Kyle's employees looked shady, even by my standards. During my interview, Kyle explained that in addition to the furniture store, he also operated a halfway house for recovering addicts. Kyle was a recovering alcoholic and addict himself. Most of his employees lived in his halfway house. As Kyle was telling me all that, I got really mad at Keith. "He set me up," I thought. "That fucker's trying to sneak me into some rehab joint without me knowing it."

"Would you like the job?" Kyle asked.

"What do I gotta do to get it?" I asked back, worried about that halfway house.

Kyle must've been reading my mind, because he laughed a little when he said, "I just need a good delivery man." Then his eyes turned serious. "Why? Do you think you should be living in the house?"

Nobody can spot an addict like another addict. Kyle knew I was in serious trouble. But he also knew better than to push too hard too fast. My first few weeks working at his store, he never talked to me directly about recovery. But he and the other employees talked about it all the time. I tried to block them out, but I couldn't: the twelve steps echoed through the aisles all day long.

I worked hard for Kyle, when I showed up. Some days I clocked in late. Some days, my shift was half over by the time I dragged my ass out of bed. I always called in with some half-baked lie about being sick. Kyle'd been "sick" throughout his twenties; he wasn't buying it. He'd fire me on principle, but he'd always hire me back a few days later, after I sat through one of his sermons about the glory of sobriety. I was usually too stoned during those talks to realize Kyle knew I was stoned.

The third or fourth time Kyle rehired me, he added a condition: I had to start hitting twelve-step meetings.

"I don't care where you go or when you go, so long as you go," he said.

"Fine."

A few days later, Kyle asked me how meetings were going.

"When do you think I've got time to go to meetings?" I asked him. "Do you know how many deliveries I make for you? I ain't got time to listen to a bunch of drunks."

"I'll keep you on the clock while you go," Kyle said.

A few days after that, Kyle and I were riding together in the delivery truck when he again asked me how meetings were going.

"Fine."

"Will you say the Serenity Prayer with me?" he asked.

"I ain't ever heard of that, but I know the Lord's Prayer. We can do that one if you want."

Kyle kept his eyes on the road. "How'd you say your meetings are going?"

"Fine."

"Every twelve-step meeting in the world begins with the Serenity Prayer."

I was busted.

"Will you say it with me?" Kyle asked. "I'll teach you." We were stopped at a light. Kyle turned toward me and said, "Just follow me."

Together we recited: "God, grant me the serenity to accept the things I cannot change, the courage to change the things I can, and the wisdom to know the difference." I guess I must've prayed part of it right, because God granted me the courage to change my address. After many months of crashing with Johnny Hawkins, the pot dealer, I moved into an apartment of my own. Well, half my own. My roommate was a punk girl I'd known for years. We split rent on a sweet place right on South Street. It was around the corner from Riley's Antiques and an easy bus ride to both Kyle's store and Second and Porter. It was also dead center of party central. Hell, it was party central for a lot of the South Street punks, especially the ones dabbling in acid. And that gave me the option of working from home. I still did most of my business on Second and Porter, simply because no other location could compete with the buyer traffic that intersection attracted at night. And since I was down there selling anyhow, I inevitably ended up partying with the boys until the wee hours of the morning.

At one of those house parties, I locked eyes with an Italian girl so gorgeous the sight of her felt like a kick in the nads. Maria Salerno was from the part of Northeast Philadelphia where rich Italians raise their children in restored Victorian homes. I'd never seen a girl like that at a South Philly party before. Her designer jeans showcased her petite curves, but they didn't cling like the jeans South Philly girls painted on. I didn't think Maria Salerno would go for my standard pick-up line, "So, youse wanna hook up with me tonight or what?" She wasn't a pick-up line kind of girl. She was a wine-me-dine-me-buy-me-a-diamond-ring kind of girl. If she hadn't been so smoking hot, I would've run for my life. Instead, I spent a weekend worming her phone number out of her and close to a week convincing her to go on a date. I spiffed myself up like I was headed to the prom and took her to a fancy Italian restaurant in Center City.

Maria and I weren't just from different parts of Philadelphia; we were from different fucking planets. Maria Salerno fell in love with a Frank Meeink that didn't exist except in her imagination. It drove me fucking crazy. Maria's brown eyes looked right through my Nazi tattoos, right over my criminal record, and right past the lines of cocaine on my bathroom counter. She wanted to see our relationship for more than it was. To me, it was an extended booty call. To Maria, it was an engagement. No matter how many times I tried to give her the brush off, she just kept coming back. And every time she came back, she brought more of her stuff along. After two months, I felt like she was living with me. I was plotting how to tell her we were through when she dropped a bomb: "We're going to have a baby."

Under the circumstances, I didn't break up with her. But I didn't ask her to marry me, either, and that seemed to piss her off, just not enough to leave. We were still together in a cold-war kind of truce a month or so later when Barry Morrison called to ask me if I'd be willing to talk to some people on behalf of the ADL.

"I don't know. I ain't ever given, like, a speech. I just talked to youse guys that one day."

"And that's all you need to do this time: just talk. Share your story so others can learn from it. Will you do it?"

I thought about it for a few minutes and figured, how bad can it be? So I committed with, "Okay," then after the fact asked, "So who am I talking to?"

"My daughter's seventh-grade class."

Shit.

BARRY DROVE ME to the suburban school himself. The whole ride, I kept coaching myself, "They're just little kids. Don't cuss. Don't cuss. Don't cuss." We walked into the classroom. The teacher had all the kids arranged in a circle. One little chair at the front was empty and waiting for me. "Oh, fuck!" I thought, as I wedged myself into the seat, "What in holy hell have I gotten myself into?" Then I reminded myself one more time, "Just don't cuss."

It was my only goal for my first public speech. Just don't

fucking cuss. Cussing, as it turned out, wasn't the challenge; crying was. I broke down sobbing minutes after I started, before I even got to the part where I joined up with the skinheads. I spilled my guts to those little kids for nearly an hour, and I bawled like a baby the whole damn time. They just stared at me. No one said a word; no one so much as coughed or squirmed around in their chairs. Not the kids. Not the teacher. Not even Barry Morrison.

I was a basket case the whole ride back to Philly. Barry kept trying to console me, saying I'd done a good job and the teacher knew it was going to be rough and the kids and their parents had all been warned beforehand, but nothing he said mattered to me. I'd blown it, and I knew I'd blown it, big-time blown it. It wasn't just that I didn't think I'd made my point or even made any sense. I was worried I'd actually scarred those kids for life. Two dozen twelve year-olds spent an hour locked up in a classroom watching my nut job Nazi ass have a complete mental breakdown. Getting my point across was the least of my worries; I was worried about getting bills in the mail for their therapy sessions.

I stayed high for days trying to forget that God-awful experience. Not even Second and Porter had a drug that could block it out. So when Barry called me about a week later and asked me to stop by his office, I figured he wanted to tell me in person that I would never, ever again be speaking on behalf of the ADL, ever, under any circumstances, about any subject, ever.

"A package came here for you." Barry handed me a large manila envelope addressed, "Frank Meeink, c/o ADL." I stared at it.

"It's from the school where you spoke last week."

I kept staring. The first round of therapy bills? Grievances from the school board and the PTA? Hate mail from twelve year-olds?

"Open it," Barry said.

The first letter sounded like the kind of letter a teacher would make a kid write to a guest speaker who'd had a breakdown in front of a bunch of seventh-graders. "Mr. Meeink, Thank you for talking to our class. You were brave to share your story." The second letter was about the same: "Mr. Meeink, Thank you for visiting us and talking about what happened to you." A few letters in, a few of the students wrote, "I'm going to try to be nicer to people from now on" and "I promise I won't ever hate anybody." I remember thinking it was nice of the teacher to have some of the kids pretend they got my point. Then I hit this letter that changed everything: "Mr. Meeink, I bet you had a long, boring ride back to Philly." That's all it said. That's exactly the kind of letter I would've chicken-scratched in seventh grade. That was the real deal. And if that was real, so were the others. Some of those kids had actually heard me through all the crying. My words had made a difference.

When I looked up from the stack of notes, I was crying again. Barry was beaming like a proud papa.

"I told you your story could help people," he said. "A lot of people want to hear you speak, Frank. I just need you to tell me if you want to keep going."

I did. Within just a couple of months, Barry and other members of the ADL team were driving me to speaking engagements all around Southeastern Pennsylvania. It was like therapy for me, only instead of lying on a couch, I stood up on a stage.

Oh Baby, Oh Baby, Oh Shit

MARIA WAS STILL IN HER FIRST TRIMESTER AND STILL convinced we were getting married when my roommate skipped town with my half of the rent in her pocket. She'd always dealt with the landlord; I didn't even know his name. And he didn't know my name, because it wasn't on the lease. When he didn't get a rent check from our unit, he busted through the door. Maria witnessed the landlord telling me I'd better be gone that night. She had overlooked my five-year Nazi "phase," my prison record, my drinking and my drugging. But an eviction notice? Now that little white trash mess caught her attention. Maria fled straight back to her family's home in Northeast Philly.

I crashed at my dad's place. Maria called me there almost every night, but I never called her. We rarely saw each other. She was scared to come to my dad's neighborhood, and I was scared of her dad's neighborhood, too. I was scared her dad would meet me with a shotgun and a priest if I showed my face within ten blocks of his pregnant daughter. After a while, she stopped calling so often. Then she stopped calling.

One afternoon a few weeks after Maria's last call, I spotted a girl in a "Sick of It All" T-shirt. Her hair was a frenzy of brown curls, bouncing like shadows across her face as she counted out worms into Styrofoam cups at the counter of a bait-and-tackle shop not far from my dad's. Even elbow deep in bait, she was amazingly beautiful and too cool to give me the time of day or even a glance. If she had, she would've busted me ogling her.

I couldn't shake the thought of the hot girl counting worms. I found out her name was Nina and that she was sixteen. I was twenty-one. Five years didn't seem like much. Unlike Maria, Nina wasn't blind to me or trying to change me or trying to marry me. She was a bad girl who liked bad boys. She was into me exactly as I was. And she was basically the same as me, just five years younger, without the Nazi "phase" or the prison record. When she wasn't counting worms, she was full-on South Street hardcore. Nina'd made her debut on South Street at the tender age of fourteen. She fell in with some former skinheads, guys I had recruited who'd drifted back into the straight punk scene while I was away. Nina and I had been seeing each other about a week when she finally confessed that her South Street buddies used to tell her stories about their wild days as skinheads, back when Frankie Meeink was still with Strike Force.

"I recognized you," she said, tracing her fingertips around the swastika on my neck. "I knew who you were the second I saw you."

Nina knew me from the start like she'd known me forever. The only thing she didn't know at first was that a girl named Maria up in North Philly was counting down to her due date. When I told Nina about Maria, she didn't care so long as we could be together. When I got the nerve to call Maria and tell her about Nina, it didn't go quite as well. Maria said if I kept seeing Nina, I'd never see my kid. I was still reeling from that ultimatum when I got horrible news. Matt Hanson, the only skinhead I still loved, was dead. Matt always fell hard when he fell in love, and every breakup left him a little more broken than the last. But Matt's last breakup was more than he could take. He called his ex-girlfriend, told her she'd ruined his life, then pulled the trigger so she would hear him die. My heart broke for my lost friend, for his poor, sweet mom, Nazi Viv, even for the girl on the other end of that God-forsaken phone call. Nina got me through. She didn't try to make me talk or cheer me up or any other useless shit;

she just wrapped me in her arms and held on tight so I wouldn't get lost alone inside the pain.

Matt's death destroyed me – I crossed an invisible line in the months after he committed suicide. I don't know which beer or line of cocaine or hit of acid pushed me over; I only know everything but my boozing and drugging started falling to shit. I tried to keep enough cash from blowing up my nose so Nina and me could get our own place, but all I could manage was renting a couch in another couple's tiny apartment. I lost Riley's Antiques because I spent the booth rent on drugs. When I showed up an entire week late for work at Kyle's store, he finally fired me for real. Riding the trolley home, I rehearsed how to tell Nina I'd lost my job so I didn't come out sounding like the failure I was. But I never got the chance to give my speech. When I walked through the door, I found her crying on the couch we called home. A shredded pregnancy test box lay at her feet. Nina looked so small, so young, so afraid. I put my arms around her and promised her over and over, "It'll be okay. Whatever you want to do, I'm with you. It'll be okay."

NINA WAS STILL considering her options when Maria called to tell me I had a son.

"What's his name?" I asked, dreading the answer.

"Jake."

It was the one name I had begged her not to pick, but she picked it anyhow. I had a bad history with that name; both the closet SHARP I'd kidnapped and my co-defendant in that case had been named Jake.

"And he'll have my last name," Maria said.

"Can I at least see him?"

She hesitated a long time before saying, "I guess. But don't you dare bring her."

I went alone. I welcomed my beautiful baby boy into the world with a whispered, "I love you," then I walked away.

I ran back to Nina, vowing to myself I'd stick by her no

matter what she decided to do about the baby. Even a year earlier, I would've pushed her to keep it because of my Catholic upbringing. But a lot had changed for me in a year's time. The world that had always been strictly black-or-white seemed so gray to me. I'd been wrong about so many things I would've sworn on a Bible were absolute facts. But nothing seemed absolute to me anymore, not even what Nina should do about the baby. I wasn't exactly the poster boy for involved fatherhood. No matter how many times I promised Nina I wasn't going to leave her, she knew the truth: I'd already walked away from two girls and two babies. No matter what I said, Nina knew that if she kept the baby, she might very well end up raising it alone, and she'd been alone too much already in her life. When I met her, she was living with her grandmother because her folks had kicked her out. After she met me, Nina barely checked in at her grandma's. Grandma wasn't happy about that. She was downright pissed when she learned her sixteen year-old granddaughter was pregnant.

I understood why. It wasn't just that Nina was so young. It was that she was so smart. She was a wild child, but the second she opened her mouth, you knew she was going to ace the fuck out of college someday. Her grandmother was afraid Nina would give up on her dreams if she had the baby. She was afraid Nina would drop out and end up counting worms for the rest of her life. So when Nina announced her decision to keep the baby, I promised I'd find a way to support us, so long as she promised to stay in school.

No pregnant teenager has ever looked hotter in a Catholic schoolgirl uniform than Nina. She kept her end of the bargain, and I kept mine. I went to Kyle and begged for my old job. When I explained the situation with Nina, Kyle not only hired me back, he hired Nina, too. While I carried furniture, she put her amazing brain to work on Kyle's computer system. Kyle even advanced us enough cash so we could upgrade from our rental couch to a studio apartment in University City.

Nina ate healthy food, went to bed early, and swore off booze and drugs while she was pregnant. Like a lot of pregnant women, she developed an aversion to certain things because they made her sick. Nina developed an aversion to Louie Lacinzi. By the end of her second trimester, she flat out hated the dude. Any time he stopped by the apartment to take me out for the night, Nina flew off the handle. She got right in his face, so close she'd ram him with her belly, and chewed him a new asshole. Louie was real patient about it. He'd take a deep breath, like he was the one going to Lamaze classes, and ask me, "Youse ready yet?" By then, I always was.

I went out every night, with or without Louie. Sometimes I went down to Second and Porter so I could make money on the side while I got fucked up. Other nights, I just went across the street to a neighborhood dive. One evening, I left the bar to make a run down South Street. I wasn't looking for anybody in particular, just a change of scenery. I ran into an ex-SHARP who'd been my sworn enemy back in the day. One look at his outfit, though, and I knew he wasn't a Sharpie anymore. Of course, he could tell I wasn't a Nazi anymore, either. So we started shooting the shit about how we'd both changed and what had happened to everybody else who used to haunt South Street. We were gossiping like a couple old ladies, when he said, "I still can't believe Brian killed himself."

"Brian who?"

"Your Brian. Brian Stugen."

The shock must've registered on my face, because he said, "You knew, right?"

"Yeah," I lied, ashamed of the truth. I fought back tears and said, "I haven't heard the details, though."

Stug hung himself. He'd been so enormous during our days with the terror squad that I couldn't imagine a rope strong enough to hold his weight without snapping before his neck did. But according to the former SHARP, Stug was so strung out on heroin, he was nothing but skin, bones, and wasted veins by the time he committed suicide.

For the second time in less than a year, Nina held me together as the pain washed over me. I laid my head on her stomach and prayed that our child would never feel the kind of pain Stug felt before he hung himself, the kind of pain Matt felt before he shot himself, the kind of pain I felt before I grabbed that rusty knife in Terre Haute. "It'll be okay," I whispered to the baby inside Nina's belly.

Nina was getting close to her due date when we realized there was no way both of us and a baby were going to fit in that tiny studio in University City. I found us a new place in Clifton Heights. If the guys from Strike Force had stopped in for a visit, they would've stroked out. Nina and me were the only white people in the entire complex.

I was still unpacking when Nina called me to meet her at the hospital. During a routine checkup, the doctor realized she'd developed toxemia; he decided to induce labor. I ran for the nearest bus. For once I was going to be there when one of my kids was born.

When I stepped onto the labor ward, there in the middle of the hallway were Nanny and Pop, all my Bertone aunts and uncles and even some of my cousins. I hadn't seen most of them since I'd gotten home from prison. I'd been too ashamed. They were all so good, so successful, so normal. And I was like my dad, a black sheep. But those were my issues, not theirs. None of that mattered to the Bertones; all that mattered was having me back. They rushed me with hugs and kisses and "How have you been?" and "Where have you been?" and "We've missed you so much" and "We love you." Then somebody asked, "How did you know to come down?"

After a few confusing minutes, we all finally realized what was going on. My aunt was having a baby down the hall from where Nina was having our baby. Nina met the entire Bertone clan between contractions. Needless to say, Nanny and Pop were nice as could be, but a little overwhelmed that they were meeting my girlfriend for the first time while she was giving birth to their great-grandson.

Nina and I named our son Matthew Francis. Like me, he was named after his father and a ghost. Nanny and Pop didn't know the significance of my son's first name, but they were thrilled by his middle name. Pop beamed as he held his little namesake. Matt was the first of Nanny and Pop's great-grandchildren they'd actually met. They'd only seen pictures of Riley. They didn't know Jake existed. Watching them fuss over little Matt, I didn't have the heart to tell them he wasn't their first great-grandson.

For a high school senior and an addict, Nina and I did all right by our newborn son. We kept things as normal as possible at home. Matt was too little, of course, to realize his mommy was doing homework between feedings. And even at seventeen, Nina wasn't quite hardcore enough to realize how many drugs daddy was doing when mommy wasn't looking.

Being with Matt every day made me miss Riley so bad I couldn't stand it. So early that summer, after Nina finished school, we dropped Matt off with my mom and boarded a bus for a three-day excursion to Illinois. Jessica was great to both of us, and Riley was like heaven. I didn't have much money to spare, but with Nina's blessing I gave Jessica the little bit I had.

On the long ride back to Philly, Nina and I couldn't wait to get to Matt. Partly, we just missed him, but partly we were worried. The rowhouse on Tree Street wasn't exactly Romper Room. But my mom had been our only option: at only three months, our son was too young to make the long trip. But I needed to see my daughter. And Nina needed to meet my daughter, because it was looking more and more like Nina would soon be Riley's stepmom.

When we walked in the front door, the rowhouse was a disaster. Although my mom swore she and John had been perfect grandparents, evidence of their imperfections was scattered around the room: empty beer bottles on the coffee table, stubbed-out joints in the ashtrays. But Matt was okay. He was upstairs sleeping, wearing a clean diaper and clean jammies, with Kirsten and Hayley playing house nearby. Still, I was furious. How dare they get fucked up when they were supposed to be looking after my son? At that point, I couldn't see that I was doing the exact same thing.

Front Office Frankie

NO MATTER HOW MANY TIMES I SCREWED UP, BARRY
Morrison never wavered in his belief that I could make a
difference if I kept sharing my story. Barry continued to arrange
speaking engagements for me during the crazy year when I was
juggling Maria and Nina and the birth of my two sons. By the time
Matt was born in 1997, I was speaking for the ADL as often as
once a week.

Driving back to Philly after one of my speaking engagements,
I got the best idea of my life. Mike Boni, a pretty big-time
lawyer associated with the ADL, was my chauffeur that evening.
Mike felt like a brother to me – an older brother succeeding
in a world I could barely imagine, but still a brother. We talked
sports nonstop. That a guy like Mike Boni seemed to think I was
worth talking to gave me hope that maybe I could make good one
day. I think that's probably why I talked about my big idea with
him in the car that night instead of letting it float out the window
into the darkness.

The idea was simple: take black kids and white kids from
different parts of Philly, kids who'd otherwise grow up to hate
each other, and put them in the one place where they'd have to
work together to make it out. Where is that place? Center ice.

The more speeches I'd given, the more I'd realized that my
real turning point had been playing football on that prison
league. If it weren't for being trapped in prison with no escape

other than that league, I never would've spoken to guys like Jello and Little G, let alone come to think of them as friends.

"I think maybe we could do the same thing with hockey," I said to Mike.

"Why hockey?"

"Because the key to making it work is the kids can't know how to skate when they join up. With football or baseball, if you're a fast runner or good with a ball, you've got an edge before you even start. But in hockey, none of that matters if you don't know how to stand up on skates." I got so excited I was practically screaming in Mike's ear. "Just think about it. We could take the shit that keeps them different and erase it with the one thing they'd have in common. No matter what color they are, they're all going to be landing on their asses. Even ice, man, even fucking ice."

Mike said, "We've got to talk to Barry about this."

Barry Morrison loved it. He called one of his contacts at the Philadelphia Flyers, and they loved it, too. The next thing I knew, Ed Snider – *the* Ed Snider, owner of the Flyers – gave the green light to my idea, Harmony Through Hockey. Barry called Mike and me in to go over the details. The ADL would provide the educational materials and the volunteers. The Flyers would supply the equipment and most of the publicity. The City Department of Recreation would let us use one of their rinks, more if it took off.

"Are you shitting me?" I asked Barry.

"No," he replied. "There is one other thing we need to discuss, though."

I braced myself, figuring it had to be bad news.

"The Flyers are hoping you'll be the head coach for the program."

That moment may be the closest to heaven I ever get. The Philadelphia Flyers wanted me. Me! The kid who used to spend months stealing supplies to build forts tall enough that he could climb up to catch a glimpse of their arena. The kid who once stole a Pathmark shopping cart and sunk it halfway into a pond so when the water froze he'd have a place to practice his slapshots. The kid who took nails to the face and got checked out into parking lots just so he could pretend he was one of the Broad Street Bullies. The Philadelphia Flyers wanted me!

Several months before the league's first season was set to start, I went to Barry's office and said, "We've got a problem." I pointed to my neck. It had dawned on me the night before when I saw myself as I passed a mirror. How could I stand in front of little kids with a swastika on my neck and expect them to believe me when I said it's bad to hate? I did it all the time when I spoke for the ADL, but except for that first group of seventh-graders, those audiences were older. Still, one of the most frequent questions I got was, "If you're no longer a skinhead, why do you still have those tattoos?" I always wanted to say, "Because they ain't lick-ons out of a Cracker Jack box." But the truth was that even real tattoos can be removed. And so long as there was a swastika on my neck and the word "skinhead" on my knuckles, a lot of people doubted I'd really changed.

"Let me think about it," Barry said.

He called a few days later with an answer to my problem. Barry had explained my situation to other ADL people, and he'd found a lady doctor who'd lost family in the Holocaust. When Barry told her about my tattoos and my life, she agreed to see me and see what could be done.

"You got any idea what that laser shit costs? I can't afford that."

"We've never been able to compensate you much for the times you've spoken for the ADL," Barry said in his gentle way. "But this we can help you with. It's not going to cost you anything."

Except a little pain. Make that a lot of pain. Getting tattoos hurts; getting rid of tattoos hurts like fucking hell. Once a month for nearly a year, I laid on a table in the doctor's office, clenching my teeth for more than an hour while she zapped away on me. Each flash of the laser bit a few more millimeters off the five-inch circle swastika on my neck. Every time the doc fired the gun, another piece of my past popped like a pimple and shot inky, bloody slime onto the towels draped around me. The swastika was the worst going on, and it was the worst coming off – that tattoo alone took half a dozen rounds with the laser, but by the time I skated onto the ice for the first Harmony Through Hockey practice, only a shadow of Nazism lingered on my neck.

My gig with Harmony Through Hockey was a fantasy come to life. I scored a free pass to come and go in the Flyers' front offices. I got free ice time every day at the West Oak Lane rink. The building wasn't well maintained, but the ice was. More importantly, I got to spend every afternoon hanging out with these cool little kids, talking about life and the lessons I'd learned the hard way. Some days, the Flyers sent their trainers down to the West Oak Lane rink to work with the Harmony Through Hockey kids. I wish I had pictures of the looks on the kids' faces, and on mine, the first time those professional NHL skating coaches arrived to give us private lessons. We had the same looks when the Flyers gave us free tickets for a "field trip" to one of their games.

The ADL supported the program just as much as the Flyers did. They sent their own brand of trainers to almost every one of our practices. After the kids came off the ice, the ADL staffers and I would gather them in a circle in the locker room and have amazing heart-to-heart conversations with them. The kids opened up about how racism affected their lives. They felt safe in that locker room discussing the very thing I'd become a skinhead to avoid: their feelings. We had twenty kids, both boys and girls, in our first test-run season. Ten were black, ten were white. The only real snag we ran into was an oversight; the rink supervisor forgot to ask the kids if they knew how to skate before letting them sign up. A couple of the white kids did, and as I feared that almost blew my whole "even ice" idea. But we worked through it in the locker room conversations. It got the kids talking about how some kids got certain advantages because of what neighborhood they lived in. The kids decided as a group that that wasn't fair; they also decided that basketball wasn't a "black" sport and hockey wasn't a "white" sport. The kids learned a lot that first season, the least of which was how to play hockey.

Before the season ended, a local television show called "Philly After Midnight" asked me if I'd come on and talk about Harmony Through Hockey. I agreed, hoping the publicity would help us get more kids involved in the second season. When I walked into the studio, I thought for a second all that acid I'd dropped was finally catching up to me: I thought I was having a flashback. In a way, I was. It was the same studio where I'd stood shoulder-to-shoulder with John Cook and Louie Lacinzi a few years earlier, during the taping of a skinhead story for morning television.

The production crew already had me hooked up to a mic when they mentioned I wasn't going to be the only guest that night. Then the host walked on the set practically arm-in-arm with a black militant professor from a local university.

"Three, two, one, and we're live."

If I hadn't thought to wear my Harmony Through Hockey jersey that night, I'm not sure anybody watching would've even known the name of the hockey program. The host had no intention of talking about Harmony Through Hockey and not much intention to let me speak. It was an ambush, and I walked into it as blindly as that closet Sharpie had walked into my apartment in Springfield. The professor slammed theories at me like the butt end of a shotgun. I ain't seen a tape of that show, but how I felt that night is burned in my mind. The professor's main point was that I was ignorant; my whole life was nothing more than a reaction to false stereotypes I held about people I didn't even know. According to the professor, that kind of ignorance isn't something a person could overcome; it was who I am.

"You didn't change," he said at one point. "You can't change."

"You don't know what's in my heart," I replied, but no one was listening.

"Hate was bred into you," the professor said. "That comes from your parents."

That made me mad. That made me want to smack the hell out of him. But I didn't. I thought about my little hockey players and the pain I'd endured so they wouldn't have to see a swastika on my neck. I sure as hell wasn't going to let them see me taking a swing at somebody on television. So I took a really deep breath, unclenched my fists, and said, as calmly as I could, "You don't even know my parents."

White supremacists aren't the only people who throw around stereotypes about people they don't know. The host and the professor missed my point or ignored it. When the show ended, I looked at the producer who'd booked me and said, "You set me up." He didn't even have the decency to answer. Had I known what I was walking into, I probably would've brought back-up just to make sure I got out of there okay – Louie Lacinzi or the Second and Porter boys. I did that sometimes for ADL speeches, especially the ones with a lot of advance publicity, in case somebody from the movement tried to shut me up permanently. But I hadn't given the TV show a second thought because it was supposed to be about Harmony Through Hockey.

That professor knew the real plan, though, and he'd brought an enormous bodyguard along with him. The dude looked like The Notorious B.I.G. He waddled over to me after it was all over and said, "I feel you, dude." Then he glanced across the studio at his boss, who was hobnobbing with the host and the producer, and said, "Don't sweat what he said. That dude's uptight." We were standing there talking about Harmony Through Hockey when the producer's assistant told me my car was waiting. Since the live show happened "After Midnight," they'd promised me a ride home. The bodyguard left the professor chatting with his fan club and walked me out in case somebody was waiting to ambush me in the alley. He wished me good luck with the hockey program as I climbed into the waiting limousine.

I asked the driver to drop me off at my dad's bar, where I

was greeted with a hero's welcome. The limo alone impressed the aging 68th and Buist boys, but it wasn't all about the car. They'd had the television above the bar tuned to "Philly After Midnight." They'd watched the whole program. I'd spent the limo ride fuming about what the host and the professor had said and what I hadn't said, could've said, would've said if I had one more chance. But the crowd at my dad's bar wouldn't have changed one word. They mobbed me with praise. "You really gave 'em hell, Frankie! Personally, I'd have shot the fucker. How the hell did youse stay so cool?"

Then my dad shoved through the crowd. He threw his arm around my shoulder and said something I'd been waiting my whole life to hear: "I'm proud of you, son." Years later, he told a friend of mine that watching me hold my own with that professor was the proudest moment of his life.

After the last game of the Harmony Through Hockey season, the Flyers hosted an awards ceremony for the kids. They set up a platform on center ice and handed out trophies. Mike Boni gave a nice speech on behalf of the ADL. I said a few words too, but I don't think I made much sense. I was too distracted by the people in the front row. My mom and John actually came to the ceremony. And sitting right next to them was none other than Dave Schultz, one of the original Broad Street Bullies from the '74-'75 Stanley Cup team.

The ADL hoped I could spread the word about Harmony Through Hockey to other cities, so they started booking me for speaking engagements all over the country. Any time I had to be gone very long, they paid me $200 a day. It more than covered the time I lost at Kyle's store, just not the cost of my beer and drugs. My habits had gotten more expensive once I started speaking and coaching Harmony Through Hockey. Just getting fucked up is pretty cheap, all things considered. Getting fucked up and then taking other shit to mask being fucked up is what gets expensive.

My eyes lit up when the ADL offered me a thousand dollars to spend a week on the West Coast. While Barry was running through the list of where all I'd be speaking, I was calculating how many weeks of drugs that grand would cover. The answer was three.

My trip to sunny California was grueling. The ADL had me speaking all over the place, giving lectures at universities, addressing a conference, meeting with various groups and officials, even headlining some fundraiser. I barely had time to enjoy the fancy hotel room they comped me. By the last night of my whirlwind tour, I was wiped out. I passed on a local ADL rep's offer to treat me to dinner. Instead, I wandered down to the hotel bar hoping to relax. I figured a couple beers would take the edge off so I could get a decent night's sleep before my flight the next morning.

A few hours later, bed was the last thing on my mind. I was trashed and shopping for a party. The businessmen at the hotel bar weren't the partying types, so I wandered outside. I heard music in the distance and followed my ears to a concert. On a outdoor stage stood George Clinton in all his funkadelic glory. I grooved out with strangers and gradually worked my way toward the front row. Somehow, I ended up talking to one of Clinton's roadies. Next thing I knew, I was partying backstage and inviting all the roadies to come back to my sweet-ass comped hotel room.

I wasn't back in Philly more than twenty-four hours when Barry Morrison called me in to his office.

"Did you have a good time on your trip?" he asked.

"It went all right."

"Are you sure everything was okay?"

"Somebody say I fucked up?"

"The feedback on your speeches was very good," Barry replied. "But I just got a copy of your hotel bill. There was more than five-hundred dollars worth of liquor missing from your minibar. Please tell me you didn't drink that much."

"Me? No." I laughed. "I had some people over one night. It wasn't just me. What do you think? I'm some kind of alcoholic?"

Barry stared silently at me for a minute, as if he wasn't sure what to say next.

"So you did use the minibar?" he asked.

"Yeah, but youse don't gotta worry about it. The ADL guy out there said my hotel was comped."

Barry shook his head. "Comped doesn't mean free. It means you don't get the bill; your hosts do. And I can't possibly ask the California office to cover $500 worth of alcohol as part of your traveling expenses. We're going to have to take it out of your honorarium."

It was my turn to stare silently for a while. Finally, Barry said, "I know you really need the money, Frank, but this is more than I can justify–"

"It's not that."

"What is it?" Barry's voice was so kind and so gentle. He really wanted the truth. Barry wasn't afraid of the truth.

I was, though. My voice broke as I confessed, "It wasn't all for the party. I think maybe I've got a problem."

V-Day

BARRY MORRISON IS THE FIRST PERSON I EVER TOLD I
thought I had a problem with alcohol. I trusted Barry like family, more than family really. I trusted him like a lawyer. Even though
he's not one, Barry treats all conversations like they carry
attorney-client privilege. So I trusted him enough to admit the
truth, just not the whole truth: drinking was the least of my
problems. My $500 minibar bill was nothing compared to what
I dropped on dope every month. My cocaine habit alone cost
me more than $200 a week. I smoked pot off and on every day.
Most days, I also downed a few Percocets. Like always, I scored
cocaine and weed from my buddies on Second and Porter, but I
always bought percs from my mom. I stopped by Tree Street
one night to stock up, and she recommended I try something new.

"What is it?" I asked, staring at the little pill she handed me.

"Oxycontin."

I'd heard the buzz about "oxys" on Second and Porter, but
I hadn't actually seen one. Oxycontin is a synthetic opium, a
super-strong pain killer doctors started prescribing in the late
1990s. Oxys were Quaaludes for the new millennium, so of
course my mom was all over them. I understood why about an
hour after I swallowed the sample she gave me. The oxy high
was like nothing else. It wasn't just that I felt no pain: I felt amazing. If it hadn't been for Nina and Matt and the ADL and the Flyers
and everything basically going well, I would've oxyed myself into
oblivion that first night.

Oxys were a prescription pad away from heroin. They were pharmaceutical-grade junk, but junk nonetheless. And I wasn't a junkie. Heroin was the one drug I promised myself I'd never try. Oxys are too close, too dangerous, I told myself the day after I took my first. A few days later, when I couldn't focus on anything but the memory of that amazing high, I conned myself into believing the cliché about how close only counts in horseshoes and hand grenades.

Not once during a meeting or before a speech did anybody ever think to ask me, "Hey, Frankie, are you high?" The people I worked with hadn't grown up around addicts. They didn't under-stand that after a certain point, addicts only seem "normal" when they're stoned. I hit that point sometime in 1997, maybe even earlier. By then, if I skipped taking something for a day or two, people got worried. I became agitated, depressed, basi-cally crazy. Sober, I acted like I was fucked up. Fucked up, I seemed okay. Only my mom and my other dealers knew I was an addict. Everybody else just thought I was an alcoholic. Even the druggies on Second and Porter gave me shit about my drink-ing. At a Halloween party, one of the guys showed up with a magic-marker swastika on his neck and beer cans shoved in all of his pockets. Everybody at the party cracked up as he weaved around the room slurring, "Trick or Treat, I'm Frankie Meeink."

I laughed, too. I got the joke; I just missed the point: when your "problem" gets bad enough to be a Halloween costume on Second and Porter, there's a pretty good chance you need help. But I wasn't ready for help. I continued to resist Kyle's campaign to get me to twelve-step meetings. And when Barry Morrison made the same recommendation, I ignored him, too. There was no way in hell I was going to walk into a room full of strangers and say, "Hi. My name is Frankie, and I'm an alcoholic," because if I did, I might have to quit drinking.

I WAS IN pretty rough shape when Hollywood and everybody else came calling. It started when a reporter from the *Philadelphia News* did a feature on how I'd turned my life around. The guy was fair about what I'd done, and also what I hadn't done, and he devoted a section of the article to Harmony Through Hockey. Working with a pro like that helped get me over the anti-media grudge I'd been nursing ever since "Philly After Midnight." So when other reporters and producers started calling, saying "We read the article about you in the *News*, and we'd like to interview you for –" I agreed.

But not everybody who called was as fair as the *Philadelphia News* reporter had been. When I appeared on Black Entertainment Television, it was "Philly After Midnight" all over again, only this time it wasn't just Philly watching me get ambushed. The BET segment aired nationwide; fortunately, it aired early on a Sunday morning, so most of America was still asleep. I was still hot about the BET experience when a young producer from *Hard Copy* started bugging me to do an interview. Even though I'd barely give her the time of day before hanging up, she wouldn't give up. She called and called. She even tried to get the ADL to convince me to do it. But I wouldn't budge. I had already vowed I was never going to let myself get set up on national television again.

If *Hard Copy* had sent a camera crew to Philly, they would've caught one hell of a dramatic scene the night I came home and found Nina on the back porch with another guy. She swore they were just outside having a smoke because she never let anybody smoke near the baby. She swore they were just friends. But something in my gut screamed, "Friends don't stand that close!" It took about a week of screaming and tears before Nina finally admitted she'd kissed that other guy. I suspected she'd done a lot more, and I wouldn't drop it. Nothing she said or did could convince me she wasn't sleeping with that other guy every time I walked out the door. "She's choosing some other dick over you," I warned myself. I warned Nina I better never see her anywhere near her little "friend" again. But it didn't matter if she saw him again; the damage had already been done. It only took one kiss to push me to the brink of insanity, and my jealousy drove Nina crazy.

Nina was seventeen and Matt still hadn't turned one when she moved back into her grandmother's house. I moved back in with my dad and Cha-Cha. At first, I tried to see Matt, but when I went to visit, Nina slammed the door in my face. My dad consoled me the only way he knew how, the same way he'd consoled himself when my mom took me away: he put me out of my misery. One afternoon I showed up at his bar and laid four-hundred dollars cash on the counter.

"You win the lottery?" he asked.

"I just cashed my paycheck. Give me one quick, then I gotta go buy some stuff for the baby and take it over to Nina."

My dad filled a glass from the tap and asked, "Is she going to let you in?"

"If she don't, I'll just leave it on the stoop."

I never made it to the stoop. I was still sitting on the same stool when my dad locked the door at closing time. It was just my dad and me and his coke dealer. I counted my money. I was doing pretty good, for me: I'd been sitting there for close to ten hours and all I'd had was maybe four or five pitchers of beer and a couple Oxycontin. I still had three hundred bucks left. I handed my dad a fiver, and he filled another pitcher. Then I slid a hundred-dollar bill toward the coke dealer, and he ran lines down the bar. When my dad kicked us out at four in the morning, I followed the dealer to an afterhours club. Within an hour, I'd snorted every dime I had left.

Needless to say, I couldn't sleep when I got back to my dad's house. I stretched out on the faded blue loveseat in the living room and tried to will my heart not to explode. I flipped on the television.

"Are you depressed?"

Of course. I just spent my kid's food money on cocaine.

"Do you ever feel like killing yourself?"

I ain't doing nobody much good alive.

"Are drugs ruining your life?"

Ding!

Without even getting up off the loveseat, I grabbed the phone. I dialed the number on the television.

"Charter-Fairmount Hospital. How may I help you?"

"I saw your ad on TV. I think I need help."

"Do you believe you have a problem with drugs or alcohol?"

"Both."

"Are you currently using and, if so, what are you using?" She sounded like she was reading off a script.

"Oxycontin." I said.

I could hear her typing my answer into a computer.

"And a lot of cocaine."

Clickety-click-click on the keyboard. She waited to see if I was going to keep going. Finally, she asked, "Is that all?"

"Does beer count?"

"Yes." Click-click-clickety-click-click and save.

She sweetly assured me I'd called the right place and that a counselor would be waiting for me to arrive; she even told me exactly which buses to take to get there.

The counselor who met me in the lobby looked a little more streetwise than the lady who answered the phone had sounded. He led me back to an office and asked me what felt like a million questions. At one point, he wanted to know, "Do you ever feel like you might hurt yourself or others?" That counselor had heard it all before; he wasn't shocked when I confessed my history of suicide attempts. He prodded me forward. "Other than yourself, who have you thought about hurting?"

"The dude who kissed my girlfriend."

The counselor looked up from the notes he was scribbling and asked, "When you've thought about hurting another person, have you ever acted on those feelings?"

I almost told the guy to go get a fresh notebook, but I wasn't

sure what kind of deal Charter-Fairmount had with the cops. I
had a bad fucking history mixing psychiatry with law enforcement. I promised the counselor I wasn't planning to do anything
to the dude who'd kissed Nina, but I wasn't willing to make the
same promise about myself. He gave me a room assignment in
Charter's inpatient rehab center.

I smoked my first cigarette in rehab. That was the one vice
I'd managed to avoid, but when I lost all the others, I needed
something. So long as there are addicts and alcoholics trying to
get clean and sober, Marlboro will never go out of business.
Neither will Folgers.

Rehab made me miss prison. When I wasn't one-on-one
with the counselor or chainsmoking my way through mandatory
twelve-step meetings, I spent most of my time playing Spades
with some older black dudes. One day, we were throwing cards
and swapping "my life sucks worse than your life" stories when
a Puerto Rican junkie sitting on a nearby couch said, "You got
some real pain." Then he leaned close so the others couldn't
hear and whispered, "Heroin will make it all go away." He fell
back onto the couch and pretended to nod out. The other card
players recognized what he was doing and cracked up laughing.
I didn't laugh; I couldn't stop staring at the smile that dude had
on his face just from remembering his last shot of junk.

After thirty days in the inpatient rehab unit, Charter released
me to a halfway house in Kensington. The location surprised
me. The large, dilapidated house was only a few blocks off the Badlands, Philly's heroin district. I guess that made it convenient
for junkies wanting to relapse. I'm not sure what I was expecting
to find at the halfway house, only that it sure as shit wasn't Muffin
Ass McCarthy. He'd disappeared from Second and Porter a year
earlier. A few of the guys accused him of running off with a
bunch of money, but the rest of us thought he'd wandered off and
died. As it turned out, he'd snuck away to rehab and worked his
way up to being the resident-supervisor of a halfway house in
North Philly. Muffin Ass hooked me up with one of the best

rooms in the place, which pissed off other residents. They gave me the cold shoulder for a couple weeks until curiosity got the best of them. They had to talk to me to get the scoop on their favorite soap opera: "Frankie and the Baby Mamas."

Nina and Matt came to visit me often. She didn't actually come out and say she wanted to get back together, but she gave me hope just by showing up. Of course, every other guy in the halfway house drooled all over himself every time Nina strutted through the front door. Then one day, to my complete shock, in walked Maria carrying Jake. She hadn't even known I was getting clean when she called my dad looking for me; she'd just decided Jake should meet his father. My dad told Maria where she could find me. The halfway house crew flipped out when the second gorgeous Italian girl blew through the front door carrying one of my sons. I would've told the guys about my third kid with a hot Italian mom out in Illinois, but it would've seemed like bragging. Instead, I begged them to help keep Nina and Maria from finding out about each other. The situation was a logistical nightmare. I never knew when either girl would show up, and I couldn't tell either what was going on. I had no intention of getting back with Maria, but I wanted to see Jake. I knew Maria would take Jake away again if she knew Nina was still in the picture. And I was afraid if Nina found out about Maria visiting, she might get pissed and give up on me for good. Things were going too good between me and Nina to chance it. Every time she visited, I got my hopes up that would be the day she'd ask me to get back together. So did the other residents. They'd huddle up on the other end of the community room, pretend they weren't eavesdropping, and hang on her every word.

None of us, not the boys, sure as hell not me, saw the big plot twist coming: while we were all trying to predict Nina's next move, Maria fell for Muffin Ass. Next thing I knew, he asked for permission to adopt Jake. If it'd been on television, that episode of "Frankie and the Baby Mamas" would've won a Daytime Emmy. I wished Muffin Ass all the luck in the world with

Maria, figuring he'd need it, and told him I'd sign Jake over to him if him and Maria made it work. I didn't want to give Jake up, but I didn't want Jake not to have a dad. Muffin Ass seemed like a good solution.

FOR SEVERAL MONTHS, I stayed clean and sober on the marijuana maintenance plan. I didn't drink or do any drug that involved snorting or swallowing. I just smoked Marlboro Lights and pot like the other guys recovering at the halfway house. We were all absolutely convinced pot didn't count because pot's not a real drug like cocaine or Oxycontin or heroin. Of course, we were stoned when we came up with that theory.

I was still living in the halfway house when Angelica Vitale, the lady producer from *Hard Copy*, called the ADL again. She explained she wanted to interview me because there was a new movie coming out that sounded a lot like my life. I agreed to the interview after I read the plot summary she sent over. It creeped me out. I'd done an informal interview with a movie producer a year earlier, but nothing had come of it. The producer had heard about a speech I gave in LA and wanted to ask me some questions, pretty basic stuff. That's all there was to it. Then theatres started showing previews for *American History X*. The movie producer who interviewed me isn't listed anywhere in the credits of that movie. I don't think she stole my story. In fact, around the same time as Ms. Vitale called me, the movie producer called again, kind of pissed off. She asked me why I'd sold my story to somebody else. I don't think she believed me when I said I hadn't.

American History X isn't my story. It's every skinhead's story to some extent. And that's why Ms. Vitale wanted to interview me; *Hard Copy* wanted to see if the movie really stacked up against the reality of a guy like me. Still leery after my media disasters, I agreed to talk to her on the condition that she had to mention Harmony Through Hockey in the segment.

Hard Copy aired their story about me, including a really

nice spotlight on Harmony Through Hockey, the same day *American History X* debuted. Angelica Vitale scored tickets so I could see the movie the first night it played in Philly. Nobody at the premier knew who I was, which was a relief because I didn't know how I was going to react. Seeing the movie was surreal to say the least. I sat in the darkness watching pieces of my life unfold before my eyes. But it wasn't me; it was the actor Ed Norton. And it was every other kid who ever got sucked up into the white supremacy movement.

I became a minor celebrity after the movie came out and *Hard Copy* aired their interview with me. The ADL's phones rang off the hook with requests for me to speak. I was so in demand I practically needed an assistant to keep track of whether I was coming or going. I got an agent instead. Admire Entertainment represents professional speakers. I'd never thought of myself as a professional speaker. At best, I was a professional used furniture mover who sometimes told stories about his crazy life into a microphone. But Admire didn't see it that way: they'd heard about my life, and they'd sent one of their agents to watch me speak. They asked what I was getting paid for my lectures.

"Two-hundred dollars a day," I bragged.

"We can get you two-thousand dollars a speech."

I damn near fainted, but I had sense enough not to agree to anything over the phone. I couldn't afford a lawyer, so my friend Mike Boni came to my rescue. He reviewed the contracts and even had a teleconference with one of the agents to go over some details. When he was sure everything was legit, he said, "Frank, this is your big break. You've earned it. Take it."

So I did. Admire booked three or four engagements for me every month, mostly at colleges, all over the nation. The only limit I put on speaking was it couldn't interfere with Harmony Through Hockey. I still suited up for practice with the kids almost every day during the season. But I no longer saw the same kids every day; the program got so big we were running it at several different rinks. Nearly eighty kids were involved. Things were going great for me professionally. I was a professional. I had agents. I worked with the Flyers. I was racking up frequent-flyer miles. I was raking it in.

And I had not one clue in hell what to do with it. Half the people I'd grown up around didn't have checking accounts, so what the hell did I know about investment portfolios? I figured I was a financial wizard so long as I was less than two months behind on my rent at the halfway house. The rest of the money just slipped through my fingers. I spent some on my kids, gave some to their mothers, even used some to travel to Illinois to see Riley a few times. But, mostly, I partied it away.

I stopped going to twelve-step meetings after the third time in a week I said, "Hi. My name is Frank and I'm an alcoholic. It's been … " I'd look down at my fancy new watch, "six hours since my last drink." The first couple nights, the recovery crowd tried to talk me back up onto the wagon. The third night, an older guy who'd been sober something like twenty years said, "You can't party like that and say you're in recovery."

I proved him wrong. I stormed out of the meeting, found the nearest bar, got totally shit-faced, and declared to the drunk sitting next to me, "I'm in recovery."

He hoisted his glass. "Me, too!"

I felt sick the next morning, not just from the hangover. I promised myself I'd get back on the right path. And I did. Every time. I'd stay clean for a couple of weeks, then I'd go on some insane bender. I'd down a month's worth of beer, oxy, acid, weed, anything and everything I could afford and survive, into one gigantic high from hell. Then I'd wake up a few days later, sober up enough to realize what I'd done, and vow to get right back on the path to recovery.

I always cleaned up before a major speech or a big interview. Angelica Vitale had restored my faith in the media, and her *Hard Copy* story had opened a lot of doors for me. I appeared in a VH1 documentary about kids and hate groups. MTV talked to me for their "Stop the Violence" campaign. Both A&E and the

Discovery Channel used clips of me in specials about skinheads. When some movement lowlifes dragged James Byrd, Jr., to his death in Texas, *The Today Show* brought me to New York so Katie Couric could interview me.

Not long after that, I returned to New York for an ADL speaking gig. Even after I signed with Admire Entertainment, I still did a lot of work for the ADL. They couldn't pay the kind of fees my agent got me for speaking at universities, but the ADL could do something even better: they could get me in front of the audiences that most needed to hear my story, the audiences I felt most comfortable talking to. One of those audiences was a bunch of inmates in a juvenile detention center in New York City. Back in my hotel room after the speech, I stared lustfully at the minibar. I couldn't do that to Barry again. I had to get out of there. So I dialed Angelica Vitale's number. She sounded thrilled to hear from me and invited me to join her and her boyfriend for dinner.

"I don't want to horn in," I said.

"You'd be helping me out," Angelica replied. "One of my good friends from high school is in town. We're picking her up in about an hour. Come with us. That way she won't feel like the third wheel. Besides, you'll like Valerie. She's really nice."

I was nervous that "really nice" might be code for "butt ugly," but I didn't have anything better to do, so I agreed. Angelica almost ran me over when she screeched a TV production van up onto the curb in front of my hotel. She gave me a hug around the neck through the driver's side window and introduced me to her boyfriend, another behind-the-scenes television type, sitting in the front seat. He didn't look too thrilled to be stuck with my South Philly ass for the night. Angelica told me to climb in the back.

When I popped the door open, the most gorgeous woman I'd ever seen in person in my entire fucking life smiled at me.

"I'm Valerie Doyle." Her long blond hair tumbled down the front of her cashmere sweater.

My mouth dropped open, but no words came out.

"You must be Frank," Valerie saved me. "Angelica's told me about you."

Angelica had told Valerie everything she knew about me, like how I'd been a skinhead and how I'd been in prison and even how I had a baby. There were just a few little details Angelica didn't know, like that I had *three* babies, that I was still seeing one of their moms as often as she'd let me, and that my home address was a halfway house.

The whole ride to the restaurant I just stared at Valerie Doyle because I figured it would be my only chance to burn her into my memory. I fully expected her to come down with a migraine or maybe a stroke or whatever she had to do to ditch me before we got seated at a table. A chick like Valerie Doyle didn't need to know all the nasty details of my life to know she ought to run. Valerie and Angelica and her boyfriend looked like they belonged at the best table in the best restaurant in Manhattan. I looked like I belonged in the alley behind the restaurant dumpster-diving for their leftovers.

Valerie didn't ditch me at the restaurant or at the club we went to after dinner. She spent the whole evening tucked up right next to me, leaning in close to whisper little comments in my ear, lightly touching my arm when she laughed at my jokes. I wasn't even tempted to take a drink that night; no way I was going to risk blacking out on this hotter than hell date. And it kept getting steamier as the evening wore on. On the ride back, Valerie and I were shooting each other looks that could've melted concrete.

We slept in the same bed that night. We kissed, but that was all. She fell asleep in my arms. I stayed awake as long as I could just so I could watch her breathing.

I'd gotten her story over dinner. Valerie had grown up in a quiet little town in upstate New York. Her parents were rich, still together, and totally devoted to their kids. They'd given Valerie every advantage and she'd put them all to good use. Since earning her bachelor's degree, she'd been climbing the corporate ladder. When she wasn't hobnobbing around Manhattan with her pal Angelica, Valerie was a systems analyst for a big company in Washington, DC.

Laying in that bed watching her sleep, I thought, "This woman is the major fucking leagues. What in the hell is she thinking hanging out with a dude like me? Hell, on my best day, I'd be lucky to make the Special Olympics. Drink in the memory, Frankie, because this lady's going to come to in the morning and kick your sorry ass back to South Philly." But she didn't. We spent the whole next day together bumming around New York. I bought a disposable camera and asked complete strangers to take pictures of us together because I knew there was no way the dudes at the halfway house were going to believe how gorgeous Valerie was unless I brought proof.

When the time came for me to catch my train back to Philly, Valerie kissed me so passionately that the thought of walking away from her made me feel like I was dying. I wanted to beg her to drop everything in her life and run away with me to anywhere, nowhere, so long as we could be together forever. But I couldn't find the words to say what I felt. I couldn't find any words at all, especially not "goodbye." I just held her in my arms and prayed some miracle would happen to keep her in my life.

"Promise me you'll call if you ever come to DC," she said.

I was afraid to believe it was really happening.

"You really want to see me again?"

"Of course! Why?"

"I'm speaking in DC next weekend."

The Rock

I LEFT VALERIE IN NEW YORK ON FRIDAY AFTERNOON, less than twenty-four hours after meeting her, thinking I'd never survive seven days waiting to see her again. She called Sunday morning and said she couldn't wait that long either. She'd already checked the train schedules. If she caught a train from New York to Philly, we could have a few hours together before she had to catch another train back to DC. I met her at the station in Center City. She took my hand and I led her onto the streets of my hometown.

"Where should we go?" she asked.

Good question. Where in the hell could I take this amazing woman without scaring her away? The halfway house? Tree Street? Second and Porter? I decided South Street was my best bet. Of course, we weren't there ten minutes when we ran right the fuck into Nina pushing Matt in a stroller. For the record, there's no good way to introduce the twenty-eight year old systems analyst you've just fallen in love with to the seventeen year old mother of one of the two kids you haven't told her about yet. Amazingly, even that didn't scare Valerie off. But it pissed Nina off royally. The girl who'd been refusing to get back together with me for months, the girl who broke up with me in the first place because I was too jealous, went freaking berserk once she saw the competition. I did my damnedest not to rub Valerie in Nina's face, but I couldn't hide my feelings. I was fucking stupid in love. Every thought of Valerie Doyle that passed through my mind left me forty I Q points lower than usual and I didn't have forty points to spare. I walked around Philly in a daze, grinning for no good reason, saying things that made no sense. I'm sure people thought I'd relapsed again.

Valerie and I talked on the phone for hours every night that first week. Then I went to DC, and it was all over after that for both of us. We vowed to spend every weekend together. The days between visits were torture. We survived as best we could on phone calls and e-mails. Valerie's e-mails read like high-class romance novels; mine read like discount porn. Nina busted into my account and read the whole collection as evidence that some bitch was trying to steal her man. She sent Valerie an e-mail to that effect, complete with South Street style teenaged punk-diva threats.

According to Nina, Valerie's reply was the most polite and professional ass-chewing Nina ever got. That's when my former girlfriend realized something about my new girlfriend that I'd known all along: Valerie wasn't a girl; she was a woman. An amazing woman who, after receiving that e-mail from Nina, told me no matter how much she loved me, she wouldn't keep seeing me if it would hurt any of my children or their mothers. An amazing woman who, after putting Nina in her place for sending that first nasty e-mail, reached out to Nina with an offer of friendship and a promise both she and Matt would always be part of the family Valerie and I would build.

Valerie wanted to make the same promise to Maria, but she didn't get the chance. Maria had replaced me with Muffin Ass and wanted nothing more to do with me. And she sure as hell didn't want to talk to my new girlfriend. Jessica did, though. A few months after I met Valerie, Jessica and Riley made their first trip to Philadelphia. With Valerie's blessing, I stayed with them on Tree Street to keep an eye on things while my mom got to know her granddaughter. Riley was too young to really notice her surroundings. Jessica noticed, though. She pulled me aside the first night and asked me why there were hundreds of tiny holes in the carpet in front of the living room couch. Nina had asked me the same question after her first visit to Tree Street. So had Valerie.

Three times, I had to explain that serious Oxycontin addicts nod off just like heroin addicts do. All three times my explanation was met with confused stares. So I used my body to demonstrate exactly how John situated himself on the couch every night after he swallowed his last oxy of the day, how his hand would go limp, his lit cigarette would drop, his head would fall forward onto his chest, his body would roll forward onto the floor, and his dead weight would snuff out the smoldering cigarette, every fucking night, like clockwork, before it could burn more than a tiny hole in the rug.

Except for special occasions like Jessica and Riley's visit, I avoided Tree Street. No matter how many times I told my mom I was trying to stay clean, every time I stopped by, she offered to sell me whatever she happened to have. I didn't trust myself to say "no" alone with my mom and my demons, so I rarely visited and never by myself.

I WAS STILL staying clean and sober, except for pot, once the second season of Harmony Through Hockey ended in May. I packed up my room at the halfway house and moved in with Valerie in DC for the summer. Three months later, Valerie followed me back to Philly. She scored a cushy consulting job in Center City, and I coached the hockey program and gave speeches. We rented what Valerie called a "shabby chic" rowhouse in a secluded section of South Philly. Valerie decorated the interior to look like something out of a magazine. I fixed up a koi pond a previous tenant had installed then abandoned in the postage-stamp backyard.

Then I learned an important parenting lesson: it's hard to keep toddlers out of koi ponds. Nina and Matt spent tons of time at our place, and Matt developed a dangerous fascination with the fish. I spent entire afternoons fishing him out of the pond.

In the meantime, Nina and Valerie gabbed away in the kitchen like sisters, making plans for dinner that night or for Jessica and Riley's next visit. Just as Valerie had promised, we'd all become a family. Except for Maria not letting me see Jake, my life was more perfect than I'd imagined it could be. I was in love with Valerie, involved in Matt and Riley's lives, friends with both Nina and Jessica, making my name as a professional speaker and being paid to play hockey. I was living the dream. That's when my life fell to shit.

It started with Percocets. I wasn't drinking anymore, but I still always wanted to go out with Valerie and our friends, who all drank socially. I knew I couldn't, but I wanted to feel something, too. So one afternoon I stopped by Tree Street and bought ten percs off my mom. That evening, while Valerie got dressed to go out, I took one. Valerie didn't know I'd taken a Percocet; she also didn't know nine more were hiding in my sock drawer. I swallowed the second one the next Friday, the third and fourth, the Friday after that. Two more for Saturday night. The rest on Sunday, for the football game, since we were having people over. Monday, I visited my mom again.

Valerie and I had been together for one amazing year, my most sober year since I'd snuck my first sip of beer at age nine. Valerie had only ever seen me smoke pot, and she had marveled at how little effect it seemed to have on me. To Valerie, "Frankie the Addict" was just a crazy character from stories of my wild past, like "Frankie the Nazi." Valerie had never actually met the belligerent, violent drunk so many people feared. She'd never seen me raise a single beer to my lips. She'd never seen me snort hundreds of dollars of cocaine up my nose in a night. Nothing in our first year together, nothing in her life, prepared my sweet Valerie to look for the signs that scream, "Next Exit: Rock Bottom."

I was up to about a dozen Percocets a day by the time Valerie realized something wasn't right. I went to bed early, slept late, took naps every chance I got. I didn't eat as much as usual. I didn't talk as much. The first time Valerie mentioned the changes in my behavior, she asked if I was coming down with something. I said, "I don't know, maybe." A few days later, she asked if I was depressed. Again, I said "I don't know, maybe." It took several weeks before it dawned on her to ask me if I was using. When she finally did, I told the truth, sort of. I admitted I occasionally took one Percocet, if I was hurting.

"Why are you hurting, baby?" she asked.

"It happened in hockey," I said, rubbing an imaginary injury on my shoulder. "I pulled something in practice."

"Should you see a doctor?"

"I'll be fine." Who needs a doctor when there's a pharmacist in the family?

One Monday morning, my mom was out of percs. But she had a fresh supply of Oxycontin. I'd been thinking about that oxy high every goddamn day since rehab. And every day I'd told myself no. But that day I compromised: Okay, one. Just one, since she's out of percs. One won't hurt. Nothing hurts when you're on Oxycontin.

After that, I took one 80 milligram oxy every morning. "It's just one," I'd tell myself. One oxy seemed like so much less than the fistful of percs I'd been swallowing. All I took was one pill in the morning, like a multivitamin. One little 80 mg oxy. It was just one. Then there was the one I needed to take in the afternoon to get me through the evening. Then just one more after that for a nightcap. Some weekends if I was certain Valerie wasn't going to be around, for an extra special treat I'd score liquid Oxycontin. I'd drizzle it over my favorite snack food. I've always loved peanut butter TastyKakes; I loved them even more when they carried me into the land of nod.

I never let Valerie see me that whacked out, though. She only saw me on my maintenance plan, about 240 milligrams per day, perfectly timed so I never felt any pain but never nodded out. I didn't act stoned; I didn't act depressed anymore either, like I had on percs. I thought I had all my tracks covered: nothing about my behavior could give Valerie any reason to suspect I was using. Except, of course, for the withdrawals from our joint bank account. Being me, I didn't even know which bank we used: I just signed all my checks over to Valerie – if I needed cash, I used the ATM card she gave me. Miss Corporate America paid a little more attention. She analyzed the fuck out of those monthly bank statements, and after a couple months she saw the pattern: $30 three times a day. Or $90 once a day. Or $270 every third day. It only took her one visit to Tree Street to do the market analysis: 80 milligram oxys went for $35 on the street then, unless you got the family discount of thirty bucks a pop.

I did my second rehab stint at Eagleville. The oxys had done a number on me. Over just a few months, I'd become so physically dependent on them that "just say no" wasn't an option anymore. The Eagleville doc tried to explain why Oxycontin is actually harder to come off than heroin, but I couldn't follow what he was saying. It had been damn near twelve hours since my last dose. The sickness was overwhelming. The pain was unbearable, like nothing I'd experienced. I was praying for death, but all I got was methadone. The doctors spent the first week weaning me off Oxycontin onto high-dose methadone, then three weeks walking me off methadone back to reality. After thirty days, they stamped me "clean" and sent me home.

I didn't make it twelve hours.

Addicts are a lot like serial killers. Serial killers only get to be *serial* killers because they don't get nabbed for their first murder. It's the same way with addicts. You've got to be damn good at doing drugs – and hiding that you're doing drugs – to become a full-blown addict.

Within hours of my release, I snuck away from the home I shared with Valerie and beelined to the rowhouse on Tree Street. I'd spent the entire thirty-day stint in rehab figuring out how to buy oxys again without Valerie catching me. Our joint bank account was off limits. So were my paychecks. I knew from then on I was going to have to find my cash elsewhere, somewhere no one would notice it missing. So I went to Tree Street, waited for my mom to turn her head, stole ninety bucks from the drug till she kept next to her recliner, then bought three oxys off her with her own money. She was so strung out I probably could've taken more. But I only took what I needed: $90 a day.

Valerie was suspicious, but without the bank statements for confirmation, she wasn't completely sure if I was using again. And she wasn't the type of person who'd accuse someone of something that serious without absolute proof. Like most people, she still believed – or maybe she wanted to believe – that people act crazy when they're on drugs like Oxycontin. People do; addicts don't. Addicts act normal when they're using and out of their minds when they aren't. So long as I never let myself go more than eight and a half, nine hours max between pills, I never jonesed myself into hysteria. And so long as I held steady at 80 milligrams, I never got so high that I nodded out. I cruised at 80 every eight hours, and no one was the wiser, except my mom.

When Nina, Matt, Valerie and I showed up at the Bertone Christmas gathering, my dad met us at the door in a Santa suit. Matt was too little to realize Santa was his grandfather. Valerie was too new to the family to know quite what she was supposed to do when Santa sang, "Ho, Ho, Ho" in her ear and shoved a half dead poinsettia at her.

"Santa, you didn't have to give me anything," she said.

"It's not from me," Santa replied, right on cue.

I walked over to Valerie, reached into the base of the plant, pulled out the diamond engagement ring Santa had hidden for me, and dropped to my knee.

"Will you marry me?"

"Yes!" Valerie answered, bursting into tears.

Valerie cried a lot during our engagement. I wish to God I could say they were all tears of joy.

JUST A FEW weeks after I popped the question, I was once again scheduled to speak in San Diego, the scene of my notorious mini-bar raid. I was running late to leave for my flight, so I frantically stuffed clothes into a duffel bag. I was almost out the door when I remembered I didn't pack any socks. My duffel bag was already bursting at the seams, so I reached for a briefcase the ADL had given me. They'd had it made special, with the Harmony Through Hockey emblem printed on it. It touched me they did that, but I rarely carried it. I'm not a briefcase guy. But rushing to catch my plane, I had to find something to stuff a week's worth of socks in; it was the first bag I saw that wouldn't need to be unpacked from my last trip. I grabbed the briefcase off the top shelf of my closet, blew most of the dust off it, opened it just wide enough to cram in the socks, and flew out the door.

I stood in line forever at the ticket counter at Philadelhia International. I checked my suitcase. I went outside for one last smoke. Then I did what all airline passengers do as their departure time looms: I emptied my pockets into a little plastic tub, laid my carry-on briefcase on the conveyor belt, and walked through the metal detector. The airport cops nabbed me on the other side.

I know this seems impossible, but it's true: I forgot I had a gun stashed in that briefcase. I guess it was par for the course. After all, I was the same genius who left the videotape of an aggravated kidnapping in the freaking camcorder. The airport cops hauled me to the Philadelphia Police substation inside the terminal.

"I swear I just forgot it was in there," I said to the officer.

"Don't worry," he replied. "It happens more often than you'd think. Obviously, we can't let you board a plane with it, but it shouldn't take too long to clear up. You live with somebody?"

"My fiancée. Why?"

"Call her," the officer said. He slid a phone across the table to me. "Have her bring down the registration papers and you can be on your way. We'll hold the gun until you get back."

I didn't pick up the phone.

"You have papers for this gun, don't you?"

"No."

He paused. "Well, so long as you're not a convicted felon—"

"I am."

"You're in a lot of trouble."

The officer left me alone in the interrogation room for a while. I couldn't fucking believe it. How in the hell was I going to explain this to Valerie? I was on the verge of tears when a huge black detective walked into the room. He shut the door behind him and laid the .380 on the table.

"What's up with the gun, Meeink?"

I spilled my guts at hyperspeed. "I'm supposed to be giving a speech in San Diego. I was running late and needed another bag and I just forgot it was in there. And I know I ain't supposed to have a gun, but I live in South Philly, you know what I mean? And some people don't like me for what I do now. And … " I paused for the first time and gulped for air. Then I concluded, "I guess I ain't going to be giving my speech."

"Guess not," the detective said. He stared at me for a really long time. "I know who you are."

My heart fucking stopped. Did he know who I'd been or who I'd become?

"And I know what you do." He stared into my eyes like he was trying to see my soul. "Keep doing what you do, Meeink."

If it weren't for that detective, things could have gone a lot worse for me that day. He made it as easy for me as possible. I was still in trouble, though: convicted felons aren't allowed to be in possession of firearms, especially hot firearms without papers. The cops transferred me to a holding tank in West Philly where I used my one call to reach Earbow Petanzi.

Even though you can't bail yourself out, the cops let you keep your cash in holding, in part so you can hire the services of the shyster street lawyers who hawk themselves down the row every morning. One who reminded me of George Jefferson strutted toward my cell.

"What're you in for?" he asked me. I was hard to miss. I was a twenty-four year old white guy in business clothes surrounded by elderly black winos and teenaged black gangbangers.

"Gun at the airport. No numbers. And I'm an ex-con."

"Ooh," he said. "You need a lawyer."

No shit. I could not risk going before a judge with nobody on my side.

"How much?" I asked.

"Two-hundred. No refunds."

I forked over all the cash I had in my pocket.

"No refunds," he reminded me.

A couple hours later, the guards escorted me and several of my cellies to a small room connected by closed-circuit television to a courtroom in another part of the city. I was shackled to a gangster, standing next to my Cracker Jack box attorney, when a video monitor popped on and revealed the lineup in the real courtroom. Earbow had been busy. He sat next to Valerie and Barry Morrison, one row back from the defense table, where Mike Boni was in a huddle with some guy I didn't recognize.

My $200-non-refundable lawyer recognized him, though.

"Is the guy on the right on your case?" he asked.

"I guess, if he's sitting with Mike. Why? Who is he?"

"That guy's famous. He used to be a federal prosecutor." Without saying another word, the small-time lawyer handed me my $200 non-refundable and walked away. The state's prosecutor recommended the judge set my bail at half a million dollars on the grounds that I had an extensive criminal record, a history of skipping parole, one escape from an institution under my belt, and a prepaid plane ticket literally in my back pocket. Then my lawyer, the former federal prosecutor, spoke. I was released about two hours later on a $200 bond. A few weeks later, the charges were dropped.

The closest I'd been to clean since leaving rehab was the

sixteen or so hours I spent in that West Philly holding tank. I was a fucking wreck by the time Valerie took me home. She thought it was stress from my ordeal. It had been a hell of an ordeal, only this time, nobody had handed me any methadone to help me cope. I wasn't home five minutes before I swallowed a double-dose of Oxycontin to make up for lost time.

My three-pill-a-day habit doubled overnight. I wasn't convinced I could sneak $180 out of my mom's till every day without getting busted, so I called my old buddy Keith and asked if he could throw me some hours at his antique shop. He helped me out, like always, for months, supplementing my speaker fees, not understanding why I was so hard up for cash. I was riding the train back from his store in Jersey one afternoon with cash in my pocket, when I made a life-altering decision: it is stupid to spend $180 a day on Oxycontin. I vowed at that very moment never to waste money like that again. So instead of getting off the train at my usual stop, I stayed on. I stayed on that fucking train. All the way to the Badlands. Telling myself the whole fucking way, "It'll be okay so long as I only sniff it. If I only sniff it, I ain't going to be a junkie. I ain't ever going to shoot it up. I'm just gonna sniff a little, to save money." In 2001, a bag of heroin only cost ten bucks in the Badlands. I slipped a dealer two fives and he handed me the key to heaven. Heroin was everything I'd ever heard it would be and more. I bought two more bags before I even climbed back on the train.

For nearly a month, I held out on two bags a day, one in the morning and one after work. Then I gave in and jumped to two bags twice a day. Then three. But I only ever sniffed, so I wasn't a real junkie. Any worries I had about Valerie busting me dissolved by summer. With the wedding just a few months away, guest lists and flower arrangements consumed her attention. I spent a little more time in the Badlands each day, making buys and chatting with my new best friend, my dealer. One morning, I only had a twenty and some change on me. I didn't want to have to make a second trip back for my afternoon bags. I picked my way around the busted appliances, toppled trash cans, and junkies that litter the sidewalks of the Badlands. I found my dealer.

"Hey, dude, will you front me, just this once?" I asked.

He clarified his policy: "No fronts. Not for nobody."

I pouted like a four-year-old.

"You don't need a front," he said. "All you need is a rig."

A needle.

A lifetime of broken promises echoed through my mind. I'll never smoke pot. I'll never snort cocaine. I'll never take oxys. I'll never do heroin.

"I'll never shoot heroin" was the only promise I had left.

"Twice the ride for half the price," my dealer said. "Go buy a rig, then come back over and I'll show you how to do it."

Every kind of dealer imaginable works the Badlands, including needle dealers. I spent a buck's worth of change on a clean rig. Then I handed a twenty to my dealer. He handed me two bags of heroin and told me to cool my heels while he finished up with another customer. But there's always another customer in the Badlands. After about ten minutes, my dealer said, "Sorry, dude, I ain't got time to help you right now." He kicked me back two dollars and pointed to a homeless junkie begging nearby. "He'll do it for you for two bucks."

I winced at the thought of the filthy bum touching my clean rig.

"Don't worry, he's a pro. He could hit your veins from across the street."

The beggar led me up into an abandoned train trestle near Kensington Avenue, through a maze of other junkies nodding out amid piles of trash and puddles of rainwater laced with urine. He found us a spot and kicked it clear of dirty needles.

"Sit down," he said.

I propped myself against the filthy metal wall. He knelt beside me. From the bowels of his tattered coat, he produced a pop bottle lid, a tiny tripod holder, and a book of matches. He demonstrated how to transform the pieces into a stove. Then he reached into his coat again and pulled out a small vial. He emptied one bag of heroin into the lid, pulled an exact measure of water up into my clean syringe from the vial, injected the water into the heroin, and lit a match. While my dose cooked down, he dug through his pockets again until he located a cigarette butt. He ripped off a little piece of the filter and floated it in my hit. He inserted the needle into the filter and pulled the cooked heroin up through it into the syringe. Then he gave me a little lecture about the importance of always checking the end of the needle for fibers so I wouldn't get "cotton fever."

While he talked, I snuck glances at the other lost souls of the Badlands. Not ten feet away from us, a man who looked like a corpse unzipped his pants and plunged a needle into his penis. The horror registered on my face. My homeless helper followed my eyes to the man, now slumped against the wall, a blissful look on his face, the needle hanging limply from his dick. "Only veins he's got left," the beggar said. He flicked his index finger hard against the pulsing vein in my right arm. "You got nothing to worry about. You got great veins."

I was still staring at the corpse man, thinking, "At least I ain't that bad," when I felt the needle prick my skin. Three seconds later, I gladly would've shoved a three-foot needle up my dick, through both balls, and all the way north until it came out my eye if that's what it took to stay feeling the way I felt when that heroin rocketed through my body. Mainlined directly into a vein, heroin is fucking nirvana. It's a feeling you can't possibly imagine until you're inside it. Unfortunately, it's a feeling you can't ever forget once you've been there.

Morning and night, every day for two weeks, I paid that same homeless dude two bucks a pop to shoot me up. I was terrified I'd overdose myself if I tried going solo. I didn't want to end up like my cousin Nick, but one day I couldn't find my helper, so I risked it. I tried to remember everything he'd taught me and to be safe, I only shot half a bag. The next day I shot a whole bag without assistance. When I didn't die, I quit worrying about killing myself.

I'd been hitting myself steady for about three weeks when Valerie scheduled a three-day binge of wedding preparations. Her schedule barely left me time to pee, let alone to hop a train to the Badlands, buy, cook, shoot up, nod out, and get back home without her noticing. By Saturday afternoon, I was pushing twenty-four hours since my last hit. My head throbbed like I'd just been whacked with a baseball bat. My bones ached like I'd just been thrown down a flight of stairs. My whole body shivered uncontrollably. I did my best to mop the sweat off my face before it dripped down onto the seating chart Valerie had me making. But when I felt the vomit cresting the back of my tongue, I had to abandon my post.

"What's wrong?" Valerie asked as I dashed past her into the bathroom.

"Flu."

Valerie wasn't stupid. She was faithful, more to God than to me. He'd let her see something in me I couldn't see through the haze: the piece of who I could be that made me worth loving. But her faith in who I could be blinded her to who I still was. She nursed me through the night. Sunday afternoon, I convinced her I was well enough to run an errand. I ran to the first dealer I could find. Twenty bucks later, my "flu" was gone.

The entire time I was using, I attended twelve-step meetings religiously, both the kind for alcoholics and the kind for narcotic addicts. Sometimes I hit more than one meeting a day. I knew I needed to go, because I knew I was losing it. I was consciously aware that I was hovering about a millimeter above rock bottom. I was way past the point of denying I had a problem; I knew I had a problem, but nobody else in my life knew. Even my mom thought I'd finally cleaned myself up because I'd stopped buying pills. Nobody knew the truth except me and the other junkies in the Badlands. But even though I knew I was in trouble, I couldn't fucking stop myself. I couldn't imagine surviving weeks of the pain I'd endured the one day I hadn't shot up. I couldn't bear the thought of living the rest of my life knowing heaven was one syringe away. I had no intention to stop using, no desire to stop, yet I wouldn't let myself stop going to twelve step meetings. "Keep coming back. It works," the recovering alcoholics and addicts promised in unison at the end of each session. I did; it didn't.

One afternoon, I curled up in bed and prepared to shoot up. I had the timing down. I knew exactly when I had to start my ritual so I'd be past the nod and back to "normal" by the time Valerie got home from work. I assembled my makeshift stove on the nightstand, carefully opened three precious bags of heroin, and reached into my backpack for a needle. I didn't have one. I didn't have time to run to the Badlands before Valerie was due home. I had no choice but to settle for sniffing. I grabbed the top book off the stack on the nightstand. It happened to be my copy of *The Big Book*. I ran a line of heroin down the cover and sniffed myself as close to heaven as I could get through my nose. But I was past the point where sniffing could take away my pain. And the guilt I felt at that moment was as painful as a kick in the groin. I was laying in the bed I shared with the most amazing woman in the world, staring at the remnants of the trail of heroin I'd just sniffed off the Bible of recovery. In my daze, I noticed the telephone number scribbled on the book's cover. It was the number of a recovering heroin addict who'd befriended me at the Eagleville rehab center. He'd said, "If you ever need to talk, just call." So I did. I told him I finally wanted to get clean for real. Then I explained my predicament: I needed to get clean without my fiancée or anybody else finding out I hadn't been clean for the past year.

"That won't work," he said.

"I can make it work."

"You're already lying to yourself. If you keep lying, you'll keep using. And if you keep using, you'll keep lying. You won't get clean until you get honest."

"But what if … ?"

"You ain't got no what-ifs left. If you're serious about getting clean, you gotta get honest with yourself. And you've got to tell your fiancée. When are you supposed to get married?"

"Next month."

"Jesus! She's walking down the aisle next month and she doesn't know the guy waiting at the altar is a junkie?"

It sounded so much worse when he said it.

He was still trying to convince me when I heard Valerie's key in the front door.

Through the phone, my twelve-step buddy coached me, "You've got to do it. You've got to tell her now."

I hung up just as Valerie walked into our bedroom.

"Sit down," I said, tears streaming down my cheeks. "I've got to tell you something."

She looked so frightened while I searched for the courage to say, "I've been shooting heroin."

I'd never seen someone cry as hard as my sweet Valerie cried that afternoon. I wanted to wrap her in my arms and promise her it would all be okay, but I was afraid to touch her, afraid even to move. The betrayal was so deep, her wounds so raw, I knew anything I did or said would only hurt her more.

When she finally spoke, she barked like a drill sergeant: "Pack your stuff!"

"Please don't kick me–"

"Don't speak!" she warned. "You are going to pack your stuff and I'm taking you back to Eagleville. You're going to do exactly what the doctors tell you to do. Then you are going to go to AA and NA and every other fucking A there is every day for the rest of your life if that's what it takes. And you are going to beat this addiction, because I will *not* be the wife of a fucking junkie. Got it?"

Yes, ma'am.

In Sickness and In Rehab

VALERIE DOYLE BECAME MY WIFE ON SEPTEMBER 15, 2001. We almost cancelled the wedding at the last minute because of September 11, but we decided that if there was ever a time people needed hope, it was then. And what's more hopeful than a wedding?

Scattered throughout the rows of chairs were all of Valerie's friends from corporate America and all her family members from upstate New York, all the Bertones, all the Meeinks who still spoke to me, staff of the Anti-Defamation League in Philadelphia, my friends from the Flyers front office, almost all of the Second and Porter boys, some of the Third and Jackson boys, and the surviving 68th and Buist boys. Louie Lacinzi stood by my side as Valerie floated down the aisle. A Rastafarian bagpiper named Rufus serenaded us on the way out.

I was a little worried a riot would break out at the reception, not because the crowd was so diverse, but because my mom and dad were in the same room for the first time in close to twenty years. In the weeks prior to the wedding, while I was still detoxing at the Eagleville rehab center, I'd had nightmares about it. I'd see Valerie's family diving for cover because my mom and dad lit into each other, which set off a Meeink versus Bertone war, which set off a Third and Jackson versus 68th and Buist war, which would've been bloody if it'd happened. I also nursed a few wedding fantasies in rehab, especially one about my dad beating the shit out of John, who he met for the first time at my wedding.

But there was no violence, thankfully, and I've got the photographs to prove it. At the reception, I asked the photographer to take a picture of me with my mom and dad. They both smiled for the shot, though I made sure to stand between them, just in case. It's the only picture I have of the three of us together.

I was 100% drug-free the day I married Valerie Doyle. A week later, I took two 40 milligram Oxycontins. A week after that, I sniffed a bag of heroin. The next day, I shot up.

I was lying in bed, wearing one of my hockey jerseys, sweating like a pig, when Valerie got home from work.

"It's hot in here, baby," she said. "Why are you wearing that jersey?" Valerie wasn't naive anymore. When I didn't answer, she knew the truth. She locked on me like a gun sight: "Take it off!"

"Leave me alone."

"Take it off now. Let me see your arms."

There was no point in resisting. I took off the jersey and revealed the fresh track marks.

"Get out!"

My mom let me move back into the rowhouse on Tree Street. Since I was there, I switched back to Oxycontin. But Oxycontin wasn't strong enough to check my rage. When John called my thirteen-year-old half-sister Kirsten a "little whore," I lost my mind. My mom chose dick like always. She sent Kirsten to her room and put me out on the street. I wandered down to Second and Porter and scored an invitation to crash at the nearby crackhouse where most of the guys were living by then. They offered me all the crack I could ever want, but I refused. I didn't want to be all cracked up; I was hell bent on heading down, down, down. I ate oxys for snacks in between shots of heroin, hoping the mix might put me out of my misery for good.

One night, Valerie hunted me down on Second and Porter and said we had to talk.

"This isn't going to work, Frankie."

I wanted her so desperately, but I had no fight left in me. "Take everything and go," I said.

I watched a tear roll down Valerie's face. She said nothing for the longest time, then she stepped in close and whispered, "I lost my husband to drugs."

I didn't respond.

"My parents are in Iowa now," she reminded me. She hesitated a long time before she said, "I have no reason to stay here."

She pulled an enormous wad of cash out of her purse. "This is your half of what we had." She shoved the money into the pocket of my coat, then she walked away.

I shot every dime of that nest egg into my veins within a month. It wasn't enough to dull the pain of losing Valerie. Nothing short of death could dull that pain. But I tried. I was shooting up in the bathroom one afternoon when the resident crackheads called me downstairs.

"Frankie! We need you."

"Later," I slurred as the heroin surged through me.

They had to wait a few minutes, until the first wave of the high passed over me, until I could manage to hold myself up against the wall and teeter down the stairs.

"What?" I asked, only it sounded more like "Whaaaaa?"

"You're outta control, dude. We love you, but you're losing it."

"Whaaaaa?"

"Dude, we're sorry, but you can't stay here no more."

You have to be fucked up to have crackheads pull an intervention on you. They were smoking crack the whole time they were telling me how messed up I was and how they couldn't handle watching me kill myself. I would've told them to go fuck themselves, but it would've come out sounding like gibberish.

I crawled up the stairs to get my stash out of the bathroom. I looked at myself in the cracked mirror over the sink. If only I'd had a needle hanging out of my dick, I would've been a dead ringer for the corpse man.

"I don't know what's wrong with me." Tears poured down my face. "This ain't who I am. This ain't who I want to be. I swear

to God I don't want to live like this no more. I don't want to fucking die like this."

There was dead silence on the other end of the phone.

"I'm checking myself back into rehab. All I'm asking is one
more chance. Just one. Wait for me. Please."

"We'll see," Valerie said.

When I showed up at the Eagleville rehab center for the
third time in less than two years, the staff skipped over most
of the normal admission rigmarole. They waltzed me past potted
plants and game tables in the common room, not bothering to
give me the tour spiel again. They marched me straight to the Dual
Diagnosis Unit, which deals with alcoholic-addicts suffering
from depression, and hooked me up with methadone.

I always entered rehab sincerely wanting to get clean. Then
after a week or so, I'd pretty much get clean, clean enough to
realize I couldn't handle the idea of staying clean. Staying clean
meant dealing with me, the me who disappeared when I was
high or drunk. Staying clean meant living with the memories, con-
fronting the monsters, wallowing in the fucking misery. Staying
clean meant being me, unprotected, forever.

During my third stay at Eagleville, I didn't even manage to
stay clean while I was still there. When the nurses weren't looking,
I stole medications issued for other patients. Some of the dudes
in the dualie unit were whacked out for real, regardless of
booze and drugs. I didn't know what they had wrong with them
or what pills the docs prescribed for them, but anytime I could
get my hands on one of those little plastic cups the nurses passed
out, I swallowed everything in it.

Of course, Valerie had no clue I was using inside the rehab
center. That was the one place she thought she could trust me
to stay clean, or at least trust the staff to keep me clean. For thirty
days, she let her guard down. For thirty days, she stopped
worrying. For thirty days, she tasted what it must feel like to be
married to someone who wasn't an alcoholic-addict. Those
thirty days gave her hope. False hope, but still hope. Valerie

decided to wait for me. She decided not to leave our marriage so long as I would agree to leave Philadelphia with her. She thought if she could just get me away from the dealers in the Badlands and the dealers on Second and Porter and the dealers in my family, I'd make it. We'd make it.

What Lies Beneath the Rock

VALERIE'S PARENTS KNEW ME IN ALL MY SORDID DETAIL. They knew their well-bred, well-groomed, well-educated daughter was about to pull into the driveway of their custom built early retirement home with a van full of furniture and her uncouth, uneducated, unemployed husband – the alcoholic ex-con former skinhead heroin addict. They were unbelievably supportive, all things considered.

My in-laws made me feel welcome in their home, even though their house was as alien to me as Jupiter. It looked like something out of the pages of magazines I'd only seen in waiting rooms. One evening, I looked at Valerie draped across an overstuffed loveseat like a Persian cat and thought, this is the kind of life she's supposed to live. This is the kind of life she did live before I came along. Valerie's parents told us we could stay as long as we wanted, but we were anxious to get our own place. Valerie polished up her resume and started searching for jobs. I got on the horn with my agent and begged her to book me into any speaking gigs she could find. Going off to speak was a problem, though, because Valerie worried I would relapse every time I left the house, let alone the state.

I thought a lot about my Nazi days after I moved to Iowa. Part of it was being back in the Midwest. Part of it was my new twelve-step sponsor, though. Bob was not a Nazi, but he was a biker, the kind of biker Scooter and Peaches had been in my prison days. I have not one doubt Bob rode herd over all the other bikers in every prison he was ever in. And he was in a lot of them; Bob spent most of his adult life behind bars. When he got out, he got clean, hardcore clean. And pushing 6′4″ and 300-pounds, that ex-con was one badass recovery sponsor. If I'd had any sense, I would've stayed clean to stay alive, because even if the drugs didn't kill me, there was a damn good chance Bob would. Bob had a real low tolerance for relapses.

So I hid mine as best I could. At first they were rare, and by recovery standards, more "slips" than full blown relapses. I'd sneak off and smoke a joint, but that was it. Bob didn't act like he was on to me. Valerie wasn't on to me because she was working crazy hours at her new job. I got cocky, then stupid.

I took a job with a moving company to fill gaps between my speaking engagements. My new coworkers were big partiers. It was a bad mix. I tried crystal methamphetamine for the first time on that job. Except that it made an eight-hour shift of hauling furniture feel like it flew by in about four minutes, I hated meth. Meth was the anti-heroin: it speeded me up, made me hyper-aware, when all I wanted was to disappear. One day, I was trying to explain the pure joy that is heroin to my meth-head coworkers, when one of the guys asked me if I'd ever been on methadone.

"In rehab."

"They say if you mix it with Colodopin, it's as good as heroin."

"Can you hook me up?"

He answered with a smile.

He brought my order to work with him the next day. Mid-morning, I washed four Coladopins down with a swig of methadone. A couple hours later, I was driving to a restaurant to pick up the crew's lunch order when a cop pulled me over.

"Would you mind taking a breathalyzer?"

"Sure," I said, like a smartass, knowing I'd pass. I hadn't had a drink in years.

I went to step out of the car and fell flat on my face.

I don't remember much after that. Here's the story everybody else tells: The cop hauled me off to the drunk tank. While I was in the holding cell, I passed out, then started puking. If I'd been anywhere else, I probably would've died. But a guard saw me aspirating on my vomit and called for EMTs. I woke up three days later with tubes down my throat, IVs in my arms, and a monitor blipping to confirm I wasn't actually dead. Valerie hovered next to my bed in the small bleach-white ICU room. She held my hand and cried while a doctor removed the breathing tube.

"What day is it?" I whispered, my throat too sore to actually speak.

"Sunday," Valerie said.

"I've got hockey." I'd joined a local men's league. We played on Sunday nights. I tried to get up, but Valerie pushed me down.

"Frank, you're not playing tonight."

I didn't understand. "Why?"

"You don't even know what you did to yourself, do you?"

I had damn near killed myself. While I was enjoying a doctor-prescribed drug-induced coma, Valerie had been in agony, waiting first to see if I'd even survive and when it looked like I would, to learn if I'd suffered brain damage. The doctors warned her to prepare for the worst. She'd called my parents. I realized just how close a call I'd had when my dad walked into my Iowa hospital room. My dad isn't an Iowa kind of guy. That he'd bought a plane ticket and flown halfway across the country told me I was lucky to be alive. Then he told me he loved me and nearly dying seemed worth it.

I was released from the hospital after about a week. Valerie wouldn't let me come home, so I moved in with my sponsor. I wasn't Bob's only "guest." Bob had had so many "guests" over the years, he'd come up with house rules we had to follow. The rules were designed to keep guys like me on the right path, one baby step at a time.

Bob's house rules made the Marines look sloppy. He was convinced that the path to recovery begins with a well-made bed. Of course, there was no way in hell I was going to tell my 300-pound ex-con host what I thought of his theory. I just made my bed, again and again, until it passed his inspection. Then I got a shower and shaved and brushed my teeth, until I passed his inspection. That was the first half-hour of every day. They were long fucking days. Looking back, I can see that he was trying to give me structure, something I'd rarely experienced. I was raised by alcoholic-addicts; I was an alcoholic-addict. About the only time I'd ever regularly eaten three meals a day was in prison. The only time in my life I'd been meticulous about grooming was when I was a Nazi suiting up for battle. Wardens and gang chiefs had parented me more than my parents had. At age twenty-seven I was a parent, but I still acted like a little kid. Like any addict, I lived only in the moment, impulse to impulse. Of course, my first impulse was to run screaming from Bob's House of Hell. I bridled under his strict behavioral codes, but not too much, for fear of Bob twisting my leg off at the hip. After a while, I stopped fighting his system. A while after that, I actually took pride in how tight I could make a bed.

Valerie was proud of me, too. She could see I was changing in ways I'd never changed during my stays in rehab. With Bob's guidance, I was actually acting responsible. I was making good decisions, little decisions, but still good decisions, like eating breakfast every morning, doing laundry before I ran out of clean clothes, or paying bills before they got sent to collection. Those are the kinds of decisions normal people make every day; they're the kinds of decisions I'd never learned how to make.

Valerie didn't invite me to come home; she asked me if I wanted to go house shopping with her. Her folks had decided to move to Arizona, and they'd offered to leave her with a down payment on a house. Her house. But she wanted to make it our home.

When I told Bob I was leaving, he said, "You're not ready."

"Valerie wants me back, man, that's all I care about."

"You haven't learned a goddamn thing," Bob said. "The only thing you can care about is staying clean. That is your whole life. Nothing else matters. You ain't shit to her or anybody else unless you're sober. And you're not going to stay sober if you leave now. You're not ready; you're still just play acting. You're doing what I tell you because I tell you. You ain't really doing the steps."

Valerie and I had been in our little Craftsman fixer-upper less than two weeks when I relapsed. When Valerie left for work, I promised to paint the living room. That's exactly what I was doing when one of my meth-head buddies stopped by. I hated being on meth, but I hated being me sober even more. I begged a rock off the guy. By the time Valerie got home that evening, I'd painted half the downstairs, ripped out all the carpets and pulled up a section of the kitchen floor. She eyed me suspiciously, but she didn't ask me if I was using. She didn't need to ask.

She would've kicked me out for good if she hadn't been pregnant.

We were so fucking close to living her dream, our dream. We had a little house. We were expecting a little baby. Riley and Matt were coming out for the summer. We were so close, if I could've stayed clean. I tried so goddamn hard. I made the bed every morning. I did the dishes every night. I went to meetings every day. But still I relapsed. Over and over again, I relapsed. I'd make it a week clean, then I'd fall. I'd make it a month, then I'd fall. But I never gave up on the dream, the dream of normal, the dream of sober.

I was clean on the December day in 2003 when our son, Little Nick, was born. I relapsed again the first week of January.

I was so fucking close to the dream, but I couldn't wake up from the nightmare. No matter how many meetings I hit, I couldn't stay clean. I couldn't stand to be me, unfiltered, unprotected.

The twelve steps only work if you actually take them. I convinced myself I was taking them. I tried to convince Bob I was taking them, but he stared me down and said, "Bullshit."

The twelve steps take you on a journey, first to surrender, then inside yourself, your real self. I couldn't go there. No matter how many times I tried to turn my will and life over to the care of God as I understood him, I couldn't let go. And no matter how many times I raced toward the fourth step, I never had the guts to take a searching and fearless moral inventory of myself.

Where would I have fucking started? The day I left a kid half bleeding to death under a toilet at Pepper Middle School just to save my own ass? The night I helped Dan Bellen pull a fucking tack hammer out of a guy's head? The night I threatened to shoot that Sharpie if he let his blood drip on my carpet? Where the fuck should I start?

And where in the hell would it end? Me snorting my kids' support payments up my nose? Paying a homeless junkie to stick a needle in my arm? Lying to Valerie every goddamn day I'd known her? Me sitting there, at that very moment, in a twelve-step meeting, pretending I gave a fuck about what all those recovering losers had to say when the truth was all I could think about was getting the hell out of there so I could get high?

The Longest Trip

IN SEPTEMBER, 2005, I FLEW BACK TO PHILLY FOR A speaking engagement. I set things up with Nina so I could surprise Matt. I would catch a train at the airport, meet Nina at the stop by Matt's school, and then we'd wait for him to walk out the door. "Surprise! Daddy's in town! Daddy's here for you! Daddy loves you!"

But Daddy didn't get off the train.

I kept riding, staring out the window at the city that made me, knowing where I was supposed to be, and knowing exactly where the fuck I was going. I kept riding until the train stop at Sommerset and Kensington. I descended the filthy blue metal stairs into North Philly's open-air underworld. The Badlands had not changed since my last descent, and neither had I. Dealers were still selling the promise of heaven for ten dollars a bag, and addicts were still buying the lie. I spent twenty bucks.

Nina found me late that night, staggering down a sidewalk in West Philly. She double-parked her car, left it running, and ran toward me screaming, "Goddamn it, Frankie!"

I stared vacantly in her direction.

"What are you on?"

"Fuck you!" I lunged toward her car.

"No!" Nina threw herself in front of the backseat window. "Don't, Frankie! Don't do this to him!"

"Get the fuck out of my way!"

"He can't see you this high."

"I'm not fucking high!" I bellowed. "I came all this way just to see my baby, and I'm going to see him. He's my fucking kid!"

"And you are your fucking father!" Nina said.

Not even heroin could've dulled the pain of that knife. I lost my balance.

Nina peeled away with little Matt still sleeping in the backseat.

About an hour later, I broke into my dad's house. I searched every fucking room. I found booze. I found pot. I found cocaine. But I didn't find one picture of me.

Nina's words echoed through my mind: "You are your fucking father!"

I was.

But I wasn't going to be anymore. I wasn't going to let my babies live their whole lives wondering why daddy chose drugs over them.

I walked upstairs to my dad's bedroom. I opened the top drawer of his nightstand and slipped his loaded .22 revolver out of its hiding place. It had been in the same drawer my whole life, at the ready, just in case.

Just in case what, Daddy? Just in case somebody turns me into a prisoner of war? A punching bag? A Nazi? A cocksucker? Or how about this, Daddy? Just in case I turn the fuck into you?

Nothing tastes quite like a gun. I savored that metallic reality as it slid past my tongue and dead-ended against the back of my throat. I felt tears streaming down my cheeks. I watched my finger tremble on the trigger. We stayed like that for quite a long time, that .22 and me, snuggled up on the faded blue love-seat, alone together in my father's house.

"I've got a gun," I confessed into the telephone to Nina, the mother of my son Matt, the namesake of my dear friend who'd shot himself while talking on the phone with his ex-girlfriend.

"Frank, do not move. Don't do anything. I'll be right there."

"I can't do this to Matt. All the kids. Valerie. You. Everybody. I can't do this anymore."

"You can. Put the gun down. Let me hear you put it down. I'll come right over."

"Promise?"

"I'll be there in five minutes."

"Nina?"

"What, Frankie?"

"I think I've got a problem."

I laid the gun on the table.

BY SEPTEMBER, 2005, I was thirty years old. I'd been drinking for twenty-one years; I'd been a full-blown alcoholic for sixteen. I'd been using drugs regularly for twelve years; I'd been an addict for ten. I'd been incarcerated twice, and I'd been committed twice. I'd done four stints in inpatient rehab, four courses of methadone, and I'd attended probably about a thousand twelve-step meetings. The longest I'd managed to stay clean was two months, nine if I didn't count pot, none if I'm completely honest. I never made it past being what twelve-steppers call a "dry drunk." I wouldn't drink, but I still thought like an alcoholic. I wouldn't use, but I still lived like an addict.

My sponsor, Bob, tried to break me out of that cycle, but I left too soon, convinced I could do it my way. But my way didn't work. It never had worked. It can't work. My way is the pat answer way, the Nancy Reagan "Just Say No To Drugs" way. Just don't drink. Just don't smoke. Just don't sniff. Just don't shoot. It's a great plan unless you're already an alcoholic-addict. It's a fine plan so long as you don't spend every fucking waking minute of every day thinking of excuses to say "yes," just one more time, just once, because just once more won't hurt, will it?

I am an alcoholic-addict. I am powerless over alcohol and drugs. I cannot stay clean and sober my way because my way *is* using and drinking. It is who I am.

The first four times, I came bounding out of rehab promising, "I'll never drink or drug again." Everybody who believed me or believed in me got their hearts broken. Addicts are full of "I'll never." An addict's life is an unbroken chain of broken promises. Real recovery begins with admitting that. I'd always promised myself that this time would be different. I'd always believed myself. I'd always broken my own heart.

The gun was still lying on the table when Nina got to my dad's house. She couldn't take her eyes off it. Neither could I.

I'd been one flick of the finger away from blowing my brains out of my skull. My kids had been one twitch on the trigger away from living the rest of their lives wondering, "Why did daddy choose death over me?"

There's only one "I'll never" I still trust. I'll never forget the taste of that gun. It lingered in my mouth as Nina drove me to a rehab center. It lingered when I begged a counselor to admit me. It lingered when I confessed to Valerie that I'd almost taken my life. It lingers still. It's my only hope. My memory of rock bottom is the only thing standing between me and hell. I am alive today only because I almost took my own life that night. The lingering taste of that gun reminds me that I chose to live.

But not the way I had been living. For the first time, I entered rehab sincerely admitting, "I really am powerless over booze and drugs." For the first time since I was awaiting trial in 1993, I dropped to my knees and prayed with all my heart, "God, please fucking help me!" For the first time ever, I let go of the lie that I could do it my way, on my own. I handed my life over to God.

I started working on this book a month later. I did my fourth step for real. I didn't just flash through my memory, picking and choosing the parts I could deal with. I actually revisited my past, all of it. In October, 2005, I drove to Terre Haute, Indiana to find Crazy Cate's. The staff couldn't believe that the skinhead who'd jumped out the window nearly fifteen years earlier had finally returned. They showed me the note I left: "PS Just another problem for me."

When I wrote that note, I was an alcoholic, suicidal, home-less seventeen-year-old skinhead on the run from the cops. The last thing I needed was another problem. So I escaped. Holding that note again at age thirty, I realized something: I'd spent my life trying to escape my problems. I'd tried to escape by hiding, by running, by leaving. I'd tried to escape by denying, by lying, by conniving. I'd tried to escape by hating, by drinking, by drugging. And every fucking time I tried to escape from my problems, all I'd done was add a new one to the list.

I have had more than a few problems. In fact, it would be fair to say I've had more than my fair share of problems. Some were forced on me; most I brought on myself. But you know what? They were all *just* problems. And I've survived every damn one of them.

I give God full credit for that. In hindsight, I look back on my life and see all the crazy coincidences, all the once-in-a-lifetime moments that happened at the right time to save me. I can't write it all off to luck; no one is that lucky.

God has taken mercy I don't deserve on me, mercy I never showed my victims. Their eyes still haunt me. I can't remember their faces, but I cannot forget the desperation in their eyes. I pray to God every day to give them peace. And I pray to God never to erase their pain from my memory. I can't make direct amends to most of the people I so brutally attacked during my skinhead years because I never knew their names. But they are in my heart now when I speak out against hatred. They are the reason I will never stop speaking out against hatred.

I've done my best to make amends to the other people I've hurt, the people who love me or tried to before I drove them away. I've been apologizing to Valerie since the day I met her. I've been apologizing to my kids since the day they were born. What I understand now, though, is that apologies only mean something if you stop doing the thing you're apologizing for. Otherwise, "I'm sorry" is as empty as the promise "I'll never."

I'm sorry I can't end this book happy by promising I'll never fuck up again. I've told the truth about everything else, so why risk lying now? The truth is, odds are I will fuck up again. I am an alcoholic-addict. Today I'm in recovery, but there's no such thing as being "recovered." It took me years to get that through my skull; it took almost blowing my brains out. I have finally learned to accept that I will live each day of the rest of my life either "in recovery" or in hell. For me, there are no other options. Just one choice, one life-or-death choice, to make every single day, one day at a time.

On May 17, 2006, I chose to return to the Badlands. A friend and I drove around for hours, looping back through the intersection of Sommerset and Kensington at least two dozen times. The dealers must've thought we were either the choosiest buyers in the history of heroin or the dumbest undercover cops in the city. As we circled the dealers, the junkies, the crack whores, the needle peddlers, and all the other lost souls who haunt the Badlands, I gave my friend, a college professor, a private lecture on how I used to buy, cook, and shoot heroin.

Late that afternoon, I leaned against a wall of windows inside a grade school. Play practice was running late, really late. It could've run until midnight for all I cared, because I wasn't going to leave that spot. Finally, the theatre door burst open.

"Dad!" Matt shouted when he saw me. I wrapped my arms around him.

Someday, when he's a lot older, I'm going to tell my son the whole story of the thirty-one-year trip I took to surprise him at school. That afternoon, though, all my boy needed to hear was the only thing I wanted to say.

"I love you."

Hurry Up and Wait

UNTIL I READ *PET SEMATARY* IN SOLITARY BACK IN 1992, I hadn't ever read a whole book cover to cover except for stuff written by white supremacists. And I'm not sure I ought to count *Pet Sematary*, considering I was flying too high on yellow jackets to remember most of it. By 2009, I still didn't have much of a frame of reference for what it means to be a serious reader, let alone what it was going to mean to be a newly published author once this book dropped. The book was scheduled to hit shelves in the spring of 2010. That meant me and everybody helping me write it had to get the manuscript absolutely set in stone almost a full year earlier. We declared the manuscript done on May 25, 2009. May 25, 2009. 5-25-09. In some parts of the world, they list the day before the month, which would make that date 25-5-09. 25509. B25509. I bet when the Illinois Department of Corrections assigned me my prison ID number, they never dreamed they were predicting the date I'd finish writing a book.

A lot of people warned me to prepare myself for a big let-down once we sent off the final copy. My professor buddy warned me. The editor warned me. The publisher warned me. Other authors I met warned me. My wife warned me. Hell, I think total strangers off the street may have tried to warn me. I listened; I just didn't fully understand what they were preparing me for until it happened.

So I'd spent five years working on this project and I finally got it done, finally achieved this amazing goal I'd set for myself, and then . . . nothing. Nothing happens when you finish writing a book. Not a damn fucking thing. Rainbows don't appear on the horizon. Cartoon birds don't circle your head chirping Disney songs. The Dunkin' Donuts clerk doesn't give you a congratulatory shot of espresso on the house. Nothing.

When an author finishes writing a book, the book itself, like the real actual physical thing that a toddler would point at and say, "Book," that thing still doesn't exist. The actual book is still nearly a year down the road, so there's nothing to autograph, nothing to hit the road to promote, nothing to hold in your hand as proof you really did it. Worse, because the book was actually written and "in production," as they say, I couldn't even distract myself by working on the book because, by then, it was totally out of my hands. I'd say to people, "I just finished writing a book," and they'd say, "Cool! Where can I get a copy?" And then I'd have to explain that it would be about a year before it would be available in stores because of the graphic design phase and the printing phase and the advance reviewer phase and the distributor phase and the phases of the moon and that awkward phase right before puberty. In the year it took for the book to go through all its phases, I educated almost every person I know on the realities of the publishing process. They'd say, "That sucks." Yeah, it kind of did. But I can't say I wasn't warned.

Fortunately, I had a lot of things to do to pass the time. I was really involved in hockey then, working on a version of Harmony Through Hockey in Iowa, at times doing some promotional work for an AHL team, playing in local men's leagues, and spending hours each week helping my youngest son, Nick, learn the fundamentals of the game. A buddy of mine was a local DJ and he'd invited me to be a guest on his show many times over the years to talk about my life and just shoot the shit. I had to remember not to say things like "shit" when the "on-air" sign was lit up, but otherwise I had a blast visiting his show. I guess I did pretty good, because I got invited to be on other shows, too, and to do some work around the studio. In the summer of 2009, I got a temporary gig filling in for one of the regular cohosts of a morning show that's a little bit of news and a lot of joking around. On one of the last days I was scheduled to be on air, we were visited by "Mr. Hollywood," as the main host called him. Mr. Hollywood's real name is Bill and he's a casting agent.

DES MOINES ISN'T Hollywood or Bollywood or even Dollywood. But in recent years, it's become a pretty popular place for production companies to shoot movies because of state legislation that gives tax incentives to filmmakers. That's why Bill and an army of directors, producers, cameramen, and tech staff had arrived in Iowa. And the people of Iowa were losing their minds trying to figure out where and when filming would take place so they could try to sneak a peek at the big-name stars in town for this particular shoot: Forest Whitaker and Adrien Brody.

The Experiment tells the story of a psychology experiment that goes bad, very bad. I won't ruin it by sharing too many details, but it's interesting and inspired by a real case. A researcher gathers volunteers to live for a couple weeks in the roles of either guards or prisoners in a fake prison he sets up where he can watch how they react. The deal is if the volunteers follow all the rules of the experiment for a couple of weeks, they'll get paid a lot of money for being involved. Because the researcher promises he will stop the experiment immediately if things get too out of hand or if there's any violence and it seems like nobody will get hurt, which attracts a lot of people hard up for money to the promise of a job that pays about a thousand dollars a day.

I'm pretty sure big-time actors like Forest Whitaker and Adrien Brody make a lot more than a grand a day for being on set. Maybe that's why casting directors like Bill try to fill smaller parts with actors who aren't so famous and even with people who aren't actors. Bill was doing the interview on the radio show to talk about a crowd scene in the movie where they were going to need lots of people to be in the background. The only pay was the glory of being able to say you were in a movie and the chance to maybe catch sight of one of the stars. Bill suggested I ought to come down to the location to be part of the scene. I didn't want to say no live on air, since he was on the show to try to drum up volunteers, but I really didn't want to do it. Mostly, I did not want to have to tell my wife why I took a day off from paid work to stand around a movie set for free.

After the show, as we were walking out of the studio, Bill pulled me aside and said again he wanted me to come down to the set. Before I could say I couldn't do it, he explained he needed some people to play small roles, too small for most professional actors, but bigger than being a face in a crowd. It would pay, not the kind of pay the stars earned, but enough to make it worth my time.

While Bill was saying all that, I was thinking to myself that Bill must not be very good at his job. One of the guys at the radio station had filled Bill in a little about my past and my speaking and the book. Bill had to be nuts to think any of the stuff I did qualified me to be in a movie. I had zero acting experience. I can give a hell of a good speech, but always off the cuff and straight from my heart. I can't memorize things word for word and recite them back and I never could. Just ask the sisters at Our Lady of Mount Carmel: I always botched Bible verses and left words out of the commandments, usually "not." I started trying to explain all of that to Bill, but he stopped me.

"Frank, I just need a guy who looks like he'd be in prison."

I hadn't ever acted a scene in my life, but I knew I was getting that part.

There were about a half dozen of us in the cast who fell in between the extras and the stars. The crowd-scene extras weren't on the set where most of the filming took place. The stars each had their own air-conditioned trailer where they could hang out comfortably between takes. Those of us in the middle sat around outside on picnic tables sweating our balls off and waiting for somebody to tell us what to do. Most of the guys in our little group were actors, just not New York or Hollywood actors. Some of them were hoping The Experiment might be their big break to get a trailer of their own someday. I was mostly just hoping I didn't make a fool of myself.

We sat around the table for nearly three hours. Nobody came to get us or told us what was going on. We just sat there, waiting and sweating. At one point Adrien Brody walked by. The wannabe Oscar winners at my table nearly wet themselves, then they returned to swapping stories about the plays they'd been in. Some of them had had bit parts in independent films. Some had acted in commercials. The longer they yammered on, the higher the sun got and the thicker the humidity hung in the air. I wasn't sure how much longer I could stand to sit around that table, pretending I was listening, trying not to have a heat stroke. I was getting pretty restless when Bill stopped by to say hi to me. He barely acknowledged the other guys at the table, but he shot the shit with me for a while and asked me if I needed something to drink. When he walked off, I could tell his visit hadn't gone over well with the actors at the table. I was sick of hearing about their "craft" by then, but I still felt kind of bad for them. Back in '93, when those dudes were vying for summer stock with Estrada, I had been trying to land a spot on Cell Block C. Now here they were yet again hoping to be discovered and the only guy the casting agent talked to was the guy with a felony record and no acting experience.

When the director called a break for lunch, I felt like I was back in prison. Those movie people split off by rank faster than gangs claim tables as turf in a chow hall. The wannabe actors and me stayed put at our table, which was behind the catering truck. The crew members took seats at the tables surrounding us. At the same time, the famous actors and behind-the-scenes big shots took their places at the tables on the front side of the truck. From my angle, I could see Bill on the other side; he was sitting at a table with Adrien Brody and they were deep into a conversation about something.

The seating may be just as segregated, but the food on a movie set is a lot better than prison chow. I was taking full advantage of the spread when Bill stood up, waved to get my attention, and called, "Frank! Bring your food. Come join us."

It turned out that Bill and Adrien's conversation had been about me. Bill had told Adrien what he knew about my past. When he introduced me to Adrien, Bill mentioned that my autobiography was coming out soon. Adrien was really nice. He asked me a lot of questions and I had some for him, too. Turns out we had a few things in common, sort of, in reverse. We were two East Coast city boys sharing lunch in Iowa. Adrien grew up in Queens, but as a kid he spent a lot of time at camps and arts programs in upstate New York, near where my wife grew up, mostly because his parents wanted to keep him away from bad influences in the city. In other words, guys like me. I'm not sure what I expected an Academy Award-winning actor to be like, but I was surprised by how down to earth Adrien was. I couldn't wait to get home and tell Valerie that I got to eat lunch with Adrien Brody.

After lunch, I got called onto the set. The director's assistant told me where to stand and when and where to move and what they needed me to contribute to the scene. Basically, they needed me to look menacing, which I didn't think would be much of a stretch. When we prepared to do a run through, I noticed the professional actors got really still. Some of them even closed their eyes. When the director said, "Action," they weren't their real selves anymore; they were fully in character. I had no clue how actors do that, how they turn themselves into a fictional character, but when it was time for our first take, I closed my eyes, too. When the director yelled, "Action!" I opened my eyes and I was B25509. I don't know if stepping back into who I used to be counts as acting, but it seemed to get the job done.

At the end of the day, I was taking a piss when the director walked into the bathroom. Paul Scheuring directs both feature films and television. He created the TV show *Prison Break*, which I freaking loved. I knew most of the first season had been filmed at Joliet Penitentiary in Illinois after the facility was shut down. So while we're standing there next to each other, staring directly and only at the wall above the urinals, I mentioned, as casually as it's possible to mention something while peeing next to another dude, that I'd done time in Illinois. While we washed our hands, we talked about Illinois's most notorious prisons, like Joliet and Menard. As we headed toward the door, Paul told me I'd done a good job on the set that day. Then he asked me if I would consider taking on a bigger role in the movie, which would require me to be on set full-time for six weeks.

If you look up *The Experiment* on a movie-industry website like IMDB, you'll see me listed as "Inmate (Uncredited)," which means my role was more than a crowd-scene extra, but not big enough to have a character name or to get listed in the full credits. I'm cool with that. I took the job for the money. I didn't have steady work at the time, just fill-in gigs here and side-jobs there. I couldn't really get a regular, full-time job because I had to be able to fly out for speaking engagements, sometimes as often as once a week. And that was only going to get more complicated once the book came out because the publisher, my speaking agent, and the ADL were collaborating to set up a tour tied to the book's release. For months, maybe even a year or more, I was going to be on the road at least as much as I was home. The book itself and all the speaking engagements and media appearances were going to help me get my message out to an incredible number of people. It was what I had always hoped to be able to do. But until that happened, I was looking for whatever work I could find to help take some of the pressure off our family budget.

I don't view any work as beneath me; if it's legit and it provides for my family, I'll do it. For a while I worked on a crew that cleans out really dirty houses, like hoarders' houses and foreclosures that have been trashed by vandals. I don't let my pride get in the way of earning an honest buck. But I gotta say, getting paid to hang out with movie stars beats the fucking crap out of shoveling dirty diapers out of a bath tub.

CLIFTON COLLINS JR. was the only big-name actor who regularly broke the unwritten rule of segregation everybody else seemed to follow on meal breaks. He almost always ate on the crew side of the truck. If I hadn't known who he was, I would have assumed he was a cameraman. Clifton looks like an old-school Hollywood character actor, which might be because he's descended from Hollywood character-actor royalty of an earlier time: his grandfather, Pedro Gonzalez-Gonzalez, acted in everything from iconic movies like *Rio Bravo* to television classics like *The Adventures of Ozzie and Harriet* and *Gunsmoke*. Before *The Experiment*, Clifton had racked up some seriously impressive acting credits of his own: *Traffic* and *Capote* to name just two. Shortly before arriving in Des Moines, he had wrapped filming *Boondock Saints II: All Saints Day*, playing the part of Romeo. Clifton Collins Jr. is a great actor, a really serious actor, all business when he needs to be, but between takes and off set he's just Clifton, one of the most humble and laid back guys I've ever met.

Clifton struck up a conversation with me my second day on set. Not surprisingly, because of the subject of *The Experiment*, everybody was always talking about what it's like to be incarcerated and how prison affects people. I shared some of my experiences in real prisons with Clifton. He told me about his good friend since childhood who goes by the nickname "Goose." Goose spent a lot of time locked up, but he and Clifton stayed close through it all. I remember in our very first conversation, Clifton made a funny comment about ramen; he was amazed by all the dishes guys like Goose learn to concoct with commissary ramen as the main ingredient. A few years later, those two coauthored a book called *Prison Ramen: Recipes and Stories from Behind Bars*. They asked a lot of people they knew who had done time to contribute recipes and memories, including me.

Once I got promoted to Inmate (Uncredited), I got moved

from waiting at a table by the catering truck to hanging out between takes in a room with all the other uncredited inmates. It was an advancement, sort of like moving from central booking to a holding cell. Not exactly a big upgrade, but at least it was air-conditioned. After Clifton and I hit it off, he rescued me from the room sometimes by inviting me to hang in his trailer. We were often on set sixteen hours a day, but much of that time was spent waiting to be called up for a scene. Clifton and I logged a lot of hours in his trailer swapping life histories; we got to be really good friends.

Days off were rare and when they happened the people who weren't local really wanted to get off set and just relax. But that was a challenge for the famous actors, because a lot of Iowans were stalking them. I happened to be in on the conversation when Clifton, Adrien, and some others were trying to figure out what to do with an upcoming free day. The only big thing going on was the State Fair, but they decided that would be a nightmare in terms of people bombarding them. So I piped up and asked if they'd be interested in doing a sweat lodge ceremony.

ABOUT A DOZEN people working on *The Experiment* drove from Des Moines to Grimes, Iowa. Grimes has a population of less than ten thousand people and those people are pretty spread out. I'd been there many times over the years to attend sweat lodges at the invitation of tribal leaders in the community. Their willingness to share their spiritual traditions with me had carried me through some difficult times. I hoped the people working on *The Experiment* might find the same kind of peace in the sweat lodge that I'd found over the years.

Grimes is the kind of town big-city types don't necessarily recognize as an actual town when they drive through. I led our little caravan past a lonesome stop light and onto a road where neighboring houses aren't in screaming distance of each other. We parked in an area that appeared deserted and set out to make the rest of the journey on foot. As I led the group through a thick woods, I worried some of them might have been thinking I was setting them up to be robbed or kidnapped. I kept reassuring everybody we were almost there. But I didn't need to say anything once we crossed the rickety bridge spanning a small creek: on the far side of the bridge, my new friends caught their first sight of the traditional lodge, hunkered down like an ancient turtle in a clearing in the forest.

I can't explain the sweat lodge experience in words to someone who hasn't done it. It's a spiritual and physical process a person has to feel for themselves in order to understand. There truly is magic in the heat, the chanting, the ancient rituals of the water pourer, the words of wisdom shared by elders. Most of the people I'd brought with me had never done a sweat before, but they were all anxious to learn about the tradition and have the experience firsthand. After it was over, everyone agreed it had been transformational, but, like me, no one could really put words to why and how it had affected them so deeply.

ON THE DRIVE back to Des Moines, I shared a car with Adrien, Adrien's stunt double, and Clifton. There's nothing like hours in a sweat lodge to make a guy thirsty, so we swung into a small g as station to grab some drinks. The automatic hinge had not yet shut the door behind us when I felt the atmosphere shift: the employees and the customers recognized Adrien and Clifton. I was directly in the sight-line of those star-struck eyes. For a few seconds, I caught a sense of what it feels like for these guys every time they go out in public. I've been under actual surveillance before, but having cops' eyes on me was nothing compared to the way the people in the gas station stared at Adrien and Clifton. It was thrilling. It was also sad.

There are no celebrities in a sweat lodge. Even on set, while it's clear that some people are bigger deals than others, there's still a sense of everybody being on the same team to get the movie made. But when celebrities walk into a small-town gas station, it's like they aren't even people anymore. People stare at them like they stare at their pictures in magazines, as if the person they are ogling isn't really in the room feeling it. All eyes are on them, and yet nobody is really seeing them. People feel like they know celebrities because they've seen them in so many movies and television shows. But people really only know the roles they have played. As I stood in that gas station, I realized it was the first time I'd actually been in public with Adrien and Clifton. I thought I understood better why they hadn't wanted to go to the State Fair. It wasn't that they minded people asking for autographs or wanting a picture; it was that they didn't want to spend a whole day being stared at while not being seen.

The only conversation I had with Forest Whitaker during the six weeks I worked on the movie was a couple days after we returned from the night at the sweat lodge. Forest told me he regretted not going with us. I spent the rest of the time between takes on the movie getting to know my fellow Inmate (Uncredited) actors, occasionally joking around with Adrien, but mostly hanging with Clifton.

Before I met him, Clifton had agreed to direct a video for the bad boy of country music, Jamey Johnson. They wanted to shoot the video in Iowa since Clifton was there for the movie and Jamey had a concert scheduled during the Iowa State Fair. Clifton had a plan for the storyline, but he tapped me for ideas about locations since he wasn't all that familiar with the area. Toward the end of filming *The Experiment,* after we'd break for the night, Clifton started working on the video project with a different production crew that he'd flown in from California. He asked me to go along with them one evening to show them some locations. We swung by my house so I could change into fresh clothes after the long day on set and Clifton and the cinematographer were like, "This is perfect!" That's how my house became a set for part of a music video. In the end, those two decided I was perfect, too, for the role of Jamey Johnson's bad-influence friend in the video for "High Cost of Living."

AFTER FILMING WRAPPED on *The Experiment,* my life went back to normal – normal for me, that is. I split my time between side jobs, speaking engagements, and dad duty. I tried to spend as much time as possible with the family because I knew my schedule was going to go insane once the book dropped and, frankly, because V and I had our hands full.

Our daughter, Jayla, was born in the spring of 2009, and looked exactly like V from the minute she arrived. She joined Little Nick, then five years old, in full-time permanent resident status in our house. For a couple years before Jayla was born and several after, my second-oldest son, Matt, was also living with us full time; his mom, Nina, and I agreed that he'd hit an age where he needed more time with his dad. Nina visited us often and Valerie and I made sure Matt got to visit her and his other family and friends in Philly often, too. But Iowa was Matt's home in those years, meaning it was where our budding teenager waged his major battles about chores, homework, and curfew. My first-born, Riley, still lived in Illinois with her mom, but she would come see us on some of her school vacations. Even my half-sister, Hayley, left Philly for Iowa and moved in with us for a couple of years while she finished high school and took classes at community college. Hayley and Matt had always been close, more like brother and sister than nephew and aunt. After I left Philly, Hayley babysat Matt often and even lived with him and Nina part of the time just to get some peace. For those two Philly kids, Iowa was Mars, but being together felt like home. The only one missing was Jake. Maria had let me see him a few times in 2005 and 2006 when I visited Philly, and even let him join all the rest of the kids and Valerie and me in Iowa for a couple weeks, but then I pissed her off and she cut off my contact with him again.

For several years, depending on the month and week, Valerie and I had as many as four teenagers, a young grade-schooler, a baby and a nut-job pug named Buttercup under our care. Valerie kept it all straight with charts and checklists. I mostly just did what she told me to do: make lunches, change diapers, drive this one that way and the other one in the opposite direction at the exact same time, and don't let anybody be late! To raise one kid, you need at least three eyes, four hands and an extra pair of feet. To wrangle five or more, you need an army or maybe just a white flag of surrender. We managed as best we could, but the truth is we were living in a madhouse – a really loving, happy madhouse, but a madhouse all the same. And once the book came out, I would need to hit the road. At the time, it was hard to imagine how we were going to handle everything: all the kids, Valerie's demanding job, my heavy travel schedule. Looking back, I think: Wow, if only it had been that simple.

The Re-Formers

SOME PEOPLE WEREN'T TOO HAPPY WHEN THIS BOOK hit the shelves in April 2010. Most were the same people who'd been mad at me ever since I first started speaking out against hate. After more than a decade, I was used to their gripes and wise to their tactics, though social media made it easier for some of them to try to scare me silent. It didn't work. A few people got mad about the book because they thought I was speaking out against them personally. Most of the folks in that camp fired off emails before they'd even read the book, thinking I was naming real names and fearing maybe I was setting them up for big trouble. But I didn't do that. I didn't use real names of anybody who wasn't already in the public realm, and I didn't rat anybody out for anything they hadn't already been tied to. I didn't write the book to settle old scores. If that was my goal, I would've just kidnapped and beat the shit out of somebody again. That vengeance only cost me about two years of my freedom; writing this book took five.

I ain't the only guy who ever turned his life around and wrote a book about it. The first was St. Augustine. He wrote a book called *Confessions*, where he spilled everything bad he ever did, from stealing his neighbor's fruit to a whole lot of the nasty with women his mother seriously did not approve of. In the 1600 or so years since he wrote that book, a lot of other former trouble-makers have gotten themselves on the right path. Most didn't make saint. I know I won't. But I have managed to become a relatively productive human being. Most days I follow almost all of the rules. I try to be good to people. I try to make a difference. I'm not likely to stab a person for taking the last piece of pizza. A dude taking the last Tastykake can still push me to the edge of insanity, but so far, so good; nobody's taken a fork to the finger.

TJ Leyden was not the first skinhead to leave the movement, but he was the first former skinhead in America to get national attention for speaking out publicly against white-supremacist hatred. Back in the day, TJ was a Hammerskin. He helped build the racist gang network on the West Coast. He spent fifteen years inside the movement, recruiting in mosh pits, and also while he was in the Marine Corps. He developed deep connections with groups like White Aryan Resistance and was set up to make the leap to leadership within the adult arena of white supremacy. Then one day his career as a neo-Nazi leader was derailed by a three-year-old. TJ was playing with his sons when a Caribbean-themed kids show popped up on television. His younger son toddled over to the set and turned it off. During speeches and in-terviews, TJ now often shares the words that inspired him to begin changing. The little boy looked up at his father and scolded, "Daddy! We don't watch niggers!" At first, TJ was proud, but the more he reflected on what his son had said, the more he realized he was setting his children up for a life defined by hatred and violence, a life that, after fifteen years, had left TJ himself hollow.

It took time for TJ to totally break free from the ideology of hate, but once he did, he reached out to the staff at the Simon Wiesenthal Center in Los Angeles, one of the leading antihate groups in the world. In 1996, TJ became a consultant to the Simon Wiesenthal Center, sharing his insights about what can be done to prevent hate-motivated violence. I think TJ has probably logged more hours than anybody giving speeches and media interviews to try to prevent the kind of damage guys like us caused when we were skinheads.

I did not know TJ when I was a skinhead. But I knew about him. And I knew about his work with the Simon Wiesenthal Center, because it was similar to what I started doing with the

ADL at about the same time. We sometimes ran into each other at conferences and kept in touch by email. For a while, TJ was the one guy I could talk to about speaking out against the movement who totally got it; I didn't have to explain why I felt I had to do it or how people reacted, both good and bad – really bad in some cases – because he was dealing with the exact same stuff.

By 2011, quite a few people who had left the movement had started publicly speaking out against it. One day TJ contacted several of us to deliver an unbelievable invitation.

GOOGLE IDEAS PARTNERED up with the Council on Foreign Relations and the Tribeca Film Festival to host the Summit Against Violent Extremism in Dublin, Ireland. The conference ran for three days in June 2011. I'd been attending hate-prevention conferences since the late 1990s. Some were small local meetings and some were huge national events. In 2009, I was invited to be part of the Reconciliation Forum, where I was humbled to be listed as a speaker alongside people like President Jimmy Carter, Bishop Desmond Tutu, and former Russian President Mikhail Gorbachev. But as amazing as some of those past conferences had been, none compared to the three days I spent in Ireland.

The Summit Against Violent Extremism blew my mind. Everyone involved was working in some way to prevent hatred and violence. Some of the participants represented nonprofit groups or NGOs, some were from government agencies and corporations, and some were survivors of extremist violence. But a good portion of the participants had come to do prevention work the same way I had: they had once been the sort of violent extremists this conference wanted to stop. The "formers" at the conference came from all parts of the world, all religions, all races. We all shared a history of hatred. In fact, there was a time when many of us had hated each other, if not by name, by race or creed. But in Dublin, we came together to talk about how formers like us could use what we'd lived to help prevent the next generation of extremists from hurting people.

Some of the most powerful, painful sessions of the conference were the ones where the survivors of violent extremism shared their stories. I remember one woman talking about how, for most people, seeing footage of the events of September 11, 2001, is a terrible reminder of one of the great tragedies in history. But while she understands the significance and why the footage must continue to be replayed, she can't get one thing out of her mind whenever she sees it: she is watching her mother die before her very eyes, again. For her, seeing the videos from September 11, 2001, is not just watching history; it is watching her mother's murder, over and over again. Every year on the anniversary, she sees it. Every time she flips through the channels and happens upon a documentary about the attacks, she sees it. Every time the media replays the videos to ensure we will never forget what happened on September 11, 2001, she and every other person who lost a loved one that day are forced to witness their deaths yet again.

I cannot imagine how hard that must be, not just the pain of the memories, but never knowing when they're going to be flashed in your face. It's like she and so many others can't escape from the worst day of their lives. How do you ever get closure on grief when the world makes you keep watching your loved one die?

Somehow, this woman had found the strength to keep going even while living with the constant reminders of her mom's death. She and the other survivors at the conference had each suffered horribly, whether extremists had brutalized them personally or killed people they loved. They had the best reasons imaginable to live the rest of their lives terrified and enraged. But they didn't. The survivors I met refused to give in to fear. They were reclaiming their lives by working to prevent future tragedies; they were honoring their trauma, their dead, not just by refusing to stay silent, but by refusing to hate. They were stronger than hate.

When I was a skinhead, I didn't think anything was stronger than hate. Hate was power. Hate was identity. Hate was everything. And it was all such fucking bullshit. In reality, it was hate that ate away at me from the inside out, making me weak. Hate was a mask I wore to cover the fact I had no clue who I was. Hate infested every thought I had and tricked me into believing the fun-house mirrors were reality. I'd stepped away from the movement earlier, but it wasn't until I watched the news coverage of the Oklahoma City bombing that I realized just how freaking stupid and chicken-shit it all was. When I watched that firefighter carrying that baby girl out of the rubble, that baby girl who looked so much like my little daughter, that's when I realized there's no strength in hate. Hate motivated that bombing. Hate brought down that building. But that's not power; that's cowardice. Only a sniveling punk-ass chicken would think he was strong because he killed a baby.

There were years of my life when I would've thought I was strong for bringing down a building. There were years of my life when I would've called a guy like Timothy McVeigh a hero. For years, I laughed at the victims of my own hate-fueled violence. I taunted the people I beat. I mocked people while they bled. I fucking videotaped an assault with a deadly weapon so I could use it to keep other people loyal to me out of fear.

When I listened to a woman talk about what it's like to watch the video of her mother's death over and over again, I felt tears well up in my eyes. I thought of my victims and I thought of my kids. And I prayed, I literally prayed to God, to please give me the strength to someday be as fully human as this woman who chooses to forgive instead of fear, to love instead of hate.

THE SUMMIT AGAINST Violent Extremism was the first time I'd been able to meet face-to-face with some people I'd long known only through phone calls, emails or Facebook. TJ and I weren't the only former skinheads in attendance. Arno Michaelis was once a notorious street soldier for the Hammerskins and the lead singer of the white-power band Centurion. Arno had wailed many a mosh pit into a frenzy of violence and unleashed hell on the streets of Milwaukee. His band had been performing the night Joe Morgan was murdered, the night I almost went back into the movement. Another guy, Christian Picciolini, was a former skinhead who had played a role in the white-power music scene in Chicago. Tony McAleer was once an organizer for White Aryan Resistance; he had been one of the most influential white-power leaders and skinhead recruiters in Canada, shaping everything from the music to the communication channels that helped the movement surge in the 1980s and early 1990s. In those days, very few women had any influence at all within the white supremacy movement; one did and she, too, was in Ireland. Angela King had done time in the federal prison system for her role in the armed robbery of a Jewish-owned store, but it was her violence toward other skinheads that had made her a legend inside the movement. Some male crew leaders used her as an enforcer, siccing her on guys they thought were out of line. I'm being dead serious here: when I was a skinhead, if I'd heard somebody was sending that particular skin chick to visit me, I would have shit my pants.

Had all of us met as a full group back when we were active skinhead crew leaders, I don't know if we would have gotten along. Considering how volatile and violent we all used to be, odds are we would have gotten blind-rage drunk and beaten each other all the way to the emergency room. But when we finally all met in person in Ireland, it wasn't who we had been that united us; it was who we had become. And one of us, Arno, had become friends with Sammy Rangel, who was also participating in the summit.

Sammy Rangel was never a skinhead, but he was a gang member. I mean, dude was a serious fucking gang member. In fact, to say just that Sammy was a gang member is an understatement nearly as big as one of his biceps, which dwarf most guys' thighs. Sammy was a high-ranked leader of a major Latin gang. He spent more than a decade in prisons in Illinois and Wisconsin. When he was locked up in Menard, he led an uprising that landed not only prisoners but also guards in the infirmary and bought him about a year in solitary. Even in solitary, the guards couldn't control Sammy: he set the adjacent cell on fire and, with it, the skinhead inside. After his release from the Illinois system, he headed to Wisconsin, where he expanded his gang's reach into the greater Milwaukee area before being reincarcerated. Sammy built such a reputation for violence within the Wisconsin Department of Corrections that on one occasion, a prison actually refused to accept him on transfer, saying they couldn't handle the security risk.

So it's ironic, or maybe miraculous, that Sammy went on to work for the Wisconsin Department of Corrections as a counselor. He has also worked for government and nonprofit agencies that try to get kids off the streets. Along the way, he's earned both his BA and a Master's in social work and he's hoping to have a PhD behind his name one day, too.

Sammy and I hit it off immediately. The very first night we met, we swapped memoirs. Each evening while we were in Ireland, once we turned in for the night, I'd work my way through a few chapters of *FourBears: The Myths of Forgiveness*, and he'd read a few more from *Autobiography of a Recovering Skinhead*. Each morning, it was as if we'd known each other for another decade. For two guys who on the surface appear to have not one damn thing in common, we have almost everything in common, like shitty childhoods and the taste of Illinois DOC "loaf" still lingering on our tongues. By the time we were about halfway through each other's books, we realized I had basically followed his path through the Illinois prison system. Sammy beat me to most of the facilities by a year. He left his mark. Sammy had played a lead role in the drama that sparked the race war between the bikers and the Latin folk that I'd walked into when I got transferred to Shawnee State Penitentiary.

The very first day we were in Ireland, before the conference had even started, Sammy, Arno, and I set out for a relaxing hike that ended up to be mountain climbing. Arno and I convinced Sammy to follow us off the beaten path. Like, literally, there was an actual path beaten down by hundreds of years of people's feet taking that route and Arno and I thought all those people couldn't possibly be right, because, you know, they had only grown up there and lived there their whole lives, generation after generation, and we had just arrived for the first time less than twenty-four hours earlier. So we took to the weeds and then the weeds sprouted branches and then the branches grew thorns and the thorns drew blood. And Sammy was cussing us every step of the way, but laughing between f-bombs. When we finally made it to the top, each one of us looked like we'd just been attacked by a pack of muddy feral cats, but the view was spectacular: rolling hills and lush valleys dotted with bright blue lakes and storybook villages as far as we could see. We stayed up there for a long time, talking about the view and life and how in the fuck we were going to get back down without dying.

Looking back, I see that hike as a metaphor for all our lives. Each one of us formers who attended the Summit Against Violent Extremism had stepped off the beaten path early in life. We'd made our lives harder than they needed to be by joining gangs, by letting hate steer our course. We'd bloodied ourselves and we'd bloodied other people, too: the victims of our crimes, the people we recruited to follow us, and even the people who tried to love us that we'd tossed aside. Each one of us had made it to the top of the mountain, to positions of leadership and influence within our gangs and movements. And from that vantage point, each one of us had come to realize that we were miserable; hatred and violence had gutted us, isolated us, ruined us. For each of us, there came a moment when we felt a need to get down off the mountain. We had all shared the experience, but not one of us had had anybody to help us when it happened. Each of us was totally isolated when we realized we wanted out because, by then, we had surrounded ourselves almost exclusively with other gang members who we, ourselves, had taught to brutalize the disloyal. There was no one we could turn to to share our doubts, our concerns, our thoughts about leaving. People who weren't in could not have understood; people who were in might've killed us.

Mountains look taller and steeper from the top than the bottom. When you're already exhausted, when you can't even remember how you got up there in the first place, when all you really want to do is fling yourself off the side onto the rocks and be done with it, that's when you have to make a choice: either commit to forging a path that doesn't kill you or stay on the mountain, miserable, until you die.

THE WHOLE TIME we were in Ireland, between conference sessions and late into each night, our little group of former gang members discussed an idea. A couple of the guys had been talking about it before the Summit Against Violent Extremism. I wasn't in on those discussions, so I can't say how the idea actually came to be. All I know is that when they shared it with the rest of us, and with others at the conference, we knew we had to make it happen.

The day we were to fly out and return to our homes in different parts of North America, we gathered in the hotel atrium. A half dozen former skinheads and a former Latin gang leader formed a circle. We each placed a hand in the middle, one atop the other, and we vowed to use what we had learned at the conference and what we had survived in our own lives to help other people find life after hate.

THOSE OF US who first put our hands in a circle in Ireland share a basic belief that people can change. We know that to be true because we've lived it. We are proof that there is life after hate. So immediately after the trip, we joined forces to form an organization called Life After Hate. A lot of other people stepped up to help get Life After Hate off the ground. Several of the groups represented at the Summit Against Violent Extremism offered resources and advice to help us get started, everything from how to file for 501(c)(3) nonprofit status to how to spread word about what we hoped to do where the people we wanted to help could actually find us.

The basic, original idea behind Life After Hate was to use what us formers knew about hatred and violence to help people still caught up in it. Just as you need the poison from the snake to make an effective antivenom, we hoped our firsthand experiences with hatred and violence could be the basis for a cure. We began with a website where people could learn how each of us had broken free from extremism and how others could as well. In time, Life After Hate also functioned as a speakers bureau, a one-stop shop for schools and other groups who wanted hate-prevention speakers. While the various individuals within Life After Hate sometimes have gotten a lot of attention for giving a major presentation or appearing on the news, the most important work the organization has ever done is the work you will never hear about in any detail: it's the conversations formers have online and by phone with people in extremist groups who need someone to light a safe path to help them find their way off the mountain.

The first few years of Life After Hate were not easy or even drama-free. While all of us who met in Ireland have had success in a variety of careers – everything from financial management to counseling to coaching hockey – each of us was the leader of a gang or extremist group earlier in life. While we've given up street life and hatred, we've still got the alpha personalities that drove us to climb the gang ranks in the first place. You've heard that phrase, "too many chefs in the kitchen." Well, try half a dozen former gang leaders on the conference call! Seriously, some of us, myself included without doubt, got in our own way sometimes, but it was mostly because we were all passionate about what we were trying to do. And the idea worked. There are people out there who aren't in prison or a grave because Life After Hate helped them.

While Life After Hate continues to thrive as an organization, the individuals involved have changed over time. I was active with the group for several years, then it was time for me to step away and put my focus on other projects. The energy created by Life After Hate inspired everybody involved to get creative, and that's led to some real innovation in how to get our shared message in front of more audiences. I've mostly concentrated on speaking and media projects, and, as always, using sports to reach kids. Arno partnered with the son of one of the men who lost his life in the Oak Creek Sikh Temple massacre and co-founded Serve2Unite. Sammy combined his firsthand knowledge of both criminality and corrections, his education, and his vast experience as a counselor to come up with an ingenious new way to help people: Formers Anonymous (FA) is a support group system for people trying to break their attachment to everything associated with "street life." While we may not all still be directly involved in the original idea we launched, a lot of good has come from that circle we formed in a hotel atrium in Ireland.

I sometimes stop to think about how my life might have been different if some of these groups had existed when I was younger. Tony MacAleer once said something about himself that really struck home for me, too: "I didn't lose my humanity when I joined a hate group; I gave it up for acceptance." What if somebody had had the wisdom and the balls to say that to me when I was fourteen and so desperate to belong anywhere and be loved by anybody that I was willing to buy into the skinheads' racism? If a group like Life After Hate had reached out to me at the right time, they might have saved my victims and me at least a couple years of my hatred. And if Formers Anonymous had been around after I got out of prison, there's at least an outside chance I might not have made the jump from hate to heroin.

I DON'T HAVE a "man cave" in our house, but I do have my own
room at Clifton Collins Jr.'s place in Los Angeles. He and I stayed
tight even after filming wrapped on *The Experiment*. He invited me
to crash at his house whenever I had speaking engagements
in Los Angeles. I stayed with him so often that he nicknamed his
one guest room "Frankie's room." For a while I was staying with
Clifton so frequently I think he might have been able to claim me
as a tax deduction.

Clifton let me stay with him because he's a true friend and
also because he believes stories like mine can help people.
So in addition to providing me with a bed, he stepped up to be a
mentor to me when various producers showed interest in
turning my story into something other than a book. For more
than a year, in between speeches, I bounced from coast to coast,
New York to LA, with pit stops in Iowa to hug Valerie and the
kids. During the worst of it, I was taking dozens of calls each week,
no matter where I was, about one project idea or another, and
flying out for so many meetings I would have to check myself
walking in the door to make sure I knew which project idea
I was supposed to be talking about. But the more I worked with
different producers to help pitch their ideas and the more I
tried to pitch a concept of my own, it was like I got caught in a
time loop: I kept having the same damn meeting with different
people. No matter if it was a feature film, a documentary or a
TV series, the meetings were always the same: a bunch of studio
or network suits would gather around a conference table, I'd
get stuck in what I swear was always the one tiny chair in every
room, they'd break eye contact with me to stare at my tattoos,
I'd answer all their questions, then they'd get really quiet and
say, "We'll get back to you."

Most didn't. A few did. Clifton, my speaking agent, and the
rights agents and lawyers affiliated with my publisher helped
me figure out what was what. But even with all their advice, not
all the projects got off the ground. A movie deal made it all the
way to screenwriting, but stalled waiting in line behind some of

the production company's other projects. It's not clear right now what, if anything, might happen with that. I also had an idea for a reality show that would be sort of like *Intervention*, but for people caught up in hate. Sammy Rangel agreed to do it with me. A well-known television production company signed on and funded a pilot episode. We shopped the pilot around to a few cable networks that seemed interested at first, but in the end nobody was willing to commit to a full season. Another former skinhead tried to get a similar idea on air more recently. He made it a lot farther than we did. Several episodes were filmed and the debut was scheduled when the TV network unleashed an advertising blitz to promote it. That's when the show's controversial title set off a frenzy of outrage on social media because people thought, from just the title, that the show was glorifying the Klan instead to trying to help people get out of it. From what I understand, people who got to see advance showings of a few episodes – critics mostly, but also some people who work with civil rights groups – thought the show had the potential to really make a difference and help people. But it seems the network decided the negative buzz was too much of a risk. First they tried changing the title. When that didn't calm the storm, they pulled the plug on the whole thing. Not one episode was ever aired because people worried that the show might glorify hatred. But how are we supposed to fight hatred if we aren't willing to look it in the face?

Stories like mine are hard to hear. I understand that. Hell, they are hard as fuck to live. But when I share my story, people seem to understand some things on a different level than they did before. Instead of just chanting, "Hate is bad, hate is bad, hate is bad," they begin to see the person on the other side of the hate. They start to wrap their brains around how a kid like I was could get sucked up into hatred. And as hard as it is to see the person underneath the label "hater," we have to do that. We have to understand how hate takes hold of a person if we really want to stop it. And if we really do want to stop the hate, we have to find it in ourselves to feel authentic empathy for that kid. We have to understand him so we can help him. We have to understand him to have any hope of stopping him before he hurts or kills somebody. That does not mean we don't have empathy for the people he thinks he hates. Not at all! It's because we care about them and keeping them safe that we have to understand the kid who is hating.

Imagine if guys like Keith hadn't given me a chance. Imagine if every time I took a baby step toward change, people had screamed "Racist!" at me and kicked me further back down into the depths of hatred. That could have happened. I'm lucky that didn't happen. The world is lucky that didn't happen. Do you even want to think about a world with me in it, twenty-five years deeper into hate and more violent than I was back in the early 1990s? Would you want that Frankie Meeink living next door to you?

Known Enough

I HAVE NEVER FELT QUITE SO OLD AS I FELT THE FIRST time I went out in public with Kristian Day. When I met him, I was pushing forty; he was in his late twenties and looked a lot like the star of *Twilight*. Every teenage girl we passed on our way to the coffee shop turned into Linda Blair in *The Exorcist*, spinning her head around backwards to gawk at him. The soccer moms waiting in line needed drool bibs by the time our order was ready. I swear I could have stripped naked in that coffee shop and not one female would have noticed.

Kristian looks like a movie star, but he works the other side of the camera. He is a cameraman for a lot of popular TV shows, including *The Bachelor*. He also makes his own independent movies and documentaries. Of course, I didn't know any of that the first time I heard his name. Kristian was shooting a movie in Iowa when one of the actors he'd flown in from LA didn't pan out. A buddy of mine tipped me off about an ad posted for an actor with some film experience to play a character named Frankie. I called the number. No answer. The voice mail greeting said the number belonged to Kristian Day. I hung up without leaving a message. About an hour later, I tried again. He still didn't answer, but this time I left a message stating my qualifications: "I've acted a couple times and my name's Frankie." He didn't call me back. I called some of the Des Moines-based film people I'd met while working on *The Experiment* to see if Mr. I-Don't-Return-Calls was legit. He was. He had produced and directed several documentaries and short films that had received rave reviews from critics.

After a few days of phone tag, Kristian hired me to play Frankie in *The Vessel*. It was a small part in a small film that never made it to theatres, but it brought Kristian and me together for something more important. As we got to know each other a little bit during filming, Kristian expressed interest in my speaking, so I invited him to tag along for a couple local talks I had scheduled. He brought his camera. Not long after that, we decided to team up on a documentary project.

Is This Heaven? explores the diversity of religions and spiritual practices in Iowa. I know "diversity" probably isn't the first word that pops into most people's minds when they think of Iowa, but it should be, at least when it comes to religion. In addition to Catholics and every denomination of Protestants, Iowa is home to the Mother Mosque of America, the second-oldest and longest standing mosque in North America. Iowa is also the site of several different types of Buddhist temples, Sikh temples, and Hindu temples. Jewish synagogues are scattered throughout the state. Religious diversity is woven throughout the history of the Iowa. The famous Amana Colonies were founded by Pietists. While fleeing persecution in the nineteenth century, Mormons crossed through Iowa, and some settled there. Quakers have long had meeting groups in Iowa. The tiny town of Fairfield is home to Maharishi University and boasts one of the largest Transcendental Meditation communities in the world. And, of course, many Native American tribes have been practicing their spiritual traditions in the area for centuries.

The idea for the documentary was that I would interview people from all these different faiths to find out what they believe and why they believe it. I was totally into it because I had become fascinated with everything about Fairfield, Iowa – mostly about how a city smaller than ten thousand people in the middle of Midwest nowhere had become a global center for meditation studies. But my interest in the project went deeper than that and it was personal. Back when I first joined the skinheads, identity theology fine-tuned my hatred. It aimed my hatred. It convinced me violence was God's way and God's will. When I was in Sangamon County Jail, it was a group of black inmates gathered for Bible study who made me feel, for the first time in a very long time, like I wasn't a worthless piece of shit. I'd been raised Catholic, but I spent most of my adult life practicing the twelve steps like religion, turning my will and my life over to the care of God as I understood him. But how, exactly, did I understand Him? How did other people understand Him? I really wanted to know. And Kristian really wanted to document my spiritual learning journey on film.

Starting in 2012, Kristian followed me around Iowa while I interviewed religious leaders and also regular people from various faiths. I asked them what faith meant to them and also what heaven meant. I talked to people who felt their faith required them to serve others, even those who held other beliefs. I also interviewed people who believed their religion demanded that they try to block other people's rights. At the time, marriage equality was a hot issue in Iowa. Some of the people I spoke with felt a religious calling to deny gay people the right to marry. By 2012, I totally disagreed with them. But there was a time in my life when I fundamentally believed in a religion that told me I had a right and responsibility to rain violence down on gay people. And black people. And Latin people. And Asian people. And Jews. And Muslims. And any white people who disagreed with me.

One of the people we interviewed for the film isn't from Iowa, but he was passing through for a concert. The first time I met Matisyahu I was riding shotgun in a car in LA traffic. The driver was a manager I was talking to about representing me back when I was shopping the television pilot. He was trying to explain to me what a manager does that's different from an agent. I was not getting it when his phone rang. He put the caller, one of clients, on speaker and said, "Matis, you're never going to believe who's in the car with me."

"Who?" Matis asked.

"A former neo-Nazi."

It wasn't the first time I was introduced so bluntly to a Jewish person who became my friend in spite of my past. Matisyahu sings reggae. He also beatboxes and raps and can wail straight-up rock, too. His music is this magical mix of cultures and spiritualism that makes me feel like I'm in a hot club on holy ground. It's trippy in a mystical way, not in an acid way.

Matis and I kept in touch after our odd first phone call. He invited my wife and me to his concerts when he came through our area. One time, he and I stayed up half the night talking about God and life on his tour bus. So I knew he would be a perfect person to interview for *Is This Heaven?*

Is This Heaven? was and still is a low-budget labor of love for everybody involved. As a result, we work on it when time and money allow. The interview footage we have so far and the editing Kristian has done along the way are shaping up to be powerful. It's turning into exactly what we hoped: a documentary that will make people really reflect on what they believe and how that shapes who they are and how they live their lives. I don't know when or if we'll ever get it finished or released, but the process of making it has helped me square up some feelings in my own soul.

MAYBE BECAUSE I spent so many years of my life only seeing differences in people and hating them for it, now I like to see the similarities. I get a real kick out of it when people's appearances look totally opposite, then I learn they are like the same person inside. Matisyahu and my friend Will Holmes are like that. Matis is a tallish, skinny, pale white Jewish guy who spent a lot of years of his life growing out dishwater-blond dreads. Will has skin the color of strong coffee, always wears his hair tucked under a tight cap that he pulls down low over his eyes, and he's built like a Sherman tank. Matis looks like a good wind might blow him off stage; Will looks like he'd tell the wind to fuck off and it would. Yet for as different as those two appear, their hearts are so similar: they are two of the kindest and also most talented people I've ever met.

Will is a product of extreme childhood abuse and one of the bloodiest ganglands in the world: Chicago. He almost died while in a gang and risked his life to break free. The physical scars from his street life weren't as deep as the emotional ones inflicted by his abuser. Somehow, he overcame that trauma, too. He moved to Iowa, worked his way up in the civil service, and became the kind of husband every woman deserves and the kind of father every kid needs.

Will isn't just an active father for his own kids; he's a father figure for his entire neighborhood and for kids in schools all over Iowa. A few years ago, he started sharing his story to help kids facing the same kind of struggles he did at their age. That's how I met him. And once I heard him speak and he heard me speak, we started speaking together some of the time. Like him and Matis, Will and I look like there would be not one similarity between us. That we were once in gangs that would have opened fire on each other given the right opportunity only furthers that point. And that's exactly what we want the kids to see: even though we look different and were in rival gangs, on everything that really matters, we have so much in common.

Except for one thing. And that one thing screws my shot at being the popular one every time we present together. Will Holmes, the speaker, is also Will Keeps, the rapper and R&B artist. No matter how on fire I am when we're talking, the minute he starts singing, it's all over. The guy has a voice that actually brings tears to my eyes. And he's using his musical talents to get his message across. Some of his R&B stuff is pure baby-making music, but his rap, in recent years, is all about getting kids to value themselves and to do right by their communities. This guy is so amazing that both teenage bad asses and cops agree to be in his videos. This guys is so amazing that he actually convinced none other than Frankie Meeink to produce some of his videos! Seriously, once I heard his music, I knew it could save some kids. I also knew it could help open better lines of communication between teenagers and police in Des Moines at a time when tensions were running really high. I jumped at the chance to use what I'd learned from my experiences on film and video shoots to help him out. Check out Will Keeps on YouTube, especially his video for "Wake Up Iowa." The man's message is powerful.

ONE EVENING WHEN I was crashing in "my" room at Clifton's out in LA, a buddy of his stopped by to visit. By then, I'd met quite a few famous people and managed not to make a total ass of myself, but I gotta tell you, meeting Slash had the potential to turn me into a screaming teeny-bopper.

When I was a skinhead, I mostly listened to white-power music. Mainstream artists had to be unbelievably good to crack through my cone of hate. Guns N' Roses busted my cone. I loved that band. I loved every song on *Appetite for Destruction*. The only thing I loved more than Axl Rose's voice was Slash's guitar solos. I loved Guns N' Roses so fucking much back then that I kept listening to them even after I found out Slash was half black. For a skinhead, that's huge.

Slash in private is every bit as cool as Slash on stage. The guy can't help it: it's who he is. He is also really smart and funny and open. He put me at ease and included me immediately in his conversation with Clifton. As the evening wore on, other friends of Clifton's popped by and the informal party broke up into various side talks. At a certain point, Slash and I ended up sitting together, just the two of us, mostly shooting the shit and sharing our histories of addiction. He told me what it's like to have other rock stars stage an intervention on you. I told him what it's like to have crackheads pull the same move. We shared some good laughs about how out of control we'd each been at our worst and some real heart-to-heart stuff about staying clean and sober.

I knew Slash had battled addiction before I met him. Anybody who's ever read an article about Guns N' Roses knows about his issues and those of almost everybody else in the band. Hearing him talk about his journey to get clean got me thinking back to those convenience-store eyes I'd once watched lock onto Clifton and Adrien Brody. In concert, Slash plays with tens of thousands of eyes staring at and through him. He's one of the most famous musicians in the world. He's also one of the most recognizable and he has been for nearly thirty years. Little kids know who Slash is. Teenagers know who Slash is. Their parents have known who Slash is since they were teenagers. Hell, I don't think that dude could visit a nursing home without a row of grannies lining up in their wheelchairs to get his autograph.

So how must it feel to go to an Alcoholics Anonymous meeting when you can't be? Even if everybody at the meeting keeps the confidentiality rules, even if they try their hardest to hold faith to the teaching that we are all the same, it's still fucking Slash sitting in the chair in the back row, and everybody knows it.

When I'm traveling and hit meetings, nobody knows who I am and what I do unless I feel the need to tell them. Even when I'm in a city to speak, until I arrive at the venue where I'm presenting, nobody knows who I am unless I bring it up. If I sat in the middle of an airport holding up a copy of this book with me on the cover, most people passing by would just keep on passing by, not making the connection or not knowing who I am even if they did put two and two together. While there have been occasional exceptions, for the most part I get to choose when I want to be known, when I want to get noticed. Guys like Slash don't get that option.

When I was a kid, laying on top of that fort my cousin and I built by the Walt Whitman bridge, my greatest aspiration was to get inside the Flyers' arena so I could see my idols play. Just watching them from the top row of seats would have been the most amazing thing I could imagine. It never even occurred to me to dream of becoming friends with them, or with movie stars, or rock stars, or movers and shakers in business and politics. People like that were so far removed from my life on Tree Street that I didn't actually believe they were real. They were just faces on the television screen, as make-believe to me as Bugs Bunny.

Maybe that's why I seem to get along pretty well with the famous people I've met. Once I actually start talking with the person, I can't quite get my brain to accept that the human standing in front of me is the movie star I've seen on screen or the rock star who played the soundtrack of my youth. I'm not sure if that means I'm a little dumb or I believe in doppelgangers, but it's how it works in my head.

I feel that same way about myself sometimes, especially if I have a lot of speeches scheduled back-to-back. I'm full-on Frankie when I speak. I'm authentically and honestly me. But I can only be a small portion of myself in a ninety-minute talk. No matter how real I keep it, I still sometimes feel disconnected from myself by the time I walk off stage, like I'm more a character or even a caricature than a real person. This book has let me go a lot deeper into my story than I can in speeches, but even it doesn't cover everything. It can't. No book can contain a human life.

MY WIFE IS far more impressed when I remember to put the dryer sheet in the laundry than she is with me meeting celebrities. Over the years, she's been able to meet a lot of them, too. Most of them have been blown away that a woman as gorgeous as Valerie is a systems consultant instead of a supermodel. But not even compliments like that have turned her head much. Valerie isn't the type to go gaga over somebody just because they've won an Oscar or a Grammy.

In fact, I've only had one celebrity encounter that truly impressed my wife, and it almost got me in major shit with her.

A woman from the ADL called to tell me a writer had asked to interview me. The writer had read my autobiography and said she wanted to ask me some questions to help her develop a fictional character for a novel. Her book was going to focus on issues of race and racism and the character she wanted my input on was a skinhead. The woman from the ADL told me the author's name and stressed that I should call her right away because she was a pretty big deal. I had to take her word for it, because I'd never heard of the person. But I made the call and scheduled the interview. The writer and her husband would travel to Iowa so she could spend a whole day asking me questions. When Valerie got home from work, I told her when I was going to be doing the interview. I was mostly just making sure we had our schedules straight so somebody would be available to pick up the kids from school. While I was running down the times and locations, the kids and the dog were all circling Valerie as she tried to untangled herself from her purse and her briefcase.

"So who are you talking to?" she asked. I could tell she was trying to sound interested, but she mostly just sounded exhausted.

"Her name's Jodi something," I said. I dug a note out of my pocket to check the name. I had no clue how to pronounce it. What came out of my mouth next sounded like "pickle loaf."

"JODI PICOULT?!?!?!" Valerie's voice pitched so high I worried the paint was going to peel off the ceiling. "Oh! My!! God!!! Frankie, seriously, are you telling me Jodi Picoult wants to meet you?"

"Yeah," I said. "Who is Jodi Picoult?"

So it turns out that Jodi Picoult is one of the top-selling authors of the last decade. Jodi and her husband travelled to Des Moines so she could interview me. Valerie spit-shined me before she left for work that morning to make sure I didn't embarrass her in front of the visiting royalty. I spent most of the afternoon with Jodi, sipping coffee and answering her questions. Later that day, Jodi went along to hear me give a talk.

I'd told her earlier that my wife was impressed such a big-time author wanted to talk to me, so when I was driving Jodi back to her hotel, she said she'd love to meet Valerie. I knew Valerie would be thrilled to meet Jodi, so I headed toward our house.

When I ushered Jodi Picoult through the front door, Valerie was standing in the middle of a mess the kids had made in the living room and she was wearing footie pajamas. I am still allowed in our house only because Jodi Picoult is not just a great writer, but a truly great person. She was so wonderful to Valerie that Valerie didn't even make me sleep in the yard that night.

I'VE GOTTEN A decent amount of attention in recent years, but I'm not famous. The closest to famous I ever felt was when word about my cable-access show *The Reich* arrived inside the Illinois prison system before I did; whether they loved me or hated me, every dude in the yard knew who I was. Then again, maybe that was a brush with infamy more than fame.

A few years ago, I had a speaking engagement in St. Louis. Back at my hotel after the talk, I popped into the sports bar in the lobby to catch a game on TV that I couldn't get in my room. I was sitting there nursing an O'Douls – because a nonalcoholic beer with an Irish-sounding name is as far as this recovering alcoholic and addict can go on St. Patty's Day now – when I saw someone across the bar who looked familiar, but I wasn't 100 percent positive he was who I thought he was. So I wound my way through the crowd to find out. I was standing right behind him when I tapped him on the shoulder and asked, "Youse ever been kidnapped?"

The closet Sharpie I brutalized in Springfield, Illinois, turned around, recognized me immediately and screamed right in my face, "Dude, I saw you on MTV!"

I was glad I finally got to apologize to the guy for what I'd done to him, but his reaction freaked me out a little. He told me that after he saw me on TV, he told all his friends how I'd once held him prisoner and beaten the hell out of him. It was like me being on television made him proud to have been my victim.

I've got really mixed feelings about becoming more well known and they get more mixed up the more well-known I become. The purely egotistical part of me loves it. When people do recognize me, it feeds something deep inside me; that same attention-starved kid who joined the skinheads freaking loves to autograph books. I try hard to monitor myself, to keep an eye out for when my ego's sneaking into the driver's seat. It's hard for me to see it happening sometimes, because that was my default setting for so many years: that's how I lived as a skinhead, as a prisoner, and most of all as an addict. When I get cocky, I'm not just a dick, I'm dangerous. There's a reason why all recovery programs stress the importance of staying humble. Humility is the only thing standing between me and heroin.

JODI'S NOVEL, *Small Great Things*, came out in 2016 and almost immediately made the number one spot on the *New York Times* best-seller list. I joke around that it's "our" book, but, of course, it isn't: as I now know, Jodi Picoult is a pretty big-time writer all on her own. Still, it was cool to meet her and to help however I could by answering some of her questions. That day we spent together, she explained the concept of the book to me and talked about the title. Dr. Martin Luther King Jr. once said, "If I cannot do great things, I can do small things in a great way." That idea is at the center of what happens in Jodi's story. It was an idea I needed a reminder of at the time I met her. I need that reminder every day, actually.

Ever since I first started speaking out against hatred, break-ing news of yet another hate crime has felt like a slap in the face. No matter how much I do – no matter how much all the other formers do and all the other sorts of people trying to stop hatred do – there's always another kid out there preparing his next attack. It feels sometimes like we're just screaming at the wind; our voices, no matter how many, how loud, how powerful, can't stop the tornado that keeps gaining strength and bearing down on innocent people. In 2016, as the presidential election heated up, the hate was everywhere and nobody could escape. The kind of uncensored hate I used to hear only inside closed-door meetings of actual white-supremacy groups was suddenly in sound bites on the news and being shared and liked by "normal" people on social media. Watching it made me wonder if anything I'd ever done had made any difference at all.

The 2016 campaign season was like a flashback for me; it felt like the build up to a gang war. And maybe it was. Only time will tell. As I write this, in February 2017, it's too early to know how it's all going to play out. But I know what I saw during the campaign: I saw one side fan people's fears, offer up scapegoats, and promise security in exchange for loyalty, just like I used to do when I was a gang recruiter. And I saw the other side respond with horror and name-calling and mocking the "stupidity" of anybody who fell for those arguments, which is exactly the sort of reaction that pushed me and every skinhead I ever met deeper into hatred than we had been before.

I find it hard some days to find the will to keep talking about how to overcome hate when it seems like hate is everywhere now. But that's when I remember the title of Jodi's book and the quotation that inspired it: "If I cannot do great things, I can do small things in a great way." One of my speeches isn't going to change the world, but it may help one kid. Maybe someday that kid will be the one who does the great thing. Or at least maybe someday that kid won't be the one who kills somebody.

Puck Daddy

MY YOUNGEST SON, LITTLE NICK, IS LIVING THE CHILD-hood I fantasized about as a kid. Actually, he's not, because in my wildest dreams I could not have imagined doing half the shit Nick is getting to do. And let me be clear, I'm talking about the stuff that really matters here: I'm talking hockey. My son Nick has ice in his veins. From the time he could walk he was grabbing for my gear. At age two, he would slam our little pug, Buttercup, into the wall and baby-talk scream, "Check in the boards!" Nick learned early not just to play well, but to play hard. He had to: Buttercup is a fucking thug.

Nick was still a toddler when we told him he was about to become a big brother. He wasn't very excited until we asked him what he thought we should name his new baby sister.

"Fargosrena!" he said, without hesitation.

Valerie and I knew at that moment Nick was going to be a great big brother. He wanted to name his little sister after the most important place in his universe: as a little kid, "Fargosrena" was the closest he could get to pronouncing Wells Fargo Arena, where the Iowa Stars played hockey. The poor kid was crushed when we told him we decided to go with Jayla, instead.

I'VE BEEN INVOLVED in hockey in one way or another ever since I can remember, as a fan trying to see the Flyers from the top of a fort made with stolen wood, as a young player honing my shots by aiming at a grocery cart I sunk into a pond before it froze for winter, and as one of the guys who survived checks through the boards and out into the parking lot at a dilapidated rink in South Philly. Those are some of my very best childhood memories.

The rinks I play now are nothing like the ones I grew up with. Hockey is serious business in the Midwest, and there's enough money in most communities to fund great facilities. In Des Moines, the biggest and best rink is inside Wells Fargo Arena, which is home to the city's American Hockey League franchise. The AHL is to the NHL as minor league baseball is to MLB; it's where the pro teams polish their new talent before they bring them up to the big game. That means the AHL is where you find the next generation of hockey greats, playing their hearts out to win those coveted spots. Most of the guys playing AHL grew up playing elite junior league hockey in the US and Canada. Some come from other parts of the world, usually hockey heavens like Norway or Finland. Some played D1 college hockey, but just like with baseball, college isn't the only or even the fastest route to the majors: some of these kids are so good at age eighteen, they get drafted straight into the pros.

The Iowa Stars were the AHL affiliate team of the NHL's Dallas Stars. They helped me get Harmony Through Hockey started in Des Moines, just like the Flyers had helped in Philly. I made great relationships with some of the Stars' front office people because of our collaboration on Harmony Through Hockey. In 2007, they offered me a position as a marketing coordinator for the team. About a year later, the franchise shifted, as happens in pro sports: the Iowa Stars became the Iowa Chops and affiliated with the NHL's Anaheim Ducks. In a front office restructure, I was offered the job of Director of Fan Development. In that position and the one before it, I spent most of my time on the phone or out in the community, helping promote the team and trying to drum up the fan base and, with it, the revenues. The people who do those jobs are as important to a hockey team as the players: the players can't play if nobody brings in the money to pay the bills. The utility bills alone are insane: it takes a hell of a lot of water and air-conditioning to keep a full-size hockey rink frozen to perfection. There are millions of dollars of other expenses, too. Pro hockey is a business, a big one.

But I'm not a business guy. Considering I had no formal education past middle school and no actual experience in marketing when I accepted the first position, I did a surprisingly good job going off gut instinct. Basically, I used my passion for the game and my firsthand knowledge of hockey fan culture to get people pumped about the Stars and then the Chops. But there were parts of each job that deserved more than just a full-time fan in the position. And I wasn't all that happy in either position, because my duties meant I missed most of the action on the ice during games.

Early in 2009, I resigned my full-time office spot with the Chops and accepted a part-time support role for the team instead. With Jayla about to be born, Valerie and I needed the scheduling flexibility the new job gave me. And I needed to get out of the front office and closer to the ice, which the new job would let me do during season, until the book came out and I'd set off on my speaking tour.

Whether I've been front office, team support staff, or just the Harmony Through Hockey coach who pops in once a week to book coaching and ice time, I've never let my work with hockey get in the way of playing. I signed up for a men's ice hockey league the very first year Valerie and I moved to Des Moines. That league and the game itself are what kept me tethered to reality while I adjusted to life in the Midwest. That league and my AA meetings are where I first met most of the people who have become my friends in Des Moines. Both places sometimes make for strange mash-ups of people. One season in the league, I was part of a line that got the nickname "The Legal System," thanks to the backgrounds of us three players: a cop, a lawyer, and me.

WHEN NICK WAS tiny, Valerie would dress him in three or four layers of clothes and a snowsuit and bring him to watch the Stars games. Like most moms, Valerie never left the house with Nick unless she had an arsenal of stuff to ward off a tantrum. The first time she brought him to a game, she packed half his toy box to make sure he wouldn't get bored sitting in a freezing cold hockey arena for two hours. I remember looking up into the stands at one point and seeing Valerie dancing a toy in front of Nick's face. He could have cared less about that toy. All he wanted to do was watch the action on the ice.

Nick was two the very first time he was in skates. The picture of him holding my hand on the ice, both of us grinning, is one of my all-time favorite photos. Before that, the trunk of my car was always full of my hockey gear, which smells like death, and our back-up stash of diapers, which would smell like death soon enough. After Nick felt those skates on his feet, whenever we headed to the arena, his "gear" had to get loaded in the trunk, too: his tiny skates, his plastic stick, his size 2T Flyers jersey. He got his first real gear when we signed him up for Mini Mite hockey. I still have the little blue puck, dated 10-24-08, from when he scored his first goal. He was five.

Nick doesn't just play hockey; he never has. Like me, Nick lives and breathes hockey. But when he plays now, at age thirteen, I gotta admit, he's better than I was at that age; he's better than I have ever been. The pride nearly suffocates me some days.

My buddy, Rob, is one of the very first friends I made when we moved to Iowa; we met through the men's hockey league. He's a real serious hockey player himself and he has a son Nick's age. He and I teamed up to coach the kids' Mini Mite team that first year. When we started gearing up for the season, we had our team practicing full ice with normal rules. Some of the kids on our team were really talented; they were all over that rink from day one. With our help, the rest were learning quickly. But a five-year-old teetering center on full ice looks like a baby penguin stranded all alone in Antarctica – at least that's how some of the parents saw it. They thought it was too much. Most of those parents never played hockey themselves, so they didn't get why Rob and I were so insistent on using full ice. The ice isn't going to get smaller, but the kids will get bigger. If they learn from day one to play full ice, then it becomes part of them; the dimensions of the rink melt into their brains and shape their peripheral vision. If full ice is all they ever know, they never have to adjust to it; it's their normal.

The only thing worse, in my opinion, than starting a kid on anything less than full ice is forcing the kid to downgrade to it. So when some of the parents in the league wanted to switch, mid-season, to playing only a third of the ice, I was not happy. Neither was Rob. We tried to convince people to at least wait until the start of the next season to make the switch so as not to mess up what the kids had already learned, but we got outvoted based on a rule they found in some USA Hockey materials.

Rob and I decided to keep our kids out of league play until they were old enough to be allowed to play the full rink. In the meantime, we got them started playing roller hockey so we could work on fundamentals. Other kids showed interest, too. Before we knew it, Rob and I were organizing a club roller hockey program that drew dozens of kids from the community. A year later, when Nick returned to ice hockey, he was playing full ice with a full year of roller hockey street smarts guiding his every move. Since then, Nick has played roller hockey year round and ice hockey during its five-month season. Rob and I continue to coach and have grown our roller hockey club, the Des Moines Xplosion, into a pretty big deal. Our teams travel all around the country to compete; Xplosion teams have won four national championships and a youth world title.

I've had a lot of support from parents and the whole hockey community in Des Moines and nationally to enable me to be so active as a coach. Unlike Harmony Through Hockey, which is a recreational and educational program, the leagues I coach now are hypercompetitive and subject to regulations the size of a Philadelphia phone book. One part of that big book puts limitations on official coaching status for people with felony records. The parents of every kid I've ever coached know about my history. It's not like I've ever tried to hide it, what with the speaking and the book and everything, but I tell them all at the beginning of each season anyhow. I follow those regulations to the letter because being able to coach these kids means the world to me. Of all the things I've achieved professionally, of all the amazing projects I've worked on and all the amazing people I've worked with, that I am trusted to coach other people's kids in this game that I love is what I consider to be my biggest accomplishment.

NICK AND ME share hockey like we share DNA; it's a bond we can't deny. And it's carried us through most of the everyday tensions that flare up between a dad and a son. No matter how mad he is that I won't let him stay up past bedtime, or how mad I am that he forgot to take out the trash, none of that matters when we get to the rink. Whether we've got blades or wheels on, once we're at the rink we're just two dudes who love hockey and each other.

The kind of traveling teams I now coach and Nick now competes on are a family affair. Valerie and Jayla are part of the giant crew of parents and siblings that come along to almost every tournament. We are one of those big noisy groups you hate to see pulling up to your hotel because you fear we'll take over the pool and eat all the good donuts before you make it down to the continental breakfast buffet. And you're basically right, but it's not the players and coaches you need to worry about; it's the parents and siblings who come along to cheer that you need to watch out for.

For Valerie and Jayla, hockey tournaments are like a weekend-long slumber party with twenty or thirty of their best friends. Valerie has known most of the other hockey moms for years and Jayla has never known life without her hockey family. They cheer Nick and his teammates on during the big games, but they also do their own thing when we're on the road, checking out the local attractions and, of course, munching donuts while taking over the hotel pool area.

Jayla is the mini-Valerie. I don't think I am her father. It's not that I think some other dude is her father; I actually suspect Valerie cloned herself. Jayla looks exactly like a tiny Valerie. She's every bit as smart as her mom and just as sassy. I try not to let her boss me around, but it's hard. She's so damn cute and kind of scary.

Jayla is my project partner. In 2016, she worked harder than Nick, helping me to build an ice rink in our backyard. In the spring and summer, she and I spend a lot of time working in the garden together. I'm not sure how a South Philly boy like me grew a green thumb, but I have and I love it. Jayla does, too, and she's a good helper when we're actually trying to get something done, but we spend a lot of time just exploring. I think she may end up being a scientist. She likes to find things in the yard, whether it's a new kind of plant or a bug she hasn't seen before, and then we go online and do a little research to learn about it.

Then again, Jayla may end up being on the crew of a show like *Jackass*. My sweet little strawberry-blonde angel of a daughter busts a gut watching videos of people falling down or getting hit in the head while doing stupid shit. Seriously, this girl has no mercy for the injured. She could spend an entire afternoon watching YouTube videos of people whacking their heads or breaking their butts. I know, because I've spent many an entire afternoon snuggled up with her on the couch doing exactly that.

Sometimes when I'm playing in the yard with Jayla or talking hockey with Nick, or driving them to school or tucking them in at night, I am suddenly overcome with emotion. I'm so incredibly grateful to be able to experience each little moment with these two amazing kids. And I'm so sad and so sorry that I missed so many of the same kinds of moments with my three older kids.

Over the years, I stayed closest with Matt, my son with Nina.

The friendship Valerie and Nina forged out of the mess I made
of that whole situation continues to amaze me. There's never
been a time that we weren't all in it together to do the best by
Matt. In the years he lived with Nina in Philly, she kept the door
wide open for me and Valerie to be a big part of his life, and
when Matt lived with Valerie and me, we made sure it was the
same for Nina.

Matt lived with us from September through May for nearly
seven years so he could go to school in Iowa. He grew from a
little kid, with a mop of curly hair we could barely comb, into a
lanky teenager with a mop of curly hair no gel could control.
He decided to return to Philly to enroll in a special high school
program. I think he also wanted to have his own room again.
Nick and Jayla love Matt, and when they were really little there
wasn't a lock made that could keep either of them from breaking into wherever he was hiding. The poor guy had zero privacy
at our house. But that wasn't the big driver of his decision to
move back to Philly. He missed his mom and he missed Philly,
itself, too. The high school program he wanted to do was just
icing on the cake.

Unfortunately, the special high school program didn't pan
out and Matt ended up at Furness, the South Philly hell school
I got kicked out of once when I was a student and once when I
wasn't. Nina, Valerie, and I were worried about him going there;
it's still a really rough school and it's not exactly known for all
the Ivy-Leaguers it produces. Something happened to Matt at
Furness none of us predicted: he became a great student. A kid
who had never really liked school much got down to business
and made honor role. He got involved in a bunch of activities,
mostly charity and activist groups. He got into science and envi-
ronmentalism and went on a trip to the Galápagos Islands.
Then one day he called and proudly announced he'd been elected
the leader of the school's feminist group.

"Well played, dude," I said, thinking my son was more like
me than he is. "That's a great way to meet the ladies."

"Dad," he said sternly. His disappointment in me dripped through the phone connection. "These issues matter."

They do matter. And I love that he's so passionate about the causes that matter to him. I just can't figure out where he learned to be so serious. I know he didn't learn it from me and I doubt he learned it from Nina. Nina's brilliant and driven, but she's not exactly known for her traditional approach to life. Even though she was a teenager when Matt was born, Nina stayed in school; she went on to earn her college degree, went to grad school to study disaster medicine and management, and held down a professional job for as long as she could stand it. But a few years back, she had to follow her heart. Nina didn't run off to join the circus; she joined the side show. Nina has become one of the most popular sideshow performers in North America. Her acts include everything from death-defying high wire motor-cycle stunts to feats of contortion, "anatomical wonders," and some routines that are right on the border of fascinating and gross. Not a lot of totally normal, honor-roll, social activists like our son Matt can say their daddy was a skinhead and their mama eats bugs for a living.

My oldest son, Jake, was born less than nine months before Matt. His mom, Maria, never forgave me for falling in love with Nina, so I didn't get to spend much time with Jake when he was little. As I watched Matt grow from a baby into a toddler and then into a young boy, it made me realize what I was missing because I'd left Jake behind when I left his mother. Maria brought Jake to see me a couple times when he was a baby and I was living in the halfway house. That's when she started dating Muffin Ass from Second and Porter. They didn't last long and he never went through with his plan to adopt Jake. But even though I have always been Jake's father, legally, I've never had any custody rights to him, and I never took any real responsibility for him. I didn't send child support. I called to talk to him sometimes, but he couldn't count on when; whenever Maria sensed those calls were doing Jake more harm than good, she would block my number. In my worst years fighting my addiction, I didn't always even remember to send him birthday cards. The day Jake was born, Maria gave him her name, Salerno, instead of mine, as if she knew even then I wasn't going to be around for him.

But every once in a while, she would crack open the door for me to get to know him. When I was working on this book, Maria agreed to meet with the researcher who was helping me out. I figured she just wanted to bitch about me, but she didn't. She told the researcher how our relationship felt from her perspective. I treated her horribly, and that came through loud and clear in the interview, but she wasn't mean about it. She and I actually got along that day. We laughed together. We even hugged each other. And she invited me to go with her to see Jake perform at a music concert at his school. He looked like a miniature Harry Connick Jr. up on stage. But it's the look on that kid's face when he realized I was in the front row that I'll never forget.

I don't know if it was Maria seeing that same look on Jake's face or her seeing that I had really changed, but after that reunion she let me start seeing him again. On one visit, I took him to the Jersey shore, where Nanny and Pop were living in retirement. Ten years after he'd been born, Nanny and Pop finally got to meet their oldest great grandson. Sadly, not long after that visit, Nanny passed away. I know it meant the world to her that she lived long enough to tell Jake she loved him.

Jake spent several weeks that summer with Valerie and me. He and Matt bonded like twins. Having two "tween" boys in the house, as well as a toddler and two teenage girls, my sister Hayley and my daughter Riley, was crazy. It got crazier when we loaded the whole crew onto a rental houseboat for a week-long vacation. Marie called to check in a lot while Jake was with us. She still didn't trust me completely with him, but she seemed to trust Valerie to make sure Jake came home to her in one piece.

For a while, things between Jake and me were almost normal for a long-distance father-son relationship that was only about two years old. Maria met and married a really nice guy and they all moved to New Jersey. Jake would tell me all about his school and his friends when we talked on the phone. We talked about once a month. Then the time between phone calls grew longer. Then he stopped calling. When I tried calling, Maria wouldn't put him on the phone. I knew better than to push it. I still had no legal rights to see him or even speak to him. I hoped maybe one day soon he'd call again. He didn't.

Kids under thirteen aren't supposed to have Facebook accounts, but I knew Jake had one and I used it to check up on him occasionally. If it hadn't been my only way to see how he was doing, I would have been pissed he wasn't using any privacy settings. I watched his page like a creeper for a few months, then, on Jake's thirteenth birthday, I sent him a friend request. He accepted right away. We had a couple "Hi. how are you?" private message exchanges, then I realized I had been unfriended and could no longer even see his page. A few days later, I got a private message from a name I didn't recognize: it was Jake, using one of his friend's accounts. He told me his mom was not happy about seeing me on his Facebook friends list, but he had a plan. He'd made a new account so we could talk; I'd be his only friend there and his mom wouldn't know about it.

Over the course of just a few weeks, Jake and I really bonded through that secret Facebook page. He got a kick out of the cloak-and-dagger feel of talking to me in secret. I liked the fact that he really opened up to me, more than he ever had on the phone or even in person. I could tell he was relaxed communicating with me that way. He told me about his girlfriend and about how he had started playing hockey. He said he sucked at it because he didn't start playing when he was younger. I coached him as fast as my fingers could type. Then one day he wrote to tell me his mom had found out we were back in touch. He said he could tell it really hurt her that he'd gone behind her back to talk to me. He didn't say he wasn't going to message me anymore, but I knew.

Nearly four years passed before I heard from him again. He contacted me through Twitter and said he didn't care what his mom thought about it, he wanted to get to know me better. So we started talking on that social media platform. I noticed he had two accounts; his mom was a follower on one, I was a follower on the other. Eventually, we traded cell phone numbers and switched to calls and texting. Jake asked if we could go on a trip together one day, once he was a legal adult and wouldn't need his mom's permission. I was thrilled. But I was surprised by where he wanted to go: Las Vegas. I warned him he wouldn't be able to do most of the things Vegas is known for until he turned twenty-one. He didn't care. That's not why he wanted to go. He wanted us to spend time together and he knew flights to Vegas were cheap.

Jake seemed more mature than most kids his age when he graduated high school. He was the kind of guy who did comparison pricing of vacation flights. He was the kind of guy who was excited to tell people how he saved his money and bought a used car, instead of wasting money on something brand new. Even though his smile was wide, there was this serious look in his eye in his graduation photos that said, "I'm going somewhere in life; get out of my way." He wanted to go into law enforcement; his dream job was to work for the FBI. Jake knew enough about my work to know I'd met a lot of FBI agents over the years, so he asked if I knew anybody who could give him advice about how to get started with the agency.

Not long after Jake made that request, I was speaking at a law enforcement conference and ran into an FBI agent I'd met several times over the years. I told him about Jake and asked if he had any advice to pass along. He shared a couple of tips on the spot, which I planned to call Jake about as soon as I got home from the conference. The next day, the agent attended my talk and then asked me out to lunch with him so he could get some more information about my son. I was so proud talking to this guy about Jake. I was proud of Jake. And I was proud to be back in my kid's life. I answered as many of the agent's questions as I could, but some were about details of Jake's education and experience that I didn't know how to answer. I sent Jake a text, hoping maybe I could get him on the phone with the guy. He didn't answer and the agent and I both had to get to our next meetings. I told the agent I'd put him and Jake in direct contact with each other once I got home and thanked him again for taking the time to help my son. After I got done with the conference that night, I shot Jake another text. No answer. I tried again the next day. He never answered. We'd been through this before, a few times. I had learned to wait and hope he'd reach out again one day.

I first learned to wait and hope for a response with Riley. My oldest child has her mother's dark hair and brooding eyes. And as she's gotten older, she seems to share her mother's opinion of me, which usually ain't good. I don't blame Riley or Jessica. I was a wreck when I met Jessica; I had just escaped from a mental hospital and was soon on my way to prison. Riley was the baby conceived in the short interval between those two institutionalizations. By the time I got out of prison, Jessica had moved on and I wanted to pull her back into my chaos; when she refused, I left. That she's let me be part of Riley's life at all says something about how big her heart is. I've been able to enjoy some really good times with my daughter and she's been able to spend enough time with Valerie and the other kids and me to be part of the family, not just my kid.

But the truth is I've always been more like an uncle to Riley than a father. I'm her funny relative from out of town who makes her laugh on vacation and sometimes sends presents. And that's great, so long as we're both in a good mood. But if she does something I'm not okay with and I say the kind of thing a dad would say, then she gets pissed. And then I get pissed. It's a cycle that's not good for either of us; it wasn't good when she was a little kid and it's worse now that she's a grown woman. I wish our relationship was better. I'm never going to give up hope of

that, but I'm not sure I can fix it without a time machine. I was
not a real dad for Riley. She knows that. Her mom knows that.
I know it, too, now. But it still hurts when they point it out to me.
I have to remind myself I've hurt them more. If I'd sent consistent child support payments instead of occasional teddy bears,
maybe things would be different now. If I'd done the hard work
of being Riley's father when she was a child, maybe she'd accept
me as her dad now. I don't expect much from Riley or from
Jessica because I haven't earned it. Over the years, I've learned
to take what I get and be grateful they still speak to me at all.

Riley was fourteen when the book researcher and I met
with her and Jessica and some of the guys from my original
Springfield crew, who are no longer skinheads, but still like family
to Jessica and Riley. We spent a whole evening together. The
researcher took turns with each person, mining their memories
as part of our process for writing the first edition of this book.
I told them the same thing I told everybody we met with: if you
have any questions, you can ask me or you can ask the researcher
if you don't want to ask me. At one point in the evening, Jessica
and the guys and I were gathered around a table, reminiscing
about some of the good times we'd shared, and Riley slid into the
booth across from the researcher. The researcher asked Riley
a few questions about her memories of me from when she was
little. Then she repeated my offer that Riley could ask any
questions if she wanted to know more about my past. Later that
night, the researcher shared with me my daughter's answer.

"I don't think I'm old enough to know more about him yet."

At fourteen, my daughter knew enough about who I had
been to know she wasn't ready to handle the whole story. I'm holding out hope maybe someday I'll be able to tell it to her myself
and hear hers in return.

Family History

WRITING THE BOOK TOOK FIVE FULL YEARS BECAUSE I
wanted to make sure I got it right. The researcher who helped
me is a stickler for details and the two of us also worked with the
team at the publishing company, who edited and fact-checked
everything all over again. But, in the end, the book had to be my
story, my version of things, my view of the world. And not everybody sees things the way I do. Hell, even in the haven of my own
home, there are days I consider myself lucky if I can at least get
Buttercup the pug to side with me. So I knew not everyone was
going to agree with my version of my story. But I was shocked to
learn about a couple things I got dead wrong.

Kids only know what their families are willing to tell them.
They fill in the gaps with what they learn on the streets or from
a screen. It's like the grown-ups in a family make one of those
connect-the-dots pictures from the bits and pieces they say in
front of a kid or when they know the kid is hiding behind the
couch eavesdropping. The thing is, not a lot of grown-ups talked
to me much when I was little and if my stepfather had ever
caught me eavesdropping, he would've knocked me across the
room. As a kid, I pieced my history together from the shrapnel
of my parents' civil war. I learned more details of my family history in the five years I spent working on the first edition of this
book than I'd known growing up. All the Bertones shared the memories, as did some of the Meeinks. But not everybody on my

mom's side was cool with me when we were working up the first edition, so I wasn't able to talk to some of them.

The book coming out opened some doors that had been shut for a while, or at least I had thought they were shut. I regret that I didn't reach out to some of my aunts and uncles earlier, but I'm glad they contacted me after they read the book. It helped us heal some old wounds and it opened my eyes about some things. So, it turns out they have a completely different version of what childhood was like in the Meeink home than the one I got from my mom since I was born. Not one of her siblings recall my grandparents ever being abusive or mean to any of their kids. In fact, they remember a really happy and loving home life, thanks to their parents. Truly, I am relieved to know this. I am sorry I got it wrong the first time around.

As with most shit involving my mom, I should have assumed she was giving me "alternate facts," a technique my mom mastered about forty years before it entered popular vocabulary. You'd think after nearly four decades, that would be my default setting with her. Most of the time it is. But she's been so consistent about her version of her childhood my whole life, I fell for it. So did friends of hers. Since I didn't feel comfortable approaching her siblings when working on the research for the book, I reached out to others who knew her when she was a kid and I got confirmation of the same sort of icy cold, punitive childhood she'd described to me. All the stories were identical; they also all traced back to the same bad source, my mom.

My relationships with most of the Meeinks are better now, but not with all of them. I still haven't seen my cousin Jimmy since I left the movement. He and Shawn live near each other in a rural part of Pennsylvania. I got to go visit Shawn once. We didn't talk at all about our skinhead days. For the most part, the aunts and uncles on the Meeink side forgave all of us for being skinheads and they seem proud of me for speaking out against hatred, even though I can't tell my story without talking about the family. It's probably been hardest for my Uncle Nick and

Aunt Catherine, because both my hate and my heroin addiction call up bad memories for them. Their youngest son, Shawn, recruited me to be a skinhead; their older son, my cousin Nick, died of an overdose. Under the circumstances, I'm grateful my aunt and uncle still speak to me; I'm blessed they still find it in their hearts to love me.

A few years ago, Uncle Nick and I were talking on the phone and I was telling him about the *Is This Heaven?* documentary project. Something really funny had happened while we were filming and I thought my uncle would get a kick out of it. While I was interviewing an elderly rabbi, he made a comment about me being Jewish, too.

"Actually, I'm Irish and Italian," I said. "I was raised Catholic."

"What's your name?" the rabbi asked. We had been introduced already. I began to wonder if perhaps he was confused, what with thinking I was Jewish and asking my name again. He was quite old.

"My name is Frank Meeink." I said it slowly and loudly, in case he was hard of hearing.

"Meeink. Yes." he said. "You're Jewish."

So I told my Uncle Nick, who's as Italian as my dad, this story about the forgetful, hard-of-hearing elderly rabbi who thought a former skinhead was Jewish, and my Uncle Nick says, "You are Jewish. I used to tell youse guys you were Jewish, but none of youse ever listened to me."

Until the moment my Uncle Nick said that, I had no memory whatsoever of him ever telling my skinhead cousins and me that we were Jewish. But as soon as he said it, I remembered. Back when we were marching around his house in our combat boots, every once in a while he'd say something like, "Do your Nazi friends know you're Jewish?" We always thought he was just busting our balls to try to get us to rethink being skinheads. We couldn't be Jewish! We were neo-Nazis. Besides, from the day we were born, our lives had been one long South Philly soap opera starring Irish girls who fell for Italian dudes. How could we be Jewish? There weren't any Jews in our family. Hell, there weren't in Jews in our whole neighborhood.

But, according to Uncle Nick, we are as likely to be German as we are Irish and there appear to be at least a couple Dutch Jews on our family tree, quite a few generations back on the Meeink side. Far enough back no one in my generation believed Uncle Nick when he told us. Not so far back to fool an elderly rabbi.

That's one of the dots that I could have used around age fourteen. How many people might have been saved from my neo-Nazi rage, had I known that? The thing is, it probably wouldn't have mattered, not to me. Because it was never really about who I hated, just that I got to hate.

I TOTALLY GET why most of my kids have been mad at me most of their lives. I'm in my forties now and I've still got my own mommy issues, and daddy issues, and stepdaddy issues. Damage done early is hard to repair, harder to forgive, and impossible to forget.

My dad and I have been hot and cold my entire adult life. He's a hard guy to hate, even for me, because he's so funny and affectionate when we are together. It's when we're apart for a while that my resentment starts building again. We sometimes go years between phone calls. When I visit Philly, I always try to see as many of his brothers and sister and their kids as I can squeeze into one trip, but I don't always let him know I'm coming to town. If I do stop by his house or the bar, we pick back up exactly where we left off the last time I walked out the door. It's like nothing has changed, because nothing really has changed. Cha Cha got himself a girlfriend and moved out of my dad's house finally, but even he's still planted on his favorite stool at the bar most nights. There were a few years where it seemed like my dad and me were both getting our shit together enough to maybe finally make our relationship what it ought to be. But for that to happen, we both need to be clean to get really honest with each other. So far, our sobriety stints haven't lined up.

It's pretty much the same story between me and my mom, except I've always been able to count on her and John to throw in a few extra plot twists. One of those twists came in 2007, when my brute of a cousin, Jerry, almost killed John. Jerry had been their supplier for years. I never heard exactly what set it off, but a drug deal went bad and Jerry muscled into the house and wrapped his giant paws around John's neck. The story I got was that right before John lost consciousness, Jerry tossed him to the floor and said, "You ain't worth going to prison over." Shortly after that, Jerry cleaned up his act. He entered rehab, got sober, and later landed a job working for a recovery center.

My mom made some huge changes after that incident, too. She kicked John out of the house and filed for divorce. She called me to apologize for not doing it a couple decades earlier, which meant a lot to me. She signed up for methadone therapy to help her break her long-time addiction to OxyContin. She was doing really great and I was really proud of her. Then one day, before her divorce from John was finalized, she learned he had gone missing. Nobody in South Philly could find him – not his drinking buddies, not his drug buddies, not my mom or my half sisters. My mom spent three weeks calling around looking for him before she finally found him filed as a "John Doe" in a city morgue. It is believed he suffered a heart attack. My stepfather dropped dead on a filth-crusted street in South Philly, with no ID in his pocket and nobody nearby who knew his name.

The news of John's death left me cold. I felt nothing, not even relief. I rarely saw him in the years before he died. He was no longer a presence in my life. Even then, John mostly existed in my memory, in the darkest corners of my mind. His death has done nothing to evict him from those places.

My half-sisters took their dad's death hard. He'd always treated them like his little princesses, even though he called his little princess Kirsten "whore" more than once. At age seventeen, just like our mom, she had a baby with a nineteen-year-old Italian guy. He was soon on his way to prison, so Kirsten and her little girl lived with my mom and John, and then with just my mom. When John was still alive and living at the house, he would volunteer to take the baby for a walk around the neighborhood. Word on the street was he used his granddaughter's stroller to transport drugs. My mom did her best to get clean after she kicked John out, but she'd already provided her kids with a lifetime of lessons in how to be an addict. Kirsten, Hayley, and I grew up in a house where using was normal and dealing was steady income. Like me, at a certain point, Kirsten followed the family tradition.

Hayley is the only one of us who made it out relatively unscathed. I think that's because she had the sense and the strength even as a kid to escape when she needed to. She not only lived with Valerie and me for a couple of years, but in Philly, she took refuge at Nina and Matt's apartment whenever things got too crazy with our mom and John. Hayley accomplished the nearly impossible: she raised herself out of the chaos. She finished her education and landed a good job in an office. She had a baby and she put that baby's needs first, no matter what, especially when things didn't work out between her and the baby's father. A few years later, Hayley met and married a totally stand-up guy who treated her and her daughter right. All three of them and a little baby girl who arrived in 2016 now live in a nice house in the suburbs.

My sisters, my kids, me and pretty much everybody else I know who knows my mom have learned to keep a safe distance, even when she's clean and things seem normal. The only thing predictable about my mom is that she's unpredictable. Whether she's sober or stoned, she can morph from angelic to toxic in a heartbeat. She's been that way ever since I can remember. But when I was a kid, she didn't have Facebook.

My mom's adventures on social media have done some serious damage. She friended most of her relatives, including my older kids, then proceeded to like funny pictures of cats and fire off unprovoked attacks. A lot of people have since blocked her. One member of the family got so frustrated she deleted her entire Facebook account to make sure my mom couldn't find a way to get at her. A national news network pulled a story about me they posted to social media after I did an interview on a morning show. It's their policy not to censor comments; if things get too out of line, though, they will pull back an entire story. My mom pushed them over that line. She flooded the page with crazy comments that weren't even about me. She was pissed off at Kirsten and hijacked a national news network's Facebook page to let me and the whole damn world know every detail of everything my mom thought Kirsten had done wrong since being born. Along the way, of course, she was dropping all kinds of personal information about Kirsten, using her real name and other people's names, too, a stunt she'd pulled with other people in the family more than once before this. It was obvious to anybody in their right mind looking at that news site that my mom's rant was disconnected from reality. When a few strangers pointed that out, she went after them, too. That's when the network pulled the story.

So, basically, my mom has become an internet troll. I hate that her online outbursts have hurt people I love, but there's a part of me that loves it when she loses her shit on social media. When I was a kid, she was a fucking master of putting on a good face in public. She would act all normal whenever she had to talk to my teachers or cops, or even to our relatives. But in private, once she ripped off that Brady Bunch mask, she could be pure evil. My mom doesn't understand social media well enough to figure out how to keep her mask on straight when she posts. Or maybe she just doesn't give a shit about hiding her true feelings anymore. Either way, a lot of people have now had a chance to see the woman who, for years, only I saw behind the closed doors of a rowhouse on Tree Street.

The City of Philadelphia officially condemned our old house on Tree Street in the early 2000s. In my opinion, they were about thirty years too late.

Ave Maria

THE BARE TREES LOOKED LIKE SKELETONS AGAINST the dark grey clouds. It wasn't cold yet, not by Des Moines standards, but the wind nipped at my face when I dashed from our front porch to my buddy's car. He and I played hockey together and sometimes carpooled when we were both working for the extreme cleaning company. Between chugs of coffee, we'd usually talk about the latest NHL news or the crazy-ass shit we'd pulled out of a hoarder house the week before. But that particular Monday morning, we were both as dreary as the weather. I was going to need at least two more cups of coffee to have the energy to pretend I was excited about going to work.

I was slurping on the one cup I brought with me when my phone rang. I didn't recognize the number, but answered it, anyway.

"Is Francis or Frank there?" a woman asked.

I knew she wasn't a telemarketer or a bill collector because they never call me Francis. Nobody calls me Francis, not even my parents.

"Yes."

"Are you Francis or Frank Meeink?" she asked, her voice robotic. She said both versions of my name so precisely I could tell she was reading them.

"Yes."

"I'm calling in reference to the paperwork we will need you to sign in order to finalize the estate of Mr. Salerno."

I could barely hear her over the sound of my own heart pounding in my ears. It was as if her voice had split in half and was coming at me from two different directions, like she was whispering up to me from the bottom of a well at the same time she was screaming through a megaphone an inch from my face. She whisper-screamed words and phrases: "I'm with the clerk's office" and "finalize the certificate" and "release the funds from his estate" and "funeral expenses" and "on his mother's behalf." And none of them fit together. None of them made any sense. As my buddy kept steering us toward the job site, as life in Des Moines, Iowa, kept rolling along like nothing had changed, this voice on the phone kept whisper-screaming in my ear about forms and faxes and signatures and how it was urgent that I sign the faxed forms immediately and return them immediately because his mother needed the funds to be released to cover the expenses.

And then there was no sound. There was no sound coming from the phone. There was no sound in the car. There was no sound on the road, in all of Des Moines, in the whole fucking world, except for my heartbeat slamming against my ear drums.

"Ma'am?"

"Yes."

"Are you telling me my son is dead?"

MY OLDEST SON, Jake Salerno, died in a single-vehicle car accident on November 1, 2014. He'd been gone more than a week when the lady from the clerk's office called me. A complete fucking stranger had to tell me my son was dead because Maria refused to make the call. Later that day, in another phone call, I asked the woman if she had any information about the funeral arrangements.

"The services were held last week."

Maria has every right to hate me. I used her, then I tossed her aside. I spent her money and dragged her through my dirt. I let her think I loved her when I knew I didn't. I got her pregnant, and then I ran off with another woman and made another son before Jake was even born. I abandoned Jake, my flesh and blood, just to escape Maria. I left her alone with that knowledge and a little boy asking "Where's my dad?" Almost from the first day we met, Maria has had every right to hate me. But I honestly did not know it was possible for one human to hate another as bad as Maria hated me. It was worse than I ever imagined: she hated me so much she refused to tell me our son died.

I have no grounds to ask Maria to forgive me for all the shit I put her through, but I'll never forgive her for not telling me Jake died. I can't find it in myself to let go of the damage that did to the other kids. Even though their time together was short, Riley and Matt got really close with Jake when Maria let him visit us. I'm not the only one Maria didn't tell; by keeping Jake's death from me, she kept it from them, too. How do you tell somebody they weren't invited to their own brother's funeral?

Valerie was devastated by the news, as was my sister, Hayley, who'd been living with us when Maria let Jake visit. The one who took the news hardest, though, was Little Nick. He'd been a toddler the last time we'd been allowed to see Jake. He did not actually remember his oldest brother. But Jake had always been part of Nick's life because Jake was part of our family. All the kids had painted their names in the doorway to our bedroom the summer we were all together; Nick walked by Jake's name every time he walked past our room. We talked about Jake and reminisced about when he had visited. The pictures we had of Jake were on display alongside all the other kids' photos in the living room and on the refrigerator. Nick even kept a picture of Jake in his bedroom. It was like he'd always had a special place in his heart for the big brother he was going to get to know someday. Nick had spent his whole little life waiting for a day that would never come.

I SIGNED THE papers. All of them. I signed them faster even than the "urgent" deadline the clerk lady gave me on the phone. My first instinct was to set those fucking papers on fire and mail the ashes to Maria with a note that said, "Fuck you, you fucking bitch!" But my friend, Pat, wisely talked me off that ledge. Pat is more than a good friend; he's also my long-time AA sponsor. Pat knows everything there is to know about me, all the good and all the bad and the worse and the worst of all. He can see where I'm headed before I even realize I'm starting to move. When I learned about Jake's death, my first call was to Valerie; my second was to Pat. Pat let me have the forms faxed to his office. When I couldn't see through my tears, he read through the paperwork so someone would know what I was about to sign. And when the first round of rage about losing Jake and the outrage about Maria not telling me curled into a fist in my stomach and started to explode, Pat looked me square in the eyes and said, "Do what they asked you to do and smile in gratitude that you had him in your life at all. Remember him. Him. Focus on your son, not his mother."

I CALLED THE lady at the clerk's office to make sure she got the forms, which I had returned by overnight mail. She had. She thanked me for being so prompt and told me that Maria had already come in to pick up the copies. She said that when she informed Maria I'd been gracious about signing everything, Maria broke down crying. A few hours after I phoned the clerk, she called me back. She and another woman from the office were both on the line. The clerk lady's robot voice was gone. She sounded genuinely human when she apologized for being the one to tell me my son had died. The other lady explained that their office had been warned I might be unresponsive or even uncooperative about signing the forms. They had been given the impression that I'd already been notified of Jake's death.

My son, Jake, was an amazing young man. Maria raised him very well. And, while I doubt I'll ever be able to get past her not telling me of his death, I also cannot imagine the depths of her grief. I'd never hurt so bad as I hurt getting that news and I hadn't even seen Jake in person for several years. What must it have felt like for Maria to learn he was gone? Jake was her world and had been from the day of his birth. On the occasions she let him spend time with me, she checked in constantly. I remember getting annoyed by that, thinking at first that she didn't trust me with him. I reminded myself I had given her a lot of reasons not to trust me. Then after a while I realized she wasn't calling because she didn't trust me, or at least not only because of that; she was calling Jake every couple of hours because she couldn't bear to be away from him. Maria was a classic, traditional, doting Italian mama: her baby boy was her everything. The kind of grief she must have suffered – that she must still be suffering – is beyond description.

I don't want to feel sorry for her, but I do. I want to stay totally focused on how fucking wrong of her it was to not call me herself, to not tell me just as soon as she got the terrible news, to not invite me to his funeral. I want to hate her for shutting me out every bit as much as she hates me for walking away. But I can't. Because every time I try to run away from my sorrow by unleashing my rage, I hear Pat's voice saying, "Be grateful you had him in your life at all." Pat saw me heading down the path I've traveled most of my life, straight toward anger to avoid the pain. He called me back from the edge. He reminded me of what matters. An amazing young man named Jake walked this planet for nineteen years. He was taken way too fucking soon. I am grateful for every second I had with him. I loved him.

Maria loved him, too. And as pissed as I am about how I found out he died, I am grateful she loved him. I am grateful she was a good mother to him. She loved Jake with her whole heart even though she hated his father. When she finally met and married a nice guy from New Jersey, she never put Jake second. She never let bad things happen to Jake. In Jake's whole life, he never once walked into his home without his mom's eyes lighting up at the very sight of him. Even though all the pieces were in place to fall the exact same way, Maria made sure my son didn't have the kind of shit childhood I did. For that, I will always be grateful.

Tears Are On the House

THE FLASHING LIGHTS AND SPINNING SCREENS MADE me carsick. Or maybe they gave me vertigo. I'm not sure what to call it; I just know casinos make me feel like I ate a couple dozen elephant ears then rode a roller coaster before entering the fun house. But there I sat anyhow, staring at a video poker machine, trying to ignore the chaos of lights and sounds all around me.

I was in Reno to speak at a law enforcement conference. I'd already done my thing, working with local cops and FBI agents on strategies to help get kids out of gangs. The conference organizers comped me an extra night at the hotel, which I really appreciated; otherwise, I would have spent hours trying to cat-nap at airport gates between connecting flights. I had hoped to get a good night's sleep at the hotel before flying out the next day.

But I couldn't sleep. I couldn't even remember the last time I'd slept through the night. It had been more than six months, maybe more than a year. The insomnia started the night I learned my son had died. For the first couple weeks, I barely slept at all. Every time I closed my eyes, my mind would conjure up images of what he must have suffered in his last moments. I blocked those terrible thoughts the only way I knew how: by focusing on Maria and how she'd let me find out. But even curled up in anger, my life-long comfort zone, I couldn't sleep through the night. Around two or three in the morning, I'd startle awake. Sometimes I remembered the vivid details of a nightmare about his accident. Sometimes it was just a clear vision of Jake's smiling face that shook me awake. I'd stay in bed, tears dripping onto my pillow, until I knew I couldn't hold back any longer. When I felt the big sobs coming, the ones that would shake my shoulders and the whole bed, the ones loud enough to echo down the hall, I'd steal out of the bedroom, pausing in the doorway where all the kids, including Jake, had painted their own names the summer we were all together. I got to where I couldn't walk through that doorway without touching Jake's name, like touching it was touching him.

I spent hours each night laying on the couch in our living room, trying to distract myself with television or the internet. When that didn't work, when the tears started welling in my eyes again, I would pace the first floor or circle our block. I never went back upstairs until it was time to wake Nick and Jayla for school. Valerie and the kids knew I was suffering. They saw it all day long; they didn't need to hear it in the night, too.

When friends asked how I was holding up, I lied and said okay. Then I would start telling them about Jake. I talked about Jake obsessively, to anyone who would listen. I would share almost everything I knew about my son with complete strangers, as if speaking his name and telling those stories meant he wasn't really gone. When no one was around to listen, I ran the same stories in my head, over and over again, like a loop of memories that, if broken, might disappear forever.

Friends assured me things would get better. Just give it time, they advised. Time heals all wounds, even one this deep, they promised. But the more time passed, the more I struggled.

Time itself was my enemy. I had wasted most of the time I'd been given to be with my son. I'd had nineteen years to be his dad and I'd spent at most a grand total of a couple months in his presence. I'd thrown away our past, telling myself it was okay because we always had the future. But we didn't. There was no next year, next week, tomorrow. There were only scattered memories of an amazing young man I had just started to really get to know and an ocean of regret so fucking deep I could not see light breaking the surface.

IT WAS AFTER midnight when I wandered down to the hotel casino, looking for anything to numb my mind. I took a seat at a video poker machine in a relatively quiet corner. I played the game mindlessly. For a couple hours, I won enough to fund more hands, which was all I wanted: a reason not to go back upstairs to my bed. As I sat there amid the flashing lights and spinning screens, the background music and tourists' chatter, I imagined how much fun Jake and I would have had if we'd been able to take that trip to Vegas together. He would've been too young to go to the casinos. He wouldn't have missed much, I thought, as I robotically entered my next series of bets. But we would have found so many other things to do, fun things to do, like taking in some shows, braving the massive amusement park rides, people watching on the Strip, just hanging out together.

I was down to only four dollars on the machine and no cash in my pocket; if I lost another hand, I would be broke. I couldn't bear the thought of returning to my room to staring at the ceiling, and I was too exhausted to wander the streets until time for my flight. Under my breath, I whispered to Jake, "Buddy, if you're here in spirit, let's hit this one." I pushed the button. The cards on the screen spun manically, then slowly began to settle into formation in three rows of five five-card hands. I hit four of a kind – four kings – on each of the three hands. I won more than $100. And I just fucking lost it.

It wasn't like what happened to me in the night, when a trickle of tears would gradually build up to sobbing. I saw those three rows of four kings and I immediately started bawling. Tears poured down my face and stained my shirt. I wanted to run out of the casino, out into the streets, away, anywhere but where I was. But when I tried to stand, my legs were so weak I collapsed back onto the stool. I leaned into the poker machine for support and to try to hide myself from the players nearby.

I buried my head on the wrist rest at the front of the machine. I was crying so hard I couldn't breathe. My chest felt like it was breaking open.

"Sir?" The security guard's voice was deep, but gentle. He leaned down next to me, like an adult bends down to whisper to a little kid, and asked, "Are you okay?"

"Yes," I mumbled, but he could tell I wasn't okay at all.

"What's wrong?" he asked. "Are you losing?"

"I'm up," I said before the next round of sobs stole my voice. The security guard used his body to block me from the view of most of the nearby gamblers. He waited for me to be able to speak again. He had to wait a long time before I finally garbled out, "My son should be here with me. He died."

The security guard had true pity in his eyes. He offered me free drinks on the house the rest of the night. I told him I didn't drink. He tried to lift my spirits by joking I could have free soda, which is free all the time anyhow. I tried to laugh a little, just to thank him for trying to cheer me up, but I lost it all over again. He stayed close to me, still using his body to block other people from seeing me. He stood over me like that for a couple more minutes, guarding me from gawkers until I could pull myself together. But I couldn't get my crying under control. He placed a hand reassuringly on my shoulder and leaned in close to my ear.

"Sir, I'm sorry for your loss. But there's no crying in the casino." He let out a tiny laugh, the kind people make when they don't want to say what they're saying. There was still pity in his eyes, but his voice was firm when he added, "It's bad for business."

I understood. I don't know how, but I got my legs under me. I staggered out of the casino like a skid row drunk. I made my way back to my room, threw myself on top of the cushy king-size bed, and stared at the ceiling. I wanted to die.

THEY SAY WHAT happens in Vegas, stays in Vegas. Well, that shit does not apply to Reno. The breakdown I had in that casino wouldn't fucking let up. It followed me home to Iowa. I was in a near-constant state of rage, interrupted only by bouts of paranoia when I saw and heard things that I knew weren't really there, but I couldn't ignore. My mental health deteriorated to a state worse than I'd ever been in when I was using drugs. My brain was acting like I was high, higher than I'd ever been, even though I wasn't. I rarely slept, but when I did manage to doze off, I slept like I was dead and woke up feeling like a corpse. When I was awake, I was hyperaware, hyperactive, hyperparanoid and so fucking hyperpissed off that I was afraid of myself. My broken heart had destroyed my brain. All I wanted to do was shut it all off. I needed the crazy thoughts in my head to shut the fuck up. I needed the ache in my heart to stop throbbing so loud it felt like it was shaking the walls of the house. About a month after my breakdown started in Reno, I popped an oxy. It didn't make a fucking dent in my suffering.

JAKE'S DEATH DID not cause my relapse. The shitty way I found out my son died did not cause my relapse. Grief did not cause my relapse. Regret did not cause my relapse. Stress did not cause my relapse. Insomnia did not cause my relapse. Me using caused my relapse. Just like every other time before, one day, one totally random day, after I'd been whispering no under my breath like a mantra for years, I said yes.

I don't need a reason to relapse. For me, everything is a reason to use. Every event in my life, every movie I watch, every song I hear, every ego boost, every slight, every sight, sound, smell, taste, touch, every bit of good news I receive, every bad thought and painful feeling that passes through my mind, every single goddamn fucking thing that crosses my path is the only excuse I need to get high. Finding the strength to say no a couple thousand times a day every day is exhausting. Saying yes feels like crawling into a warm bed for a good night's sleep. When I'm high, I don't think about how bad I want to use. When I'm stoned out of my mind is the only time my addict brain shuts the fuck up. Only when I'm high does my brain stop screaming, "Use. Use! USE!!!!!"

The problem this time was it wasn't just my addict brain that was screaming at me; something else had broken loose inside me and it was crying out louder than anything I'd ever experienced before in my life. Whatever started to happen to me in Reno just kept getting worse and worse, even after I started popping pills again. I held it to oxy. Just a few a few times a week, nothing like the eighty mg every eight hours I'd done at my worst. Just enough to try to take the edge off feeling the hurt so bad I was scared I might hurt myself on purpose or somebody else on accident. Just enough to try to silence the crazy thoughts that wouldn't shut up inside my mind. But low-dose oxy didn't stand a chance against what was happening to my brain. So I upped the dose a little more each time, until I got it high enough that I actually would have seemed high to other people. Of course, because of that, I needed to follow the oxy with just a little sniff of meth to bring me back in balance to "normal" so nobody had to know. But every time I asked an oxy to carry me away from the hell inside my head, I was reminded of where I really wanted to be.

I vowed I would only sniff when I went back to heroin. I made that promise to myself like I was reading straight off the script I first wrote in the Badlands. Tragedies always end the same fucking way.

VALERIE WAS AWAY on a business trip. Nick and Jayla and I ate a bunch of junk food for dinner, then Jayla settled in to watch a video while Nick and I went upstairs to finish up a project. Over the past weekend, the whole family had pitched in for a coordinated swap of bedrooms. We got everybody's stuff moved before Valerie caught her flight out of town. The only thing left to do was to assemble a new, larger bed for Nick's room. Nick was so happy to be in his new room, he skipped his regular nightly protest when I said it was bedtime. When I went back downstairs, Jayla was already sacked out on the couch. I put an extra blanket on her and kissed her softly on the forehead. I flipped the television to ESPN. I wasn't worried about waking Jayla. Once that girl is asleep, she's out until we pry her eyes open the next morning.

I called Valerie. We talk on the phone every night whenever one of us is away from home. I filled her in on the progress on the great bedroom swap. She gave me a quick rundown on how her meetings were going. I asked her if she was done for the night. She said she was going to go out for drinks with some of her coworkers.

I got pissed. I always get pissed when this subject comes up. Usually I pout about it. Sometimes I snark off, all passive-aggressive like a teenager. Sometimes I even yell. None of it is at Valerie, but it flies in her direction. She knows it's my issues blowing up inside my head, but that doesn't make it any easier on her when she has to deal with it.

I've got more issues than a politician, and Valerie going out for drinks with her coworkers taps about half dozen of them, mostly of the trust and jealousy variety with a little bit of ego-maniac thrown in on the side. I trust Valerie completely. It's other fucking dudes, liquored up and loose next to my gorgeous wife, that I don't fucking trust. And I don't trust strangers in some hotel bar a thousand miles away to protect her if something goes wrong. And I fucking hate it that those strangers, and Valerie's coworkers, and Valerie herself can go out and enjoy a drink or two and then stop, just fucking stop, while there's still alcohol behind the bar and drugs for sale on the street outside. That's the stream of shit that flows through my head when I think about my wife having a drink or two with coworkers. The shit that comes out of my mouth at Valerie isn't much better. Neither one of us was happy with the other one when we hung up, but we said, "I love you," and meant it.

I paced around the kitchen and living room for a while, trying to shake off the thoughts of some asshole in a business suit slurping a martini and drooling at the sight of my beautiful Valerie, laughing and enjoying herself and not seeing that fucker closing in on her. I got so fucking pissed at him and at every other white-collar-wife-stealing ass wipe in my imagination that I wanted to put my fist through the refrigerator. "It's in your head," I told myself. "Youse gotta calm down," I coached myself.

And I knew I had to. I was home alone with the kids. Valerie was in another state. This was not the time for me to go apeshit. But I felt so fucking disrespected and so totally alone. I knew I had to get myself under control. So I made another phone call.

When my dealer dropped off the heroin, he said, "It's really good. Go easy."

That night wasn't the first time I'd shot up since I relapsed. I'd shot up twice already, both times when I was home alone with no worries of Valerie or the kids walking in and finding me nodding off. But that night was the first time I shot up Frankie style, old Frankie style, like I had back in Philly, not giving a fuck where I was, where anybody else was, or if the shit I was cooking was likely to kill me. I cooked everything my dealer gave me in one big hit. The last thing I remember thinking before I stuck the needle in my vein was that I had survived years of Badlands heroin; what in the fuck could Iowa heroin do to me that I hadn't lived through before?

MY MEMORIES OF what followed are like shards of a filthy mirror. An EMT down on his knees, calling "Frank! Frank! Frank!" into my face. My tattooed arms limp, lifeless, seemingly not under my control, draped across the marbled grey vinyl of our kitchen floor. A cop towering over me, hands on hips, feet planted wide, saying something about heroin laced with elephant tranquilizers and people dying. The cop's legs framing my view of my two youngest children in the next room. Jayla was still sound asleep on the couch, just as she had been when I shot up. But Nick, Nick was not the same. My confident, happy twelve-year-old's eyes were wide like a lost toddler's. I was still flat on the kitchen floor, peeking through the cop's legs, watching Nick stare vacantly at the EMTs who were working on me, the whole time cradling his sleeping sister like a teddy bear. When our eyes finally met, when my son realized I wasn't dead, the terrified innocence drained from his face. He met my gaze like a man, a man who had been forced to grow up in the last thirty minutes.

Most of what I know about what happened is based on what others have told me. Nick was awakened by a loud crash and ran downstairs. He found me unconscious on the kitchen floor. He tried to revive me himself, but when that didn't work right away he called 911. He didn't want to alarm his little sister, so he left her asleep on the couch; he chose to be alone with my body, unsure if I was dying or maybe already dead, until help could arrive.

The EMTs brought me back around without needing to use Narcan. I hadn't overdosed. The dirty mix I'd shot had taken me down fast. I didn't nod off; I was knocked to the floor, unconscious, within minutes of hitting my vein with the needle. The cop grilled me about what I had used. I tried to lie my way out of it, but he told me not to waste my time, since they'd found the syringe on the floor next to my arm. He asked me what else I had in the house. I told him the truth: nothing. I had cooked everything I had into that one shot. The EMTs wanted to transport me to the hospital, but I refused. For reasons I still don't understand, the cop said they weren't going to arrest me, but that they couldn't leave the kids with me. I had to get a responsible adult to come be with the kids or they'd have to call in social services.

They had me off the floor and in a chair when Valerie called me. Concerned by the sight of the ambulance and squad car in front of the house, neighbors had texted Valerie to see if we were all okay. She didn't sound angry or worried. I couldn't tell if she didn't know what I'd done or if she'd just flipped into emotional autopilot from years of experience. I told her everything was all right and I'd call her back in a little bit. I called my sponsor, Pat, and our other good AA friend, Dan, who immediately rushed to the house. Once Dan and Pat arrived and passed muster with the cop, the police and EMTs left on the condition I was not to be left alone with the kids and I was to be checked out by a doctor. Pat and Dan agreed and took charge. They got Jayla up and ready for school without her knowing any more than daddy wasn't feeling so good. We all piled into Dan's car. Nick was scary silent. Dan dropped both kids at school, then drove me to the hospital.

I was checked out and released within a couple hours, but I wasn't okay. Dan and Pat kept watch over me because I was so woozy and dizzy I couldn't sit up without tipping over sideways and I kept dozing off. For several days before I shot up, I'd been fighting a blocked sweat gland that had gotten infected. I tried to convince Dan and Pat, and mostly myself, that was the reason I was feeling so bad. They knew better. So did I. They drove me back to the hospital. This time I was admitted for observation.

I couldn't stay awake. The nurses would come in to take my temperature or check my blood pressure and ask me how I was feeling and I'd drift off before I could answer. When I'd open my eyes, I'd see a different nurse, or a doctor, and either Dan or Pat. Those two were taking turns, one babysitting the kids and one babysitting me. One time when I opened my eyes I saw a beautiful angel hovering over my bed. When she smiled down at me, her tears dripped onto my cheek.

THE HOSPITAL AGREED to keep me while Valerie worked her magic and got me on the waiting list for a bed at one of the best rehab facilities in America. I stayed in a regular hospital room for a few days, but then they needed the bed and moved me to a room that reminded me of a holding cell. I was in there with four other people. Two were out of their mind crazy and waiting for admission into a psychiatric ward. The other two, like me, were addicts awaiting openings in rehab. The day before I was to fly to a rehab facility in Oregon, the hospital told Valerie they couldn't keep me any longer.

She let me come home for that one night. Nick was so happy I was going to get help that he didn't act mad at me. Jayla just wanted daddy time. Both kids were all over me the whole evening. It was the best medicine I could have been given. They helped me pack. Jayla tucked little love notes in my suitcase. Nick threw in a couple that read like mini locker-room pep talks.

Valerie didn't take her eyes off me for one second the entire night. One minute her eyes would fill with tears, and she'd hug me and tell me she loved me, and beg me to get well. But just seconds later, the rage would flash across her baby blues, and she'd retreat to the far side of the room. She didn't say what she was feeling in those moments, not in front of the kids, but I knew.

When I boarded the flight for the Hazelden Betty Ford Center in Oregon the next day, the kids' notes were already in my suitcase. I figured the only other mail I would get from home would be divorce papers.

No Promises But One

THERE'S MORE THAN ONE REASON THE REHAB CENTERS
run by the Hazelden Betty Ford Foundation are world famous,
and they aren't all related to the amazing quality of the treatment
program. When the car pulled onto the property, I thought,
"I definitely ain't in Philly anymore." The place looks like a high-
end resort. The grounds are spectacular. The interiors could be
featured in one of Valerie's decorating magazines. The food they
served me at every meal was over-the-top fantastic. Even the
activities they had for us to do during free time made it seem like
I was on vacation at the Kennedy compound. I actually played
lawn games with guys with names like Blair and Skipper. If that
had happened anywhere else, I would have felt out of my
element. But the Blairs and Skippers inside Hazelden were fighting the exact same battle I was. Social class doesn't mean shit on
rock bottom.

The Hazelden Betty Ford facility in Oregon specializes in
helping addicts who have experienced significant trauma in
their lives. Valerie battled a red-tape army of insurance regulations to get me that specialized placement. When she told me
that's where I was going and why, I thought back to the time the
public defender in Springfield, Illinois, asked me if I'd ever
experienced any trauma. I remember thinking about it for a minute, then asking back, "Does being raped count?" I honestly
didn't know; I was just throwing out a guess like I was taking a

test I hadn't studied for, a test that was worth up to twenty years of my freedom.

Being raped counts. So does losing a child. So does a lot of other stuff. Huge stuff, the kind of crazy things people can barely believe I survived. And also really little stuff, the kind of shit I used to think I was stupid to even remember. Those little memories show up sometimes in my mind, not like the grainy black-and-white movies in my head of the major scenes from my childhood, but more like blurry Polaroids, taken by a stranger. I always sort of assumed that was a result of doing too many drugs. Seriously, I've split my adulthood between being an active addict and being active in recovery programs. When I was using and things in my head were foggy, well, no shit: I'm fucking higher than the moon! And when I've been sober, even for years at a time, and I've struggled to remember things, I've always written it off to brain damage caused by all the drugs and all the blows I've take to the head in fights, in hockey, and, yeah, back on Tree Street. There are all kinds of totally legitimate reasons that a guy with my kind of history can't always remember everything clearly, whether it's some freaky fragment of a flashback to childhood or where in the holy fuck I put my car keys every single fucking morning.

The staff at the Hazelden center seemed almost more interested in my mental state than my relapse. They did something no other rehab counselors had ever done for me before with my full cooperation: they put me through the full battery of medical, psychological and every other kind of assessment they have that I don't even know the names of. A few places I'd been in before had done a lot of those tests, but not all of them, and not at a time in my life I was willing to give honest answers to all the questions.

I REMEMBER SITTING in Hazelden, talking to one of the counselors, and he asked me if there was anything from my childhood that I thought about all the time. There was. It was this stupid thing that went down once between John and me, such a small, insignificant little incident that I never even thought to include earlier. Because it didn't matter. Because it shouldn't matter. But the thing is, it did. It still does.

I've spent a lot of time doing carpentry and odd jobs in recent years. I've picked up side projects here and there to earn some extra cash for the family. More often, I've been working on our house. Our fixer-upper is looking really good, but it's a work in progress that won't ever be done. I'm not skilled in any trade, but I've graduated to better-than-average DIY guy, which is a really good thing since Valerie is a full-blown Pinterest addict. Between the side jobs and my honey-do list, I spend a lot of time with a tape measure clipped to my belt.

Every time I reel the thin, shaky, metal tape out of its square metal case, every single fucking time I hear the soft scrape of the metal on metal, I am in the kitchen on Tree Street. John is hanging with some of his friends, pounding back beers, bragging about work he probably never even did, and toying with a tape measure. He said to me, "Frankie, youse can read a tape, can't you?"

I was just learning to read a ruler. John had never let me touch his tape measure or any of his other tools, so I didn't know if I could read a tape measure.

"Maybe," I said.

John handed me the tape measure and told me to find something along the lines of five and eleven thirty-secondths. I didn't understand what he wanted me to do. There were no "thirty-secondth" divisions on the ten-cent plastic ruler I used at school. I couldn't read the tape measure, at least not with the precision John demanded. I kept staring at it, hoping the tiny line I was supposed to find would wiggle or light up or somehow lead me to it and out of John's line of fire. His friends were starting to grumble and smirk as they watched John watching me like an alley cat eyes a baby mouse. I looked up at him. I didn't need to say I couldn't find the mark. He burst out laughing.

"Of course you can't read it, because you're a dumbass!"

John got off on his friends' laughter. He loved nothing more than dogging me in front of an audience, showing off how tough he was by picking on a little kid.

"Maybe instead of laughing at me, you could teach me."

I meant it; I wasn't trying to be a smartass. But the only thing that registered with John was that I'd disrespected him in front of his friends. My punishment was immediate.

"Get upstairs! You're grounded!"

I probably was grounded already. In those days I was grounded more than I was free. I trudged up the stairs to put myself back into my cell of a bedroom. I didn't make it to the top step before I heard John thundering three steps at a time behind me. He took me down with one punch.

Being a dumbass got me grounded. Being a smartass got me beaten.

It wasn't the worst beating John ever gave me. Hell, it wasn't even in his top twenty. But laying there on the top step, listening to him and his friends laughing about how stupid I was, something about that stuck deep inside my memory.

Every fucking time I use a tape measure, I'm back in that kitchen, then I'm back, alone, on that step listening to them laugh.

THE DOCS AT Hazelden officially diagnosed me with post-traumatic stress disorder as well as depression. I've been treated for depression on and off over the years, but the PTSD diagnosis threw me. Except for combat veterans, I've always thought PTSD was some bullshit. I couldn't accept the idea that I had post-traumatic stress disorder because the kind of shit I've lived through isn't all that different than the shit a lot of people I know have survived. To me, putting a label on it, on me, seemed like wussing out, like only I couldn't handle it. But the more I learned about PTSD while I was at Hazelden and since my release, the more I realize I really do have it. And, most likely, so do a hell of a lot of other people I know.

I've had a lot of labels slapped on me in my lifetime – skinhead, felon, addict, to name a few. I never balked at any of those terms. I wore them with pride. Hell, I tattooed proof I was a skinhead all over my body for the whole world to see. But I cringed at being diagnosed with PTSD, at being labelled with a mental illness. I think that probably says a lot about our society's attitudes toward mental health. I know it says something about my ego. While there were a bunch of forces at play, in the end I chose to be a skinhead, a felon, and even an addict. I didn't choose PTSD. It happened to me. All kinds of really awful shit has happened to me and all of it has hurt me. I have PTSD because the wounds are still inside me, still unhealed, still festering. As a skinhead, felon, and even as an addict, I was in the driver's seat; I was the one doing the victimizing. The PTSD diagnosis forces me finally and fully to accept an uncomfortable truth: I am also a victim.

Intellectually, I've known that for years. It doesn't take a genius to look at my life history and see the patterns: I was victimized and then I turned that pain outward and made other people suffer. And if I they acted like a victim while I was victimizing them, it fueled my rage. I could see my stepfather's ugly mug in the face of every dude who ever fought back. But the second they gave up, the very instant they curled into a ball and begged me to stop, they were me, cowering on the stairs, or in the kitchen, or on the floor of my bedroom, waiting helplessly for John's final blow. John made me a victim and he taught me to hate victims. He taught me to hate myself.

SOME EXPERTS SAY there's a link between post-traumatic stress disorder and addiction itself. I'm no expert, but I can't accept that, at least not for me. PTSD did not cause me to become a heroin addict. I, alone, make the choice to use. I have to hold tight to that truth, because without it, I'm dead. If I can blame PTSD for my addiction, then I can use it as an excuse to get high every day until I die. I can't let myself go there.

But I now understand that having untreated PTSD has

been a huge barrier to me staying clean. It's like I've been fighting my addiction with one hand tied behind my back for years. Thanks to the twelve steps, I've packed a powerful punch with that one hand, but now it's a fair fight.

The counseling I'm getting to help manage the PTSD is letting me see the triggers before I step on the landmines. I'm learning how to calm myself, instead of wanting to numb myself. I've never denied the traumatic events in my life, but I've never been willing to admit how much the trauma itself still affects me. I'm learning to do that. It's not easy because I have to set my ego aside and be totally vulnerable, which is not exactly my comfort zone. But I'm gradually getting better at it. Even Valerie has noticed I'm different now. If anybody would know, she would; she's a twenty-year veteran of my war with addiction.

Valerie and I love each other, but we love our children more. Our first priority is to make sure our kids have a healthy and safe home to grow up in, like I didn't. We are determined to break the cycle. The love Valerie and I have for each other has to come second to that. We're hopeful we can do it together, but we've come to the conclusion that if we can't, then we have no business staying together. I think we've got good odds now that we're working not only with knowledge of recovery, but also of managing PTSD. But even great odds ain't guarantees, so I'm praying a lot for all of us.

SO, NOW YOU know why I never promise that I'll never fuck up again. I'm sitting on a lifetime of experience that says I probably will. And I did. More than once over the past twenty years. I still won't promise I'll never relapse. I can only promise I'll keep fighting. With each relapse, I get more depressed about my addiction, more expert in my recovery, more determined to keep dragging my ass back up out of hell. But each fall takes a greater toll on me. Worse, each fall takes a greater toll on everybody I love.

In 2005, when I relapsed in Philly, I ransacked my dad's house looking for any shred of evidence to prove I ever existed in his life. I reeled through his living room, his bathroom, his bedroom and into his kitchen looking for one single scrap from my childhood, a yellowed drawing or a school photo of me as a kid. I found nothing. It was like I'd never been there.

In 2016, while my youngest son tried to revive me on our kitchen floor, he was surrounded by photos of himself and his sisters and brothers. My kids are everywhere in our home. Their photos, their art work, their trophies, their clothes, their toys, their memories inhabit every square inch of the home Valerie and I have built for them. And there I lay, unconscious, in the middle of that home, with my poor baby trying to get me to open my eyes, to prove I was still there.

My son found me unconscious on the floor and he knew. At twelve years old, Nick knew. He may have wanted to wish I'd had a heart attack or a stroke, but he's my kid so he just fucking knew: Dad relapsed, again. Dad's not Dad, again. Dad chose drugs over me, again. And my sisters, again. And my brother, again. And Mom, again and again and again. And Jake.

Nick knew it all. At age twelve, Nick knew that his dad was and will always be an addict and addicts will turn anything into a reason to use. At age twelve, Nick knew I had turned my grief about Jake into a reason to use. At age twelve, Nick knew if Jake were still alive, I'd have found another reason. At the tender age of twelve, my youngest son, Nick, knew full well that there's a difference between a reason and an excuse.

When I was back in my right mind and back home again, after some time in the hospital and about a month in rehab, Nick called me on my bullshit. He wasn't willing to pretend it hadn't happened or to believe it would never happen again. He wasn't the same around me as he'd been before he found me on the floor. We did some counseling sessions together to figure out how to work through all of it; we're going to be working through this for years. In those sessions, hell, even in the kitchen, the living room, and the car, he's thrown some truths at me that hit like knives. He's got every right. He's got every right in the world to say to me every single fucking thing I ever wanted to say to my dad after I found him passed out drunk or stoned out of his mind. I'm praying if Nick screams it all out at me long enough and loud enough, it will save him from the cycle. Maybe it'll even help me. But saving me isn't his job, just like saving my dad wasn't my job. Nobody can save anybody else. We've got to save ourselves from ourselves and, sometimes, from the people who love us.

I don't expect Nick to ever forget finding me on the floor. I hope someday he'll be able to forgive me completely, but that's gotta happen on his timeline. Until then, we've mostly figured out how to be father and son again. It's funny, because what helped us turn the corner was him pulling exactly the kind of shit I would pull if I was him. Little dude found the hustle in the heartache. That kid had one counseling session under his belt and the next thing I know he can't do any of his chores because of "trauma." He even tried to strong-arm guilt me into buying him a bunch of shit.

I wish I could fix it with an XBox and a month off from washing dishes. God, I wish that was all it took to erase the past! But I know if I fall into that trap, it's not going to work; it's going to make things worse. Nick needs a father now more than ever to help get him through what his dad did to him. Finding me on the floor gave Nick all the ammo he needs to try to fight my authority. I love the kid too much to let him win that war.

I worry a lot that my worst life decisions have scarred my kids. I worry the image of me on that kitchen floor is going to dog Nick the same way John's fucking tape measure still haunts me. I'm hoping the fact that I even worry about such things is a sign maybe I'm doing okay as a dad, most days, anyhow. I don't think my dad spent much time worrying about how his using affected me. Sure as shit John didn't worry about me one bit. But that's not a lot of comfort when I wake up in the middle of the night thinking about how Nick must've felt seeing me out cold on that floor, or how much Jayla missed me while I was away at rehab or how Matt and Riley felt getting yet another phone call telling them I'd done it again. It's no comfort at all when my mind turns to Jake. To the future we never get to have as father and son. To the past I didn't give him.

Those were the kind of thoughts that started crossing my mind once I gave in and said yes to an oxy. Those were the thoughts that first got me thinking about shooting up again. They weren't the only thoughts that sounded to me like a good excuse to use, but that stuff about Jake was definitely top of the list. That's the worst part of the guilt I feel as a father, even worse than all the years I missed with Jake: it's knowing that while my grief for him is and always will be pure, I still found a way to turn that grief into just another excuse to get high. At the time, it made perfect sense to run from the pain straight into the tip of needle. Now, sober again, I feel like I pissed on my own son's grave.

The Twelfth Step

I'VE BEEN TO AA MEETINGS IN BIG CITIES AND TINY
towns all over the country. When I pack up to go on the road for
hockey or for speaking engagements, I already have the times
and locations of meetings mapped out for wherever I'm going to
be. I hit meetings between games during hockey tournaments.
I hit meetings before or after speeches, sometimes both. No one
knows who I am when I enter those meetings. I'm not the guest
speaker who just got a round of applause from five hundred
university students. I'm not the author whose book signing is
being promoted on the radio. I'm not the dude somebody saw on
MTV or CNN or in a couple movies.

"I'm Frankie and I'm an alcoholic/addict."

That's all that matters in an AA meeting. Because in an AA
meeting, we all have the same story. There's no judgment because every person in the room has been to rock bottom at least
once. From the first-timer who's still got the taste of his last
shot of whiskey in his mouth to the wise old elephants who could
break a Vegas casino with the stacks of years-clean chips
they've amassed, every single person in the room knows what it
feels like to be in hell. So no one accuses anyone else of being
on fire.

I've been working the twelve steps since I first started
trying to get clean and sober in the 1990s. Looking back, there
were times when I wasn't really working them; I was just
punching in, then zoning out. But there have been more times,

huge blocks of years, when I've thrown my entire mind, heart, and soul into the twelve steps. If I hadn't, I have no doubt I'd be dead already.

A person never graduates and moves on from the twelve-step process. No matter where they are on the steps, if they relapse, they go back to step one and work the program all over again. But even if they never relapse, they are never done with the program. That's because of the twelfth step. As it is written in the original *Big Book of Alcoholics Anonymous*, the twelfth step reads, "Having had a spiritual awakening as a result of these steps, we tried to carry this message to alcoholics, and to practice these principles in all our affairs." The twelfth step requires those who make it there to stay around, to give back, to use what they've learned to help others.

I've spent many years on the twelfth step for alcoholism and addiction. After each relapse, with a lot of support from a lot of people, especially my AA family, I've worked my way back to step twelve. I'm the most solid in my recovery when I'm on step twelve, when I'm able to use what I've learned to help others. Bill W., the founder of AA, didn't add the twelfth step just to keep people coming back forever; he put it in there because he knew it would help keep people clean and sober.

I now realize I twelve-stepped my way out of hatred. I didn't set out to take that approach; I just got lucky. Before I fully understood what the twelve steps were, I stumbled my way down a similar path to free myself from the hatred and violence that once defined me. Ever since the Oklahoma City bombing, when I first volunteered to use what I'd been through to try to help others, I've been doing the twelfth step for hatred: I've been sharing my awakening with others in hopes maybe it will help somebody else.

Trying to help other people isn't a selfless act. In fact, it's selfish. When I focus on helping people who are struggling with my same demons, I, myself, am more resistant to those demon's temptations. I've given a lot of thought over the years to why that is. Other people may have different takes on it, but for me it comes down to one word: empathy.

Empathy means you understand how somebody else is feeling. It doesn't mean you agree with them. It doesn't mean you pity them. All it means is you take the time to consider what the world looks like from their perspective. There's as much empathy as there is coffee at an AA meeting; everybody in the room knows exactly how everybody else is feeling. We don't judge because we've all been there. We have compassion because we know how bad it hurts.

I know from personal experience that the AA approach works. It may not seem like it has worked for me, but don't let my history of relapses fool you. Yes, I have relapsed. A lot. But every single time I've relapsed, I've also climbed back up on the old wagon with the help of the twelve steps. Knowing those steps are there, knowing other alcoholics and addicts are there to support me with compassion and without judgment, has given me the will to keep trying. I owe my life to AA.

Lately, I've started to think America needs to hit a meeting. Seriously, step back for a minute from whichever side you agree with and just look at how politics are playing out these days. Judgments are being flung in every direction. Compassion has all but evaporated. Everybody is labeling everybody else. Everybody is screaming and nobody seems to be listening.

I'm not saying there isn't a lot of shit going on that's worth screaming about. A lot of what's going on is scary. Some of the people in the so-called alt-right sure sound like they are advocating the same kind of things I was all for when I was a skinhead. They don't look like we did, but they sound just as hateful. There was a movement within the white supremacy movement back in the 1990s to try to clean up the image of racism. Even some of the top-ranking skinheads of that era started to argue we'd get more done if we stopped brawling and bashing, and focused instead on moving a political agenda. Of course, guys like me wanted no part of that. We were more interested in leaving blood on the streets than moving bills through Congress.

The internet has changed everything, including the white supremacy movement. I had to meet skinheads to get recruited and indoctrinated. Now any kid with Wi-Fi can do that all on his own. The actual white supremacy groups that are out there have become experts at using technology to promote their ideas. Of course, they aren't the only extremists doing this: hate groups and terrorist organizations worldwide are using technology to reach people, to recruit people, and to rally people to commit violence.

But it's not just the people in hate groups and their recruiting targets who are being affected by these changes. We are all being affected, at least all of us who use social media. Controversies about fake news and algorithms brought a lot of this to mainstream attention in 2016. I'm not even going to pretend to understand how sites and apps like Facebook and Twitter actually work, but like the rest of the world I now understand that they show us users more of what we "like." As a result, every time we log on to social media, it gives us more of the same. With each click on a conservative post, one user sees more and more conservative posts. At the same time, another user clicks to the left and gets more and more liberal content in their feed. Given enough clicks, it feels to the one user like everyone agrees with her and to the other that everyone agrees with him. The technology is set up to let us wallow in a make-believe world where everybody thinks just like we do. It lets us reinforce all of our own pre-existing beliefs and, at the same time, makes it look like everyone else is confirming that we are right.

There was no social media when I was a skinhead. Other skinheads reinforced my beliefs and I reinforced theirs. We didn't associate in any meaningful ways with people who weren't skinheads, so the only version of reality we heard was the one we already believed, the one we parroted back to each other day in and day out. We intentionally isolated ourselves not just from people of different races and religions, but from people who held different opinions, especially people who held the opinion that we were wrong.

For me, the scariest thing going on in America today isn't what's happening in Washington, even though some of that shit's pretty fucking terrifying; it's what's happening in people's everyday lives all across the country that has me really worried. I'm seeing too many people who aren't willing to listen to anyone they even suspect might disagree with them. I'm seeing too many people labeling and stereotyping people who don't look and think exactly like them. I'm seeing regular people throwing out the kind of hateful words online and out in public that us skinheads used to spout off full volume, mostly only in back alleys when we were blind drunk. And I'm seeing otherwise nice, "normal" people at rallies and protests with the exact same look in their eyes we used to have when we were stalking Center City, hunting for victims.

Hate is hate. Hate is a process and that process does not discriminate. Hate can suck in both Republicans and Democrats. Hate can infest people of any race, religion, gender, sexual orientation, and ability. Nobody's got a corner on the hate market. You don't have to be a skinhead to fall victim to hate.

Hate happens when we stop seeing individuals and start seeing only labels. Hate happens when we believe stereotypes about groups instead of getting to know actual people. Hate happens when we scapegoat our problems onto other people, believing our own bullshit to justify why we are right to hate them. Hate happens when we are too proud to admit we are afraid of people who aren't just like us. Hate happens because it is easier than being honest.

Nobody can bullshit their way through an AA meeting, not if those old elephants are in the room. They've heard it all before. They've survived it all before. That's why they don't judge. That's the basis for their compassion. They don't preach. They listen. And then, because they've been listening very closely, at the right moment, they are able to ask the right question, the one that helps somebody else find their own footing on the path to recovery.

I think in today's political climate, we all need to take a lesson from those old elephants. We need to stop being so fast to judge each other and start taking the time to really listen. That's the only way we're going to break through the roar of the hate to find the sources of the fear beneath it. And I guarantee you the fear is there. It is always there, lurking beneath the hatred.

If we really want to stop hate from taking center stage in our culture, once we find the fear, we need to show some compassion. The best way, the only way, I know to do that is through empathy. If I can put myself in another person's position, if I can embrace even for a few minutes what it feels like to be them, then I can understand better what's motivating them.

Whether I'm talking to a skinhead in a jail cell or an addict in a detox unit, I don't stand a chance in hell of helping another person until I know what's really driving their actions. I can't know that unless they open up to me. And they won't ever open up to me if all I do is point a finger in their face and scream "racist" or "junkie," then lecture at them about how they are ruining my life. To get them to talk, I have to stop judging them. To keep them talking, I have to show them a little compassion.

Nobody ever cured a drunk by dunking him in a vat of gin. We aren't going to stop the spread of hate by adding more hate to the mix. Hating haters is still hating. To break the cycle, we've got to figure out what's beneath the surface of the hatred; we've got to aim our efforts at the fears beneath the hate. Anything less than that just putting a Band-Aid on a bullet wound.

TOWARD THE END of my stay at the Hazelden Betty Ford Center, I got a meeting with a counselor the other staff members call the guru. Everybody who goes there gets one meeting with this guy. It's a life changer. After about five minutes in his presence, I understood why he earned his nickname. It felt like the dude had mind-melded me; it was as if he popped right inside my head and my heart and knew not only everything I had ever done, but understood every thought and feeling I'd had throughout my life.

At one point in the conversation, he asked me to give him a quick rundown of everything I'd been involved in the past few years. I ticked off a list that started with this book coming out and the speaking tour and the trip to Ireland, then it diverged into flow charts of all the different kinds of work I've done with hockey, all the different movies and documentaries and TV shows I've been in or tried to get off the ground, and all the stuff Valerie and I do to keep our marriage sane in the midst of all the chaos of our careers and the kids, so many things about all the kids, especially Jake. The list ended with me out cold on the kitchen floor.

"You've lost your purpose," he said with such authority I expected a bush to catch fire outside the window and stone tablets to appear on the lawn.

He said my problem wasn't what I was doing or how much I was doing, but that I'd lost sight of why. He asked, "When is the last time you felt absolute clarity about your purpose in life?"

I thought it over for a minute, then said, "When I was working on my book."

"Then you should write another one."

So I did. I don't know if a second edition counts as another book, but working on it helped me get back my clarity of purpose. I hope it's helped you find something you needed, too.

Epilogue

ON APRIL 1, 2017, FRANK'S MOTHER WAS FOUND DEAD in South Philadelphia. A toxicology report revealed that she succumbed to a lethal overdose of morphine and fentanyl.

Acknowledgements

FRANK MEEINK AND JODY ROY WOULD LIKE TO THANK the following individuals and organizations for their contributions to *Autobiography of a Recovering Skinhead*:

For introducing them to each other, Quay Hanna.

For funding to underwrite research costs, Ripon College and the FaCE Phase I grant program of the Associated Colleges of the Midwest.

For research assistance, Matt Birschbach and Tony McClintock.

For feedback on early drafts, Deano, Micah, Jackie C., Stuie, Nancy L., and The Eclectic focus group.

For sharing their memories, "Margaret"; "Big Frankie"; "Nanny"; "Pop"; the "Bertones"; "Uncle Nick" and the Meeink aunts; "John"; "Kirsten"; "Hayley"; "Louie Lacinzi"; "Crazy Cha-Cha"; "Jeremy"; "Clark"; "Jessica"; "Maria"; "Nina"; "Valerie" and her family; Barry Morrison; Michael Boni; "Bob"; "Aunt Joan," the former coach of the Eddie O'Malley team; "Squints"; "Vicey"; "Earbow"; and other "boys" from the corners of Second and Porter, Third and Jackson, and 68th and Buist; current and former employees of the Philadelphia Public Schools; the Catherine Hamilton Center; the Indianapolis Fire Department; the Terra Haute Police Department; the Springfield Police Department; Sangamon County Jail; the Sangamon County Public Defender's Office; the Sangamon County State's Attorney's Office; the Illinois Department of Corrections; and the University of Illinois-

Springfield (formerly Sangamon State University) Telecommunications Department. To these and many others who took the time to sit for interviews, thank you!

For turning Frankie's vision of Harmony Through Hockey into reality, the Philadelphia Flyers, The Anti-Defamation League, and the City of Philadelphia. For helping establish the program in the Midwest, Global Spectrum, Schlegel Sports, the Iowa Stars, and the Iowa Chops.

For supporting Frank throughout this process, everyone at F&G and the White House.

For their patience, understanding, and assistance during the years Jody devoted to this project, Jerry, Claudia, Vida, Jean, Carol, Tammy, Ric, Cody, and all of the students and faculty of the Ripon College Department of Communication. Special thanks to Shawn K. for his unwavering emotional support and for being on the stairs when the call came.

For believing *Autobiography of a Recovering Skinhead* can make a difference, Rhonda Hughes and the team at Hawthorne Books and Literary Arts.

For being the perfect editor for the first edition of this book, Adam O'Connor-Rodriguez.

For uttering not one word of complaint when Jody moved yet another book project and, at times, Frankie himself, into the house, Pookie.

For accepting Jody as her "other husband," and for loving and believing in Frankie even through the worst of times, "Valerie."

Finally, Frank would like to thank Jody for transforming his story into a book, Jody would like to thank Frank for entrusting her with the privilege, and they both would like to thank the Higher Power for everything.

Resources

Against Violent Extremism Network
www.againstviolentextremism.org

Al-Anon/Alateen
www.al-anon.alateen.org

Alcoholics Anonymous
www.aa.org

Anti-Defamation League
www.adl.org

Exit USA
www.exitusa.org

Formers Anonymous
www.formersanonymous.org

Hazelden Betty Ford Foundation
www.hazeldenbettyford.org

Life After Hate
www.lifeafterhate.org

Narcotics Anonymous
www.na.org

National Association of Students Against Violence Everywhere
www.nationalsave.org

Southern Poverty Law Center
www.splcenter.org

To learn more about Frank's work, to see clips of his presentations, or to inquire about booking him to speak in your area, please visit *www.frankmeeink.com.*

Interview with Frank Meeink and Jody M. Roy, Ph.D.

ADAM O'CONNOR RODRIGUEZ (AOR), SENIOR EDITOR FOR Hawthorne Books, conducted this interview with Frank Meeink (FM) and Jody M. Roy, Ph.D. (JMR).

AOR   How did this project come about?

FM   Jody came to me first on another book project she was working on and asked if I'd be interested in being interviewed for a chapter for the book. I said sure – she was recommended by a good friend of ours, Quay Hanna. She drove down to my house from Wisconsin; it's about a six hour drive, and first thing, we went out to dinner and talked and she reminded me again that I was just a chapter in the book and I assured her I knew that I was more than a chapter. She laughed and said, "We'll look into that later on." That was our first real meeting.

JMR   Frank's response was slightly more colorful than "I'm more than a chapter" but that was the essence of it. For that particular project, the day after we had dinner together, we sat for about two and a half or three hours of interview, just sort of a basic run-through of everything, and I was convinced by the end that yes, Frank was more than a chapter, no doubt about that. But also, Frank seemed comfortable talking about the book project even at that point.

FM   What I really felt comfortable with was two things: one, that she knew the lingo. I'd tried to work on this project with other people before, but to have to describe and define every piece of the movement – like what SHARPs are, Skinheads Against Racial Prejudice – to have to define all that stuff bogged me down talking until I wasn't enjoying it. But when I talked to Jody, she would sometimes know more of the history than I did.

And second, she knew other things, like that some people have businesses in civil rights and sometimes those groups will use fear to get more donations. When I talked to her about that, she knew what I was talking about already; she knew what I was getting at. So I felt comfortable enough that I could say whatever I wanted, because I wouldn't say something like that around most people. Of course, most civil rights groups are very legitimate, great groups, but when I said that some weren't, she knew exactly what I was talking about. And I remember thinking right then that I felt comfortable with her.

AOR   What was the process you used to get the story from spoken to written?

JMR   We had that first short interview for the other project and we decided we'd move forward, but I had to finish working on the other project, some work I was doing wearing my academic hat. We actually got started about a year and a half later, just because of things we both had on our plates at the time. Step one was to do a great deal of interviewing, but also to do some site visits. This was a gut instinct on my part – I believed Frank would remember things better if he could see them. You have to remember – for four and a half years, Frank was pretty itinerant, at times homeless. There aren't the kinds of records most people would have from their teenage years. We can't look in the high school yearbook. We can't look at family pictures in photo albums. We can't cross-reference things to a grade sheet. Trying to pin things down and get the discussion going, it seemed it might be better if we left the home and office space and got in the car. In October of 2005, I picked Frank up and we started toward the end of the story – we did Indiana and Illinois. It was our first trip ever together and it was quite a commitment. We were on the road for six days, twenty-four hours a day of work on the book interrupted only by sleep, naps really. I had Frank on tape basically the whole time, whether he was talking about things that had happened in Philly when he was a little kid or talking like, "Wow, I'm standing in the parking lot of Crazy Cate's for the first time in fifteen years" – we captured it all. Part of that was so that I could go back and piece the timelines together, but it was also of course to capture his voice, because I needed tons of exposure to that.

After that trip, we went back to our separate corners, and I went into research mode really trying to nail down the dates. The following May, we spent seven or eight days on the East Coast doing the same thing – interviewing people, visiting the scenes of various events. And that was important for me because I had to get a feel for what some of these places looked like. One example: having not grown up on the East Coast, my concept of an urban alley is based on Chicago or St. Louis or Indianapolis. I had no idea that what Frank considers an alley, I would consider an outdoor hallway; I needed to see the compression of South Philly and how close things are to even begin to evoke that sense of space within the book. That trip was very important for that purpose. It was also important to meet people and capture their voices for purposes of dialogue in the book.

Somewhere in between those two trips, we realized we were off by a year on the time layout for the book and for his life. It took months to figure that out. As Frank talks openly about in the book, he not only was itinerant, he also lied about his age as a teen – it's not like we could ask somebody, "Well, what was Frank doing when he was sixteen," because when Frank was sixteen, people thought he was eighteen or nineteen. For several years, the timelines are convoluted and without touch points. Ultimately, what became the touch points were the arrest dates and counting back from that to Crazy Cate's and counting back back back and realizing we had an extra year in there. We were off base due to confusion about his age and lying about his age when he was a teenager, and also because he just doesn't have the date markers most people rely on. Frank can't assume it was summer when something happened because he wasn't in school then; he dropped out at fourteen. Actually, his memories of what was going on in sports and what songs were playing heavy rotation on the radio became very important. Without Guns-N-Roses, we never would've figured out parts of that timeline.

FM   And on the lying about my age – most of my life I was either running, head of, or hanging with older guys, which included older girls. So most of my life, I wanted the girls to think I was older, so I was fourteen telling everyone I'm sixteen because the girls we're hanging with are sixteen.

JMR   Whenever we'd try to nail down when these things happened, I'd be talking to someone for the book and I'd ask, "Do you know how old Frank was when this happened?" And the universal answer was sixteen. Frank was sixteen for about five years according to most people who knew him. Figuring out the timeline was the hardest part of the book. We rarely were able to pinpoint a particular week or something; unless somebody keeps a daily record from birth on, they're not going to be able to do that. But to get it into some kind of causal order was a key issue to me, and that took a long time. So after we got that down and did the site visits and the interviews and everything else, then I started the original rough draft. After that it's been I draft and proof, then Frank reads and gives me feedback, then draft, proof, read, feedback, again and again for about two years, until we decided to move with it.

FM   With the timeline, since I've been speaking about my life
      for the past ten or fifteen years, I remember when Jody
and I first started this project, I thought, "Well, I've been telling
this story, but am I standing on a stage as the fisherman who's
been telling people the fish was two foot big when really it was
just one foot?" What was good about our trips was that it seemed
like the fish really was two foot, because to hear other people tell
their versions of the story, they actually make me sound worse –
in my version of the story, I threw a lucky punch one night. But
in other people's versions, I was an animal. That was one of the
good things about interviewing other people and me being very
open and telling them they could say anything they wanted
about me. Sometimes when Jody would do interviews, I'd leave
so they could be as honest as they wanted about me.

JMR   I had lots of good reasons to have complete faith in Frank
      when we started this project, but you just don't know.
Part of the reason that I wanted to do the Indiana and Illinois trip
first and in that specific order is because I was going on an old
theory that if there's going to be a lie, something exaggerated, it's
going to be something big. I knew what it was going to be. For me,
the most unbelievable thing in the entire story was the escape
from Crazy Cate's; there was just no doubt in my mind that if there
was a lie, that would be it. So we got in the car together on a Saturday afternoon and it was about 9:00 am Monday that we showed
up at the Catherine Hamilton Center in Terre Haute, Indiana.
So we're standing in the parking lot, and Frank said, "So, is this
the first time youse ever been to a nuthouse with an escapee?"
And I said, "Why, as a matter a fact it is, Frank." But we walk in and
sure enough, coincidentally several staffers who were working
that day remembered the incident very well. So I'm listening to
these people who'd been admissions staff, orderlies, *et cetera*,
when this wild and wacky event happened fifteen years earlier, and
the story they're telling me is dead-on with Frank's memory.

AOR   Several notable memoirs have been in the news lately for having stretched facts and in a few cases, invented the whole thing. Some critics might say that a few scenes in *Autobiography of a Recovering Skinhead* stretch credibility. What is your response to people who question the truth of the book?

FM   When we started writing this, it was maybe two months after James Frey got called out, so me and Jody had that conversation right away, she was like, "People question memoirs now" and I said I understand. I remember thinking that I was going to be so truthful that sometimes we'd go into a two-hour story that probably wasn't even useful to the book, but was just something I'd talk about. The point I'm trying to get at is that if I have a big, pure glass of milk sitting in front of me and I'm dying of thirst, but you put one little drop of poison into that, I'm not going to drink the glass at all. I don't want there to be one little drop of lie in this book; I want the milk to be okay.

JMR   The thing that's so tough, though, from a writing perspective, is that to reduce thirty-one years to less than three hundred fifty pages is by definition an exercise in lying by omission. While that is a great frustration, I don't think we missed the mark on anything major – we've checked and double-checked and triple-checked against his memory recalled on different occasions, against documentation, and against memories of unbiased witnesses when possible – but we skipped talking about that girlfriend and we didn't talk about the time he wore the tan T-shirt. You have to do that or you devolve into levels of detail no reader could tolerate.

FM   Me being honest, sometimes when I read how Jody put something or maybe how it was edited, if it didn't sound right, I was quick to say so, and it's never been in my favor. I've never said, "No, I was such a badass in that fight." It's always been the opposite, like, "Maybe that guy wasn't in a good fighting mood and I got the best of him." I always put the worst spin on myself. I'm very good at self-deprecation. I don't take myself too seriously. Anyone who questions the truth of the book can do the same thing Jody and me did – they can ask people, they don't have to just go on me. Sometimes the reality of it was even crazier than it looks in the book. So they can ask the people who were part of it. We toned things down in the book a little. So they'd probably get a better story if they went and checked it out themselves, actually.

JMR   To the extent possible, I verified Frank's memories, either against other people's recollections, though obviously that's not always possible, or against actual documentation. For example, the account in the book of the incident in Springfield that Frank ultimately went to prison for his role in – the source of the writing about thought process comes from Frank's recollections, but the action in that section of the narrative is derived from police statements – I pulled case files in those situations. But the fact of the matter is that this book is Frank's reflections on his experiences – we did the best job we could to confirm, to authenti cate. As an academic, my impulse is, "If we can't footnote it, it doesn't exist," but the flipside is that this is not a scholarly book.

FM   Having someone else write the book – because if I wrote my own book, who knows how it would turn out; it'd be one page long. But working with Jody, knowing she knows how to ask the right questions – that's why I often backed off and let her do the interviews with people: she'll ask the questions that ultimately will get the truth out. Sometimes maybe she put together their version and my version to get to the whole story. Almost all the major stories in the book are other people's versions put together with my words.

JMR   Not surprisingly, certain things Frank remembered expe riencing, some of which are in the book, other people

428 FRANK MEEINK / JODY M. ROY, PH.D.

sometimes didn't remember a particular detail. The other side of that is that I interviewed some people who told me stories of which Frank has no memory, especially from when he was a small child.

FM   Even from when I was a teenager – I mean, by then I was already a full-blown alcoholic – and I'm not trying to say, "Oh, I was an alcoholic and I don't remember the story so I'm going to tell it any way I want." But most of my life back then was hear-say – people told me what I did. A lot of stuff would happen and years later people would say, "Remember when you did this?" And I'd say, "I vaguely remember or I kind of remember being there," that type of stuff. And that's not to blame it all on the alcohol, because the rage inside me was ready to come out anyway.

JMR   Two things I can remember here: One is, it's not only Frank who has that issue, we had an awful lot of witnesses to these events who, at the time or now or both in some cases, struggle with substance abuse issues. Sometimes we had not only an alcoholic primary, but some of the secondary witnesses also were severely inebriated or have become so over time. And tragically, many of them died very young. Now, that said, what is particularly interesting is how much of Frank's memory lined up with the actual document trail that existed and also lined up with the most credible witness in particular situations – the person who wasn't inebriated that night. I was shocked – and Frank might remember this during the first read-through – I said to Frank, "I can't believe how dead-on your memory is."
Finding the bus depot in Indianapolis is a fantastic example of this. That was our first stop on our first trip together and we get there and Frank didn't recognize the bus depot. I remember having this sinking feeling in my gut, but I told myself "have faith." Next thing I know, Frank befriended a homeless man who became our tour guide that afternoon. The man had lived on the streets of Indy for a really long time. Frank described what

he remembered – and the description from the opening of the chapter "Caught on Tape" comes from Frank's conversation with this homeless guy, me following them through downtown Indy, Frank's describing the bus station as we walk and all of a sudden, this guy says, "I know where you're talking about, that's when they used to let off in the parking lot." We followed him for two or three blocks and when we rounded a corner, these two buildings opened up and Frank said, "This is it" and the homeless guy said, "Yeah, this is where they used to drop off Greyhound." I just stood there in amazement. It was like what Frank had been saying in this conversation appeared before my eyes. His memory of the scene was completely accurate; he just didn't know how to find the place on foot because he'd never walked there.

AOR Frank, you've become a well-known public speaker. What drives you to continue to tell your story to live audiences?

FM I truly believe there are people who have a gift, and I definitely have a gift when I'm onstage or when I'm interacting with kids who grew up like I did; I just have a way of connecting with them. I never studied to do it or nothing like that. I just don't bullshit them at all. My big point when I'm talking is that I want to connect with the people I'm talking to in however way I can do that. There are times in my life where I'm like, "Maybe I should just chill out and stick with my other career doing hockey or whatever," but whenever I think I might not want to speak anymore, I always have those kids who come up to me and are all, "Thank you; I felt the same way." A part of my story that I get great feedback for is when I was a little kid and I used to go home from school every day and wish I'd get hit by a car. That's all I wanted. I didn't want to die, I just didn't want to go home. I have so many kids come up to me and say, "I felt that same way at one time." I like when I get to do the universities, because I have free reign on whatever I want to say and I can curse and yell and do whatever I want and I have tons of fun with it and people laugh and have a good time and leave with a message. It's funny, the way I started was speaking to little kids. A guy asked me to speak to suburban little kids in Philadelphia, like fifth, sixth, seventh graders and I'd go there and be real raw with these kids and think I was doing damage to them; I used to think my talk wasn't good, that I was scarring these kids for life talking to them the way I did. Then I'd get these letters back and the kids would thank me and that was one of the first times in my life I thought that maybe I had a purpose, maybe I'm not going to be one of these guys who grew up in my neighborhood with a needle in their arm in an abandoned house whose family don't know they're dead for a month. I thought maybe I might not end up being that guy.

AOR   Notable figures such as Cornel West and Morris Dees have endorsed this book, even claiming that it "has the power to change lives." What has the support you've received on the book meant to you?

JMR   I don't let a lot of people read stuff in progress. Frank has shared drafts with several people and received a lot more feedback on it than I have, because it's just not the nature of how I work. I love working with a good editor, but I've got to be ready for that stage. I've only had maybe six people read very early drafts, and they were colleagues who I asked to give feedback on particular issues and they've like it, but they haven't seen this final version. What I'm trying to say is that my first feedback on the final book is from Morris Dees and Cornel West, and that's really cool. Though I'm only truly concerned about one audience on this, and he's sitting next to me right now, and he's comfortable with it, so if he feels that I sound like him, I've achieved that.

AOR   Do you agree that the story has the power to change lives?

JMR   Absolutely – if I did not agree with that, I would not have become involved in this project.

FM   And I would say the same thing: talk about how I am today, that I'm not a religious person but consider myself spiritual. And if I put the two together, being religious or spiritual – for me only now – religion is "I live this life afraid that when I die, I go to hell if I'm bad." Spirituality is "I feel like if I'm bad now, I'm going to go back to the hell that I've already come from." And I don't ever want to go back there. I don't want to feel the feelings I felt before, and if one person reads this and understands that – you always hear that expression, "If this will only help one person," and I think this book will help more than one and people who read it will also be able to help people in similar situations.

JMR   That was a large part of my motivation to get involved with this. Creative nonfiction was not the genre in which I was schooled to write. But having gotten to know Frank and to work with him over the years, I've watched his story develop live. I've watched it impact people, whether it's maybe a young kid who's into the skinhead thing, but it has very little to do with the skinhead part per se. It's about – maybe it's a kid who hates for those kinds of reasons. Maybe it's an African-American kid who hates the guys from a block down in a rival gang. Hate is hate; that's a big issue. And addiction is addiction. That's the other big issue in this book and in his story. Frank is living proof that simultaneously those issues are unbelievably difficult to overcome and it's a constant battle – you're always recovering, never "recovered" on all those fronts – but also that it's possible to keep getting up after getting knocked down. That is the power of his story, not only for people trying to get up now, but also for people trying to reach out a hand of assistance.

AOR   While this book is titled *Autobiography of a Recovering Skinhead*, it isn't just a book about the white supremacy movement. It is at different times a memoir about: child abuse, the tragedy of a broken American family, a gang member, a prison story, drug addiction, a love story, a coming of age story, the power of sports, and finally, a man's redemption. Besides the skinhead story, what are the other most important parts for people to look at?

JMR The first time I heard Frank speak in long form was in front of about 400 college students. He did a great job, and college students are a hard audience to keep, because unlike high school students they can get up and leave whenever they want to; it's not like there's attendance for an evening open lecture. People were riveted by the presentation and then they started in on questions and we were there for a really long time. This kid asked one of those questions that just sticks with you. He asked, "What do we do?" And Frank didn't even pause – his answer was brilliant. He said, "Just love them." This is the most important issue in the book. When you start looking for some of the cause and effect patterns in Frank's life, what you see is the patterns of so many issues that plague American youth. The skinhead issue happens to be what Frank wound his way into, but the same would be true of other gangs. The same would be true of certain kinds of cliques. It would be true of the recent phenomenon of shootings in high schools. When you see neglected or physically abused kids, you see this negative path that begins to spiral out of control, and you go back and ask yourself what would've happened if at some point in Frank's life, someone had loved a little more. So many things that should have been safety nets for Frank – not all, because Nanny and Pop and a couple of other relatives did the best they could – when he started falling, they weren't there, whether it was the schools or some family members or certain neighbors; too many people turned the other way and didn't act – as Frank would say, "Just love them."

FM One part right in the beginning of the book, when I start getting into the movement, I talk about how these two older skinhead guys ask me what it was like going to school in Philadelphia and how it must've been so hard for me – that was one of the first times in a long time that someone asked me about myself. To me, that was someone asking, "How was your day?" "How's your life?" Because my mom or dad or no one, when I got home from school, never asked "How was your day at school? What did you learn?" Never. And for once someone was asking, "How was your day?" And I think that's what made me love them guys first and foremost is that they asked these questions no one had asked in years. It comes down to just asking the kids in your life, whether it's your own kids or neighbor kids – don't let them get off with "Uh, it's okay." Make them answer you, "What teachers do you like? What teachers don't you like? Why don't you like them?" Get kids talking – at least they know that someone knows something about them, because maybe they're not getting that at home.

AOR   Family is a subject that runs all through this book – family brings you into the skinhead movement and is instrumental in your drug addiction, but family also helps you get out of the skinhead movement and helps you stop using drugs – has family been supportive of you since you left the movement? Are they supportive of the book?

FM   Like everybody, I have two families, my dad's side and my mother's side. And they never talk to each other, so I've always had that tear. My dad's side of the family, they're amazingly supportive. Loving, loving family. My grandmother just passed and I flew home for her funeral. The first thing that made it weird was when they brought out the old pictures, we're all eating at my cousin's house and she brings out the old photo albums, and you see the years that I'm gone. You see where I stopped coming around for Christmas when she pulls out the Christmas pictures. And that kind of hurts, but then you see where it picks back up. They're very supportive of the book, supportive of me getting out of all that stuff and happy I don't drink or use because they know my dad, so they know what I am potentially if I do drink or use –

and my dad's a great guy, don't get me wrong, and they love him – but he doesn't live to his full potential, he still lives to hang out with his friends and he's fifty-something years old, and that's where I was headed.

I don't talk to my mom's family very much – aunts and uncles and cousins included. And it's funny, I became a skinhead on that side of the family. And a lot of them aren't racists, great people, but I've just lost that connection, maybe talk to them on Facebook every once in a while.

Ironically, my cousin on my dad's side who I was very close with, beautiful Italian girl, married a northeast Philadelphia Jewish guy, and he's probably my greatest contact now in the family, we keep in touch more than anyone else in the family. It's funny I guess, when people look at it and think, "Oh, you're a former skinhead and you're closest now to your cousin-in-law who's Jewish" but it's just because we're similar people and great friends. It just happened that way.

They're all really happy with the book. I know they wish they could've did better for me in life, but it wasn't all up to them. They tried to step in many times, but I was too far gone. I was too far into having an alliance with somebody else and I turned my back on them and they didn't turn their backs on me and I think they feel bad, but I try to reassure them they're some of the main reasons I got out, because I wanted to be invited to the family parties, I didn't want to be the guy who, when they're thinking of having a family get-together, they say, "Do we really want to invite Frank? Do we want to hear all that Nazi bullshit again that he always brings to the party?" I didn't want to be that guy. And to know that now when something's going on, even though I live four states away, they still call me now to let me know something's going on if there's any way I can make it back home.

JMR   And part of it, too, with Frank's dad's side of the family – there were so many years where he not only disappeared from the pictures but they had no idea what was going on with him and no real way to get a hold of him to find out. And like Frank said earlier, he would usually prefer to leave the room while I'd interview people and he'd say, "Tell Jody everything and if you have questions, you can ask her or if you want to later, you can ask me."

I remember meeting with the Bertone aunts and uncles and cousins in Philly and the question they asked me that blew my mind was they wanted to know why Frank had gone to prison. This was in 2006, thirteen years after the fact, but they didn't want to ask him because they didn't want to embarrass him. They'd heard stories, the 68th and Buist rumor mill, but they weren't sure what was true and what wasn't, because the lines of communication were so severed by that point between the two sides of the family, basically since Frank was two. It was fascinating to me that it had gone that long and they really didn't have a clue about Frank – for example, nobody knew how bad it was between Frank and his stepfather for a long, long time.

AOR   You were incarcerated in an adult prison as a seventeen-year old kid. How did doing that time shape who you are?

FM   I learned to become a man in there. In the movement, I was surrounded by boys; even the older guys were scared little boys. And when I went to prison, I met people who were real men. Real men in the fact that they handled themselves like men. I didn't even know how to shave. A dude had to teach me how to shave in there. I only had a little goatee then, but I'd never shaven in my life; my father never gave me that lesson, my stepfather never gave me that lesson, and I'll never forget that prison is where I learned to shave; it's where I learned to talk a little deeper and mean a little bit more about what I say. I don't want to put forward that guys in prison are great representatives of men because, even when I give talks I'll say that they're not the real tough guys – the real tough guys are the men who pay their bills and take their kids fishing every weekend, those are the real tough guys.

I definitely became a man in there, and I learned that up until that point, I feared men because of my stepfather – I had a fear of men. And once I got in prison and learned that I can handle myself and do it with a streetwise dignity, that fear went away. Until then, I was always afraid of adult men. If you were a friend of mine and you had a dad, I didn't want to be around the room with him – for one, I was probably trying to recruit you into the movement, so I didn't want your dad to be involved in our talk, but I also had this fear that all fathers and father figures were mean. But in prison, I learned that I am a man and not all men are like that.

JMR   One of the things I've noticed in Frank, and this is coming from that fear as a child that lingers, is that as a kid on Tree Street, the only time Frank could eat comfortably was very late at night after John was asleep or passed out. And I've noticed now, having spent a lot of time with Frank, that he still consumes nearly half of his calories in any twenty-four hour period standing at the kitchen cupboard in the middle of the night, or eating pickles out of the fridge or if we're on the road, raiding hotel vend-
ing machines, because it's safe.

FM   I still do that every night, I wake up and I have to go downstairs and eat, because my body tells me, "Yo, this is the time that you normally eat" and I do – I feel comfortable eating what I want, and my wife even says she knows there's some issues there, like sometimes subconsciously I still might even hide what I ate, because when I was a kid, I wasn't allowed to go downstairs and eat, so if I ate something that came in a wrapper, I had to bury the wrapper at the bottom of the trash. I still do that, and I don't know if that's a fear of men or habit.

JMR   The fear of men issue was overcome from everything I've
       seen. But some patterns that started because of that fear
are still there, and that's a behavior pattern I don't think he'll ever
shake – it's not like he's eating at 2:00 a.m. because he's scared
of who's actually in the room, it's that his whole experience from
ages ten through thirteen was so intense that it programmed
certain behaviors that will always be there. It's as if your stomach
is only comfortable eating at that time.

FM   It's even hard for me today to discipline my kids forcefully
       and not think, "Am I treating them like my stepfather
treated me?" I know I'm not; I know I treat my children a million
times better than I was treated, but when it comes time to discipline them – and I don't hit my kids or anything – I make sure to
not cut too deep with my words. And sometimes I think maybe I
need to do that; that they need to see I'm really disappointed in
something they did but I can't go there because my biggest fear
is that they're going to go to their bedrooms and feel what I felt.
And it's hard to go up to that line, but I have to do it daily with
them.

AOR   So you've moved toward softness with your children because
       of the way you were treated?

FM   I would say so, but of course my kids and their friends think
       I'm strict, but I'm just a guy who says all the old things my
grandparents used to say. Like my kids'll say, "All my friends are
going to go to the mall," and I'll say, "No you're not" and they'll
say, "but Johnny's dad said he could go" and I'll say, "Well I'm not
Johnny's dad." I say all them old things. But I'm also like this
super fun dad, so their friends like to be around because I do take
the kids fishing, I play sports with them in the backyard all the
time. I think I'm a good dad, and I think my kids think I'm a good
dad – a little strict maybe, but I would never discipline them the

way I was. If my kids do something stupid, I would never call them idiots, I couldn't say that to them. Maybe I did learn something from my stepfather – do the exact opposite of whatever he did.

AOR   Sports, especially hockey, play a huge role in both your up-
          bringing and the transformation you undergo in this book.
What can sports do for someone's life? Why are they so powerful?

FM   Sports in general, especially real team sports like basketball,
          football, and hockey, make you learn to rely on other people
and if you don't – if you try to be a puck hog or a ball hog – a real
coach is going to make you play the whole team in practice so you
see how good you really are compared to how good you think
you are. It makes you gel more as a team, and once you start thinking together on the ice and in the locker room, you start to accept
each other for what you are. Just like when I was in prison, obviously we didn't have hockey – no skates with blades or big sticks
to play with in there – but when we played football, once the guys
saw I'd do anything for the team to win, they didn't care I was a
skinhead, they didn't care what my political beliefs were, they
just knew that when I came out there to play, I cared about what
happened to the team. Once the other inmates thought I was a
good enough player and a good enough teammate, they started to
stand up for me.
Sports are universal. I just did this conference in Washington, DC, the PODER Reconciliation Forum, and I met a guy who
does the same exact thing I do with hockey, but with soccer – and
he does it with the south Sudanese and the north Sudanese. He
does the same thing and has the same results. Once you get kids
out of an environment where they're expected to hate their neighbors and you teach them to just have fun, that's all they're going
to want to do. Because for a kid, it's a relief to just have fun and not
have to live up to the expectations of adults that you hate someone you don't even know.

AOR   You founded an organization called Harmony Through
        Hockey based on these principles. What has working with
the organization taught you?

FM   I founded Harmony Through Hockey in 1997, and thank-
        fully, the Philadelphia Flyers saw my vision and jumped right
on board, told me that however they could make it work they
would. When they got on board with it, it just took off. In the City
of Philadelphia, to have a sports team back you in a big sports
city like that made my program really well received by everybody,
from upper class to lower class. And once the kids started to
come, they didn't just play sports – we had racial counselors come
in while they were in the locker rooms getting dressed and they
brought up issues that had the kids talking openly. Sometimes the
talks went good and sometimes they didn't, but at least they
were talking. It was always a racial mix, we tried to do about half
and half between black and white and then we started trying to
make it like a quarter Asian, quarter Latino, quarter white, quarter
black and let in both boys and girls. Once you put all that hockey
equipment on a little kid – and by our insurance, we had to put so
much equipment on them that normal players don't have to
wear, like neck guards, all kinds of stuff – you don't even see their
skin color. All you see is a little-sized hockey player who's learning to skate. Race goes right out the window – the only color you
care about is the jersey on the kid's back.
One of the good things about Harmony Through Hockey, is
every year, we always get one kid who's kind of a bully and a
loudmouth, kind of picks on other people, always says something
about another kid's sneakers, that kind of thing. But once we
get all the hockey equipment on – and they all wear the same stuff,
so no one's better or different – every single one of them is going
to fall, because they've never ice skated before. It breaks that barrier down, that nobody there is better or worse than anybody
else in the program, and they all have to learn to work together.

One of my strong rules is that you cannot laugh at each other – if someone falls, you are not allowed to laugh. And the first week, sometimes the kids laugh, because it is kind of funny when a kid falls and screams or throws his gloves or something. I make sure to hold back my laugh, but the kids will start to laugh at first, but other kids in the program will step up and say, "Hey, don't forget about the rules, don't laugh at him." And that's what I want.

AOR In the book, you say that it isn't one big moment that changed your views on race. Looking back on it, what do you think really did change those views?

FM What I remember really made me think was meeting the two furniture guys I worked for. They were both Jewish, both recovering from drugs and alcohol, both had antique companies, and both knew my history – and at the time I was still basically a skinhead – and they took me into their companies because they saw something in me. Those two people cemented home what I'd already been learning – because I'd already at that point started to accept that blacks, Latinos, whites, Asians, were all equal, I could admit that – but something still held me back from accepting Jewish people, because it'd been drilled home for so long that Jews were secretly evil, there were all these conspiracy theories.
Something else that really started to get me, and I don't think we talk about this much in the book, is that every animal on this earth, has children – elephants carry babies for a certain amount of time, twenty-three months, kittens are born in two months, humans carry babies for nine months. And no matter the race or any other differences, we learn to walk at the same time, at about one year, we start to learn how to talk at the same time – that drove home that we're all human, we all care about the growth of our children. The DNA of all human beings is so similar that during the O.J. trial, maybe God was pointing out to everyone else that O.J. was guilty, but for me, hearing all about DNA, God was point-

ing out how equal every one of us are as human beings, and how
dare me judge the people who'd stepped into my life.

Even in prison, guys stepped into my life who helped keep me
sane. Little G, if we would have continued our friendship
when we got released, I know we would have been best friends
because we were almost exactly the same type of human being;
we were built exactly the same, we were both the same thing on
the football field. Off the football field, we both cared about girlfriends we had on the outside, breaking both of our hearts. We
both swore they were cheating on us. You don't get more human
than a man whose heart's breaking and able to share with another
man whose heart's breaking, that's all human. And we both regretted how we treated our girlfriends – all that stuff, to me that was
God stepping in, slapping me on the head telling me, "Who are
you to judge anyone, Frank?"

AOR   While most names are changed in this book, all the characters are real people. Are you worried about the reaction people
in the book will have to its publication?

JMR   Of course. But the folks I'm most concerned about on that
        count probably won't read it for about ten years, Frank's
kids. Some people might mistake this book as an exposé of the
movement, but if they take the time to read it, they'll very
quickly realize that's not the case – Frank reveals nothing about
the movement that isn't available on the internet with two clicks
of a mouse. He's talking about stuff that happened twenty years
ago, and the book is about one young man's particular experience in sub-corners of the movement. Still, Frank had no intention
to out anybody from the movement who isn't already a public
figure or, for that matter, to bring unwanted attention to other
people in his life. Most names, some descriptors, are changed –
of individuals and groups. Frank never did "rat anybody out." He
doesn't do it here, either.

Some people might read the book as a testament to recovery from substance abuse, and there is that element. The book is truly Frank's fourth step, a searching and fearless moral inventory. We put in a lot of miles in cars and airplanes to take this particular fourth step. But it's also a family history for his kids, because Frank doesn't have that – as he said, the pictures are missing from the photo albums for a decade or so – and Frank's kids were very much in my mind at times writing the book.

AOR   This book has a cinematic quality to it. Can you see this book being turned into a movie?

FM   I absolutely do. From the people who I've talked to about it, some see it more as a dark comedy because of the way I am about the mistakes I've made in life, how I'm willing to mock myself. And I don't see it happening so I become a big, rich person. But it's a great story and it's true and of course I didn't live my life to make it into a movie, but then I look back on it, and I know it can entertain someone and get a positive message across. I'd be fooling myself if I thought I could have a great message without entertaining. My story, for whatever reason, is entertaining. People like looking and saying, "Thank God I'm not that guy."

About the Authors

JODY M. ROY, PH.D., IS THE VICTOR AND CARRIE PALMER Endowed Chair of Leadership Values and Professor of Communication at Ripon College. The recipient of more than a dozen professional awards, Roy was named the Jeanne Robertson Outstanding Professor by the National Speakers Association in 2004 and Wisconsin Professor of the Year 2005 by the Carnegie Foundation and CASE.

Since the late 1980s, Roy's research has explored the diverse ways in which hatred is communicated within American society. Her scholarly studies have included analysis of organized hate movements in the nineteenth and twentieth centuries, as well as critique of the roles hatred and violence play within American popular culture. More recently, Roy has focused her studies on communication surrounding incarceration. Her publications include *Love to Hate: America's Obsession with Hatred and Violence* (Columbia University Press, 2002).

Throughout her career, Roy has translated her work as a scholar into accessible resources and programs teachers, parents, and others can use to improve their communities. In 2001, she founded Students Talking about Respect (STAR), a nonprofit organization that offered K-12 schools free access to hate-prevention resources. In 2004, STAR merged into the National Association of Students Against Violence Everywhere (SAVE), which works with about a quarter million students per year. Roy served as chair of SAVE's board of directors from 2008

to 2010. Since then, she has become involved in a prison education initiative and has collaborated with a group of currently
incarcerated men to develop materials designed to help prevent
youth crime and to prepare prisoners for successful re-entry
into society. In 2014, the curriculum developed by Roy and her
colleagues in the Ripon College Department of Communication
was awarded the National Communication Association's Rex
Mix Prize as the top undergraduate communication program in
the country.

FRANK MEEINK coaches national-championship youth roller
hockey teams and has worked in support positions for professional ice hockey teams. He is the founder of Harmony Through
Hockey, a member of the Against Violent Extremism Network,
and has been a member, consultant, and speaker for a wide range
of nonprofit groups dedicated to preventing hatred and
violence. Meeink has been on the national lecture circuit since
the late 1990s, sharing his amazing life story with students,
educators, community leaders, government officials, adult and
juvenile offenders, and those struggling with alcoholism and
addiction. In 2015, Meeink was one of three "Civil Rights Heroes"
honored by the Anti-Defamation League during the Voices
In Harmony: Houston in Concert Against Hate event. This is his
first book.